Biosocial
Psychopathology

Donald I. Templer, PhD, Professor of Psychology at the California School of Professional Psychology–Fresno, received his doctorate in clinical psychology from the University of Kentucky in 1967. He has written more than 100 journal articles and 20 book chapters, most often in the areas of neuropsychology, schizophrenia, and death. Dr. Templer is the co-editor of *Preventable Brain Damage: Brain Vulnerability and Brain Health* (Springer, 1992). He has over 1000 citations to his credit, with one of his earlier articles being declared a citation classic by *Current Contents* in 1984. He is an author of six assessment instruments. His Death Anxiety Scale has been translated into many languages and used on all six continents. A synthesis of this research is found in his book (with R. Lonetto), *Death Anxiety* (1986). He is a fellow of the American Psychological Association, the American Psychological Society, and the American Association of Applied and Preventive Psychology.

Dorothy A. Spencer, PhD, Director of the Kauffman Library and Professor at the California School of Professional Psychology–Fresno, received her M.S.L. from Western Michigan University School of Librarianship in 1970, and her Ph.D. in biomedical communications/adult and continuing education from the University of Nebraska in 1981. She has served as an Associate Professor at the Medical College of Georgia Library, and as the Director of the Kern Health Sciences Library, Bakersfield, California. Dr. Spencer is a Distinguished Member of the Academy of Health Information Professionals of the Medical Library Association and has written and lectured extensively on various topics related to health sciences information, technology, and education. She teaches research proposal development and participates in a variety of research activities.

Lawrence C. Hartlage, PhD, directs the Augusta Neuropsychology Center in Augusta, GA, and consults to the courts and to rehabilitation hospitals concerning head injuries and their sequelae. He has served as president of the National Academy of Neuropsychology, and of the American Psychological Association division of neuropsychology. His academic appointments have included professor of neurology at the Medical College of Georgia and at Indiana University Medical Center, and Marie Wilson Howell visiting scholar at the University of Arkansas. He has edited the *International Journal of Clinical Neuropsychology, Clinical Neuropsychology*, and *Neuropsychology and Special Education*, and served as consulting editor to *Archives of Clinical Neuropsychology, International Journal of Psychophysiology*, and the *Journal of Consulting and Clinical Psychology*. He is the co-editor of *Essentials of Neurological Assessment* (Springer, 1987) and *Preventable Brain Damage: Brain Vulnerability and Brain Health* (Springer, 1992).

Biosocial Psychopathology
Epidemiological Perspectives

Donald I. Templer, PhD
Dorothy A. Spencer, PhD
Lawrence C. Hartlage, PhD

Springer Publishing Company
New York

Copyright © 1993 by Springer Publishing Company, Inc.

Springer Publishing Company, Inc.
536 Broadway
New York, NY 10012

93 94 95 96 97 / 5 4 3 2 1

Library of Congress Cataloging-in-Publication Data

Templer, Donald I.
    Biosocial psychopathology: epidemiologic perspectives /
Donald I. Templer, Dorothy A. Spencer, Lawrence C. Hartlage.
        p.   cm.
    Includes bibliographical references and index.
    ISBN 0-8261-8290-9
    1. Psychology, Pathological.   2. Psychiatric epidemiology.
I. Spencer, Dorothy A.   II. Hartlage, Lawrence C.   III. Title.
    [DNLM: 1. Mental Disorders—epidemiology.   WM 100 T287b 1994]
RC454.T44   1994
616.89—dc20
DNLM/DLC
for Library of Congress   93-25832
                                                                          CIP

Cover and interior design by Holly Block

Printed in the United States of America

CONTENTS

v

PREFACE

The focus of this book is the biological and social epidemiology of psychopathology. Epidemiology studies the relationship between various factors such as age, sex, race, occupation, and frequency and distribution of disease in populations. It explores cycles and patterns of disease, and the onset of disease.

A medical disorder can be best understood, and its etiology can be best determined, by focusing upon what sort of people are most vulnerable to the disorder. Such an approach will be taken with psychological disorders. Demographic variables will be heavily stressed. Age, sex, country, ethnicity, socioeconomic status, religion, and geographical distribution are among the most important demographic variables.

Two important words in epidemiology concerning the rate of occurrences of a disorder are *prevalence* and *incidence*. *Prevalence* refers to the number of cases per unit of population. If there are 1,000 schizophrenics in every 100,000 persons in the community, then the prevalence of schizophrenia is 1,000 per 100,000.

Incidence refers to the number of new cases, incidents, admissions, or some sort of occurrence, divided by the number of persons at risk, in a given period of time. For example, in a given county there may be 15 babies born with Down's syndrome for every 1,000 births to women over 40 years of age.

The present epidemiological approach has some similarities to the "medical model" of psychopathology that posits discrete disease entities, as with the physical disorders. It is the orientation of this textbook that psychopathology can be understood both in terms of discrete entities and continua, with some conditions conforming more to a disease entity conceptualization; others, more to a dimension of psychopathology model; and still others to a combination model. A disorder that fits very well the disease entity conceptualization is Down's syndrome, which is caused by a chromosomal abnormality and is associated with mental retardation and a characteristic appearance. A person either has Down's syndrome or he/she doesn't, and it is pretty clear if he/she does or doesn't. On the other hand, the anxiety disorders fit much less well into a disease entity framework. Everybody has anxiety, and the difference between the so-called normal person and the one with an anxiety disorder is one of degree.

It is the position of this textbook that the causes of psychopathology are of two sorts, biological and social (Figure 1). The biological causes of psychopathology are both intrinsic to the individual and deriving from external sources. One of the most important intrinsic factors is genetic endowment. Included among the numerous other intrinsic biological factors are the neurotransmitters and other brain chemicals, hormones, and cardiovascular functioning. Extrinsic biological factors causing psychopathology include brain injuries, infections, toxins, drugs, and alcohol.

The social causes of psychopathology can be grouped into three categories. One is the cultural context in which a person is reared and lives—ethnicity, social class, religion, national, and geographic abode. The second category, that of interpersonal influence, consists of experiences relatively specific to the individual such as occurred with his/her family of origin, teachers, present family, and various past and present significant others. One's liabilities and deficits that limit one's success in life and determine the behavior that others exhibit toward one are also fundamentally in the interpersonal category. The third category, that of present environmental circumstances, overlaps with the interpersonal experience category, but also includes an array of other factors such as one's work, income, physical health, gains and losses, physical environment, and various stressors.

The chapters of the book have been placed in four categories: disorders of brain abnormality, disorders of subjective experience, disorders of self-control, and disorders of interpersonal maladjustment. As one moves from Part I

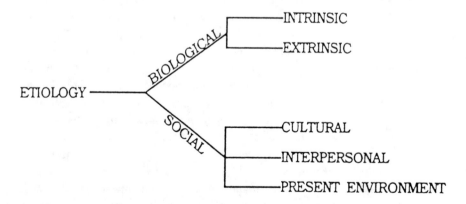

FIGURE 1   **Etiology of psychopathology.**

through Part IV, the disorders become less biologically rooted and the symptoms less internally generated and more likely to be directed by interpersonal variables. The more biologically rooted disorders tend to be more pervasive, impacting upon comfort and happiness, upon the ability to control one's behavior and upon effective interpersonal relationships. Information on disorders that begin in childhood is so voluminous that it exceeds the scope of a single chapter and has not been included in this book.

PART I

DISORDERS OF BRAIN ABNORMALITY

AT HIGHER RISK FOR BRAIN DISORDERS

Persons with Family History

Children with Prenatal Difficulties

Children with Perinatal Difficulties

Persons Who Abuse Drugs

Persons Who Abuse Alcohol

Poorly Nourished Persons

Lower Socioeconomic Status Persons

High Risk Takers

Elderly Persons

Persons in Dangerous Occupations

Persons with High Blood Pressure

Persons Who Play Contact Sports

Persons with Poor Health

Military Personnel in War

Divorced Persons

Sexually Promiscuous Persons

Persons with Downs Syndrome

Persons in Developing Countries

ONE

Brain Disorders

When one considers all persons who have head injuries, epilepsy, strokes, dementia, and other brain disorders, such persons constitute an appreciable percentage of the general population.

Although brain afflictions produce a multitude of symptoms, the most often reported are in the cognitive domain, with memory impairment being most salient. Associated with the decline in intellectual faculties is poor judgment. Emotional lability is very common. The patient may cry one minute, laugh the next, and be angry the next. Poor impulse control and deterioration of personal habits and ethical behavior are not uncommon. The patient who displays these general features is often referred to as "organic."

HEAD INJURIES

Templer, Hartlage, and Cannon (1992) made a distinction between "impact damage" and "chemical damage." Impact damage occurs in motor vehicle accidents, sports injuries, assaults, and a large variety of accidental injuries. Examples of chemical damage are those that result from alcohol abuse, drug abuse, agricultural neurotoxicity, and industrial neurotoxicity. Impact damage is usually observable, but chemical damage is usually unseen. Impact damage is usually instantaneous; chemical damage is more likely to be insidious and occurring over a period of time. Chemical damage is usually diffuse. Impact damage is more likely to have focal components. In this section we are dealing only with impact damage.

3

Traffic accidents account for roughly half of all head injuries. Males have considerably higher rates of head injuries than do females. Persons in lower social classes also have considerably higher rates of head injury.

Loss of consciousness is associated with increased probability of permanent sequelae, and the severity of such sequelae are positively correlated with the time the victim is unconscious, disoriented, or amnesic. Unconsciousness of over 24 hours justifiably causes worry to clinicians and to loved ones.

Depth of coma is also associated with less favorable prognosis. The depth of coma is often gauged by the Glasgow Coma Scale, which assesses eye-opening response, motor responsiveness, and verbal responsiveness (McClelland, 1988). Severity of sequelae is also positively associated with age. Persons over the age of 40 are more likely to have long-lasting symptoms than are persons under 40. Those over 40 are also more likely to die if they have a head injury.

In a concussion there may be loss of consciousness with the impact and headache, dizziness, and confusion upon awakening. In the postconcussion syndrome, these symptoms may exist for years after the injury. Concussions have traditionally been regarded as functional rather than structural, although this notion is now being seriously challenged. In a contusion, there is a bruising of brain tissue. The symptoms are the same as in a concussion but tend to be more severe. In a laceration there is an actual tearing of brain tissue. This is more likely to result in a coma or death. The consequences are usually more severe than in a concussion or contusion.

A distinction is often made between open and closed head injuries. In the former the skull is penetrated, and in the latter it is not. Open head injuries tend to be more serious and often are the results of automobile or other accidents and battlefield or other violent situations. The symptoms produced are to a large degree a function of the brain area damaged. The closed head injury is more likely to produce the general symptoms of brain pathology, such as memory loss and confusion, and less likely to produce focal symptoms.

A subdural hematoma (entrapped and usually clotted blood under the outer layer of the brain) ordinarily results from a head injury. Estimates of the frequency of such after an injury vary from 1% to 10%. Older persons are more susceptible to subdural hematomas because their lesser brain mass leaves more room for the development of a hematoma after injury. Altered mental functioning has long been recognized as a common symptom, and this observation is buttressed by research. In one study 58% of patients with subacute or chronic subdural hematoma had mental changes great enough to warrant a psychiatric diagnosis. Delirium was the most common change, dementia the second most common, and coma the third most common (Black, 1984). In addition to mental changes, headache is very common after a subdural hematoma. Surgical removal of the hematoma is often required.

On a microscopic level, the two most common types of brain damage appear to be diffuse axonal injury and focal cerebral contusions. The former is characterized by the scattered shearing of axons, mainly in the cerebral hemispheres. In severe cases there are often midbrain lesions that cause coma. Residual effects include decreased arousal, slowness of information processing, apathy and impoverished behavior, and vigilance deficit. Focal cerebral contusions most commonly occur in the frontal and temporal lobes. Their residual effects include impulsivity and tangential thinking (Benedict, 1989).

Memory difficulty is perhaps the closest to a universal symptom for head injury patients and those with other brain disorders. Amnesia is one sort of memory problem. Immediately following a brain injury or associated coma is posttraumatic amnesia, in which the patient is unable to remember anything from one moment to the next. This is associated with disorientation and bewilderment. In retrograde amnesia the patient is unable to recall material from a period of time before the accident to the time of the event. In anterograde amnesia the patient is unable to recall the material from the time of the event to a point of time thereafter. Retrograde amnesia time is even more important in regard to prognosis than is the amount of time unconscious (Berg, Franzen, & Wedding, 1987)

However, the memory problems, which are more common and which have more negative consequences with respect to occupational, educational, and social functioning, are the problems that consistently occur over many weeks, months, or years. Such memory problems can be divided into immediate (also called short-term) memory and long-term memory. Research, both with brain-disordered persons and with normal persons, has revealed that these are two sorts of relatively distinct memory systems (Levin, Benton, & Grossman, 1982). Short-term memory is a temporary entity that holds information for up to a minute. It is very much interfered with by material and distractions subsequently presented.

In the past it had been assumed that minor head injuries have little or no long-term effect. However, evidence in recent years suggests that such an assumption may not be warranted. In one study, 424 patients who suffered minor head trauma, having unconsciousness of 20 minutes or less and hospitalization less than 48 hours, were evaluated 3 months after the injury (Rimel, Giordani, Barth, Boll, & Jane, 1981). Seventy-nine percent complained of persistent headaches, and 59% reported memory problems. The patients' mean scores were in the brain-damaged range on most parts of the neuropsychological test battery. Of the patients who had been employed before the trauma, only 34% were employed 3 months later. In another study, 70% of brain-damaged patients continued to suffer from considerable memory impairment a year after the injury (Brooks & McKinlay, 1983).

Brooks, Campsie, Symington, and Beattie (1987) did a 7-year follow-up with 134 head-injured persons who had a coma of at least 6 hours and/or posttraumatic amnesia of at least 2 days. Before the injury, 86% of the patients were employed, but only 29% were employed at the time of follow-up. Factors associated with greater likelihood of return to work were being under the age of 45, having a technical/managerial job as contrasted to an unskilled job, being able to carry on a conversation, understanding a conversation, having a higher IQ and higher scores on neuropsychological tests, having better self-care and personal hygiene skills, as well as less subjective distress, better impulse control, and more favorable interpersonal relationships.

Recent research with boxers, who apparently suffer from numerous small concussions and mini-hemorrhages, shows that an accumulation of relatively small blows to the head can produce severe consequences. Research has indicated that brain damage does occur in many boxers, even those of championship caliber. Significant association has been found between the number of fights a boxer has had and cortical atrophy demonstrated by CT scans (Ross, Cole, Thompson, & Kim, 1983).

Posttraumatic epilepsy is too often an additional curse to the brain-injured person that could begin months after the injury and even when progress had been regarded as generally satisfactory. The probability of posttraumatic epilepsy is a function of the nature and severity of the injury. In general, the research literature indicates posttraumatic epilepsy in 10%–15% of patients with depressed fractures, 35% in those with hematomas (blood clots), 35%–45% in patients with penetrating head injuries, about 5% in patients with closed head injuries, and about 35% for patients who had been comatose for 3 weeks or more (Guidice & Berchou, 1987).

Research based upon men with posttraumatic epilepsy acquired in World War I, World War II, the Korean War, and the Vietnam War shows great variability in regard to seizure prognosis (Caveness et al., 1979). Another generalization is that there is an increase both in brain-injured men who cease to have seizures with time and in those who begin to have seizures over time. From 65% to 75% of the men brain-injured during war were fortunate enough not to have seizures. Of those persons who did have seizures, 5% had seizure onset in the first week, 10% in the first 6 months, and 29% in the first 2 years. However, within 5 or 10 years about half of the patients ceased having seizures with or without treatment.

INFECTION

Encephalitis means inflammation of the brain and is usually caused by an infection. Meningitis is inflammation of the meninges (covering of the brain).

Meningitis tends to be somewhat less serious than encephalitis, although the two often occur together. The symptoms of encephalitis and meningitis are headache, disorientation, drowsiness, weakness, vomiting, fever, stiffness of the neck and back, and sometimes coma or convulsions. Although most patients do not die, encephalitis is feared because of the severity of the sequelae, which include intellectual, speech, and motor deficits. In the 1920s there was an epidemic of encephalitis lethargica (sleeping sickness) that damaged tens of thousands of brains in the United States alone. The victims of the epidemic were especially affected by parkinsonism, a gross tremor caused by involvement of the extrapyramidal areas of the brain. The sequelae in children often include behavioral problems such as aggressiveness, destructiveness, hyperactivity, and psychopathic manifestations.

General paresis is the syphilitic affliction of the brain. There is gross atrophy throughout the cortex, which results in intellectual and personality deterioration and motor and sensory problems. Slurred speech especially characterizes the paretic, who has difficulty pronouncing such words as "Methodist Episcopal." A very classical symptom of general paresis is the Argylle-Robinson pupil, which does not respond to light but does show normal accommodation for distance. In about 10% of AIDS patients neurological symptoms are the first to be manifest and may include forgetfulness, concentration difficulty, mild confusion, mental slowness, unsteady gait, and coordination difficulty. Dementia eventually appears in a large percentage, probably the majority, of AIDS patients. Unfortunately, AIDS is always fatal. Those in the United States who are at high risk for AIDS include homosexual men, Haitians, hemophiliacs, intravenous drug users, and persons who engage in unsafe sex.

ABSCESS

An abscess is a localized collection of pus surrounded by inflamed tissue. The symptoms of a brain abscess include headaches, blurring of vision, confusion, language difficulty, and seizures. The source of the infection is usually the middle ear or the sinuses, and therefore frontal lobe and medial temporal lobe abscesses are the most common. Other sources of infection are the teeth, the lungs, and the heart. Treatment consists of antibiotic drugs and surgical removal. Since the mortality rate is about 20%, prompt and rigorous diagnosis and intervention are essential.

BRAIN TUMOR

Brain tumors (neoplasms) occur in 40 of 100,000 persons. The most common type of brain tumor is the glioma, which is a tumor of the glial cells—the supportive cells in contrast to the actual neurons. The second most common type is the meningioma, a tumor of the meninges or covering of the brain. Because of their location and because they are benign and encapsulated, surgical intervention with a reasonably favorably prognosis is usually possible. The pituitary tumor is the third most common. Because of the important functions of the pituitary and because it is not surgically accessible, a pituitary tumor is a most serious condition.

Location of the tumor is one of the factors that determine the symptoms of a brain tumor. Symptoms relatively common in frontal lobe tumors are dementia, motor difficulty, seizures, and poor emotional control. Parietal tumors often cause sensory symptoms, spatial orientation defects, calculational deficits, apraxia, and difficulties in music ability and facial or color recognition. Temporal lobe tumors frequently result in auditory problems, visual problems, memory impairment, and seizures. Occipital lobe seizures result primarily in visual dysfunction. Hypothalamic tumors are most commonly seen in children and result in various problems such as emaciation, obesity, vomiting, improper temperature and blood pressure regulation, low blood sugar or diabetes, and hypogonadism, or precocious puberty. Cerebellar tumors, which are ordinarily found in children, produce incoordination, gait difficulty, headache, and dysarthria. The symptoms of pituitary tumor include headache, visual problems, and hypothalamic dysfunction because the pituitary is just beneath the hypothalamus. Limbic system tumors are likely to produce psychiatric disorder.

In addition to classification of brain tumors on the basis of type and location, they can be classified as primary or metastatic. In primary tumors the origin of the tumor is in the brain. In metastatic tumor, the origin of the problem is in another part of the body, with lung cancer and breast cancer as the two most likely sources of trouble.

Since the brain is the organ of behavior, it is understandable that a brain tumor can produce almost any sort of emotional, cognitive, sensory, perceptual, or behavioral problem. However, there are certain symptoms that are more characteristic of brain tumors. The most common is headaches. Headaches are apt to be persistent, especially as the tumor progresses. Blurring of vision is caused by a choked disk, also referred to as papilledema. Because of increased pressure of cerebral spinal fluid, there is swelling where the optic nerve meets the retina. Vomiting, seizures, memory and general intellectual decline, language problems, emotional lability, and personality deterioration are other manifestations. A brain tumor can cause hallucinations and simulate a variety of so-called functional psychiatric disorders. In fact, cases have been reported in which neurological signs were minimal or absent, and the patients even responded favorably to the psychotropic medication appropriate for the psychiatric diagnosis but with late discovery of a brain tumor (Binder, 1983). As with all major brain syndromes premorbid personality determines reaction to the tumor. Some persons become compulsive, some antisocial, a few euphoric, and, needless to say, many become depressed.

ABNORMAL MOVEMENT DISORDERS

The various abnormal movement disorders have several common clinical features. They are increased by anxiety, exertion, fatigue, and psychomotor stimulants such as caffeine. They are decreased by relaxation and apparently by biofeedback in some cases. They are generally absent during sleep. They can be momentarily suppressed by concentration and effort. The abnormal movement disorders' common anatomical feature is the involvement of the basal ganglia, which is the origin of the extrapyramidal tract that modulates the voluntary muscle movements mediated by the pyramidal tract. The basal ganglia is composed of three major parts. The corpus striatum (also called striatum) includes the caudate nucleus, the putamen, and the globus pallidus. The other two major parts are the subthalamic nucleus and the substantia nigra. The three important neurotransmitters of the basal ganglia are dopamine, acetylcholine, and gamma-aminobutyric acid, which is usually referred to as GABA. Dopamine and GABA are inhibitory transmitters; acetylcholine is an excitatory transmitter.

In parkinsonism the most apparent symptom is tremor, and the most debilitating is akinesia. The tremor involves primarily the hands and feet and may be either unilateral or bilateral. It is a resting tremor since it is seen more when the extremities are stationary than when they are being moved. Akinesia (deficient movement) has several different components in parkinsonism. One of these is cogwheel rigidity in which muscular resistance, such as pushing the examining neurologist's arm, consists of a series of movements rather than a continuous pressure. The gait contains marche a petits pas (walk in small steps) in addition to a somewhat accelerating forward propulsion movement. When parkinsonism patients seat themselves, they characteristically do not reposition themselves, and when seated they remain immobile. Their arms stay on their laps or chairs and are not used in gesturing. Their legs are not crossed. Parkinsonism patients are said to have masked facies because their faces are immobile, without expression, gesturing, or blinking. The voice is often quavering, with a low volume. Parkinsonism is associated with insufficient dopamine and excessive acetylcholine.

Athetosis is a slow and twisting movement of the limbs. Athetosis can be regarded as the opposite end of the spectrum from chorea, in which the movements are of greater amplitude and less regularity. Athetosis becomes apparent in early childhood. It usually results from prenatal problems such as anoxia and is often associated with cerebral palsy and mental retardation. In athetosis there is an excess of dopamine. In chorea there are many jerklike movements of the limbs and the trunk. The face has intermittent frowns, grimaces, and smirks. The gait is jerky. In the very early stages of chorea the movements are sometimes mistaken for anxiety or restlessness, discomfort or clumsiness (Kaufman, 1985). Chorea is associated with an excess of dopamine.

DEGENERATIVE DISORDERS

Huntington's Chorea

Huntington's chorea is transmitted by a dominant gene. It typically begins in the late 20s to the mid-40s. In about 10% to 15% of the cases Huntington's chorea begins before the age of 20, and the diagnosis then is juvenile Huntington's chorea. The earlier indications of the disorder are more behavioral than motor or cognitive. The patient insidiously exhibits a deterioration in personality (i.e., slovenly habits, irresponsibility, lower moral standards, and emotional lability). Next comes the choreic or jerking movements of the hands, arms, legs, and body. There is also intellectual decline. The road is downhill in all of the realms until the patient becomes bedridden a decade or two later and dies. There is considerable degeneration in the frontal lobes (which explains the personality deterioration) and in the caudate nucleus (which explain the choreic movements). There are deficits in the neurotransmitters acetylcholine and GABA. Treatment of Huntington's chorea is symptomatic. Persons with relatives suffering from Huntington's chorea should be informed of their risk for the disorder and of the probability that any children they might have will develop it.

Dementia of Old Age

There are two basic types of dementia of later life: primary degenerative dementia and multiinfarct dementia. In primary degenerative dementia there is considerable cerebral degeneration. This results in a deficit of cognitive ability, especially memory. Recent memory (e.g., for events earlier in the day) tends to be worse than memory for events of years ago. Other symptoms are poor judgment, emotional lability, irritability, impaired judgment, and childlike behavior.

Over half of the cases of primary degenerative dementia and of senile dementia generally can be attributed to Alzheimer's disease. It accounts for almost half of nursing home admissions. Symptoms are memory and general intellectual decline, apathy, indifference to personal hygiene and other aspects of social decorum, and speech and language problems. Fifty percent of persons die within 3 years of the onset of symptoms, and 95% are dead within 5 years. The immediate cause of death is usually secondary infections.

The clinical course of Alzheimer's disease is often divided into three relatively distinct stages (Schneck, Reisberg, & Ferris, 1982; Swihart, Baskin, & Pirozzolo, 1989). The first is the forgetfulness phase, in which there are such problems as misplacing objects, not remembering where the car is parked, difficulty in remembering names and appointments, decreased initiative, comprehension deficits, and topographic disorganization. In the second stage, the confusional phase, there is obvious deterioration to the point of great memory impairment, aphasia, disorientation, and poor judgment. In the third phase, the dementia phase, the patient becomes extremely disoriented, completely unable to function, bed-ridden, and incontinent. At the end of the scenario is death.

Wragg and Jeste (1989) reviewed 30 studies on Alzheimer's disease and found a considerable extent of mood disturbance and psychosis. From 40% to 50% of Alzheimer's patients are reported to have depressed mood, and 10% to 20% had depression serious enough to be called a depressive disorder. The reviewed studies reported from 3% to 17% of patients with elevated mood and indicated that from 10% to 70% of Alzheimer's patients have delusions; most of the studies report between 30% and 38%. Persecution delusions were the most common; however, Wragg and Jeste cautioned that it may sometimes be difficult to distinguish psychosis from confusion in Alzheimer's patients.

Cerebral atrophy is found in Alzheimer's disease, but the degree of atrophy is quite variable and is not highly correlated with degree of dementia. The diagnosis of Alzheimer's disease is dependent upon neuritic plaques (patches of neural pathology) and neurofibrillary tangles (tangles of delicate, threadlike fibers in and connecting neurons), which do not correlate greatly with degree of dementia. These degenerative changes are especially prominent in and near the hippocampus, accounting for the gross memory difficulty.

Even though Alzheimer's disease is recognized as an established disorder, it should be kept in mind that the "normal" aged brain undergoes at least some of the same changes as in Alzheimer's disease, only to a lesser degree. The vast majority of patients dying of any cause after 70 years of age have neuritic plaques and neurofibrillary tangles, and less than 1% of persons over the age of 80 have no such lesions.

Alzheimer's disease can begin anywhere from middle age to very late in life. It ordinarily occurs after age 65. When the disorder begins before age 69, it is referred to as presenile dementia of the Alzheimer's type. This form has a more rapid and malignant course and is associated with a stronger family history of the disorder.

Common sense tells us that a family member with Alzheimer's disease can place great stress upon a family. Research has demonstrated that over half of the caretaker family members are clinically depressed, that they have three times the number of stress symptoms, and receive more psychotropic medication than control persons (Cohen & Eisdorfer, 1988). Some of the more disturbing behaviors are incontinence, wandering (especially during the night), inappropriate sexual behavior, eating and self-feeding difficulty, and poor orientation and reality appraisal. Although the course is downhill, these problems are to some extent amenable to behavioral and environmental modifications such as making bathrooms more accessible and providing more light at night.

The cause of Alzheimer's disease is not known. However, it is possible that, as seems to be the case with schizophrenia, there is more than one cause and that it is a syndrome of closely related disorders. It does appear that first-degree relatives have a morbidity risk that is four times as great as that of the general population. However, it is uncertain whether this risk is a function of heredity or environment or both. Neurotransmitter irregularities and a slow virus have also been suggested to have etiological significance. There is some evidence that immunological factors may play a role in the disorder. There has been speculation that stressful life events may be an etiological factor.

The incidence of Alzheimer's disease increases very sharply with age. Female rates are twice male rates in the United States and in European countries. However, the opposite has been reported in Japan. It certainly appears that a generalization that 1% of elderly persons have Alzheimer's disease would be conservative. The prevalence of Alzheimer's disease is increasing, at least in the more developed countries of the world. This increase appears to be a function of the increasing life expectancy brought about by public health and medical advances.

The relationship that appears to exist between Alzheimer's disease and Down's syndrome is not clearly understood (see Chapter 3) (Mortimer & Schuman, 1981). There appears to be an excess of relatives of Alzheimer's disease patients who suffer from Down's syndrome. Furthermore, a strikingly large percentage of Down's syndrome patients exhibit Alzheimer's-like changes in the brain by age 35–40. There are other disorders that tend to be associated in some intriguing fashion with Alzheimer's disease. For example, relatives of Alzheimer's disease patients have an excess of hematologic cancer such as leukemia.

Also in the realm of epidemiology is the interesting but less than conclusive evidence that Alzheimer's disease patients are more likely to have a history of head injury. There is also some evidence that the patients tend to be born relatively late in their mothers' childbearing years. It has been reported that Alzheimer's disease patients have a family history of immune system disorders.

Pick's disease is a dementia that is similar to Alzheimer's disease, and at times the early-stage differential diagnosis is difficult. Pick's disease has more deterioration in personality, and Alzheimer's disease has more decline in cognitive abilities. Pick's disease patients tend to be socially disinhibited and display rambling speech and anomia (difficulty in finding words for objects). About a third of Pick's disease patients exhibit echolalia, a symptom that is ordinarily associated with schizophrenia. Eventually, dementia masks the more specific deficits, and death takes place about 10 years after onset. There is considerable frontal lobe atrophy, and that likely causes the poor judgment and impulse control. There is a good deal of temporal lobe atrophy, which likely causes the speech difficulty. Onset is usually in the 50s, earlier than in Alzheimer's disease. Male and female incidence is about the same, unlike Alzheimer's disease, in which there are twice as many females. There are from 50 to 100 times the number of Alzheimer's disease patients as there are Pick's disease patients. Exceptions occur in Malaysia, where Alzheimer's disease is apparently nonexistent, and in Stockholm, Sweden, where there are a great number of Pick's disease cases (Strub & Black, 1981). The etiology of Pick's disease is not known.

In multiinfarct dementia there are a number of tiny strokes. The symptomatology is similar to that of primary degenerative dementia. However, there tends to be somewhat less intellectual and personality deterioration and more focal neurological signs such as speech and motor impediments.

It should be borne in mind that senile dementia is found in only a distinct minority of the elderly (Butler, 1984). It has been estimated that at least 75% of that population maintains sharp mental functioning, although perhaps with some slowing of thought and memory, and that only 5% are senile (Kay, Britton, Bergman, & Foster, 1977). The prevalence rates of senile dementia are reported as 2% among persons in their late 60s, 4% among persons in their 70s, and 20% in their 80s and beyond (Roth, 1978).

Furthermore, a sizable percentage of the elderly demented, with estimates ranging from 15% to 40%, have reversible dementias that can be treated (Besdine, Brody, & Butler, 1980). These reversible dementias have a wide range of etiology, from depression to therapeutic drug intoxication. As pointed out by Besdine et al., the aging brain is extremely sensitive to cardiac, hepatic, pulmonary, and renal failure, endocrine abnormalities, water and electrolyte disturbances, anoxia, nutritional deficiencies, infections, hypothermia, and hyperthermia.

NEUROTOXINS

Arsenic, copper, manganese, and mercury are metals that are toxic to the brain. Mercury and manganese poisoning are most often encountered in industrial settings. Lead poisoning is encountered in both industrial and nonindustrial situations. Young children in impoverished environments are more prone to lead poisoning from the paint that flakes off the walls. Leaded gasoline fumes can be toxic, and this is the reason for legislation requiring the use of unleaded gasoline in newer cars. Various chemicals are injurious to the brain. Agricultural workers are prone to the toxic effect of pesticides. Carbon dioxide is toxic to the brain, and persons who make suicide attempts with carbon monoxide sometimes have even less to live for because of the ensuing brain pathology. Common toxic brain symptoms are disorientation, concentration difficulty, emotional lability, delusions, hallucinations, lowered intellectual ability, speech difficulty, gait difficulty, and memory problems. Lead poisoning sometimes produces retardation in children.

CEREBROVASCULAR PROBLEMS

CEREBROVASCULAR ACCIDENTS

There are three types of cerebrovascular accidents, or "strokes." The most common type is thrombosis in which a blood clot forms in a section of the artery narrowed by atherosclerosis (deposits of fatty materials). In the embolism, tissue from another part of the body (e.g., the lungs) becomes lodged in the artery. In the hemorrhage there is a bursting of the blood vessel. Hemorrhages usually produce the most serious consequences and are most likely to result in death. Strokes are most common in persons over the age of 60. About 10% of strokes are fatal, and in about another 30% death will occur within a few months (Berg et al., 1987). For those who survive stroke, speech difficulties, motor deficits, and memory loss and other cognitive impairments are common. Strokes account for about a tenth of the total mortality in the United States and are the third leading cause of death.

About 80% of stroke victims are over the age of 65. However, strokes are by no means rare in young adults. Research indicates that strokes in young adults tend to be associated with current alcohol consumption, history of heavy drinking, and alcoholic binges (Taylor & Combs-Orme, 1985). Alcohol-induced hypertension is the underlying mechanism most frequently postulated, although other mechanisms have been suggested. Black men, both African Americans and black men in Africa, have a high incidence. This is probably because black persons are prone to high blood pressure. Even after controlling for ethnicity, the rate of stroke is more common in the southeastern United States. This is ordinarily attributed to a high-cholesterol diet. The incidence of strokes is higher in males than in females. The risk of stroke is greater with hypertension, elevated serum cholesterol, high blood and urine glucose levels, abnormal triglyceride levels, tobacco smoking, and cardiovascular disease.

TRANSIENT ISCHEMIC ATTACKS

In transient ischemic attacks the blood supply to the brain is temporarily interrupted, with a resulting loss of some neurological functioning. Restoration of blood flow usually takes place in from 3 to 30 minutes (Kaufman, 1985). Motor and speech problems are commonly experienced. Fortunately, the pathology is functional rather than structural. However, a transient ischemic attack represents a stern warning. About a quarter of persons who have such an attack will suffer an actual stroke within a year.

EPILEPSY

Epilepsy is sometimes defined in nontechnical terms as an "electrical storm" in the brain. About 1 of 200 Americans has epilepsy. Although we ordinarily classify persons as epileptics and nonepileptics, the fact that everyone has the potential for seizures is vividly illustrated by the fact that seizures are produced by electroconvulsive therapy (ECT). Seizures as an alcohol withdrawal symptom are not uncommon. Anoxia (insufficient oxygen), hypoglycemia (low blood sugar), fever, fatigue, excessive water intake, flashing lights, pain, and various drugs can all lower the seizure threshold. Some epileptics sometimes can have a seizure triggered by listening to music, watching television, or solving mathematics problems or even in response to a particular person's voice.

Epilepsy can be classified with respect to etiology as either primary or secondary. Symptomatic or secondary epilepsy results from a brain injury. The etiology of primary or idiopathic epilepsy is often unknown, and there is more apt to be a genetic factor. Also, it is more common in males.

Seizures can also be classified as centrencephalic (also called generalized seizures) or focal (also called partial seizures). In the centrencephalic seizures there is an immediate loss of consciousness, and the electroencephalogram (EEG) abnormality is the same on both sides of the brain. In the focal seizures there is, at least initially, not a loss of consciousness, and the EEG abnormality is confined to one side of the brain. Centrencephalic seizures originate in the subcortical regions, and the discharge quickly spreads to the cortex. Focal seizures originate in a specific cortical locus.

There are two major kinds of centrencephalic seizures, grand mal and petit mal. Jacksonian and psychomotor seizures are among the more common types of focal seizures.

GENERALIZED TONIC-CLONIC

The generalized tonic-clonic, or grand mal, seizure is not only the most common type of seizure but it is what most people think of when they hear the word *epilepsy*. In about half of epileptics with grand mal seizures, the seizure begins with a brief aura that consists of such experiences as an uneasy feeling in the stomach, dizziness, a peculiar odor, ringing in the ears, or an apprehensive, uneasy feeling of something bad going to happen. The aura is frequently described as preceding the seizure but is actually part of the seizure. After the aura there is sometimes a brief crying-type noise caused by forced expiration of air. The convulsion itself is divided into the tonic and clonic phases. In the tonic phase after the person falls to the ground, there are muscular spasms that usually last less than a minute. In the clonic phase there is alternating flexion and extension of the body muscles that produces jerking movements of the arms and legs. Sometimes incontinence of urine and/or feces occurs, and occasionally there is erection and ejaculation. Consciousness is resumed from a few seconds to several hours after the seizure stops.

In status epilepticus there is a series of grand mal seizures with one rapidly following the preceding one. The most common cause is the imprudent discontinuation of anticonvulsant drugs by the epileptic. This is a very serious medical problem that necessitates immediate intervention since death can occur. Intravenous administration of anticonvulsants is needed. However, large dosages of anticonvulsants can cause respiratory arrest, hypotension (abnormally low blood pressure), and cardiac arrhythmias (abnormal heart rhythms). Therefore, it is important to determine whether the patient has a genuine status epilepticus seizure or the simulated seizures or conversion symptoms associated with a psychiatric disorder (Lechtenberg, 1982).

Infantile seizures are grand mal seizures that occur primarily in the first week after birth. They are 15 times more likely to occur in premature infants. Anoxia, intracranial bleeding, and hypoglycemia are among the more common causes of infantile seizures. Such seizures are cause for concern for the parents. Research has determined that among infants who experienced such seizures and were followed up at varying ages in childhood, 52% were apparently normal, 20% had died, and 28% displayed severely abnormal development (Lombrose, 1978). In another study, 35% of the children had died, and of the survivors 19% were retarded and 15% had borderline retardation (Holden, Mellits, & Freeman, 1982).

In contrast to infantile seizures, febrile convulsions ordinarily should not be of grave concern to parents. Febrile convulsions occur in from 2% to 5% of all children between 6 months and 5 years of age. They usually occur soon after the onset of febrile illness. They are usually grand mal seizures of short duration. Males are more susceptible to febrile convulsions than are females. There may be a genetic predisposition. In most cases there are probably no neurological or neuropsychological sequelae. Testing at age 3 shows that children with febrile convulsions do not differ in IQ or academic proficiency from their siblings without such a history (Spreen, Tupper, Risser, Tuokko, & Edgell, 1984).

ABSENCE SEIZURES

Absence or petit mal seizures are characterized by a lapse of consciousness that lasts a matter of seconds, usually less than a minute. The person does not fall to the floor or exhibit involuntary movements except for possibly a few twitches of the face and eye muscles. It is common for a child's eyes to blink at the same frequency as the abnormal EEG. Petit mal seizures occur frequently for those so afflicted, occasionally as often as several hundred times a day. Petit mal epilepsy is almost exclusively a disorder of children, with the greatest incidence occurring between 4 and 8 years of age. Females are somewhat more likely than males to have petit mal epilepsy. In about 40% of children with absence seizures one or more tonic-clonic seizures occur at sometime in their life (Kaufman, 1985).

JACKSONIAN SEIZURES

Jacksonian seizures are characterized by a muscle twitching or numbness that moves from one part of the body to the next. The march of symptoms can be explained by the progression of the abnormal electrical activity up or down in the vicinity of the central sulcus. The manifestation of the seizure is motor (twitching) if in the precentral gyrus and sensory (numbness) if in the postcentral gyrus. Sometimes the Jacksonian seizures and other focal seizures culminate in a grand mal seizure.

PARTIAL COMPLEX

Partial complex, or psychomotor, seizures are sometimes called temporal lobe seizures because that is the area of the brain where the abnormal discharge usually occurs. At one time it was thought that psychomotor epilepsy was uncommon or even rare. However, it is now known that about three fifths of epileptics have at least occasional psychomotor seizures (Stevens, Milstein, & Goldstein, 1972). Psychomotor seizures can produce behavioral, perceptual, thought, and affective effects. These can include hallucinations, stereotyped automatism such as chewing movements, and occasionally somewhat more complex organized behavior. The patient is unable to remember what happened during th. seizure. On rare occasions in temporal lobe epilepsy, patients engage in violent behavior. However, it is probably more common for an attorney to use this defense with an ordinary criminal when no effective legitimate defense can be mustered. It is difficult to either prove or disprove that a given crime is a function of temporal lobe epilepsy. Gunn and Bonn (1971) reported that in 434 epileptics with temporal lobe epilepsy, violence was very uncommon. They also found that of epileptics in prison only 10 of 150 claimed a seizure within 12 hours of their last offense.

Furthermore, other research shows that psychomotor epileptics are no more prone to psychosis and other psychiatric manifestations than are other epileptics (Stevens et al., 1972). In one study, in which 57 psychomotor episodes were induced in a routine workup in a neurological clinic, there was not a single instance of aggression and only one instance of threatened aggression. The behaviors were of a very simple sort, such as chewing movements and unbuttoning of the shirt (Rodin, 1973). In other research, in which psychomotor seizures were actually observed, violence was seen in less than 0.1% of patients (Delgado-Escueta et al, 1981). And this violence was neither sustained nor goal-directed nor very serious. Shoving, pushing, and screaming were the sort of aggressive manifestations observed.

INTELLIGENCE AND PERSONALITY OF EPILEPTICS

As is the case with almost every type of brain disorder, the IQ of the average epileptic is less than that in the general population. However, the overlap is considerable, and some epileptics are gifted. Among famous geniuses and famous historical epileptic persons are Julius Caesar, Mohammed, Van Gogh, Dostoevsky, and William Pitt. It is the impression of some clinicians that an "epileptic deterioration" of intellect occurs over an extended period. Consistent with this observation is the demonstrated neuronal loss in the hippocampus; patients with more seizures exhibit greater hippocampal neuronal loss.

Mental health professionals frequently used to say that epileptics characteristically have personality features that include explosiveness, stubbornness, resentfulness, irritability, and a paranoid trend. If some epileptics have these traits, they may not be intrinsic to epilepsy but caused by the ignorance and discrimination that society delivers to persons who are in some way handicapped or different. Actually, research has not provided clear evidence of an "epileptic personality."

Nevertheless, there does appear to be evidence that epileptics have more psychopathology than do nonepileptics. They seem to be more inclined to depression, anxiety, and psychosis. They have a high suicide rate (Matthews & Barabas, 1981). A disproportionate number of persons in prisons are epileptic (Herman & Whiteman, 1984). Although less than 1% of the general population has epilepsy, 12% of persons in institutions for the mentally ill have epilepsy (Sherwin, 1982).

Studies show that about a quarter of epileptics with normal IQ have had one or more psychiatric hospitalizations (Stevens et al., 1972). However, it is difficult to generalize from hospitalized epileptics to epileptics in the general population. To permit such generalization, Kogeorgos, Fonagy, and Scott (1982) assessed the psychopathology of epileptics being treated in a neurological clinic. These epileptics were found to have appreciably more disturbance than either normal control subjects or other neurological patients. The degree of anxiety, depression, and hysterical-type behavior was especially striking.

A tiny percentage of epileptics have such frequent seizures that they must be institutionalized. Fortunately, the vast majority of epileptics have their seizures well controlled by medication so that they can lead normal lives. This control often initially requires a combination of both clinical skill and trial and error to get just the right anticonvulsant and combination of anticonvulsants and their optional dosage so that seizures are controlled but the patients are not too drowsy to function effectively. There are a number of anticonvulsant drugs on the market, the "old standbys" being Dilantin® and phenobarbital. Nonpharmacological interventions are employed in a minority of epileptics (Hartlage & Telzrow, 1986). Ketogenic (high-fat) diets are modestly effective and are especially useful when there is concern about drug toxicity. Biofeedback and reinforcement contingency programs also are employed. Surgery is an option when the seizures are not controlled by more conservative methods. It may consist of excision of scar tissue that is an epileptogenic focus, the severing of fibers in the corpus callosum that connect the two hemispheres, lobectomy (lobe removal), or hemispherectomy (removal of either the left or the right cortical hemisphere).

There has been considerable discrimination against epileptics. In 1976 five states had involuntary sterilization laws for epileptics: Arizona, Delaware, Oklahoma, South Carolina, and Utah. It was not until 1969 that West Virginia repealed its law prohibiting epileptics from marrying. Epileptics still must face their joint handicap of seizures and an ignorant world that does not understand them.

That epilepsy is more common in the developing countries should be no surprise in view of the less adequate health care and lack of necessities of life. In Africa the incidence is estimated at an astonishing 10%. Malnutrition, parasitic and other brain infections, febrile convulsions, and birth injuries are causes of epilepsy that are much more common in Africa than the United States. Less adequate medical care for epilepsy exists in the developing countries. Nigeria, one of the more developed African countries, has only seven neurologists and five neurosurgeons in the entire country, with a population of 80 million (Osuntokun et al., 1987).

CEREBRAL PALSY

Cerebral palsy is the general term applied to a group of closely related conditions resulting from damage to the developing brain that may occur before, during, or after birth and that result in loss or impairment of control over voluntary muscles. Ordinarily, cerebral palsy results from interference with the oxygen and nutrient supply to the brain before, during, and just after birth. This deficient supply can result from various conditions such as prematurity, an awkward birth position, a twisted umbilical cord, German measles (rubella) or other viral diseases in the mother, a toxic disorder such as lead poisoning, induced labor, and forceps injury during delivery. Prematurity seems to account for cerebral palsy more than any of the other conditions. Prevention to reduce at least some cases of cerebral palsy by measures such as better obstetrical care is possible.

Motor impairment is ordinarily most prominent and can range from mild clumsiness to confinement to a wheelchair. The motor difficulty usually involves one or more of the following forms: spasticity, athetosis, and ataxia. Spastic patients have excessive muscle tension and sometimes have contractures (permanent fixation of a joint such as a wrist in an abnormal position). The athetoid patient has slow involuntary movement of the hands and feet and may have slurred speech. The ataxic patient has a staggering gait and often falls.

About half of cerebral palsy patients are retarded, but the retardation usually is mild. However, it should be pointed out that some persons with cerebral palsy are intellectually gifted. It is unfortunate that cerebral palsy patients with normal intelligence are too often regarded as retarded by casual acquaintances because of such symptoms as speech difficulty and poor coordination.

DEMYELINATING DISEASES

Multiple sclerosis is the best known of the demyelinating diseases. It is also called disseminated sclerosis because the demyelinization (degeneration of the myelin sheath around an axon) is disseminated or scattered throughout the nervous system. Its cause is unknown, although some suspect a slow virus. Consistent with this possibility is the fact that a disproportionate number of multiple sclerosis patients in Denmark were born in March, April, May, and June (Templer et al., 1992). It is more common in cold than in warm climates. Persons who migrate from a high-risk to a low-risk zone maintain the risk associated with their zone of origin, even 20 years after migration. Multiple sclerosis is about eight times as common in immediate relatives of persons with multiple sclerosis than in the general population. However, the evidence for genetic etiology is unclear. Females are almost twice as likely as males to be afflicted. Symptoms of multiple sclerosis are numerous and varied and may include weakness, impaired vision, tremor, ataxia, paresthesia (abnormal sensations such as tingling or burning), pain, sphincter impairment, dizziness, or changes in muscle tone, although most symptoms are primarily of a motor, sensory, and perceptual nature. Appreciable intellectual deterioration is ordinarily not noted. Depression and euphoria are not uncommon. Symptoms frequently remit, change, or reappear in a seemingly mysterious fashion. Although the long-term prognosis is unfavorable, it is common for 30 years to pass from the onset of symptoms to complete incapacitation and death.

PARKINSON'S DISEASE

The most common type of parkinsonism is Parkinson's disease, also known as idiopathic parkinsonism or paralysis agitans. The typical age of onset is in the 60s. One percent of the population over age 50 has Parkinson's disease. The cause is unknown, although there is some tendency for it to run in families. It is slightly more common in males.

The symptoms of Parkinson's disease are quite insidious, and it is common for family and friends to notice the symptoms before the patient does. Other persons may observe a slightly stooped posture, slight stiffness of movement, and "mumbly" speech. However, the diagnosis cannot be made until three characteristic signs appear: tremor, rigidity, and bradykinesia (slowness of movement). The tremor is ordinarily the part of the triad that patients first notice. It is often manifested in the patient's handwriting, which is often quite small in addition to the irregular lines produced by the tremor. The muscular rigidity can cause headaches, low back pain, and leg cramps. Muscular rigidity contributes to the bradykinesia by interfering with the synchrony of agonist and antagonist muscles. For example, when the biceps are being flexed, there is movement difficulty if the triceps are not in proper operation.

The percentage of Parkinson's disease patients reported to have dementia ranges from 33% to 81% (Passafiume, Boller, Keefe, Grant, & Kenneth, 1986). It is not known why some Parkinson's disease patients have dementia and some do not. However, it has been suggested that there are two forms of the disorder, one with pathology of only the substantia nigra and not producing dementia, and the other with cortical pathology as well and producing dementia.

Drugs that increase the neurotransmitter dopamine activity are beneficial for Parkinson's disease and other forms of parkinsonism. Some of those drugs directly increase dopamine activity, the best known of these being L-dopa. Other drugs do so indirectly by suppressing the neurotransmitter acetylcholine. These are referred to as anticholinergic drugs.

NEUROLOGICAL SOFT SIGNS

A neurological soft sign is a minor motor or sensory deficit that is not associated with definitive evidence of central nervous system abnormality. Poor coordination is perhaps the most common of these soft signs. Others include tremor, inability to perform rapid alternating movements of hands and feet in a fluent and rhythmic fashion, and inability to recognize objects placed in the hand when blindfolded.

Neurological soft signs have traditionally been regarded as of minor or inconsequential importance. However, in recent years it has become increasingly clear that soft signs in children are often associated with or predictive of psychological difficulties (Shaffer et al., 1985). They are more common in children who are psychiatric patients and in children who are impulsive, distractible, dependent, sloppy, socially immature, uncooperative, and poor readers. A disproportionate number of adult schizophrenics have soft signs.

A very important study followed up 63 male and 27 female adolescents who had soft neurological signs but were free of definite neurological disorder or retardation in a pediatric exam at age 7. These adolescents were compared with a control group of 63 males and 27 females who were also 17 years of age (Shafer et al., 1985). The index subjects had significantly lower IQs and were more likely than the control subjects to have psychiatric diagnoses. Perhaps the most salient finding is that all 6 of the girls and 12 of the 15 boys with an anxiety-withdrawal disorder were in the index group. The difference was also significant when IQ was controlled for. Thus, it appears that soft neurological signs can predict not only lower IQ and conduct problems but unfavorable subjective state as well.

SPECIFIC DEFICITS IN PSYCHOLOGICAL FUNCTIONING

In addition to the general deficit in intellectual functioning that is found in retarded individuals and in many brain-disordered persons, there are specific deficits that are of interest and concern to neuropsychologists and neurologists. Some of these deficits are of a receptive sort; that is, they are concerned with taking in and processing information. Other deficits are of an expressive sort; they are concerned with the execution of movements and communication. The specific psychological deficits are ascertained through clinical observation, through specific questions or tasks, or through standardized and comprehensive neuropsychological test batteries.

APHASIA

The aphasias are disorders of the spoken language. In expressive aphasia the person knows what he or she wants to say but is unable to do so. The affected person may have the frustrating experience of saying the wrong words or saying item in the wrong sequence, of only being able to grunt, or of saying nothing at all. In anomia, the patient is unable to retrieve a particular word from his or her vocabulary. For example, he or she may want to retrieve the word for what he or she is writing with but is unable to find the word *pencil*. In receptive aphasia, also called sensory aphasia, the patient is partially or totally unable to comprehend the speech of others.

A classical distinction has been made between Wernicke's aphasia and Broca's aphasia, the former being a receptive aphasia and caused by pathology in Wernicke's area of the temporal lobe, and the latter being an expressive aphasia and caused by pathology in Broca's area of the frontal lobe. Actually, most brain-disordered persons with one of these aphasias have both, although the second may often be to a lesser degree. A neuropsychological distinction is sometimes made between nonfluent aphasia, which roughly corresponds to Broca's aphasia, and fluent aphasia, which roughly corresponds to Wernicke's aphasia.

Distinctions in speech pathology are made among aphasia, dysarthria, and aphonia. In aphasia the patient is unable to express his or her ideas. Aphasia reflects some sort of permanent or temporary brain abnormality. In dysarthria there is defective clarity, speech, or rhythm of speech. Dysarthria may or may not be a function of brain disorder. An example of brain-disorder dysarthria is the general paresis patient who has difficulty saying "Methodist Episcopal." Another example is that of the patient with cerebellar damage who displays a scanning or staccato type of speech. In aphonia, which is a function of defect in the peripheral speech apparatus, the person is unable to speak.

ALEXIA AND AGRAPHIA

Alexia refers to the complete inability to comprehend written language. Dyslexia refers to the partial inability to comprehend such. Dyslexia is a common problem encountered by school psychologists. Agraphia refers to the inability to write. Agraphia refers not to a simple deficit in the motor ability needed to move a writing instrument but to a deficit in the symbolic aspect of writing. Alexia and agraphia may or may not be found in the same person. Both are the result of pathology in various parts of the brain.

APRAXIA

In apraxia, the patient is unable to perform the acts he or she wishes to perform in spite of adequate motor skills and intelligence. In ideomotor apraxia the patient is unable to carry out his intention or comply with a request in the execution of a simple act such as stirring coffee with a spoon or waving good-bye. In ideational apraxia the patient is able to carry out the simple elements but not the totality of relatively complex activity.

In construction apraxia the patient has gross difficulty in spatial relations tasks such as drawing geometric figures or constructing simple objects with sticks or blocks. The exact nature of the difficulty is a function of the locus of the brain pathology. In dressing apraxia, as the name implies, the patient has difficulty in coordinating and executing the movements necessary to dress himself or herself.

AGNOSIA

Agnosia refers to an inability to recognize what is familiar. In visual agnosia, the patient is unable to recognize familiar visual presentations such as objects, persons, faces, or colors. In auditory agnosia the patient is unable to recognize familiar sounds such as voices or music. The patient with tactile agnosia is unable to recognize an object he touches or holds while blindfolded.

THE NEUROLOGICAL EXAMINATION

SENSATION

The neurologist assesses touch, pain, temperature sense, position sense, and vibration sense. He or she does this by such techniques as fingertip number writing, having the patient recognize objects placed in the hand, inducing mild pain, and determining whether or not two sharp close points are felt as two or one.

COORDINATION

Cerebellar abnormality and a number of different neurological conditions are associated with coordination difficulty. If a patient can not touch his or her nose, this is called dysmetria. If he or she reaches for and misses a point in space, it is called pastpointing. Sometimes the coordination difficulty consists of inability to start and stop movements smoothly and quickly.

REFLEXES

The neurologist assesses the adequacy of reflexes by tapping the muscle tendons at the major points. An excessively brisk reflex, a diminished reflex, and the absence of reflex can indicate various sorts of nervous system disturbance. In the pathological reflexes the reflexive movement is inherently abnormal rather than differing in degree from normality. One of the better known of these is Babinski's reflex or Babinski's sign. In the adult with pyramidal tract damage (and in the normal infant) the toes fan outward and upward instead of contracting when the patient is stroked on the sole of the foot.

GAIT

Different neurological conditions produce different sorts of abnormal gait (style of walking). Persons with cerebral palsy exhibit a scissors gait in which one leg is placed in front of the other. Patients with lower motor neuron damage display a steppage gait, lifting their knees rather highly in the air. Cerebellar damage often results in a wide-based gait. The characteristic gait of parkinsonism is that of rather small steps with somewhat of a lunging forward. In a spastic gait, caused by damage to the upper motor neuron, there is increased muscle tone that interferes with coordinated muscle movement.

MUSCLE STRENGTH AND TONE

The neurologist ordinarily assesses muscle strength in a very gross fashion by asking the patient to push and pull against him or her in various ways. The neurologist not only assesses degree of strength but also appreciable differences between the strength on the right and left sides of the body. Diminished strength on one side of the body could indicate brain pathology on the contralateral side of the brain. Muscular atrophy, either bilateral or unilateral, is noted by the neurologist.

CRANIAL NERVES

Because of the intimate association of the brain and the cranial nerves, the assessment of cranial nerve functioning is important. As an example, visual acuity, which is a function of cranial nerve II (optic), is tested by such means as having the patient read and by determining if the examiner's finger can be seen in each of the four visual quadrants.

NEUROLOGICAL TESTS

ELECTROENCEPHALOGRAM (EEG)

The EEG is a recording of the electrical activity of the cerebral cortex. The frequency of the brain waves, their voltage, and various abnormalities such as "spikes" (very high voltage waves) are noted. EEGs are especially useful in epilepsy. Degenerative conditions and brain tumors can produce a relatively "flat," low-amplitude EEG. An abnormally slow EEG can indicate a number of conditions, including seizure activity, degenerative disorder, inflammation of the brain, brain infection, metabolic disorders, and various drugs, such as antidepressants, barbituates, other sedatives at very high dosage, and antipsychotic drugs at very high dosage. An abnormally fast EEG can indicate barbituates and other sedatives at low dosage, antianxiety drugs, and anxiety.

Lumbar Puncture

The lumbar puncture or spinal tap is made to withdraw a sample of the patient's cerebrospinal fluid. Central nervous system abnormalities can alter the color of the fluid such as making it bloody. Laboratory analyses can detect a variety of infections and chemical abnormalities.

Brain Scan

The brain scan consists of passing material containing radioisotopes through the brain and mapping the brain on an x-ray film. Abnormal brain tissue retains more radioscopic material than normal tissue does, and this is indicated on the film. Brain scans are especially valuable for determining the presence of a brain tumor.

Angiogram

Angiography consists of passing a radio-opaque solution into the arteries of the brain so that the arteries and veins can be observed on special x-rays. This permits visualization of vascular pathology such as blockage or hemorrhage, in addition to displacement such as may be caused by a tumor. Angiography is often used when a tumor has already been found and the neurosurgeon wants to determine the blood supply to the pathological region.

Computerized Axial Tomography (CT Scan)

The CT scan consists of tens of thousands of x-rays that are computer-processed so as to detect minute variations in tissue density. CTs can detect and elucidate a variety of brain abnormalities, including tumors, atrophy, subarachnoid hemorrhages, hematomas, and trauma.

Magnetic Resonance Imaging (MRI)

MRI i· ·n imaging technique that is similar to the CT scan in what it can detect, b·t it produces greater clarity and specificity and is superior in terms of providing a three-dimensional perspective. It is less invasive for the patient but is more expensive than a CT scan.

POSITIVE EMISSION TOMOGRAPHY

Positive emission tomography, usually referred to as a PET scan, is a technique primarily geared to brain physiology rather than structure. Specifically, it reveals metabolic activity of the brain both normal and abnormal. As the name implies, it detects energy in the form of positrons. It can be useful in seizure disorders, strokes, Huntington's chorea, and Alzheimer's disease and in research.

NEUROPSYCHOLOGICAL TESTING

The work of the neuropsychologist is heavily focused on testing psychological functions that are impaired in brain-damaged or other brain-disordered persons. Ordinarily, an intelligence test is administered along with the neuropsychological tests that are designed for specific types of impairments. However, if the brain pathology is not diffuse and substantial, the decline in general intelligence may be fairly small. One of the reasons for this is that some parts of IQ tests are highly dependent upon previously acquired elements of intelligence, such as vocabulary and store of knowledge. These skills are usually less affected by brain pathology than are memory, abstract thinking, sensory and perceptual and motor functioning, and capacity for new learning.

The most widely used neuropsychological test battery is the Halstead-Reitan Battery. The initial work was done in the 1940s by Ward Halstead, who was attempting to construct a measure of "biological intelligence," that is, intelligence that is relatively independent of educational and other acquired skills. Halstead's student, Ralph Reitan, further developed the battery.

One of the Halstead-Reitan subtests is the Category Test of abstract reasoning, in which the person being examined is required to sort projected geometrical designs by such principles as shape, size, number, and color. In the Tactile Performance Test the subject is blindfolded and timed as he or she places wooden geometric designs into the appropriate holes in the formboard, as a child would work on a puzzle. After this is done with each hand, the subject's blindfold is taken off, and he or she attempts to draw the shapes of the designs from memory. In the Seashore Rhythm Test the subject must specify whether sounds are the same or different. The Speech Sounds Test is similar to the Rhythm Test, but speech sounds are used. In the Finger Tapping Test the subject is asked to tap a key something like an old Morse code telegraph key as rapidly as possible, first with one hand and then with the other. In the Time

Sense Test the subject must estimate the amount of time it takes a sweep hand to rotate around a clock face. In the Critical Flicker Fusion Test the frequency of a flashing light is lessened until the flashing light is seen as fused or steady. The person with brain pathology is more likely to require a lower flashing frequency for the light to be perceived as fused. The Aphasia Screening Test assesses various types of aphasia. In addition to the so-called impairment index, the proportion of tests that are in the impairment range, the neuropsychologist considers the precise score of each test and their parts, differences between left- and right-sided functioning, and qualitative observations.

The second most widely used neuropsychological battery is the Luria-Nebraska Neuropsychological Battery of Charles Golden. The Luria-Nebraska, which is newer than the Halstead-Reitan, is a modification of the procedures of Russian psychologist Alexandria Luria. These procedures were designed so that each task assesses a relatively unique neuropsychological function. This is in contrast to the Halstead-Reitan tests, which seem to assess a greater array of functions per task.

The Motor Functions, Rhythm and Pitch, Tactile and Kinesthetic Functions, Visual Functions, Receptive Language, Expressive Language, Writing and Reading Scale, Arithmetic Scale, Memory Scale, and Intelligence Scale tests assess what the names imply. Failure on the Pathognomonic Scale almost certainly implies abnormality in the central nervous system. The Left Hemisphere Scale contains items involving the motor and tactile functioning of the right arm. The Right Hemisphere Scale, in like manner (with the left arm) assesses the integrity of the central sulcus area of the right hemisphere. An advantage of the Luria-Nebraska is that it can be administered in 2–3 hours, in contrast to the approximately 8 hours needed for administration of the Halstead-Reitan. However, the latter has some advantages over the former, such as being better able to detect subtle brain pathology in highly intelligent persons.

NEUROPSYCHOLOGICAL REHABILITATION

There are a number of psychologically oriented rehabilitation techniques and procedures. One of them is biofeedback, which is often used in enabling the patient to regain muscle usage. Electrodes are placed on the muscle under consideration, and the electrical impulses are recorded on an electromyograph. The patient can gauge the extent of desired movement by looking at the electromyograph and thereby gradually improving the muscle movement. Biofeedback has also been used for speech improvement in cerebral palsy and stroke patients and in the treatment of urinary and fecal incontinence. Another technique for increasing muscle movement is to apply electric shocks to the

NEUROLOGICAL	NEUROPSYCHOLOGICAL	INTELLIGENCE	ACHIEVEMENT
ANATOMY & PHYSIOLOGY	LANGUAGE, MEMORY, CONCENTRATION, PROBLEM SOLVING ABILITIES	VERBAL AND NON-VERBAL INTELLIGENCE	APTITUDE & ACADEMIC ACHIEVEMENT

FIGURE 1.1   Spectrum of neuropsychological functions and associated assessment procedures.

From Templer, D. I., Campodonico, J. R., Trent, A., & Spencer, D. A. (1991) *The neurological spectrum: A theoretical formulation.* San Francisco: Western Psychological Association.

limb sufficient to produce reflexive movement. Fine motor control is improved by such techniques as repeatedly executing a movement such as the turning of a screw.

Verbal functions, such as speech, reading, and writing, are frequently defective in brain pathology. The laborious repetition of various sounds or words is sometimes employed. Training for alternative verbal functions and modes of communication is also carried out. Psychologically oriented techniques can be employed with kinesthetic, memory, spatial relations, and spatial orientation deficits. Destroyed neurons cannot be restored or replaced. However, other parts of the brain can take over the functions previously governed by the damaged areas. Also, new brain circuits can be established. Since the 1980s there has been a mushrooming of the employment of remediation strategies for head-injured persons. Remediation strategies assume some sort of neuronal growth such as collateral sprouting resulting from the exercise of neuronal circuits. Remediation strategies for head injuries differ from the other category of rehabilitation, cognitive rehabilitation, which involves compensation for cognitive impairment. An example of the latter would be carrying a memory notepad. It is apparent that the remediation techniques are far more ambitious in that they attempt to bring about actual neurological recovery rather than only strategies that enable the patient to make greater utilization of intact brain structure and functioning. Benedict (1989) reviewed the remediation literature and appropriately concluded that much of the evidence falls short of being clear and unequivocal but does provide sufficient encouragement for further and better research and for more and better treatment engineering.

THE NEUROLOGICAL SPECTRUM

The concept of the "neurological spectrum" was intended to span the continuum of functioning from biological foundations to acquired skills, as illustrated by Figure 1.1 (Templer, Campodonico, Trent, & Spencer, 1991; Templer Campodonico, Trent, Spencer, & Hartlage, in press). There are different assessment procedures that parallel this spectrum of functioning. The adjacent assessment segments were found to correlate more highly with each other than the distal segments do. The spectrum conceptualization emphasizes that the different assessment tools of the various disciplines, such as neurology, neuropsychology, and special education, differ at point of application in degree rather than in any absolute qualitative sense, at least on the theoretical level. Such a perspective not only facilitates interdisciplinary collaboration but clarifies the diagnostic, intervention, and prognostic issues.

AT HIGHER RISK FOR SCHIZOPHRENIA

Persons with Family History of Schizophrenia

Northern Europeans

Persons of Northern European Ethnicity

Adolescents and Young Adults

Lower Socioeconomic Status Persons

Persons Who Live in Colder Climates

Persons with History of Prenatal and Perinatal Difficulties

Persons with Abnormal Neurological Test Findings

Persons with Soft Neurological Signs

Persons with Brain Disorders

Persons with Below-Average IQ

Persons Who Had Behavioral Problems as Children

Persons Who Act Out

Persons in Urban Localities

Persons with Multiple Psychiatric Diagnoses

Persons with Interpersonal Difficulties

TWO

Schizophrenia

Morel, a Belgian psychiatrist, in 1857 reported the case of a 14-year-old boy who had previously been a good student, well mannered, and well adjusted. Within a period of a few months his intellectual ability declined, and he lost contact with reality. Morel coined the term *dementia praecox*. *Dementia* is a French word meaning loss of mental ability, and *praecox* means occurring at an early age. It is good that this old term has been abandoned. In the first place, many schizophrenics exhibit little or no intellectual impairment, and some, in fact, are brilliant individuals with considerable academic and vocational attainment. Second, in some patients, schizophrenia may not appear until they are in their 30s. The word *schizophrenia* was devised by Swiss psychiatrist Eugene Bleuler in 1911. (The Greek word *schizein* means to cleave or split, and *phren* means mind.) Bleuler maintained that in schizophrenia there is a split between the affective and cognitive components of the mind. This may be the origin of the "split personality" commonly mentioned in the popular press.

SYMPTOMS AND CHARACTERISTICS

Bleuler maintained that there are four primary symptoms of schizophrenia. Bleuler's "four A's" are looseness of *a*ssociations, inappropriate *a*ffect, *a*mbivalence, and *a*utism. Inappropriate affect (emotion) is often displayed by a flatness or blunting. Schizophrenics' voices often have a bland or rather lifeless quality. Autism refers to the schizophrenic's preoccupation with fantasy

33

life, delusional material, hallucinations, and in general the inner world of experience to the exclusion of the external world. Ambivalence refers to concurrent positive and negative emotions directed toward the same person or object. A man may love his wife and hate her at the same time. Ambivalence is the least useful of the "four A's" because it is characteristic of people in general rather than schizophrenics in particular.

It is the opinion of many psychologists, that the Bleulerian "looseness of associations," often referred to as a "thought disorder" or a "thinking disorder" or "cognitive slippage," is the cardinal characteristic of the schizophrenic. In 1961, one of the authors (DIT) administered an intelligence test to a schizophrenic woman in a state hospital. One of the questions required naming four U.S. presidents since 1900. She replied "Eisenhower, Washington, Mt. Washington, Mt. Everest." Each of the last three components of her answer was related to the item before it, but her train of thought led her far away from the question. Occasionally, schizophrenics are so thought-disordered that they are incoherent to the extent that their verbiage is referred to as a "word salad."

Kurt Schneider (1959) described the "rank order symptoms" of the disturbed inner world of the schizophrenic. In "audible thoughts" the patient hears a voice saying his or her own thoughts. In "voices arguing" there are auditory hallucinations of voices arguing. Another rank-order symptom is "voices commenting on one's actions." In "influence playing on the body, somatic passivity," there is the belief that invisible influences such as x-rays are having an influence on one's body. In "thought withdrawal" the patient believes that thoughts are being extracted from him or her. In "thought insertion" patients believe that the thoughts of another person are inserted into his or her mind. In "diffusion" or "broadcasting of throughts" the patient is convinced that those around them can read their thoughts. In "made feelings" the schizophrenic believes that other persons can insert various mood states such as anger or sadness into them. In "made impulses" ego-alien impulses are complained of. They are similar to "made volitional acts."

Mellor (1970, 1982) found that 119 (72%) of 166 schizophrenics had one or more of these rank-order symptoms. The more disturbed schizophrenics were more likely to have such. Although not all schizophrenics have these symptoms, some clinicians contend that they are pathognomonic (conclusively establishing the diagnosis) of schizophrenia. Schneider's first-rank symptoms seem to be rather universal symptoms of schizophrenia. (Carpenter, Strauss, & Bartko, 1974).

Bleuler's secondary symptoms of schizophrenia are hallucinations and delusions. Although schizophrenics sometimes experience visual hallucinations and even olfactory hallucinations, auditory hallucinations are unquestionably the most common. The preponderance of auditory hallucinations consist of voices, frequently voices calling one's name. Occasionally, schizophrenics receive command hallucinations such as instructing the patient to kill himself (a state of affairs that is most serious and frequently leads to hospitalization and suicidal precaution decisions from the prudent clinician).

Romme and Escher (1989) reported a study in which they attempted to understand the hearing of voices from schizophrenics' accounts of their experiences. They described the period in which the voices began as "the starting phase." The schizophrenic persons described this as an experience that began very suddenly and was anxiety-producing. Seventy percent of the respondents said that these experiences began in some sort of emotional or traumatic experience such as an accident, divorce, death, psychotherapy session, spiritism, illness, being in love, moving, or pregnancy. Some of the interviewed persons regarded the voices as aggressive, causing chaos in their minds, and generally negative. However, some persons viewed the voices in a positive sense such as being helpful or strengthening them or raising their self-esteem. Romme and Escher described the next phase as "the phase of organization: Coping with the voices." Different persons in this phase chose various strategies: ignoring the voices, listening to only the positive voices, and setting limits upon the voices. In the "phase of stabilization" some patients accepted the voices as part of themselves and of life and were often able to either follow the commands of the voices or to choose their own ideas. Romme and Escher maintained that one third of the schizophrenics were able to cope with the voices, and two thirds were not able to cope with them.

Many delusions are of a paranoid sort. The schizophrenic may feel that people are trying to kill him, injure him, embarrass him, discredit him, spy on him, follow him, steal from him, or harm him in some way. Some delusions are of a grandiose sort (e.g., thinking that one is Jesus Christ or the Blessed Virgin). It is common for persecutory and grandiose material to be combined in the same delusional system (e.g., thinking that one has been sent by God to save the world and that many people want to harm him because they are jealous of his special powers). Delusions of references are common. With such, the patient may feel that people are talking about him or looking at him or in some way referring to him. It is fairly common for schizophrenics to feel that television programs have special reference to them or that they can obtain personal messages from television.

The schizophrenic is ordinarily viewed by other people as peculiar or at least "different." Eccentricities, mannerisms, awkward word usage, grimaces, inappropriate smiling, and inappropriate laughter are all common. Schizophrenics are often rather careless or indifferent about their personal appearance. The "deteriorated" or "regressed" schizophrenics may rock back and forth, sit motionless for hours, disrobe, or openly masturbate. Their habits pertaining to personal cleanliness alone may impede them from functioning in the mainstream of society.

The general public is often told that mental patients are no more dangerous than the average person. Although such public education may reduce the stigma of mental illness, it does not appear to be completely accurate. In one study it was found that 45 (45%) of 99 schizophrenics, in contrast to only 34 (33%) of 104 nonschizophrenics, exhibited "violent" (hitting, kicking, or shoving) behavior on a psychiatric inpatient unit (Shader, Jackson, Harmatz, & Appelbaum, 1977). In a study of first admissions of 253 schizophrenics to a psychiatric hospital in London, 6% had repeatedly threatened the lives of others, and an additional 13% did so on one or two occasions. Twenty-two percent had contact with the police for bizarre or inappropriate behavior (Johnstone, Crow, Johnson, & MacMillan, 1986). In another study in London over half the families of schizophrenics reported behavior that was severely distressing, threatening, or noisy (Gibbons, Horn, Powell, & Gibbons, 1984).

About 100 persons each year are arrested by the Secret Service for causing or attempting to cause problems at the White House. In a report on 328 such cases over a 3-year period, 91% were found to have a schizophrenic diagnosis. At 12-year follow-up, 31 of the 217 males had murder or assault arrests during this period. A schizophrenic woman was arrested for assaulting a woman she incorrectly believed to be the First Lady (Gottesman & Bertelson, 1989). Parnas, Schulsinger, Schulsinger, Mednick, and Teasdale (1982) conducted a study in which high-risk children (specifically those with schizophrenic mothers) were assessed at age 15 and then had the determination of presence of schizophrenia 10 to 12 years later. Many who later became schizophrenic exhibited classroom disciplinary problems at about age 15.

A long-standing diagnostic rule is that disorientation is a symptom of brain syndrome but not of schizophrenia. However, it has been reported that about a quarter of chronically hospitalized schizophrenics incorrectly state their age by 5 years or more, with a younger age being more frequently given than an older age. Age orientation tends to be associated with temporal disorientation such as not being able to state the year or the length of their hospital stay (Stevens, Crow, Bowman, & Coles, 1978). The age-disoriented patients did significantly worse than correctly oriented schizophrenics on a number of knowledge and intellectual ability tests administered by Liddle and Crow (1984), who concluded that the disoriented schizophrenics have "organic-type" psychological deficits.

There is considerable evidence that schizophrenics tend to score below average on intelligence tests. Children who later become schizophrenics have lower IQs than their normal siblings. In general, it appears that schizophrenics tend to have below-average premorbid IQs and that these IQs become even lower after onset of the disorder, especially when they become very disturbed. There tends to be an increase in IQ after improvement. The lower IQ of schizophrenics is probably a function of two factors: the same brain abnormality that produced the schizophrenia and psychiatric disturbance in the realms of thought disorder, concentration difficulty, anxiety, depression, and hallucinations, and other psychotic preoccupations.

Schizophrenia is quite a heterogeneous category, representing a number of different conditions. Some schizophrenics, particularly those on the long-term care wards of state and veteran's administration hospitals, are difficult to differentiate from their retarded or brain-damaged roommates. The so-called pseudoneurotic schizophrenics (Hoch & Polatin, 1949) suffer terribly from their fears, anxieties, dreads, and preoccupation with bodily functioning and ills.

In the 1950s and 1960s a massive amount of research was carried out on the reactive versus process differentiation of schizophrenia. The reactive schizophrenic was said to become ill at a relatively later age and with considerable environmental stress. Psychosocial and psychosexual functioning are at a higher level, and prognosis is better. The process schizophrenic has more genetic etiology, an insidious onset at an earlier age, and a history of more inadequate functioning; their prognosis is less favorable. The original conceptualization of two distinct types evolved toward a continuum, with the reactive schizophrenic at one end and the process schizophrenic at the other. The Templer and Cappellety (1986) conceptualization of primary and secondary schizophrenia is similar to that of process and reactive schizophrenia in that in both there is essentially a distinction between endogenous and exogenous etiology. In the older conceptualization the exogenous factors were thought to be in the interpersonal realm, and in the Templer and Cappelletty conceptualization the exogenous etiological factors are of a biological origin such as head injury and infection.

DIAGNOSIS

Although almost all schizophrenics have noticeable paranoid tendencies, such are paramount in paranoid schizophrenics. On the average, thinking disorganization is less for paranoid schizophrenics than for other schizophrenics, and they are brighter. Sometimes these reasonably well integrated schizophrenics actually convince authorities such as the FBI that their delusional material is actually true.

The disorganized (formerly called hebephrenic) schizophrenic tends to be cognitively and socially impaired to a greater extent than other schizophrenics. His or her behavior is very childlike and includes giggling, laughing, inappropriate smiling and grimacing, silly gesturing and speech, and inattention to personal hygiene.

The catatonic schizophrenic's catatonic stupor consists of maintaining a rigid posture for hours at a time. There may be apparently stubborn resistance to change in position. On the other hand, the clinician sometimes observes waxy flexibility in which the patient's limbs and body will assume any position they are placed in. At times "catatonic excitement" takes place which consists of erratic, excited, apparently purposeless, and sometimes dangerous behavior. Both catatonic schizophrenia and hebephrenic schizophrenia are much less common now than several decades ago (Templer & Veleber, 1981, 1982). The reasons for this are not known.

It should be borne in mind that a catatonic state does not invariably mean schizophrenia. Catatonia can be produced by hyperparathyroidism and other metabolic disorders, medial temporal lobe dysfunction or damage, midbrain lesions, brain degenerative diseases, neurosyphilis, cerebral cysts, encephalitis and various drugs including PCP, hallucinogenic drugs, and amphetamines (Lechtenberg, 1982).

The undifferentiated schizophrenic has clear characteristics of more than one type of schizophrenia. The residual type of schizophrenic is diagnosed when the patient has a past history of psychotic episodes but is not currently floridly psychotic.

The symptoms of childhood schizophrenia are the same as these of adult-onset schizophrenia. Childhood schizophrenia has an even worse prognosis than its adult counterpart. Follow-up research shows that the adult is almost invariably schizophrenic, with prominent negative symptoms of schizophrenia, perhaps especially poverty of thought and drive. About 2% of schizophrenics have onset in childhood.

EPIDEMOLOGY

THE GEOGRAPHY OF SCHIZOPHRENIA

Statements about the geography of schizophrenia should be made with caution, especially on an international level, because of differences in criteria and diagnostic practice in the various countries and possible differences in recording. Nevertheless, although one may question the schizophrenia rates in any given country and between pairs of countries, the big picture seems to indicate that the rates of schizophrenia are not the same throughout the world.

Torrey (1980) maintained that schizophrenia has not always existed to the extent it does today and that prior to 1800 it was virtually unheard of. Torrey maintained that if the psychotic episodes prior to then are examined they appear to be more transient and possibly a function of an acute brain syndrome due to, for example, an infection or nutritional deficiency. The prevalence and distribution of schizophrenia expanded greatly in the 19th century. Schizophrenia seems to be rare in the remote and technologically undeveloped parts of the world. Even in the industrialized countries the distribution of schizophrenia is far from uniform. In Europe, the prevalence appears to be high in the western part of Ireland, the Scandinavian countries (especially northern Sweden), the northwestern coastal region of Croatia, Poland, and the Soviet Union; it appears to be low in the Mediterranean countries.

Scheper-Hughes (1979) reported rates that are generally consistent with the Torrey contention of schizophrenia prevalence in various countries. From high to low, they are Republic of Ireland, 7.37; Sweden, 6.97; Austria, 5.29; New Zealand, 4.86; Israel, 4.78; Scotland, 4.74; Northern Ireland, 4.20; England and Wales, 3.63; United States, 2.93; Canada, 2.39; Poland, 2.38; Italy, 2.06; Chile, 1.62; Ceylon, 1.42; Spain, 1.33; Japan, 1.31; Cyprus, 1.09; Greece, 1.06; Portugal, 1.01; Brazil, .73; Ghana, .52; Mexico, .34; Kenya, .29; Senegal, .26; and Nigeria, .02.

In the United States the prevalence is higher in the more populated states (Templer & Veleber, 1981), and there is greater prevalence in the inner city. Schizophrenia rates are higher in countries with lower January temperature, lower July temperature, higher geographical latitude, and higher per capita income (Templer, Hintze, Trent, & Trent, 1991).

SEASONALITY OF SCHIZOPHRENIC BIRTHS

It is well established that schizophrenics tend to be born in the colder months of the year. There are negative correlations between temperature of month and number of schizophrenics born (Templer & Austin, 1980; Templer, Ruff, Halcomb, Barthlow, & Ayers, 1978; Templer & Austin, 1980). The most viable explanation for this association seems to be the "harmful influence" hypothesis of McNeil, Raff, and Cromwell (1971), which contends that there are harmful effects surrounding birth or during gestation, such as infection or nutritional variables. Consistent with the harmful influence hypothesis is the finding of greater seasonality over the 20th century in Europe than in the United States, a phenomenon attributed by Templer, Ruff, Barthlow, Halcomb and Ayers (1978) to the greater prosperity and protection from the elements in the United States. On the basis of this technology-based explanation, Templer and Austin (1980) predicted and found a decrease in the seasonality of schizophrenic births from 1900 to 1960 in Missouri. To further test the harmful effects hypothesis, Templer and Veleber (1982) determined that schizophrenics with presumably a lesser genetic predisposition, namely, paranoid schizophrenics, had greater seasonality of birth than did catatonic and hebephrenic schizophrenics. Apparently, with a greater genetic predisposition, less of a harmful influence is needed for the development of schizophrenia.

SOCIOECONOMIC STATUS

In a classical sociological study, Faris and Dunham (1939) found that the incidence of schizophrenia was inversely related to socioeconomic status. They reported that the areas in the outermost of concentric circles around the center of Chicago represented a lesser incidence of schizophrenia. As reviewed by Eaton (1985), the passage of years has not altered the generalizations of Farris and Dunham. Schizophrenia is more prevalent among less prosperous, less well educated, and less well occupationally placed people. There are two common explanations for the higher prevalence among less privileged people. The first is that the hardships and deprivations of low socioeconomic status force a retreat from reality. Most of the evidence supports the second explanation—the so called drift hypothesis, which purports that because of the devastating effects of the disorder the schizophrenic drifts into lower social status.

GENDER

The incidence of schizophrenia seems about the same in the two sexes. However, there is some research evidence that schizophrenic males tend to be more withdrawn and passive than normal men, whereas schizophrenic women are more assertive, physically aggressive, and sexually active than normal women. Male and female schizophrenics differ on several other premorbid, behavioral, and clinical course variables. Male offspring of schizophrenic mothers have more soft neurological signs than do female offspring (Rieder, Donnelly, & Herdt, 1979). Male schizophrenics are more likely to have a premorbid schizoid personality (Wolff & Barlow, 1980). Male preschizophrenics have more aggressive and delinquent behavior, and female preschizophrenics are more shy and withdrawn (Watt, 1978). The peak age of onset is later for female schizophrenics (Loranger, 1984). The causes of these gender differences are unclear, but there has been speculation on the possible roles of hormonal, brain, and in utero factors (DeLisi, Dauphinais, & Hauser, 1989).

MANIFESTATIONS OF SCHIZOPHRENIA AS A FUNCTION OF CULTURE

Torrey (1980) pointed out several examples of the content of thoughts and delusions differing from one subculture to another in addition to changing over time. Educated schizophrenics in Brazil have delusions focusing upon electricity, whereas less advantaged schizophrenic Brazilians have delusions focusing upon spirit possession. Similar differences are found between urban and rural schizophrenics, respectively, in Ecuador. It has been reported that delusions of grandeur are uncommon among nonliterate Africans, who are reluctant to challenge the gods. Before World War II, the delusions of Japanese schizophrenics focused upon the emperor, but after the war they focused on the United States and the Communist party. In the past century delusions of European schizophrenics have tended to shift from God and the devil to agents of the government. Torrey suggested the generalization that schizophrenic behavior is often that which is more outrageous for the culture. As an example he reported that in Japan, where family ties are very important, schizophrenics often assault family members.

DIGRESSION TO EXOTIC PSYCHOSES

There has been a good deal written about the so-called exotic psychoses exhibited by people in remote or undeveloped parts of the world. Whether such is schizophrenia colored by the cultural milieu or different and distinctive other psychoses is a controversial matter. In the *indigo* psychosis, among Indians in northwestern Canada, there is purported to be a compulsion to eat human flesh. Attacks of *piblobtog* among Eskimos may include tearing of clothing, wandering off, and rolling in the snow. In *susto* there is a belief among the Indians in Bolivia and Peru that their soul has been stolen. In the Orient, there is the *koro* symptom, a delusion of penile shrinkage.

BIOLOGICAL ETIOLOGY

GENETICS

Heston (1966) found that children separated from their schizophrenic mothers at birth have an incidence of schizophrenia that is much higher than that of children separated from nonschizophrenic women and comparable to the incidence of schizophrenia in children raised by the schizophrenic mothers. Kety, Rosenthal, Wender, and Schulsinger (1968) found a much higher incidence of schizophrenia in adopted children with schizophrenic biological mothers than in adopted children with nonschizophrenic mothers. An important aspect of the findings of Kety et al. is that about half of the biological half-siblings were paternal and about half maternal. This rules out the possibility that intrauterine conditions rather than genetics constitute the crucial variables. Slater (1968) reviewed 16 reported cases of monozygotic twins being reared apart. The concordance rate was 62.5, comparable to that for monozygotic twins reared together.

The closer the genetic relationship to a schizophrenic, the greater the probability of becoming schizophrenic (Shields, 1975). About 1 of 100 general population persons become schizophrenic. However, if a person is a first-degree relative of a schizophrenic, such as a sibling or a child, the chances are about 1 in 10. The probability of an ordinary sibling and a fraternal twin of a schizophrenic becoming schizophrenic does not differ in spite of the more similar environment of twins. However, about half of identical twins of schizophrenics also become schizophrenic. Whether or not the twins are separated at birth has no bearing on the probability of becoming schizophrenic.

BRAIN ABNORMALITY

Brain Atrophy

A number of studies using computerized tomography have demonstrated that schizophrenics tend to have larger ventricles than do normal persons, presumably the result of atrophy. Andreason, Olsen, Dennert, and Smith (1982) found symptomatology differences between schizophrenics with large ventricles and those with ventricles smaller than those of the average schizophrenic patient. The former had "negative" symptoms such as affective flattening, avolition, and anhedonia, and were functioning at a lower level. The smaller-ventricle patients exhibited "positive" symptoms such as delusions, hallucinations, and bizarre behavior. Thus, the patients with large ventricles seemed to resemble brain-damaged persons more. Weinberger, Cannon-Spoor, Potkin, and Wyatt (1980) found that schizophrenics whose CT scans evidenced greatest atrophy had the poorest premorbid adjustment. These authors inferred that their findings implicate a neuropathological process that occurs early in development. On the basis of both the Andreason et al. study and the Weinberger et al. study it would appear that it is the so-called process or primary schizophrenics who are more likely to have enlarged ventricles.

In one study it was found that the offspring of schizophrenics who became schizophrenic had larger ventricles than those of the 13 nonschizophrenic offspring. Thus, it would appear that a combination of having a schizophrenic mother and having neurological abnormality increase the likelihood of schizophrenia (Schulsinger et al., 1984). Another important imaging study was carried out with 15 monozygotic twins who were discordant pairs for schizophrenia (Suddath, Christison, Torrey, Casanova, & Weinberger, 1990). Twelve of the discordant pairs were correctly identified by mere visual inspection of the magnetic resonance imaging (MRI). Suddath et al. appropriately inferred that, since the identical twin pairs have identical genetic endowment, their findings would appear to be of neuropathologic origins.

There is an impressive accumulation of evidence that schizophrenics tend to have abnormality in the medial temporal cortex, especially the hippocampal region (Torrey, 1991). Postmortem studies have found below-normal volume in this region (Jeste & Lohr, 1989). MRI has confirmed the below-normal reduction in volume (Suddath, et al., 1990).

Left–Right-Sided Brain Differences

There is evidence of left-sided brain involvement in schizophrenia. Flor-Henry (1969) found that temporal lobe epileptics with left-sided foci were more apt to have schizophreniform psychoses, and those with right-sided foci were more likely to have affective disorders. Auditory threshold research has demonstrated left-sided deficits in schizophrenics (Gruzelier & Hammond, 1976). Schizophrenics tend to have abnormal evoked potentials (EEG response to sensory stimulation) on the left side of the cortex (Reveley, Reveley, Clifford, & Murray, 1983). Most normal individuals have slightly greater brain mass on the left than on the right side. However, there tends to be a reversal of this tendency in schizophrenics (Luchins, Weinberger, & Wyatt, 1982).

Abnormal EEGs

Schizophrenics tend to have abnormal and/or atypical EEGs. Itil, Simeon, and Coffin (1976) found that adult schizophrenics, schizophrenic children, and children designated as having a high risk of becoming schizophrenic all tend to have fewer alpha waves (8–10 cycles per second, characteristically observed in normal persons resting with eyes closed) and more beta (fast) activity than normal control subjects. Furthermore, hallucinogenic drugs tend to change EEG in a psychotic direction, and antipsychotic drugs tend to produce EEG changes in an opposite direction.

Thickening of the Corpus Callosum

The corpus callosum, which is the major commissure connecting the left and right cerebral hemispheres, is found at postmortem to be thickened in 20% of schizophrenics (Rosenthal & Bigelow, 1972). On a number of psychological tasks, schizophrenics have shown deficits apparently related to inadequate communication between the two hemispheres. For example, Beaumont and Dimond (1973) reported that schizophrenics had difficulty matching patterns separately flashed to each visual field. They suggested a similarity between schizophrenics and persons who had a surgical commissurotomy for intractable epilepsy.

Deficit in Cerebral Blood Flow

Schizophrenics have less cerebral blood flow in the frontal lobes than do normal control subjects. Since cerebral blood flow correlates rather highly with indices of neuronal metabolism, one might have predicted lower frontal than occipital metabolism in schizophrenics, and such actually has been found (Buchsbaum, 1990).

Pregnancy and Birth Complications

McNeil and Kraij (1973) concluded that schizophrenics tend to have suffered from a disproportionate number of pregnancy and birth complications. In a subsequent study it was found that the children of schizophrenic women who had pregnancy and birth complications were more likely to become schizophrenic than children associated with normal pregnancy and birth (Parnas et al., 1982). Such findings are consistent with the below-average IQ of children who later become schizophrenic. It should be further noted that when identical twins are "discordant" for schizophrenia, the twin who develops schizophrenia is of lighter birth weight and length.

Neuropsychological Testing

Chronic schizophrenics are difficult to distinguish from patients with generalized chronic brain disorders on psychological tests designed to assess brain pathology. Goldstein and Nelson (1984) pointed out that the overlap between schizophrenic and brain-damaged patients is so great that when schizophrenics incur brain damage it is often difficult to distinguish them from schizophrenics who have not had head injuries.

Head Injuries

Davison and Bagley (1969) reviewed six studies of history of head injury in persons who later became schizophrenic and concluded that the incidence is two to three times greater than in the general population. Research subsequent to the Davison and Bagley (1969) review supports their inferences. Davison (1983) found that of 291 persons who had been unconscious at least a week and followed up from 10 to 24 years later, schizophreniform psychosis developed in 2.4% of the cases. Wilcox and Nasrallah (1987) found that 22 (11%) of 200 schizophrenic patients, but only 1% of 134 control surgical patients, had head injuries before the age of 10. It does not appear that most of these persons were already schizophrenic or preschizophrenic, and the head injury was coincidental or precipitated a psychosis in persons so predisposed. One basis for arguing against this possibility is that such patients do not have a disproportionate number of schizophrenic relatives. Schultz (1932) reported that in 240 cases of schizophrenic manifestations after head injury family history was no greater than expected in the general population.

Excessive Dopamine Activity

The "dopamine hypothesis" is one of the most viable of all the formulations that attempt to integrate a diversity of biological findings into etiological suggestions. This hypothesis is that the neurotransmitter dopamine has excessive activity, perhaps especially in the limbic region of the brain. Antipsychotic drugs decrease dopamine activity, and drugs that worsen or bring about schizophrenic symptoms such as amphetamines and psychedelic drugs increase dopamine activity. The antipsychotic drugs block dopamine receptors and cause their parkinsonian side effect because of this blocking (Hoffer, Osmond, & Smythies, 1954). Autopsy findings and research with positron emission tomography (PET) combine to indicate a high density of dopamine receptors in the basal ganglia (Gottesman, 1991).

Brain-Related Biological Findings

Left-Handedness

There have been a number of studies reporting that a disproportionate number of schizophrenics are left-handed (Manoach, Maher, & Manschreck, 1988). These findings are consistent with the fact that a disproportionate percentage of brain-damaged and brain-dysfunctional persons are left-handed and the fact that schizophrenics have a disproportionate number of brain anomalies. Manoach, Maher, and Manschreck (1988) found that 31% of their schizophrenics used their left hand for writing and that these schizophrenics had more thought disorder than their right-handed schizophrenics. Specifically, the left-handed schizophrenics had significantly more thought derailment, less understandability, more poverty of information, and more total thought disorder. Monoach et al. inferred that their findings seem to indicate that a sizable proportion of left-handed schizophrenic individuals are left-handed because of a disruption in the pattern of hemispheric dominance. However, not all studies have reported disproportionate left-handedness in schizophrenics, and a study by Green, Satz, Smith, and Nelson (1989) suggests inconsistent handedness may best characterize schizophrenics.

Deficient Sensory Gating

Research indicates that schizophrenics have a deficit in sensory gating, that is, the ability to filter and disregard extraneous stimuli. The schizophrenic over responds to a bombardment of various stimuli, which is said to account for his/her poor performance on tasks that require concentration or attention. In one experiment it was found that schizophrenics responded excessively to the less relevant of a pair of auditory stimuli and that 50% of their first-degree relatives had this same gating deficit. The relatives who had the more pathological scores on the MMPI were more likely to have this filtering difficulty (Siegel, Waldo, Mizner, Adler, & Freedman, 1984).

Minor Physical Anomalies

Schizophrenic persons have an excess of minor physical anomalies. These anomalies are in the head and hands and feet and are presumably associated with abnormal fetal development or occurrence in the first trimester. Examples of minor physical anomalies are a curved fifth finger, third toe longer than the second, and low-seated ears. Green, Satz, Gaier, Ganzell, and Kharabi (1989) found that their schizophrenics had a significantly greater number of these anomalies than did controls. A remarkable number of their female schizophrenics had a larger or smaller head circumference than control. Both the female and male schizophrenics had a remarkably higher incidence of mouth anomalies such as a furrowed tongue. Patients with minor physical anomalies, were more likely to have an earlier age of onset.

Eye Movement Dysfunction (EMD)

Eye movement dysfunction (EMD) refers to a deviation from normal eye movement in following a moving target. Various studies have found from 50% to 85% EMD in schizophrenics, contrasting with from 8% to 22% in nonschizophrenics (Szymanski, Kane, & Lieberman, 1991). Studies have found EMD in from 34% to 58% of schizophrenic patients first-degree relatives but in only 5% to 13% of first-degree relatives of patients with other psychiatric disorders. Furthermore, monozygotic twins concordant for schizophrenia have greater similarity of eye tracking than discordant monozygotic twins (Clementz & Sweeney, 1990). EMD, like other biological markers of schizophrenia, strengthens the already strong suspicion that schizophrenia has a complex yet not clearly understood biological etiology.

Slow Virus

Evidence has been found for the existence of a "slow virus" that remains dormant for years or decades. Torrey and Kaufmann (1986) reviewed a number of antemortem studies of brains of schizophrenics, using CT and radiosensitivity measurements that consistently reported pathology often associated with a history of central nervous system infection. The possibility of a slow virus certainly meshes with the geographical and temporal distribution of schizophrenia. Torrey and Kaufman pointed out that the fact that schizophrenia did not exist before 1800 and the rapid development in schizophrenia after 1800 is consistent with the fact that viral diseases do not exist without a critical number of people to spread them. Furthermore, infectious diseases flourish more in densely populated areas and among low socioeconomic people. Infectious diseases also have a seasonality.

Drug Induced Psychosis Analogy

In some persons, some drugs can produce psychotic states quite similar to schizophrenia. These drugs include the hallucinogenic drugs, PCP, amphetamines, methyphenidate (Ritalin®), and cannabis. Others, however, are more likely to produce different sorts of psychoses (e.g., having more visual than auditory hallucinations).

In spite of the large number of biological differences between schizophrenics and nonschizophrenics, there is no single abnormality that all schizophrenics have. Park, Templer, Canfield, and Cappelletty (1992) introduced the concept of "cumulative biological risk," which proposes that the greater the number of biological risk factors, the greater the probability of a person's becoming schizophrenic.

PSYCHOLOGICAL ETIOLOGY: FAMILY RELATIONSHIPS

Much clinical impression based material about schizophrenia and family dynamics has appeared in the clinical literature. There has been an especially large amount written about the so-called schizophrenogenic mothers. Frieda Fromm-Reichmann thought them to be hostile, critical, cold, domineering, and demanding. The "double bind" term of Bateson, Jackson, Haley, & Weakland (1956) has generated a great deal of research and formed a large part of the clinical lore in the treatment of schizophrenia. According to the double-bind hypothesis, the schizophrenic-to-be receives a duplicity of messages from his mother. He is told that his mother loves him, and yet he senses underlying hostility, so this duplicity of messages leaves him confused and anxious. Most of the research has not supported the double-bind and schizophrenogenic mother positions and has not supported the other speculation about schizophrenic etiology through interpersonal relationships (Dohrenwend et al., 1987).

TREATMENT

ANTIPSYCHOTIC DRUGS

The antipsychotic drugs, also called major tranquilizers and neuroleptics, were introduced in the early to mid-1950s and revolutionized the treatment of schizophrenia. Prior to that time a large percentage of patients were restrained by straitjackets or by being tied to their beds or chairs. The state hospital census throughout the country dropped dramatically in the 1950s and 1960s. However, it should be emphasized that the lowered census of hospitals is ordinarily ascribed to patient improvement rather than to "cures."

In a comprehensive and massive project (May, 1968), five treatment modalities were compared: (1) antipsychotic drugs, (2) electroconvulsive therapy, (3) psychotherapy conducted by psychiatric residents and psychiatrists, (4) antipsychotic and psychotherapy combined, and (5) milieu therapy, consisting of the standard hospital environment providing the usual nonspecific treatment modalities such as industrial therapy, recreational therapy, and occupational therapy. The treatment results, ascertained by a variety of criteria, were quite clear. Antipsychotic drug treatment with psychotherapy and antipsychotic drug treatment alone were equally effective and superior to the other therapies. Milieu therapy alone and psychotherapy alone were the least effective treatments. Electroconvulsive treatment provided intermediate results.

Since the compelling investigation by May (1968), numerous studies have conclusively documented the efficacy of the antipsychotic drugs. Among the various antipsychotic drugs available in the United States, the largest single group is the category called phenothiazines. The oldest of these antipsychotic drugs is chlorpromazine, which is also the earliest of the phenothiazines. The brand name of chlorpromazine is Thorazine® in the United States and Largactil® in Canada and Britain. Table 2.1 contains categories, generic names, and brand names of antipsychotic drugs frequently prescribed in the United States. Antipsychotic drugs vary greatly with respect to antipsychotic capability per milligram. These differences are ordinarily expressed in chlorpromazine equivalent units. All of these drugs have central nervous system–depressant properties. One of the dominant considerations in choosing antipsychotic drugs is the degree of sedation desired. Chlorpromazine is often administered to quickly slow down very agitated or violent patients. Haloperidol, which has low sedation properties in relation to antipsychotic properties, is often given to frail or elderly persons.

The therapeutic dose range is so broad that finding the right dosage to stabilize the patient is to a large extent a matter of trial and error. A review of the literature shows that between 100 and 2,000 mg/day in antipsychotic drug–chlorpromazine equivalent dosages was virtually unable to predict relapse (Baldessarini & Davis, 1980). This is probably a function of several factors, not all of which are equally or fully understood. Correlations between blood level and dose are typically around .50, indicating that only about 25% of the variance can be accounted for by dose. And patients on the same neuroleptic dose can vary 10-fold in their neuroleptic blood level (Lieberman et al., 1986). Even the consideration of blood level has its complexities and

TABLE 2.1 Common antipsychotic drugs

CATEGORY	GENERIC NAME	BRAND/TRADE NAME
PHENOTHIAZINES	Chlorpromazine	Thorazine
	Fluphenazine	Prolixin
	Mesoridazine	Serentil
	Perphenazine	Trilafon
	Thioridazine	Mellaril
	Trifluoperazine	Stelazine
NON-PHENOTHIAZINES		
Butyrophenone	Dropiderol	Inapsine
	Haloperidol	Haldol
Dibenzodiazepine	Clozapine	Clozaril
	Loxapine	Loxitane
Diphenyl-butylpiperidine	Pimozide	Orap
Indolene	Molindone	Moban
Thioxanthenes	Chlorprothixene	Taractan
	Thiothixene	Navane

uncertainties in that only about 10% of the antipsychotic drug blood concentration is available to the brain (Charlesworth, 1991).

In general, the effectiveness of the various antipsychotic drugs does not differ greatly except for the sedation consideration. Clozapine (Clozaril®), a drug used for 30 years in Europe but rather recently marketed in the United States, deserves specific mention. It is an atypical antipsychotic drug in that it seems to be more active at limbic than at striatal dopamine receptors. It is probably for this reason that it has fewer extrapyramidal side effects. An even more important and relatively unique virtue of clozapine is that it appears to work effectively in patients who may not respond to the other, longer-established antipsychotic drugs. The greatest disadvantages of this drug are side effects, especially seizures and potentially very dangerous blood abnormalities. For this reason the current prevailing opinion is that clozapine should be used only for schizophrenia that does not respond well to other antipsychotic drugs.

Although the evidence that antipsychotic drugs are effective for schizophrenia is overwhelming, research does not provide a clear picture of the time course. Most of the relevant reports in the literature have not used control subjects. Keck, Cohen, Baldessarini, and McElroy (1989) reviewed the small number of studies in which subjects have been given placebo or a nonantipsychotic sedative (to control for the sedative effects of antipsychotic drugs independent of the antipsychotic effects). Keck et al. concluded that the antipsychotic-treated patients exhibited improvement within hours of initiation of drug treatment but control subjects also manifested this rapid improvement. It is possible that some of the improvement in schizophrenic inpatients may be a function of various factors, such as sedative effects, hospitalization, and treatment milieu.

Those who work with schizophrenics become exasperated by their reluctance to take medication and consequent necessitated rehospitalization. From 24% to 63% of schizophrenic outpatients and from 15% to 33% of inpatients are noncompliant and take fewer antipsychotic drugs than prescribed (Van Putten, 1974). Such reluctance is associated with paranoid delusions regarding the medication, hostility, and dysphoric response to extrapyramidal side effects. Many patients who stop taking their medication feel more energy and experience no immediate return of schizophrenic symptoms. Thus, they believe they no longer need their medication.

Equally as certain as the efficacy of the antipsychotic drugs is the fact they have side effects, including dry mouth, blurred vision and other eye problems, constipation, liver dysfunction, drowsiness, impotence, inhibition of ejaculation, skin conditions, weight gain, and body temperature alterations.

The more disturbing side effects are extrapyramidal, the most common being pseudoparkinsonism, including muscle rigidity, tremor, stooped posture, shuffling gait, drooling, akathisia (inability to sit still), and masklike face. The parkinsonian symptoms are caused by one of the apparent therapeutic mechanisms of the antipsychotic drugs, namely, a decrease in dopamine level. Many patients receiving antipsychotic drugs are also administered antiparkisonian drugs.

Persistent tardive dyskinesia is an extrapyramidal symptom that develops after a number of years of antipsychotic drug administration. It consists of involuntary movements around the oral region such as lip smacking, sucking movements, and jaw movements. Tardive dyskinesia in advanced stages appears to be irreversible. Paradoxically, it can sometimes be temporarily relieved by increasing the dosage of antipsychotic.

It has been suggested that schizophrenic patients can be taught to monitor their relapse signs, such as anxiety, tension, insomnia, and depression, and take a more active role in their treatment (Hamera, Peterson, Handley, Plumlee, & Frank-Ragan, 1991). In the Hamera et al. study all of their 51 patients were able to recognize prodromal signs. Forty-nine of the 51 patients reported taking one or more self-regulatory actions. The most frequent action was to focus on existing activities such as to "get busy." Other frequently reported actions include resting, taking prescribed medication, and contacting health care professionals. There were also self-defeating behaviors such as using alcohol or illicit drugs. The authors suggested that schizophrenics could be taught to monitor early nonpsychotic indicators more effectively, which may improve their functioning and prevent hospitalization.

MEGAVITAMIN THERAPY

Megavitamin therapy for schizophrenia is part of a more general position of psychiatric treatment termed "orthomolecular psychiatry." A. Hoffer (personal communication, 1990) stated, "If all the Vitamin B3 were removed from our food, everyone would become psychotic within a year. This pandemic psychosis would resemble pellagra and it would resemble schizophrenia." Hoffer then went on to describe the similarity of the mental disturbances of the two disorders with clinical material, most of this written in the early part of the 20th century or earlier. Pellagra can be effectively treated with large quantities of vitamin B, with removal of, or at least lessening of, the physical and mental symptoms. Hoffer and other notable psychiatrists, such as Osmond and Hawkins, have administered B3 to thousands of schizophrenics since the early 1950s. Their rationale, besides the analogy with pellagra, includes the assumption that schizophrenics have a greater need for vitamins than does the average person. This assumption is based in part upon research that schizophrenics excrete less niacinamide, pyridoxine, and ascorbic acid after loading with these vitamins than do normal subjects.

In addition to vitamin B3, the megavitamin therapists typically employ other B vitamins and ascorbic acid (vitamin C). They recommend abstinence of caffeine, avoidance of excessive sleep, and a hypoglycemic diet. The bulk of the controlled studies have not demonstrated the effectiveness of megavitamin therapy (Ban, Lehmann & Deutsch, 1977). However, megavitamin proponents have not regarded to this negative research evidence as a mortal blow. Instead, they (Osmond, 1973) maintain that the other camps of researchers have not properly administered the megavitamins. They even go so far as to question the suitability of double-blind research, which they maintain is insensitive to changes in a small percentage of patients. Osmond, Hoffer, and their colleagues also maintain that megavitamin therapy is a long-term therapy that should be evaluated over a period of years rather than weeks. They further maintain that it should not be an isolated treatment but rather incorporated into a global regimen that includes standard treatments for schizophrenia.

PSYCHOTHERAPY

Research following that of May (1968) also casts doubt about the efficacy of some modes of psychotherapy, particularly dynamic or insight oriented psychotherapy. Supportive counseling and commonsense advice on how to adjust to the disorder seem to be preferable. In one study, schizophrenics were randomly assigned to either psychoanalytically oriented or support-oriented individual therapy. Patients who received the former treatment had lengthier hospitalizations and when discharged were less likely to return to their jobs and household functioning (Stanton et al., 1984). It appears that the same sort of generalization can be made regarding group therapy and milieu therapy (Lehman, Possidente, & Hawker, 1986).

FAMILY COUNSELING

Schizophrenia places a burden upon the family as well as on the patient (Lefley, 1989). Relatives are upset by the patient's abusive and/or assaultive behavior, mood swings, unpredictability, offensive behavior in public places and social circumstances, conflict with neighbors, losing or squandering money, property damage and sometimes fire hazards, sleeping during the day and keeping family members awake at night, medication noncompliance, paranoia, and insufficient motivation for productive activity. Many families need supportive counseling and guidance in making the best possible adjustment. There are still mental health professionals who believe the contention common in the 1950s and 1960s that schizophrenia is caused by faulty family relationships. Such a contention lacks research support and can make family members feel guilty. However, there is research evidence that family members' expressed negative emotion toward the schizophrenic member is associated with an exacerbation of the symptomology and rehospitalization (Day et al, 1987). However, some authors suggest that the exacerbation of schizophrenic symptoms can cause the negative emotions in the relatives.

Torrey's (1988) book *Surviving Schizophrenia: A Family Manual* contains a wealth of scientifically based yet practical advice and information for the families of schizophrenics. It is apparent that the largest single entity is that of the family. Torrey recommends that families of schizophrenics join self-help groups. Most of these groups primarily involve mutual support and information exchange and are associated with the National Alliance for the Mentally Ill, which has over 1,000 chapters around the world. Torrey recommends limiting patients' use of caffeine, alcohol, nicotine, and street drugs.

BEHAVIOR MODIFICATION

There are many behavior therapists who use laboratory-based learning concepts such as reinforcement, schedules of reinforcement, shaping, and extinction in working with schizophrenics. Some of this is done with individual patients, but "token economy" and related programs on a ward level are more common. The patients are given rewards of various kinds for socially desirable behavior such as making their own beds. These techniques have documented efficacy in the development or modification of specific behaviors, and in some cases the patient is able to progress to a less intensive level of care.

PROGNOSIS

Schizophrenia with more of a mood component has a better prognosis. Family history of mood disorder (depression and/or mania) is also associated with a better prognosis. One study found that schizophrenics with neuroendocrine test findings similar to those of depressed patients had a better prognosis (Targum, 1983). Research has demonstrated that the rehospitalization rate is lower for brighter than for duller schizophrenics.

AT HIGHER RISK FOR RETARDATION

Children Who Receive Inadequate Medical Care

Children of Mothers with Prenatal Difficulties

Children of Mothers with Perinatal Difficulties

Poorly Nourished Children

Children with Substance Abuse By Mother During Pregnancy

Children with Infantile Seizures

Children from Poor Families

Culturally Deprived Children

Children Born to Mothers Over 40

Persons Who Live in Poor Countries

THREE

Mental Retardation

EPIDEMIOLOGY

It is generally believed that about 3% of the general population is retarded. Traditionally, mental retardation has been defined as scoring in the bottom three percentiles on intellectual tests. However, a precise assessment is not possible because not all retarded individuals are brought to the attention of the authorities. The recorded prevalence of retardation rises with age until the teens or 20s and then decreases (Kushlick & Cox, 1973). This may at first appear surprising since retardation is generally regarded as a lifelong condition. The explanation for this seemingly contradictory fact is twofold. Retardation is often not recognized in infancy and early childhood. A youngster is often not institutionalized until adolescence, when his/her increased size, strength, and sex drive make management more difficult. However, the reason for the sharp decline after the 20s is probably more real than apparent. The retarded, especially the more severely afflicted, do not, on the average, live as long as normal persons do.

It has been long recognized that the prevalence of retardation in males is higher than in females. There are several explanations for this phenomenon (Munro, 1986). One is that males are more susceptible to various Y-chromosome-related factors that can cause brain damage, such as congenital abnormalities and prematurity (Gruenberg, 1964). Another explanation is that of X-linked mental retardation (Herbst & Miller, 1980; Labrisseau, Messier, & Richer, 1982; Scarbrough, Cosper, & Finley & Smith 1984). In addition to there being more actual retardation among males it would appear that a given degree is more likely to be labeled retardation in males because of the greater male tendency toward assertive and disruptive behavior. In a very ingenious study involving a household survey it was found that the numbers of male and female retarded identified on the basis of IQ did not differ. However, there were twice as many males who failed the adaptive behavior portion of the evaluation (Mercer, 1973). Research indicates a substantial excess of males among the mildly retarded but not among the more severely retarded (Baird & Sadovnick, 1985; Herbst & Baird, 1983). This is probably a function of the lower life expectancy of more severely retarded males (Munro, 1986).

The much larger prevalence of retardation in some nonwhite groups are rather consistently reported in the literature. Research studies show an increase in prevalence in black children as a function of age and a decrease in white children. In fact, in a study by Jones (1979) there was actually a higher retardation of whites at ages 3–4. This could be viewed as consistent with the fact that motor development of blacks is higher than that of whites at younger ages (Hartlage, 1981). Explanations for the increasing rate of retardation as a function of age and ethnicity usually include those centering around socioeconomic status, education, and nutrition.

CLASSIFICATION OF RETARDARION

There are various retardation classification schemes, with different terminology and IQ cut-off points. However, the one most commonly employed by those who work with the mentally retarded in the United States is that of the American Association on Mental Deficiency (AAMD). Table 3.1 contains the AAMD classification criteria for degree of mental retardation. Since the Wechsler tests have a standard deviation of 15 and the Stanford-Binet and Cattell

TABLE 3.1   AAMD classification of IQ test scores and descriptive retardation terminology

Descriptive Retardation Terminology	Range in Standard Deviation Units	Standford-Binet and Cattell Scores	Weschler Scale Scores
Borderline*	-1.10 to -2.00	83-68	84-70
Mild	-2.01 to -3.00	67-52	69-55
Moderate	-3.01 to -4.00	51-36	54-40
Severe	-4.01 to -5.00	35-20	39-25
Profound	-5.01	<20	<25

[a]This caregory was included in the 1959 manual only. Adapted from: Rick Heber. *A Manual on Terminology and Classification in Mental Retardation*, Monograph supplement to the *American Journal of Mental Deficiency*, 64, 1959, p. 59; Herbert J. Grossman (Ed.); *Manual on Terminology and Classification in Mental Retardation*. Washington: American Association on Mental Deficiency, Special Publication Series No. 2, 1973.

tests have standard deviations of 16, the IQ categories differ slightly. At the lower IQ range there is an excess of what is expected on the basis of the normal curve. It has been estimated that 89% of the retarded are mildly so, 6.0% moderately, 3.5% severely, and 1.5% profoundly (President's Commission on Mental Retardation, 1972). The prevalence of mental retardation with an IQ below 50 is about 4 per 1,000 children (Abramowicz & Richardson, 1975). If IQ were distributed entirely according to the normal curve, 1.2% of children would have an IQ this low. The excess in retardation appears to be a function of brain damage and other medical conditions.

While the AAMD system would classify individuals with (Wechsler) IQ scores up to 84 as borderline mentally retarded, not all clinicians like the borderline category. If someone with an IQ of 84 is considered borderline-retarded, then 16% of the general population is at least of borderline retardation. Most persons with IQs in the low 80s appear dull but not subnormal. In diagnosing and classifying mental retardation, IQ is not the only factor considered. Social functioning is also weighed in the decision.

Education systems often make the distinction between educable mentally retarded (EMR) and trainable mentally retarded (TMR). In general, persons in the former category have IQs between 50 and 80; and those in the latter category, from 30 to 50. The former are capable of learning some academic skills such as reading, writing, and arithmetic. The TMR are mainly taught social and manual skills.

LIVING ARRANGEMENTS OF THE RETARDED

The majority of retarded persons live in the community rather than in institutions. In fact, only 3.5% of the estimated 6 million or so retarded persons in the United States are in institutions (Keirtz, 1977). The more severe the retardation, the greater the chances the person will be institutionalized. In one study (Saenger, 1966) it was found that all children with IQs under 20 were institutionalized within a short period after the retardation was observed. However, only one in nine children with IQs in the 20–49 range were so institutionalized. And only 1 in every 90 children with IQs over 50 were institutionalized. Table 3.2 shows the percentage of mentally retarded persons in Manitoba in different living conditions as a function of severity of retardation (Fishback & Hull, 1982).

BEHAVIORAL AND PSYCHIATRIC PROBLEMS

A substantial percentage of retarded persons also have mental, emotional, or behavioral disturbances. One study found that only 13% of retarded children brought to a clinic were free of psychiatric disorder. Thirty-eight percent of the children were classified as having psychosis; 26%, behavioral disturbances; 16%, personality disorder; 5%, neuroses; and 2%, transient situational disor-

TABLE 3.2   Current living situation of persons with mental retardation by level of intellectual impairment, including percentage distribution within each level

	Borderline	Mild	Moderate	Severe or Profound	All levels Combined
Independent living	4.4	5.2	0.8	0.0	3.2
Family or relative	72.0	62.1	51.8	26.0	54.4
Foster home	11.6	9.4	13.6	4.9	9.8
Other residences	8.6	13.4	5.1	5.3	9.0
Community group home	2.4	2.8	5.9	5.8	3.8
Institution	1.1	1.1	22.8	22.8	19.8

Source: Fishbach, M., and Jull, J.: Mental retardation in the Province of Manitoba: Towards establishing a data base for community planning. *Canada's Mental Health 30*, 16–19. Used with permission.

ders (Gath & Gumley, 1986). In another study, 27 of clinic attenders were diagnosed as having conduct disorders; 13, neurotic disorders; 9, hyperactivity; 5, childhood psychosis; 1, manic depressive disorder; and 1, unclassified (Reid, 1980). In still another study (Corbett & Harris, 1977), psychosis specific to childhood was reported in 17% of retarded children, adjustmental reaction and emotional disorders in 4% of the sample, and special symptoms or syndrome not elsewhere classified in 12%. Even in those with Down's syndrome, who have traditionally been regarded as placid and good-natured, considerable psychiatric disturbance has been found. In a study of Down's syndrome children in special education classes, only 31% were found to be well adjusted. For the 193 children with Down's syndrome, 21 were found to have unsocialized disturbance of conduct; 17, psychosis with origin specific to childhood; 18, hyperkinetic conduct disorder; 9, mixed disturbance of conduct and emotions; 6, disturbance of emotions specific to childhood and adolescence; and 2, infantile autism.

Menolascino (1977) provides the figures for 543 persons who had dual diagnoses of both retardation and some sort of psychiatric disorder. The diagnoses were schizophrenia (25%) organic brain disorder (19%), adjustmental disorder (19%), personality disorder (13%), affective disorder (8%), psychosexual disorder (6%), anxiety disorder (4%), and other mental disorders (6%). The fact that a quarter of these retarded persons were schizophrenic should not be surprising in view of the large amount of evidence presented in Chapter 2 indicating that a substantial percentage of schizophrenics have some sort of brain abnormality. The fact that 34 (6%) of the patients had a paraphilia and that the largest category was pedophilia (12 cases) is interesting. Thus, the study of Menolascino can neither strongly support nor strongly alleviate the fears of many persons in the community that the retarded are likely to molest children. Six patients had an exhibitionism diagnosis, and four had a transvestism diagnosis.

Next to the overall severity of mental retardation, problem behaviors appear to be the most significant factor influencing initial placement in institution. And maladaptive behavior such as hitting, kicking, biting, fecal and urinary incontinence and public masturbation are the largest cause of readmission to institutions. The same picture is found in studies regarding employment. Poor interpersonal skills constitute a major source of problems related to securing and retaining employment among mentally retarded persons. Inappropriate behavior was the major reason for return to employment training from job placement (Schalock & Harper, 1978). Foss and Peterson (1981) surveyed job placement personnel and found not "refraining from exhibiting bizarre or irritating behavior" and not "controlling aggressive behavior" were the two principal reasons for job dismissal.

Drooling is a common problem with some groups of the retarded, especially those with cerebral palsy. Because of the poor coordination of the tongue, lips, and cheek movements, saliva and other mouth contents are often directed out of the mouth rather than down the throat. This can cause such problems as skin infection, odor, and wet clothes, in addition to the social impediment aspect of this symptom (Gourash & Putg-Antich, 1986). There are a variety of treatments, including physical therapy, oral appliances, speech therapy techniques, chin cups, drugs, surgery, and behavior modification.

Rumination consists of the regurgitation of previously ingested food and its reconsumption and/or drooling from the mouth (Starin & Fuqua, 1987). Estimation of rumination among the institutionalized retarded was given as 9.6% by Ball, Hendricksen, and Clayton (1974). The resulting health and social problems include dehydration, weight loss, malnutrition, lowered resistance to disease, aspiration pneumonia, tooth decay, halitosis, and foul odor caused by the contact of the body and clothes with vomitus (Feldman, 1983). Mortality rates as high as 20% have been reported (Kanner, 1972). The physiological mechanisms consist of sudden contraction of the abdominal muscles, forcing the gastric contents of the stomach into the esophagus, and then into and out of the mouth. This is sometimes self-induced by the stimulation of the palate with the tongue and finger (Starin & Fuqua, 1987). However, the causes of this phenomenon are not known. The various suggested etiologies include genetics, dilation of lower end of the esophagus, dilation of the stomach, gastric hyperacidity, insufficient chewing, and boredom. There have been a number of successful reports of behavioral intervention, usually involving some sort of punishment. Electric shock has been reported most often, but pinching and noxious tastes have also been employed.

MULTIPLE HANDICAPS

It has been contended that the multiple handicaps in the retarded are devastating and that they combine in a multiplicative rather than in only an additive fashion (Munro, 1986). One study found that 22.5% had multiple physical impairments (Richardson, Katz, Kooler, McLaren, & Rubinstein, 1979). Wolf (1967) found that two thirds of students in special education classes for the retarded had three or more additional physical or emotional handicaps. The number of handicaps is, as expected, correlated with the seriousness of the retardation.

About a fourth of blind children are also mentally retarded (Munro, 1986). Levinson (1962) reported that 0.8% of the mentally retarded have severe visual impairment. Grunewald (1975) reported that 2.7% of the retarded in Sweden are visually handicapped and that this is 15 times higher than in the general population. Other research in Sweden reported that 1% to 9% of mildly retarded and 10% to 15% of more seriously retarded had severe vision problems (Hagberg & Kyllerman, 1983). A Canadian study reported that 8% of all persons with retardation suffer visual impairments (Clarke, Clark, & Reiman, 1958).

Kodman (1963) found that hearing impairment is three to four times higher in retarded than in normal children. Lloyd (1970) reviewed studies of hearing impairment in the institutionalized retarded and reported it to be from 10% to 15%. A study found that 14.6% of noninstitutionalized retarded had hearing impairments (Reynolds & Reynolds, 1979). In general, the more severely retarded have a greater prevalence of hearing deficits.

In a study with noninstitutionalized retarded persons it was found that 51.2% had speech impairments and that such problems were three and a half times more frequent than hearing problems. The prevalence for the institutionalized was reported as 57% to 72% in one study (Spradlin, 1963) and from 18% to 94% in another study (Mathews, 1971). Another study found significant language deficits in 81.5% of the institutionalized retarded. This study reported deviate or delayed articulation skills in 44%, voice deviations in 23.3%, and stuttering in 4.4% of the retarded persons studied.

The mortality rates for the retarded are high (Munro, 1986). One study found that the mortality rate for the mildly retarded was 1.7 times the general population rate, and for severe retardation it was 4.1 times greater (Forssman & Akesson, 1970). For ages 1–19, the death rate for the mildly retarded was twice that of the general population; for the severely retarded, 7 times; and for the profoundly retarded, 31 times. One study found that 98% of persons with mild and moderate retardation reached age 20, but only 92% of the severely retarded reached this age (Herbst & Baird, 1983).

ETIOLOGY

Zigler (1967) has suggested a plausible two-group approach to mental retardation etiology, as displayed in Figure 3.1. This conceptualization explains the
excess of persons at the lower end of the retardation range over what is
expected on the basis of the widely assumed theoretical distribution of intelligence according to the normal curve. The familial retarded are those who
have no medical abnormality but whose genes place them in the lower end of
the normal curve. The organic retarded are those with some sort of medical
abnormality. The authors believe such a formulation has considerable appeal
and propose a short stature analogy. The man who is 5 feet, 2 inches tall
probably is short because he has short parents. The man who is 4 feet tall
probably has some medical abnormality.

However, according to the conceptualization of other authorities, the upper
curve, which accounts for both normal persons and those with familial retardation, is accounted for by both genetic and environmental factors. Indeed, there
is evidence that some retardation can be produced or at least be exacerbated by

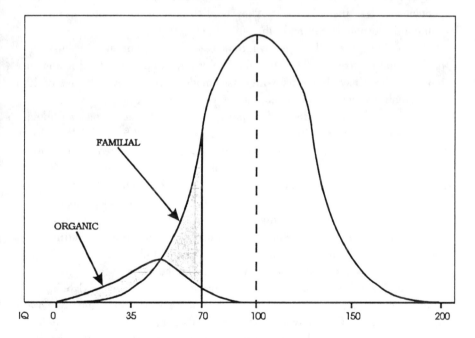

FIGURE 3.1 **Distribution of intelligence as represented in the two-group
approach.** *Source:* Edward Zigler, "Familial Mental Retardation: A Continuing
Dilemma." Science, 155 (January 20, 1967). p. 293. Copyright © 1967 by the
American Association for the Advancement of Science.

culturally impoverished environments. The precise roles of nature and nurture are unclear and such is a controversial issue. However, both factors unquestionably have an influence. There is no doubt, however, about the fact that mild and borderline retardation tend to run in families.

A study distinguished among residents of an institution for the retarded between those who had physical signs of an underlying medical condition and those that did not. Five percent of the parents of the former group and 15% of the parents of the latter group were found to be retarded (Penrose, 1963).

SPECIFIC MEDICAL SYNDROMES

DOWN'S SYNDROME

Down's syndrome used to be called Mongolism because of the Mongoloid-like facial features. One in about every 700 or 800 births (largely related to the mother's age) is that of a Down's syndrome child. Roughly 10% of the institutionalized retarded have Down's syndrome. The characteristic appearance is readily recognizable and includes a small chin and ears, slanting eyes, and a large fissured tongue. Persons with Down's syndrome have a life expectancy of less than 50 years. They tend to have heart problems and are vulnerable to pneumonia and other infections.

Ninety-five percent of Down's syndrome cases have 47 chromosomes instead of the usual 46 (trisomy 21). Over the age of 30, the probability of a woman having a Down's syndrome baby increases moderately, but over the age of 40 the probability increases dramatically.

Down's syndrome has diseaselike properties insofar as it is not distributed evenly either geographically nor temporally. In some small Scottish islands the prevalence for this disorder is 14 times greater than expected. Stoller and Collman (1965) pointed out that in Australia there are intervals of 5–7 years between maximum peaks of incidence, that urban peaks were higher than rural peaks, and that rural peaks followed a year after urban peaks suggesting a slow spread of infection out of the high contact urban areas into the rural ones. There is a close relationship between the incidence of infectious hepatitis and the incidence of Down's syndrome 9 months later. Stoller and Collman suggested that hepatitis or some sort of virus attacks the ovum of the mother. As stated in Chapter 1, a disproportionate number of persons with Alzheimer's disease have Down's syndrome. Down's syndrome persons, dramatically more than those without Down's syndrome, develop Alzheimer's Disease or Alzheimer-like brain changes and dementia in their 30s or 40s. Thus, we then have a person who is already intellectually subnormal becoming even more subnormal. Institutionalization is often necessary at this time (Gourash & Puig-Antich, 1986; Miniszek, 1983).

It has been said by a number of authorities in the area of mental retardation that Down's syndrome patients have characteristic personality features— lively, good-natured, affectionate, adaptable, placid, and relatively free of behavioral problems. Some research and considerable annecdotal reports have provided confirmation for some of these contentions.

PHENYLKETONURIA

Phenylketonuria (PKU) is a recessive gene–associated congenital disorder in which the protein phenylanine is not normally broken down into tyrosine. The resulting incomplete metabolites are harmful to the brain. The diagnosis can be established in infancy by testing for phenylpyruvic acid in the urine. The retardation can be prevented or lessened by diet very low in phenylalanine. In countries that have effective screening programs the fully developed condition is now seldom seen. However, before the neonatal screening and dietary treatment were available, patients with PKU probably accounted for about 1% of the institutionalized retarded (Stein & Susser, 1980). About 1 out of 15,000 Caucasian births is found to result in PKU. PKU occurs most frequently in persons of European, especially Celtic, origin, and it is rare in Negroid and Semitic peoples (Poskanzer, 1980). The retardation in untested victims is severe or profound. Other features include tendency to seizures, slightness in body build, and light coloration of hair and skin.

Persons with PKU tend to have behavior problems that include emotional lability, temper tantrums, aggressiveness, severe fright reactions, hyperactivity, frequent stereotype movements, frequent rocking, negativism, and catatonia. Even those put on low-phenylalanine diets in infancy tend to have behavior problems.

There seems to be no doubt that the low-phenylanine diet greatly improves the prognosis. One study found children whose special diet was introduced from 4 to 135 days from birth had IQs ranging from 77 to 127, with a mean of 93. Their IQ was lower than the IQ of their normal siblings but much higher than the IQs of untested children with the disorder. The research is unclear in regard to when the children should be taken off the low-phenylaline diet, but there are indications that midadolescence is best.

HYDROCEPHALUS

Hydrocephalus is the accumulation of excessive amounts of cerebrospinal fluid within the brain. In children without cranial suture closure there may be observable enlargement of the cranium. Some "crib cases" in institutions for the retarded may have grotesque heads as large as their bodies. This condition occurs in infancy or early childhood and fortunately is rather rare. Life expectancy is usually quite short. However, in recent years surgical techniques such as placing shunts into the ventricles to drain the excess fluid have been developed, and some afflicted persons survive until adulthood, although with at least some mental and physical impairment.

MICROCEPHALY

The microcephalic individual has an abnormally small head and brain, is usually short in stature, and is moderately to profoundly retarded. Microcephaly, which appears to be caused by a variety of intrauterine conditions, is rare.

CRETINISM

Cretinism is associated with a characteristic appearance that includes small stature, a rather large head, a flat nose, and a somewhat protruding forehead. Cretinism results from a thyroid deficiency, and the condition can be reversed if detected early and thyroid extract administered. Cretinism is more common in mountainous regions because of the low iodine concentration in the soil. Iodine is needed by the body to manufacture the thyroid hormone.

LESCH-NYHAN SYNDROME

Lesch-Nyhan syndrome (also known as juvenile hyperuricemia syndrome) was first reported by Lesch and Nyhan (1964) as an X-linked recessive disorder of uric acid metabolism. The disorder occurs exclusively in male children. The patients have spastic motor problems, as in cerebral palsy. They are normal at birth, become irritable by 2 months of age, and by 2 years show increasingly aggressive and self-destructive behavior (Jablonski, 1991). Severe self-mutilation is almost invariably present and is perhaps the most disturbing and dramatic characteristic of the disorder. It is very common for patients to chew their fingers and lips to the point of amputation. They also commonly bite and hit other people around them. Physical restraints and removal of teeth are frequently employed. There is some evidence that administration of the precursor of the neurotransmitter serotonin results in a reduction of self-mutilating behavior. The improvement is temporary, however, as patients frequently develop a low tolerance to the treatment (Nyhan, Johnson, Kaufman & Jones, 1980). At least one study has reported lessened self-injurious behavior through positive reinforcement for noninjurious behaviors (Anderson, Dancis, & Alpert, 1978).

FRAGILE X SYNDROME

Fragile X syndrome is a recently recognized medical syndrome associated with retardation. Nevertheless, next to Down's syndrome, it is the most common type of chromosomal abnormality retardation (Hagerman, McBogg, & Hagerman, 1983). One of every 1,000 to 1,500 boys and 1 of every 2,000 to 2,500 girls have this syndrome. Girls usually have milder cases of the disorder. It is so named because part of the X chromosome is fragile and prone to breakage. Although it had been known since the late 19th century that there was an excess of retarded males, the first report of sex-linked retardation in association with severe mental retardation was that of Martin and Bell (1943). It was not until 1969 that there was documentation of an X marker chromosome in some males (Lubs, 1969). The overwhelming preponderance of our knowledge about the syndrome was published in the 1970s and 1980s.

The characteristic physical features include macroorchidism (large testicles), large ears, a large head circumference, a high or prominent forehead, elongated face with heavy features, and a prominent chin. However, not all of these features are present in all patients. Most occur in fewer than half of such persons. Probably the most common feature is that of the large ears, which occurs in about 90% of the patients (Hagerman, McBogg et al., 1983). The second most common feature appears to be macroorchidism. Fragile X syndrome is found in persons from a wide variety of ethnic backgrounds.

In addition to general intellectual retardation, there are salient speech and language disturbances that include rapid rate, erratic rhythm, a disorganized and repetitive style, dysfluency, litany-like phraseology, poor articulation, and echolalia (Bregman, Dykens, Watson, Ort, & Leckman, 1987).

Behavioral abnormalities may include attention deficit, hyperactivity, gaze aversion, aggression, and self-injurious behavior. Bregman, Dykens, Watson, Ort, and Leckman (1987) reviewed several studies covering 532 fragile X syndrome patients and found an autism rate of 23%.

DIGRESSION TO "IDIOT SAVANTS"

The idiot savant is a person who is generally retarded but has special abilities in certain very specific cognitive functions. They often can tell the day of the week on a certain date centuries earlier. In addition to calendar calculation, idiot savants are often talented in mathematical computations (e.g., being able to multiply a 9-digit number by another 9-digit number in a few seconds). Some idiot savants are able to play musical instruments, although they cannot read music. They have IQs ranging from borderline all the way down to less than 30. Various explanations, such as exceptional eidetic imagery or exceptional memory, have been postulated. However, we do not have a good grasp of what mechanisms are involved in these sensational abilities. Furthermore, we do not know what determines whether or not a retarded person is an idiot savant.

NUTRITION

Severe malnutrition seems to do more permanent harm to children than to adults. The two major disorders of extreme malnutrition in childhood are marasmus and kwashiorkor. Marasmus results from insufficient calories, and kwashiorkor is caused by insufficient protein. The pure forms of marasmus and kwashiorkor are not common. When one of these disorders is present, the other ordinarily is also present. This combined syndrome is referred to as marasmic kwashiorkor. Also, these two disorders are ordinarily superimposed upon some degree of in utero malnutrition and upon deficiencies of vitamins and minerals.

Marasmus is ordinarily manifested in the first 6 months of life. The infant's growth is greatly stunted, with only about half the weight of age-expected norms. There is muscular wasting, loss of subcutaneous fat, and deficient hair growth. The infant is typically apathetic but often irritable when handled. There is a deficit of both brain cell size and brain cell number and aberrant auditory evoked potential.

Kwashiorkor is ordinarily manifested between the first and third years of life. Apparently it is not observed earlier because of the protein in the mother's breast milk. However, when the child is weaned to a protein-deficit diet, the kwashiorkor begins. Severe diarrhea is the rule. Edema produces the characteristic bloated abdomens we see on television. The child is usually apathetic and somnolent, but echolalia and crying spells are also observed. In kwashiorkor, cell size is reduced, but apparently there is not a reduced number of brain cells. EEGs are abnormal, with a tendency toward reduced alpha- and increased slow-wave activity.

It is difficult to estimate the additive effect of prenatal nutritional deficiency in marasmus. However, we do know that when an infant has marasmus, the mother almost invariably suffered from at least some degree of nutritional deficiency. The fetus has the advantage of obtaining nutrients directly from the food consumption of the mother and from placental transfer, evidenced by the fact that the fetus survived during pregnancy. Nevertheless, both human autopsies and animal research clearly demonstrate deficient brain weight in utero and at birth. The compromised brains and behavior are strongly predictive of cognitive deficits later in childhood. A number of studies show such deficits on psychometric instruments.

Too many psychologists, physicians, nurses, and educators naively assume that lower IQ in economically underprivileged persons is a function of either genetics or less adequate education or both. It is, however, apparent from the above-reviewed research that nutrition often plays a contributory if not a major role in the development of subaverage or subnormal intellect.

TREATMENT, PROGNOSIS AND PREVENTION

The more severely retarded individuals are a social problem insofar as they have to be cared for by others. The problems of the mildly retarded are associated with their inability to cope with the demands of a society that tends to discriminate against them. Their rate of crime and delinquency is higher than the rates for persons with normal IQ. Nevertheless, because of special education classes, workshops that teach vocational skills, and enlightened parents, professionals, and communities, many retarded individuals are rather successful as measured by the conventional yardsticks of society.

Although mental retardation can not be "cured" a modest degree of prevention is possible through such means as genetic counseling, counseling regarding childbearing in women beyond the age of 40, PKU testing, nutritional attention, avoidance of alcohol and certain drugs during pregnancy, and better perinatal care. There is an accumulation of evidence pointing to intrauterine malnutrition lowering childhood IQ.

Token economy programs are effective in modifying the behavior of retarded individuals. As is the case with chronic schizophrenics (see Chapter 2), the patient is given tokens or awarded points that can be used for food, privileges and various rewards. Such programs have been demonstrated to increase self-care such as bathing, brushing teeth, and being appropriately dressed. Token economy programs are effective in teaching and maintaining work skills in the retarded. They are also effective in the classroom.

Di Lorenzo and Ollendick (1986) did a review of the use of punishment in the mentally retarded. They began their review by a refutation of the notion that punishment consists of an extremely painful stimulus that is administered in isolation and without a context of a well thought out and multi-faceted treatment plan. Di Lorenzo and Ollendick reviewed six sorts of punishment that have been used with the mentally retarded. These are overcorrection, time out from reinforcement, punishing stimuli, physical restraint, response cost, and extinction. Di Lorenzo and Ollendick acknowledged that extinction is usually not classified as a punishment and that technically speaking it is not a punishment. However, they categorized it thusly because there is a reduction in the future probability of response when the procedure is used correctly.

Physical restraint is ordinarily used by mental health professionals to restrain violent persons such as schizophrenics, manics, persons under the influence of PCP, brain damaged persons, and retarded persons to prevent them from harming themselves or another person. However, the physical restraint here addressed is that systematically used to modify behavior. This physical restraint can be viewed as similar to or a variation of time out for reinforcement. It has been reported to be successful for treating inappropriate eating behavior, self-destructive behavior, hitting others, and soiling (Matson & Di Lorenzo, 1984).

Although both definitions of time out and time out procedures differ from study to study, essentially it consists of taking the patient from a more desirable to a less desirable situation such as an empty room. Di Lorenzo and Ollendick (1984) reviewed the previous parameters of time out. One of these is duration. If the duration is too short it may not be effective but if it is too long the patient may not have the opportunity to learn more adaptive behaviors. Most studies have used time outs that range from 5 to 20 minutes. It appears that continuous schedules of reinforcement are more effective than intermittent schedules of reinforcement for initial suppression of the targeted behavior but that intermittent schedules of reinforcement are better for the maintenance of the suppression.

Antipsychotics comprise the category of psychotropic drugs that are used most often with the retarded. About half of the institutionalized retarded receive these drugs. This usage does not mean that a large percentage of the retarded are psychotic. The usage reflects the fact that the antipsychotic drugs have sedative and calming properties and, therefore, reduce aggressive, inappropriate, sexual, destructive, and excessive behavior, and reduce burdens upon ward and school personnel. However, as pointed out by Bruening, Davis and Poling (1982), there is presently inadequate research justification for this large scale use of antipsychotic drugs with the retarded. The overwhelming preponderance of research with antipsychotic drugs has been with schizophrenic patients, and inferences based on that research to the retarded may or may not be warranted. This is especially the case when the side effects (see Chapter 2 on schizophrenia) are considered.

Antianxiety drugs, antidepressant drugs, lithium, and psychomotor stimulants have also been used with retarded persons, but to a far lesser extent than is the situation with antipsychotic drugs. The efficacy of these other drugs with the retarded is also not buttressed by a good deal of research evidence. It should be noted that a substantial proportion (perhaps about a third) of institutionalized retarded receive anticonvulsants for seizures.

The sheltered workshop has for decades provided a work environment in which the retarded can feel like productive citizens and through which they can hopefully develop skills and work habits needed to function successfully in the main stream of employment. The tasks performed by the students in a sheltered workshop are ordinarily of a repetitious sort that would be found very boring by persons of average intelligence. Sheltered workshops ordinarily have contracts with industry for assembling, sorting, finishing, renovating, or manufacturing new goods. Some of the workers in the sheltered workshops eventually obtain employment in the regular job market, and others remain in the workshop for an indefinite period. It should be pointed out that most sheltered workshops are not financially self-sustaining. They are regarded as worthwhile because of the training and the enhancement of human dignity that they provide.

PART II

DISORDERS OF SUBJECTIVE EXPERIENCE

AT HIGHER RISK FOR ANXIETY DISORDERS

Females

Children with Soft Neurological Signs

Persons with Family History of Anxiety Disorders

Persons Who Experience Trauma

Persons with Mitral Valve Prolapse

Persons with Schizophrenia

Persons with Brain Damage

Persons in Stressful Circumstances

Black Persons

Persons with Endocrine Disorders

FOUR

Anxiety Disorders

T here is no universally agreed upon definition of anxiety. Nor is there complete agreement on the best means of assessing anxiety. Three general means have been employed. One is that of subjective report, such as what is obtained when a patient or subject answers a series of questions on an anxiety scale. The second is the ratings of an external observer, such as a clinician filling out a rating scale. The third is through various physiological indices such as changes in heart rate, blood pressure, or electrical skin resistance. The three general assessment procedures do not correlate with each other to a remarkably high extent.

The experience of anxiety has both a cognitive and a somatic component. Examples given by Hilbert (1984) of the former are thoughts such as "I may have a heart attack," "I am going to faint," "I may panic in front of others," and " I might die." Examples of the latter are "butterflies" in the stomach, neck stiffness, faintness and headache.

ANXIETY DISORDER CATAGORIES

PANIC DISORDER

In panic disorder there are attacks of great anxiety that occur rather suddenly and unexpectedly and that are not produced by specific stimuli such as in simple phobias. As the disorder becomes more extended, some stimulus specficity is often found.

AGORAPHOBIA

In agoraphobia there is a fear of going into situations that produce anxiety. These situations and localities may include stores, tunnels, highway travel, waiting in line, and being alone. The patient very often becomes a virtual invalid confined to the home. Panic disorder and agoraphobia often occur together. It is very common for agoraphobic patients to report feeling nervous, tense, dizzy or faint, and agitated. Likewise they often experience palpitations, weak legs, trembling, and shaking.

SOCIAL PHOBIAS

As the name implies, the fear of social situations is the phobia present in this type of anxiety disorder. Such situations might include speaking in public or in school or at work, eating in the presence of others, hand tremors while writing in the presence of others, and urinating in a public urinal.

SIMPLE PHOBIAS

In simple phobias the focus of fear is a very circumscribed entity such as an object or animal or insect. While patients recognize that their phobias are irrational, anticipatory anxiety is common and patients become anxious upon approaching phobic situations.

Torgersen (1983) factor-analyzed a large number of fears and reported five distinct factors. Factor 1 was labeled "separation fear " and included such experiences as journeys, being a passenger on a bus, and crowds. Factor 2 was labeled "animal fears," including fears of mice and insects. Factor 3 was called "mutilation fears" and included experiences relating to hospitals, blood, and doctors. Factor 4 was labeled "social fears" and included such social situations as eating with strangers and being watched while writing. Factor 5 was labeled "nature fears" and included fires, cliffs/heights, and the ocean. It would appear that Factor 1 identifies agoraphobia symptoms, Factors 2 and 3 contain mainly simple phobias, Factor 4 relates to social phobias, and Factor 5 is a mixture of simple and agoraphobic features.

OBSESSIVE-COMPULSIVE DISORDER

Obsessions and compulsions tend to be present in the same person and they often occur at the same time or with one immediately following the other. Obsessions are thoughts that are ego-alien, obtrusive, unpleasant, and diffi-cult, if not impossible, to rid oneself of. Common obsessions include thoughts about doing or saying something embarrassing or harmful; about dirt,

contamination, infection, or disease; about becoming ill or dying; about religious matters; as well as doubts, uncertainties, and guilt.

It has long been recognized that patients with an obsessive-compulsive
disorder tend to have features of the obsessive-compulsive personality. Research has demonstrated that obsessive-compulsives do have the personality
features ascribed to them in the clinical literature: "orderly, obstinate, uncertain, dependable, pedantic, inconclusive thinking and acting, constancy of
mood, and dislike for change." They show high neuroticism and low extraversion; high needs for achievement and autonomy; low needs for affiliation,
dominance, and change; and a tendency toward worry, guilt, phobic symptoms,
aloofness, and conscientiousness (Rosenberg, 1968). Obsessive compulsives
tend to be above average in intelligence (Templer, 1972). They are depression-
prone.

POSTTRAUMATIC STRESS DISORDER

Posttraumatic stress disorder occurs after some major trauma, such as fire,
natural disaster, accident, battle experience, rape, violence, death of a loved
one, injury, being a prisoner of war, torture, or a concentration camp experience. The patient typically has difficulty keeping thoughts of the traumatic
experience out of his or her mind. Dreams of the event frequently occur. Sleep
difficulty, physiological arousal, concentration difficulty, and depression are
often experienced.

Horowitz and Wilner (1976) differentiated between the "intrusive" and
"denial" symptoms of posttraumatic stress disorder. The former include invasive thoughts and dreams, hypervigilance, sleep disturbances, and pangs of
strong emotion. The latter include emotional numbing, constricted thought
processes, inattention, and amnesia. Laufer, Brett, and Gallops (1985) postulated four sets of symptoms and went on to describe four sets of corresponding
scales. Their Intrusive Imagery Scale includes troubling thoughts and frightening dreams. Their Numbing Scale includes loss of interest, believing life is not
meaningful and that whether other people care does not matter. The Hyper-
arousal Scale includes sleeplessness, irritability, tenseness, and exaggerated
startle response. The fourth scale is called Cognitive Descriptions and includes
memory and thinking problems.

GENERALIZED ANXIETY DISORDER

In generalized anxiety disorder the patient is almost always anxious, and the
anxiety is not necessarily tied to specific stimuli. The specific symptoms are
generally the same as in other anxiety disorders and may include trembling,

twitching, muscle tension, restlessness, easy fatigability, shortness of breath, palpitations, accelerated heart rate, sweating, dry mouth, dizziness, nausea, diarrhea, flushing, frequent urination, the feeling of a "lump" in the throat, exaggerated startle response, difficulty concentrating, difficulty sleeping, and irritability.

ALTERNATIVE DIMENSIONAL CONCEPTUALIZATIONS

Although the traditional diagnostic nomenclature for anxiety disorders is useful and contains conditions that have long been recognized, an alternative (yet not mutually exclusive) conceptualization of anxiety has been put forward (Templer, Corgiat, & Brooner, 1984). Specifically, it is proposed that any anxiety case can be plotted on three dimensions: stimulus specificity versus nonspecificity, sometimes present versus always present, and cognitive versus somatic components (see Figure 4.1). The phobia is obviously most stimulus-specific. The phobia and the panic states are by definition not manifested all the time; generalized anxiety disorder and the obsessive-compulsive states are. Freud spoke of "free-floating anxiety" and Wolpe of "pervasive anxiety." The obsessive-compulsive disorder would appear to have the highest cognitive component.

One potential advantage of this three-dimensional conceptualization over the traditional disease-entity-based classification is that most anxiety cases do not neatly fall into the pure types. Phobics tend to be generally more anxious than the average person. Patients with a generalized anxiety disorder are not equally anxious at all times and all circumstances. The presently proposed formulation perhaps especially facilitates the understanding of the categories of phobias in relationship to each other and to the other anxiety disorders. The simple phobias are the most circumscribed with respect to stimulus and with respect to time. Agoraphobia is the least circumscribed and resembles generalized anxiety disorder. Social phobia occupies an intermediate position.

Trent (1990) assessed the feasibility of a dimensional formulation in heterogeneous psychiatric outpatients and found three factors. Factor 1 was called "morbidity," and patients high on this factor were high on measures of severity of anxiety and anxiety temporal constancy. Factor 2 was called "cognitive-somatic"; Factor 3, "acute-chronic."

The above conceptualization is not the first that has included a quantification of pervasiveness. Speilberger, Gorsuch, and Lushene (1970) made an important distinction between trait anxiety and state anxiety. The former refers to the usual anxiety level of the patient or research subject, and the latter refers to his or her anxiety at the present time. On one side of the Spielberger et al. State-Trait Anxiety Inventory form the subject is instructed to answer the items

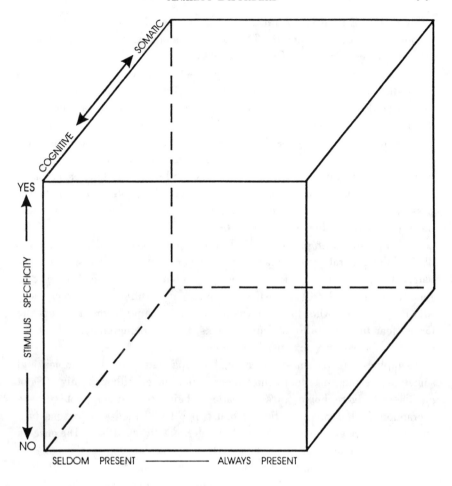

FIGURE 4.1 Three dimensions of anxiety.

"as you generally feel," and on the other side the instructions are to indicate "how you feel right now."

EPIDEMIOLOGY

Panic disorder is a familial syndrome. One study found that 17.3% of first-degree relatives of panic disorder patients were found to have this disorder, and another 7.4% were regarded as probably having the disorder. The comparable percentages for control relatives are 1.8% and 0.4%. The risk is twice as high for females as for males (Crowe, Noyes, Pauls, & Slymen, 1983). In another study a fifth of first-degree relatives of panic disorder patients had a panic disorder diagnosis, and one third had some type of anxiety disorder diagnosis (Harris, Noyes, Crowe, & Chaudhry, 1983).

Although panic attack ordinarily has its onset in the 20s, in one study of 524 panic-disordered persons it was found that 73 of them were 55 years or older. Of these older patients 57 had their first panic attack before the age of 55 and 18 had onset after age 55. It was found that in late-onset panic disorder patients had fewer symptoms during their attack and were less avoidant than those with onset before 55. The latter group tended to resemble the younger panic disorder patients. The authors suggested that the late onset panic disorder patients could be basically depressed. They also entertained the possibility that late onset panic disorder could be a different type of panic disorder (Sheikh, King, & Taylor, 1991).

Not all persons with panic attacks deserve a panic disorder diagnosis. Up to 35% of the general population have experienced panic attacks, which fortunately are ordinarily very few in number (Norton, Dorward, & Cox, 1986). Jones and Barlow (1990) suggested that an important difference between those who do and those who do not develop full blown panic disorder is that the former fear the possibility of future attacks, that is, being anxious about the prospect of becoming anxious, in a vicious circle.

Agoraphobia is the most severe and incapacitating of the phobias and sometimes results in virtual confinement to the home. Although only 10% of phobias are agoraphobia, 50% of patients being treated for phobias have agoraphobia. One survey indicated that 6 per 1,000 thousand persons in a community were agoraphobic (Agras, Sylvester, & Oliveau, 1969). The onset is usually in the late teens to the early 20s.

Agoraphobia is a familial disorder. One study showed that 8.6% of first-degree relatives of agoraphobics had agoraphobia, in comparison to 4.2% of controls. Thirty-two percent of the first-degree relatives of agoraphobics had some type of anxiety disorder. There was found to be a disproportionate number of alcoholics among the relatives, especially male relatives of agoraphobics (Harris et al., 1983).

Research justifies the differentiation of agoraphobia and social phobia as distinct syndromes. In one study (Amies, Gelder, & Shaw, 1983), agoraphobics were 86% female and social phobics 40% female. The onset of agoraphobia tended to be in the 20s and 30s, and the onset of social phobia in the teens. The social phobics were from higher social status backgrounds.

In one study 8% of the general population were found to have phobias, but only 0.2% were receiving treatment (Agras et al., 1969). In terms of types of phobias, 42% consisted of illness or injury; 18%, storms; 14%, animals; 8%, agoraphobia; 4%, death; 5%, crowds; 5%, heights. Phobic symptoms tend to occur in childhood or youth and to be long-lasting.

The preponderance of phobics are female. Most studies show about 80% of agoraphobics to be women. The preponderance of animal-phobic patients are female. However, social phobias are rather equally distributed between the sexes.

Obsessive-compulsive disorder has traditionally been regarded as an uncommon disorder, constituting less than 1% of inpatients and outpatients. However, recent studies have indicated that between 1.2% and 2.4% of the general population have this condition (Karno, Golding, Sorenson, & Burnam, 1988). The sex distribution seems to be equal. A disproportionate number have been found to be first or only children, although statistical significance was not obtained with the females (Kayton & Borge, 1967). The authors attributed this finding to concentrated exposure to adults without the modifying experience of siblings; high achievement expectation for firstborns, especially males; and relative parenting inexperience. They maintained that these factors lead to the intellectualization, emotional isolation, and hypertrophied superego that are characteristic of obsessive-compulsives.

Some white Americans stereotype black Americans as being carefree. However, the review of Neal and Turner (1991) on anxiety in black Americans does not mesh with such stereotypes. There is some evidence that, at least with some anxiety disorders, they may have a higher prevalence than whites. Anxiety disorders are the most frequent diagnosis in black women and the second most common diagnosis in black men (Gray & Jones, 1987). After controlling for education, birthplace, and socioeconomic status, American blacks seem to have about two or three times the number of simple phobias that whites have (Brown, Eaton, & Sussman, 1990). American blacks exhibit more phobias regarding closed places, storms, water, spiders, bugs, mice, snakes, bats, and harmless and unrestricted animals. Black children are apparently more afraid than white children of the use of other persons' dishes, glasses, eating utensils, and towels and of snakes, thunder, lightning, going to the doctor, going to the dentist, germs, animals, teachers, policemen, and postmen. Agoraphobia is also more common in blacks than whites; low-income blacks have the highest prevalence (Blazer et al., 1986).

In the past decade or so there has been increased recognition that coexisting psychiatric disorders are very common. In one study it was found that 73% of 90 psychiatric inpatients had a coexisting anxiety disorder (Garvey, Noyes, Anderson & Cook, 1991). In other studies it was found that major depression patients who had a coexisting anxiety disorder had a less favorable prognosis (Hecht, Von Zussen & Wittchen, 1990). There is other research in which an anxiety disorder was viewed as the primary one. Panic disorder patients with secondary depression have exhibited less favorable prognoses (Garvey et al., 1991).

There is considerable research indicating that persons with generalized anxiety disorder, phobias, and panic disorder have an excess mortality rate. The causes of death that are of high risk are suicide and cardiovascular disorders (Allgulander & Lavori, 1991).

BIOLOGICAL ETIOLOGY

GENETICS

Panic disorder is definitely familial and very likely a genetically determined disorder. A disproportionate number of persons with panic disorder have first degree relatives who have panic disorder (Crowe et al., 1983). There is a higher concordance of panic disorder in monozygotic than in dizygotic twins (Torgersen, 1983).

Turner, Beidel, and Nathan (1985) compiled all 89 cases in a total of 19 studies that determined the degree of concordance in obsessive-compulsive twins. Forty-two (68%) of the 62 pairs of monozygotic twins were concordant and 20 (32%) were discordant for the disorder. For the 27 sets of dizygotic twins, 4 (15%) were concordant and 23 (85%) were disconcordant. However, Turner et al. appropriately cautioned that the effects of heredity and environment could not be completely ascertained because none of the twins were separated since birth. The authors pointed out, however, that the rates of concordance of the obsessive-compulsive monozygotic and dizygotic twins are about the same as the typical rates given for schizophrenic twins. As stated in Chapter 2, the schizophrenia rates for monozygotic concordant twins raised apart are about the same as for those raised together. The incidence of obsessive-compulsive disorder in persons with Tourette's disorder (a tic disorder that often includes the utterance of strange noises and offensive words) is quite high, ranging from 33% to 89% in several different studies (Turner et al., 1985). Furthermore, obsessive-compulsive symptoms are commonly seen in first degree relatives of persons with Tourette's disorder (Montgomery, Clayton, & Friedhoff, 1982).

Turner, Beidel, and Nathan (1985) proposed a reasonable formulation, also suggested by previous authors, that obsessive-compulsive disorder has a twofold etiology: a high arousal, anxiety-fraught, neurologically based component and a psychological component. Turner et al. tied this conceptualization to the work of Torgersen (1983), in which there were very high anxiety disorder concordance rates for twins but usually not for the same anxiety disorder. Thus, the developing body of research gives further support to the proposal that there is genetic transmission of anxiety proneness rather than a specific anxiety disorder.

It was found that 41% of 76 first-degree relatives of patients with anxiety neurosis also had an anxiety neurosis (Crowe, Pauls, Slymen, & Noyes, 1980). *Neurosis* is an old term that is roughly equivalent to the contemporary category of anxiety disorders. The authors concluded that this family morbidity risk is as high as any in the psychiatric genetics literature. Shields (1961) found that identical twins brought up separately correlated highly on a measure of neuroticism. Furthermore, identical twins brought up separately were more similar in neuroticism than fraternal twins raised together. A genetic basis for degree of anxiety is also suggested from the research showing greater similarity for identical than fraternal twins on autonomic measures such as heart rate and palm and skin resistance (Martin, 1971).

It has been demonstrated that dogs can be bred for fearfulness (Murphree & Dykman, 1965). Even when such dogs were separated from their mothers at birth, they showed less exploratory activity, less approach to humans, and a greater amount of posturing and freezing in response to a noise. Rats and chickens have also been bred for anxiety.

STARTLE REACTION

The startle reaction described by Landis and Hunt in 1939 is strikingly similar across the life span, across cultures, and across other primates. With a loud noise such as the firing of a gun, the head will jerk forward, the eyes will blink, the body will stoop somewhat forward and down, the shoulders will raise and draw forward, the elbows will bend, the hands will turn backward and downward, the fingers will flex, and the knees will bend. Landis and Hunt viewed this as an innate and biologically based preemotional reaction.

INNATE FEARS

There can be no doubt about the fact that some fears are innate rather than learned. This was vividly demonstrated in the classical work of famous ethologist Konrad Lorenz. Lorenz found that if a shadow passed sideways or backward over a baby chick, nothing happened; but if the shadow is passed over the chick in a forward direction, the chick reacted with panic, even though the chick might be only a couple of days old and had never seen a hawk. The V-shape shadow sets off an innate release mechanism for a fear reaction.

There are several different types of fears that are innate in children (Goodwin, 1986). Almost all children are afraid of the dark after age 3. Children in different cultures are often afraid of the same sort of monsters. Fear of strangers develops in children from 6 months to 1 year of age. The same sort of thing is observed in chimpanzees. It is uncertain whether or not fear of snakes is innate in humans. However, chimpanzees fear snakes even if they have not previously seen one. Fear of heights is definitely innate in infants. Fear of being looked at and stared at is common in a variety of animals. Two potential enemy dogs of the same sex will often stare at each other, but if one is more fearful and deferent, it will turn its eyes away.

BRAIN ABNORMALITY

As reviewed by Kettl and Marks (1986), there appears to be an association between obsessive-compulsive disorder and brain pathology. There have been a number of reports of obsessive-compulsive symptoms in persons with encephalitis, encephalopathy, and Parkinson's disease. Obsessive-compulsive manifestations are occasionally reported after head trauma. One study found that one third of 33 patients with obsessive-compulsive disorder had suffered birth injury. There have been a number of reports of obsessive-compulsive epileptics. Various studies have reported abnormal EEGs in obsessive-compulsives, ranging from 11% to 65%. CT scans have indicated brain atrophy in child and adolescent obsessive-compulsives but not in adults. However, it must be borne in mind that many obsessive-compulsives exhibit no evidence of brain pathology. Furthermore, the high intelligence of obsessive-compulsives as a group would seem to legislate against the possibility of considerable brain pathology in the typical obsessive-compulsive patient.

Temporal lobe epilepsy and tumors in the vicinity of the third ventricle are associated with anxiety (Strub & Black, 1981), and it has been suggested that such implicates the hypothalamus and limbic system in the production of anxiety (Mackenzie & Popkin, 1983). Furthermore, it is well established that certain endocrine disorders, most notably hyperthyroidism, are associated with high anxiety. A disproportionate number of panic disorder patients seem to have neurological abnormalities that include bloodflow irregularities in the parahippocampal region, and (approximately 5%) have focal neurological signs (Bigler, 1988).

CARDIOVASCULAR ABNORMALITY

Cardiovascular symptoms are very common in panic disorder patients' description of panic attacks. However, the origins of the chest pain, palpitation, shortness of breath, and feeling of impending fainting are not clear. Nevertheless, it appears that these symptoms are not strictly the imagination of the patient. One study demonstrated more cardiac rhythmic irregularities and other physiological abnormalities, such as rapid heart rate, in panic disorder than is expected in normal persons. Research demonstrates that these symptoms were especially noteworthy during panic attacks but also tended to be present with more than chance expectancy during nonattack periods (Shear et al., 1987).

It has been reported that a substantial percentage of patients diagnosed as having an anxiety neurosis have mitral valve prolapse, a minor heart condition that occurs in about 10% of the general population (Crowe et al., 1979). This condition occurs more frequently in women and may be familial. These findings may be viewed as consistent with the fact that anxiety neurosis patients demonstrate impaired capacity for work, as demonstrated by treadmill performance and production of lactic acid during exercise.

BRAIN ANATOMY AND NEUROCHEMISTRY

Gray (1985) provided a good presentation of the neuropsychology of anxiety. Antianxiety drugs and related drugs, such as alcohol and barbiturates, appear to exert their relevant effects upon the septal-hippocampal system. Lesioning of the septum and hippocampus produces the same behavioral changes in animals as do the antianxiety drugs. Stress increases activity in the septal-hippocampal system, and this activity is counteracted by antianxiety drugs. This counteraction seems to be mediated by the reduction of flow of norandenergic and serotonergic impulses to the septal-hippocampal system under conditions of stress. Also, antianxiety drugs facilitate the inhibitory transmitter gamma-aminobutyric acid (GABA).

The classical James-Lange theory of anxiety holds that the physiological processes such as increased heart rate are followed by feelings of anxiety. However, Walter Cannon, a student of William James, contended that the physiological processes occur immediately after the anxiety that originates in the brain. Contemporary research seems to support the position of Cannon about anxiety originating in the brain (Goodwin, 1986). There seems to be an anxiety center in the brain, a bluish cluster of cells in the pons called the locus ceruleus (the Latin words for "blue nucleus"). Norepinephrine, a neurotransmitter associated with increased physiological arousal, originates from those cells. Electrical stimulation of the blue nucleus of rats produces what in humans would be called physiological indices of anxiety. Surgical destruction of the blue nucleus decreases indicators of anxiety in animals. Drugs that produce anxiety promote the firing of cells in this nucleus. Drugs that alleviate anxiety inhibit firing.

PHYSIOLOGICAL AROUSAL

It has long been recognized that there are autonomic nervous system correlates of anxiety. Sympathetic nervous system components of anxiety are rapid or irregular heart rate, irregular or rapid breathing, elevated systolic blood pressure, inhibited salivation and dry mouth sensations, sweating, coldness in the extremities, muscular tremor, and salivary and urinary acidity. Parasympathetic components of anxiety are diarrhea, gastric distress, and increased urination (Trent, 1990). Sympathetic activation is primarily mediated by the posterior hypothalamus and parasympathetic activation by the anterior hypothalamus.

Patients with anxiety disorders were found to have a higher level of physiological arousal, including elevated systolic blood pressure, greater muscle tension, and higher skin conductance levels (Martin, 1971). Furthermore, anxiety patients have slower autonomic habituation (attenuation of response with repeated stimuli in experimental situations). It has been reported that anxiety disorder patients needed a higher dosage of a sedative to achieve drowsiness than do normal subjects (Shagass & James, 1956).

It has been suggested that obsessional patients are prone to excessive arousal and that their cortical response to sensory stimuli are enhanced because of low inhibitory activity (Beech, Ciesielski, & Gordon, 1983). Such contention meshes with research evidence of a deficiency of inhibiting neurohormones in obsessionals (Thoren et al 1980). Obsessive-compulsives demonstrate considerable resistance to habituation, that is not showing a reduction in physiological response after repeated presentation of a stimulus such as a tone. Furthermore, Eysenck (1979) actually reported an increased response to repeated stimulus presentation in some obsessive-compulsive individuals.

LACTIC ACID

Infusion of sodium lactate produces an anxiety attack in patients with a panic disorder diagnosis. Medication that blocks naturally occurring anxiety attacks also blocks sodium lactate-induced attacks. One study demonstrated that panic disorder patients who were vulnerable to lactate-induced panic also had abnormally low rate of blood flow from the left to the right hemisphere of the brain, around the region of the hippocampus. In addition, these patients had an abnormally high rate of whole brain oxygen metabolism (Reiman et al., 1986).

Lactic acid injection into non–panic disorder patients produces panic attacks. In fact, lactic acid administration has virtually become a diagnostic test for panic disorder (Goodwin, 1986). The mechanisms for this action are not understood, but there are suggestions that calcium has a role.

HYPERVENTILATION

It appears that hyperventilation plays an important role in panic attacks. One study had panic disorder patients and generalized anxiety disorder patients voluntarily hyperventilate. The panic disorder patients reported more symptoms and markedly greater stress after such hyperventilation than did the generalized anxiety disorder patients. Furthermore, the panic disorder patients had a higher heart rate and a greater partial pressure of carbon dioxide, indicating correspondence between the subjective and the biological aspects of the symptoms. Furthermore, 75% of the panic disorder patients reported that the symptoms after hyperventilation are similar to the symptoms they have in actual life situations (Rapee, 1986).

PSYCHOLOGICAL ETIOLOGY

CLASSICAL CONDITIONING

Classical conditioning, at least theoretically, lends itself very well to explanations of why and how some stimuli acquire phobic properties. In a famous experiment over 70 years ago, Watson and Raynor found that a loud noise would elicit fear in an infant named Albert, but a white rat would not. After a number of pairings of the white rat and the noise, the white rat (now a conditioned stimulus) would produce fear in Albert.

RESISTANCE TO EXTINCTION

The recalcitrance of much phobic and compulsive behavior can perhaps be better understood by experimental work demonstrating that avoidance learning is very resistant to extinction. In a study by Solomon, Kamin, and Wynne (1953), dogs could avoid receiving electric shocks by jumping from one compartment of a box to the other. This avoidance response became very resistant to extinction. In the second phase of the Solomon et al. study a glass partition was put up to keep the dogs from jumping and to facilitate their learning that the shock was no longer received on that side. Yet that did not extinguish the jumping response. In the third phase the dogs were actually punished for jumping. However, this punishment paradoxically increased the resistance to extinction.

LIFE EVENTS

Research has indicated that patients with panic disorder experienced more important life events the year before onset than did control patients. Moving to a different home, a different neighborhood, or a different city were the events that most differentiated the panic disorder patients from the control persons (Roy-Byrne, Geraci & Uhde, 1986). We entertain the possibility that moving to a new location may produce separation anxiety similar to the postulated separation anxiety produced when an agoraphobic goes outside the home and a school phobic leaves home to go to school. However, since the panic attack does not necessarily occur immediately after a stressful event, panic disorder patients frequently do not associate the negative experiences with the panic attack, but state that attacks came on "out of the blue" (Jones & Barlow, 1990). Research indicates that the majority of agoraphobics experience precipitating events, such as death of a relative or friend, physical illness in themselves or a friend or relative, or they witness the traumatic experience of another.

It is possible that the etiology of agoraphobia could be a function of both specific traumatic experiences and predisposition. Roberts (1964) reported that 60% of agoraphobic women had specific traumatic experiences in temporal proximity to their first anxiety attacks. Such experiences included being on the way to a hospital to visit a sick child and hearing of a husband's infidelity. However, 50% of the agoraphobics had neurotic traits, usually including phobias, from childhood.

It is easy to believe research showing that the greater the trauma, the greater the seriousness of the posttraumatic stress disorder. In one study it was found that combat exposure and exposure to abusive violence in Vietnam veterans were associated with greater symptomatology (Laufer et al., 1985). In another study, rape victims had higher posttraumatic stress disorder fear levels if a weapon was present (Becker, Skinner, Abel, & Cichon, 1986).

There is reason to believe that posttraumatic stress disorder is worse in those who have a greater previous history of negative life events. Perhaps an analogy might be that influenza is ordinarily worse in sickly than in healthy persons. It was found that women who were raped and who had major life events such as the death of a loved one a year before had a more unfavorable adjustment than rape victims who had had less serious life events. The women who had had no notable negative life experiences a year before had less unfavorable life adjustment (Ruch, Chandler, & Harter, 1980). Consistent with these findings is another study that reported that survivors of Australian brushfires who had more serious previous negative life events had more serious cases of posttraumatic stress disorder (McFarlane, 1988).

Current negative life events also influence the degree of posttraumatic stress disorder symptoms. Perhaps a reasonable analogy might be that of a person with a reactive depression who becomes more depressed when additional adverse circumstances develop. In the above-cited research of McFarlane (1988), the brushfire victims who had more current unfavorable circumstances had more posttraumatic stress disorder symptoms. Similar findings were reported for Vietnam veterans (Green & Berlin, 1987).

Even though the Falklands War that Britain fought with Argentina was brief (April–June 1982) and did not involve many casualties as wars go and even though it was a war supported by the British public, in comparison to the American involvement in Vietnam, there were soldiers who suffered from posttraumatic stress syndrome. In one study it was found that of a group of 64 combat veterans who were still in the military 5 years after the war, half had some posttraumatic stress problems, and 22% had the complete syndrome. Veterans who had more intense combat experience, such as having killed someone or having helped in the treatment of casualties, were more likely to be still suffering from the syndrome (O'Brien & Hughes, 1991).

Although obsessive-compulsive disorder has traditionally been regarded as a condition that is very much ingrained and that has its genesis in early childhood or basic personality structure or neurological status (depending upon one's theoretical orientation), there have been a number of reports of its being precipitated by life events (Bridges, Goktepe, & Maratos, 1973). In a systematic study by McKeon, Roa, and Mann (1984), obsessive-compulsive disorder patients had a significantly greater number of objective negative-impact life events, such as illness in the patients or in relatives in the 6 months prior to onset, than did controls. A negative correlation between number of life events and premorbid personality problems such as obsessional, anxious, or self-conscious personality traits was found. The reasonable-sounding explanation of McKeon et al. was that less stress is needed for onset in individuals who are more predisposed to the disorder.

TREATMENT

DRUGS

Benzodiazepines

The antianxiety drugs, also known as anxiolytics or minor tranquilizers, are of demonstrated efficacy in the treatment of anxiety (see Table 4.1). The benzodiazepines are the antianxiety drugs most commonly employed. The most commonly used of the benzodiazepines are diazepam (Valium®) and alprazolam (Xanax®). They are more likely to be effective if the anxiety is not accompanied by severe depression, pronounced obsessive-compulsive features, or schizophrenia. As is the case with other drugs with sedative properties, there is associated tolerance and withdrawal symptoms. However, the potential for addiction is considerably less than for other sedative drugs, such as the

TABLE 4.1   Common antianxiety drugs

CATEGORY	GENERIC NAME	BRAND/TRADE NAME
BENZODIAZEPINES	Alprazolam	Xanax
	Chlordiazepoxide	Librium
	Clorazepate	Traxene
	Diazepam	Valium
	Lorazepam	Ativan
	Oxazepam	Serax
	Prazepam	Centrax
	Temazepam	Restoril
OTHER	Buspirone	Buspar
	Clonidine	Catapres
	Hydroxyzine	Atarax, Vistaril
	Meprobamate	Equanil, Miltown
	Propanderol	Inderal

Note: Sedative and sleep inducing drugs are not included. See Chapter 12, Drug Abuse.

barbiturates. Deaths from overdose of these drugs is fortunately rather rare except when they are combined with other drugs or alcohol.

Goodwin (1986) described the use of the benzodiazepines and their advantages over other drugs in the treatment of anxiety and other problems. They relieve anxiety without greatly reducing alertness, impairing coordination, or interfering with normal thinking processes. They relax muscles and are effective in relieving spasticity from strokes and back strain. They prevent epileptic seizures, and they abort status epilepticus—prolonged seizures that may be fatal—better than the other drugs. Benzodiazepines are the safest, most effective drugs for treating alcohol withdrawal and the agitated states produced by many street drugs. They are good for insomnia.

Beta Blockers

Research has indicated that beta blockers are also effective in the treatment of anxiety. Beta blockers are primarily used in the treatment of cardiovascular disorders, especially high blood pressure. They slow down the sympathetic nervous system (e.g., decreasing blood pressure and slowing heart rate). Beta blockers seem to be more effective in decreasing the somatic symptoms of anxiety, such as tremors or palpitations, than the psychic symptoms of anxiety, such as worries or obsessions. Beta blockers are sometimes used in combination with antianxiety drugs. However, the bulk of the controlled research comparing the efficacy of beta blockers with that of benzodiazepines shows the latter to be superior in the treatment of anxiety disorders (Noyes et al., 1984).

Tricyclic Antidepressants

It is noteworthy that panic attacks respond less well to antianxiety drugs than to antidepressant drugs. It has been suggested that the efficacy of the antidepressant drugs appears to be related to their apparent ability to reduce noradrenergic activity. In one study, evidence of norandrenergic activity was greater on days when patients had panic attacks than on days they did not (Ko et al., 1983).

Although obsessive-compulsive disorder is classified under anxiety disorders, it is widely recognized that it is often associated with depression, and the symptomatology responds favorably to antidepressant drugs, even when patients are not especially depressed (Insel et al., 1983). Another study found that the antiobsessive effects of antidepressants are at least partially independent of their antidepressant effects in the treatment of obsessive-compulsives. The authors suggested that the dual effect could be a function of some sort of neurochemical differentiation, for example, the serontonergic action in the control of obsessive-compulsive symptoms and the noradrenergic action in the control of depressive symptoms (Mavissaklian, Turner, Michelson, & Jacob, 1985).

Tricyclic antidepressant drugs have potent serotonin uptake-blocking properties, thus increasing serotonin availability. Furthermore, research has demonstrated a negative correlation between improvement in the obsessive-compulsive disorder and degree of the metabolite (breakdown product) of serotonin in the cerebrospinal fluid. Tricyclic antidepressants such as imipramine and amitriptyline that do not have as potent serotonin uptake-blocking properties are less effective in the treatment of obsessive-compulsive disorder than is clomipramine, which is a relatively new tricyclic antidepressant with potent serotonin uptake-blocking properties. It appears to be the best drug for this disorder (Benkelfat et al., 1989).

As stated by Steketee, Grayson, and Foa (1985) and echoed by others, obsessive-compulsive disorder patients have historically been regarded as rather intractable. Certainly, the benefits from insight-oriented psychotherapy do not seem to be great. Kringlen (1965) found that only 20% of obsessive-compulsives treated with such psychotherapy were in an improved condition at the time of follow-up from 13 to 20 years later. Other authors have come to similar conclusions. However, Steketee, Grayson, and Foa reviewed more recent treatments using behavioral techniques that seem to provide a somewhat more optimistic perspective. Neither obsessive-compulsive disorder nor behavior therapy are extremely homogeneous entities; and these reviewers attempted to specify what sort of techniques are apparently effective for the various symptoms of this disorder. The aversion procedures include punishing a compulsive behavior by an electric shock and "thought stopping" (punishing a thought with spoken words). In general, the research does not produce unequivocal evidence of their efficacy. A reasonable-sounding approach is to reduce the patient's general anxiety in the hope that this alleviates the obsessions and the compulsions. It appears that some obsessive-compulsive patients have profited from relaxation training. However, controlled research is needed before we can obtain a definitive perspective with respect to treatment efficacy. "Paradoxical intention," that is, focus on and attempted intensification of disturbing thoughts (Solyom, Garza-Perez, Ledwidge, & Solyom, 1972), seems to be effective for some patients. As is the case with relaxation training, successful case studies have been reported, but controlled research is needed. In exposure and response prevention the patient is exposed to obsessive cues but prevented from engaging in ritualistic behavior. As an example, patients with hand-washing rituals would be directed to touch objects they regard as contaminated but would not be allowed to wash their hands. Controlled research indicates that response exposure and response prevention, as in the example above, are effective (Steketee, Foa, & Grayson, 1982).

There is some research evidence that a combination of behavior therapy and drug therapy may be more effective than either treatment by itself. Marks et al., (1988) found good results with a combination of clomipramine and behavior therapy (exposure in vivo and response prevention). We offer the suggestion that since obsessions are more internally generated, they may be relatively more benefited by drugs and that since compulsions are behavior, they may be relatively benefited more by behavior therapy.

A number of behavioral techniques have also been employed with children. In the use of Bandura's principle of modeling, the fearful child observes other children or adults safely engaging the feared object or situation. This can be done live or on film. As with adults, systematic desensitization has been employed with children for such fears as school, loud noises, water, separation, physical examinations, gaining weight, and the dark. In implosion the child is requested to visualize in a vivid fashion the feared object or situation. In flooding, the child is placed in the actual situation until the anxiety dissipates. Operant approaches have also been employed in which the child is rewarded by approaching the feared object or activity. This has been used in school phobia, nocturnal anxiety, toilet phobia, and separation anxiety. One sort of operant technique is that of shaping, that is, the rewarding of successive approximations of the ultimate target behavior so that the child gradually comes closer to the goal.

It is apparent that both behavioral and psychotropic treatment of the anxiety disorders are effective. And sometimes concurrent use is better than one modality alone. It is difficult to say which is better, behavioral or psychotropic treatment. Certainly neither is a uniform entity. However, we tentatively suggest the following generalizations related to the dimensional conceptualization of anxiety introduced earlier in this chapter: that behavior techniques are better when the symptoms are externally generated, stimulus-specific, not present all the time, not severe, and when anxiety is the primary disorder, and that drugs are the treatment of choice when the anxiety is internally generated, not stimulus-specific, severe, pervasive, and secondary to a more fundamental disorder such as schizophrenia.

AT HIGHER RISK FOR MOOD DISORDERS

Depression

Females

Persons with Family History of Depression

Lower Socioeconomic Status Persons

Persons with Recent Loss

Persons Who Lost Parent In Childhood

Persons with History of Depression

Introverts

Persons with Negative Life Events

Mania

Higher Socioeconomic Status Persons

Persons with Family History

Jews

Persons with Above Average IQ

Persons with History of Mania

Extroverts

High Need for Achievement Persons

Persons Who Act Out

FIVE

Mood Disorders

The mood disorders (also called affective disorders) comprise depression and mania, depression being much more common than mania. Only a fairly small percentage of persons who become depressed also have manic episodes in their lives. However, most individuals with mania have experienced or will experience depression. In unipolar mood disorder the person has only recurrent depression, while in bipolar disorder episodes of both depression and mania occur. A third type, with recurrent attacks of mania only, is characterized as a form of bipolar disorder. Bipolar disorder was formerly known as manic-depressive illness.

The symptoms of depression include sadness, crying, pessimism, guilt, self-denigration, concentration difficulty, loss of appetite, insomnia (and perhaps especially early morning awakening), decrease in sex drive, somatic preoccupation, suicidal ideation, fatigue, loss of interest in recreational activities, and preoccupation with death. It is probably because of the various somatic components of the depressive syndrome that the first health care professional ordinarily seen is the primary care physician (Ormel, Koeter, van den Brink, & van de Willige, 1991). Not all depressed people have all of the elements of the depressive syndrome. Some depressed people have increased appetite, and some depressives sleep more than when they are not depressed. The depression symptom constellation that differs appreciably from that ordinarily encountered is called atypical depression. Mild depression, especially if it is long-standing, is often referred to as "dysthymia" or "neurotic depression."

Sometimes clinicians speak of "masked" or "hidden" depression, in which the depressed person is successful in hiding his/her depression from associates. Clues to the depression will then be subtle, such as cessation of one's favorite recreation. However, depression is ordinarily not difficult to diagnose. It is apparent not only from the patient's mental content but from his or her facial expression. Research using frame-by-frame film analysis has demonstrated that depressed persons walk with a lifting motion of the leg in contrast to normal control subjects, who propel themselves forward (Sloman, Berridge, Homatidis, Hunter, & Duck, 1982).

Depression often causes cognitive deficit, and scholastic performance is adversely affected. In one study (Whitney, Cadoret, & McClure, 1971) students who were depressed upon entering their freshman year of college were found to have lower grade point averages than those of nondepressed students. The authors inferred that depression rather than ability was responsible for this inferior school performance since there was a nonsignificant correlation between depression and score on a college aptitude test.

CATEGORIES OF DEPRESSION

Depression is frequently divided into types, although none of the designations are remarkably clear-cut.

Reactive versus Endogenous

Depression is said to be reactive when it results from immediate environmental factors, especially loss of a spouse or a job. It is described as endogenous when there is no clear precipitating stress. Mendels and Cochrane (1968) reviewed seven factor-analytic depression studies and found that there were eight items that loaded significantly and positively on at least four of the studies. These items, stated in the direction of endogenous depression, were the presence of psychomotor retardation, nonreactivity to environment (the depression not being at least temporarily changed by events), loss of interest in environment, lack of self-pity, lack of precipitating event, middle-of-the-night insomnia, and visceral symptoms.

Unipolar versus Bipolar Depression

Unipolar depression (Perris & Gallant, 1976) is that in which any previous affective disturbances have been depression, in contrast to bipolar depression in which the depressed person has a history of one or more manic episodes. The bipolar depressive tends to have a younger age of onset and responds better to the mood-stabilizing drug lithium. The unipolar depressive tends to respond better to tricyclic antidepressant drugs. Unipolar depressives tend to have unipolar-depressed biological relatives, and bipolar depressives have bipolar-depressed relatives. However, bipolar depression runs in families to a greater extent than does unipolar depression.

PSYCHOTIC VERSUS NONPSYCHOTIC

The delusion content of nonpsychotic depression is often mood-congruent insofar as it includes nihilistic, self-deprecatory, or guilty beliefs. Research indicates that psychotic depression is more severe and is more likely to include psychomotor retardation, cognitive disturbance, guilt, hopelessness, hypochondriasis, anxiety, insomnia, suicidal ideation, risk of suicide, and brain abnormality. Also, psychotic depressed patients ordinarily respond poorly to antidepressant drugs alone but respond well to a combination of antipsychotic and antidepressant drugs and to ECT.

Persons with psychotic depression ordinarily have fewer hallucinations, less bizarre behavior, and less thought disorder than do schizophrenics. However, at times differential diagnosis can be difficult. The diagnosis "schizoaffective" is sometimes applied to those cases in which there is a mixture of thought disorder and mood disorder.

PRIMARY VERSUS SECONDARY DEPRESSION

Depression is said to be primary when it is the fundamental psychopathology entity. Depression is secondary when it is derived from some other psychopathological condition, such as alcoholism or schizophrenia.

PREVALENCE FACTORS

Depression competes with anxiety for being the most widespread psychological affliction. While only a small minority of people become psychotic in their lifetime, almost everyone becomes at least mildly or transiently depressed on occasion. The exact prevalence of depression in the general population is difficult to ascertain. However, Murphy, Simons, Wetzel, and Lustman (1984) reviewed eight general population surveys in the United States and Canada that reported point prevalence rates from 3.5% to 5.8%. Rorsman et al. (1990) found an incidence of first depressive episode to be 4.3 per 1,000 in men and 7.6 per 1,000 in women. Up until 70 years of age the cumulative probability of suffering a first depressive episode was 27% in men and 45% in women.

Research indicates that depression in children is quite prevalent. One study reported that 5% of the general population of 9-, 10-, and 11-year-olds were depressed (Kashani et al., 1981). Other investigators concluded that 1% of high school juniors and seniors were seriously depressed, and 14% were mildly depressed. Estimates of lifetime prevalence of depressive disorder have ranged as high as 35% (Kendler, Neale, Kessler, Heath, & Eaves, 1992b).

The reports of gender difference have indicated that females have from 1½ to 3 times the risk of diagnosed depressive disorder as males, not only in the United States but around the world (Kendler et al., 1992b). However, in India and Papua New Guinea, males have twice the rate of depression of females (Weissman & Klerman, 1977). Males and females have somewhat different manifest depressive symptomatology, perhaps as a function of societal expectations of what is masculine and feminine behavior. Men are more likely to exhibit social withdrawal, weight loss, and sleep disturbance; women are more likely to display crying and self-depreciation.

One study found that men who have never married have higher depression scores than do married men. However, married women obtained higher depression scores than women who have never been married (Radloff, 1975). It was suggested that marriage is a mental health advantage for men but not for women. Research indicates that persons with less education, less income, and lower or no employment are more likely to be depressed (Warren & Mc-Eachren, 1983).

Elderly persons are at greater risk for depression. Furthermore, the prognosis is less favorable in older persons, both in regard to the depression and to death from various causes, including suicide (Kivela, Pahkala, & Laippala, 1991).

The incidence of mood disorder, especially bipolar mood disorder, is quite high among the Amish in Pennsylvania (Egeland & Hostetter, 1983). However, it is difficult to discern whether this is a function of their religion and associated life-style or of genetics. There is almost no migration into the community and consanguinity is rather high.

It is indeed difficult to compare the rates for affective disorder in various parts of the world. However, a number of observers have maintained that affective disorders are less common in Africans, and there does seem to be a low suicide rate in African countries. The depressive syndrome has been found to be quite similar in diverse cultures. However, clinical impressions of less guilt and suicidal tendencies and more somatization and hypochondriacal features in developing countries have been reported.

Ball and Clare (1990) investigated symptom differences between Jewish and non-Jewish depressives in London. Jews had a significantly higher proportion of persons with hypochondriasis than did non-Jews, 80% and 30%, respectively. Guilt was less common in the Jews (48%) than in the non-Jews (92%). Ball and Clare tied these differences to cultural and religious factors. They related their hypochondriasis findings to the clinical and research literature that shows somatic concern to be very common in Jewish culture in nonpsychiatric populations. They attributed the comparatively high guilt of non-Jews to the emphasis upon guilt in Christianity.

ETIOLOGY

BIOLOGICAL

Everyday observation indicates the plausibility of biological factors in the etiology of depression. The mood of many normal persons varies as a function of amount of sleep, caffeine intake, alcohol consumption, exercise, time since last meal, and fatigue.

Possible Genetic Predisposition

The concordance rate of depression in identical twins is much higher than the concordance rates for fraternal twins, ranging from 40% to 100%. In general, the concordance is about five times as high for identical as for fraternal twins. The rates are similar regardless of whether the twins were raised together or apart.

Neurotransmitters

The biogenic amines are the focus of a large amount of theory and research in depression. The two neurotransmitters that are dealt with most often in the literature on depression are serotonin and norepinephrine. Since these amines do not cross the blood-brain barrier, direct and measurable manipulation of the bioamines in the brain is not possible. However, there has been a convergence of diverse evidence suggesting the importance of their role. The two most commonly used categories of antidepressant drugs, the tricyclic antidepressants and the monoamine oxidase (MAO) inhibitors, both raise the serotonin and norepinephrine levels, although by different mechanisms.

Endocrine Functioning

Depression commonly results from a number of endocrine disturbances. Depression can result from malfunctioning of the pituitary, adrenal cortex, and thyroid and parathyroid hyperfunctioning. Some women taking birth control pills, which contain synthetic estrogens, experience depression as a side effect (Klerman, 1980). And some women have mood changes as a function of their menstrual cycle (Hurt et al., 1992).

In addition to having elevated cortisol levels in the blood serum, depressed patients, especially those endogenously depressed, are much less likely than normals to have suppression of cortisol levels with administration of dexamethasone, a synthetic cortisol-like hormone. The so-called dexamethasone suppression test is frequently used in research with depressed patients. Dexamethasone suppression tends to return when the depression remits or turns into mania or hypomania. There is evidence that the sleep difficulty of depressives may be related to their neuroendocrine dysfunctioning. In one study, the depressed subjects not only had a significantly greater plasma cortisol concentration than did control patients but exhibited an increase in cortisol concentration shortly after sleep onset (Jarrett, Coble, & Kupfer, 1983).

Depressed persons frequently report decreased libido, reduced sexual activity, and diminished ability to achieve orgasm. An obvious question is whether this decreased sexual functioning is strictly a function of lessened interest or attitude or whether physiological processes are also involved. The latter is supported by sleep research, which found men with major depression to have less time with an erection during sleep than do normal men. This difference could not be attributed to sleep efficiency or REM (rapid eye movement) sleep time. At follow-up in three of the men in whom the depression had remitted, appreciably more time of penile tumescence during sleep was found (Thase, Reynolds, Glanz, Jennings, & Sewitch, 1987).

Cortical Atrophy

A disproportionate number of depressed persons, especially the depressed elderly, have cortical and/or subcortical atrophy and other degenerative changes (Emery & Oxman, 1992). Differential diagnosis between a severely depressed person's associated temporary memory and concentration difficulty and the brain-disordered person who is depressed has long been recognized as a difficult diagnostic problem. Emery and Oxman contend that instead of a dichotomy there may be a continuum with very evident brain disorder on one end and "functional" impairment or "pseudodementia" at the other end.

Seasonal Affective Disorder

In seasonal affective disorder persons tend to be depressed in the fall and winter and normal or hypomanic in the spring and summer. It has been speculated that this phenomenon could be related to seasonal rhythms of activity in other mammals. It has also been conjectured that this affective disturbance is associated with amount of daylight. Research has found bright artificial light in the morning and evening to have an antidepressant effect in depressed patients, both those with seasonal affective disorder and those without (Rosenthal et al., 1985). However, subsequent research indicates that such treatment may not be effective in more severe cases (Terman et al., 1989), and the evidence of the efficacy of the treatment in nonseasonal depression is conflicting (Yerevanian, Anderson, Grota, & Bray, 1986).

A question that logically follows is whether some relatively normal persons also have mood changes as a function of season. In fact, as early as 1922, Emil Kraepelin suggested that some cases of manic-depressive illness might represent an exaggeration of the season fluctuations found in relatively normal persons. Kasper et al. (1989) provided artificial lighting to normal persons with slight seasonal mood fluctuation and to normal persons with no seasonal mood fluctuation. The lighting improved mood for the former but not the latter.

PSYCHOSOCIAL

Roy (1981b) assessed the risk factors in depression by comparing 94 depressed patients with 94 patients with personality disorder diagnoses. A family history of depression, parental loss before the age 17, and unemployment were the risk factors for women; parental loss before age 17 was the only significant risk factor for men. Parental loss before age 17 was the most significant variable for both men and women. Roy (1987) found that being unemployed, having a poor marriage, having three or more children under the age of 14, and a family history of depression were risk factors for depression.

One of the better studies demonstrating the role of life events in producing depression is that of Paykel et al. (1969). The authors interviewed 185 depressed patients and 185 normal control patients about events experienced in the preceding 6 months. The patients were interviewed after clinical improvement was observed in order to minimize the influence of affective state on memory or judgment. The depressed patients reported three times as many events as did the control subjects. Paykel et al. did a further analysis by dividing events into entrances and exits from the social field. The entrances included engagement to marry, marriage, birth of a child, and a new person in the home. The exits were death of close family member, separation, divorce, family member leaving home, and son drafted for military service. The depressed and control persons had a similar number of entrances, 21 and 18, respectively. However, the depressed persons had a significantly greater number of exits, 46 and 9, respectively.

Research on the correlates of depression in children has also been carried out. Depressed children are more likely to have lower IQ and academic achievement and more likely to be rated by their peers as unhappy and unpopular. Depression in the girls tended to be inversely associated with family income and positively associated with depression in the mother (Lefkowitz & Tesiny, 1985).

A rather consistent finding is that depression is more prevalent in urban than in rural areas. Explanations for this finding include greater social stability and integration, more supportive interpersonal networks, and the greater beauty of rural areas (Crowell, Blazer, & Landerman, 1986).

Although some disorders, such as schizophrenia, ordinarily occur primarily in individuals who are predisposed, at least some depression occurs in the majority of persons who are harshly dealt with by life events. The economic difficulties of farm families, even though such families are ordinarily noted as stable and nurtured by the work ethic and other traditional American values, have caused depression throughout rural United States and Canada. Hefferman and Hefferman (cited in Farmer, 1988) studied 40 Missouri families who left farming between 1980 and 1985 and found that nearly 100% were depressed at the time they left farming. Even several years afterward, about half of the men and three quarters of the women were still depressed.

Depression can be emotionally contagious. Mental health professionals often report feeling drained after working long hours with depressed patients. However, the impact of depression is especially apparent in family members. Coyne et al. (1987) found that over 40% of family members were depressed themselves. The husbands tended to be especially bothered by their wives' fatigue, hopelessness, worrying, and lack of interest in normal social activities.

Perhaps the children of depressed mothers are especially adversely affected by their mother's depression. In infancy there is less favorable mother-child interaction than with nondepressed mothers. Research indicates that depressed mothers gaze less at their infants' faces, feel more anger toward their babies, display less warmth, feel that parenting is more stressful and less rewarding, physically interact with their children to a lesser extent, have more negative attitudes toward their infants, and more generally lack sensitive reciprocity and expression of pleasure from the company of the child. Both children and adolescents of depressed mothers exhibit a high incidence of diverse psychopathology, with depression being one of the more notable problems (Gelfand & Teti, 1990).

Seligman (1974) proposed the learned helplessness theory of depression, which essentially states that animals and people eventually become passive and depressed after insurmountable stress. Seligman and others have done experiments in which animals or humans were subjected to inescapable electric shock or inescapable noise or unsolvable problems. These subjects, when later placed in other problem-solving situations, generally gave up. In fact, the experimental situation behavior of normal persons provided prior frustrating experiences was found to be similar to that of depressed persons not given the prior frustrating experience.

The syndrome of postpartum depression has long been recognized. In one study it was found that 12% of women had sufficient depression to justify a depressive diagnosis in the 9-week period after childbirth (O'Hara, Neuaber, & Zeboski, 1984). In that study it was found that complications during pregnancy, stresses related to child care (e.g., poor health of child), and previous history of depression were positively associated with depression. A more recent study found postpartum depression to be correlated with personal and family history of depression, social maladjustment, stressful life events, and levels of estriol (O'Hara, Schlecte, Lewis, & Wright, 1991). The composite of the literature on postpartum depressions shows it to be caused by biological, psychological, and social variables.

THE DEMOGRAPHY OF SUICIDE

In the United States suicide is the 11th most common cause of death, and between the ages of 15 and 44 it is the 4th most common. Females attempt suicide more often but males employ more lethal methods and have a higher suicide rate. There is a positive correlation between age and suicide rate and in males the relationship continues through the 80s. Chinese Americans, Japanese Americans, and Native Americans have higher rates than whites. Blacks have lower suicide rates than whites. Catholics have a lower suicide rate than Protestants. Police officers and physicians, especially psychiatrists, have high suicide rates. Catholic priests have low suicide rates. Divorced and widowed persons have the highest rates, and married persons have the lowest rates. The western states have high suicide rates, and San Francisco has traditionally had one of the highest in the country. Suicide is more common on Mondays and in the spring (Lester, 1992).

A number of studies have compared suicide rates of ethnic groups within various countries (Lester, 1983). In the Bahamas, non-Bahamians were found to have a higher suicide rate than Bahamians. The suicide rates in Israel were reported to be higher in European-born Jews than in Oriental and eastern African–born Jews. In another study in Israel, suicide rates were highest in European Jews, lower in Asian and Israeli Jews, and least in African Jews. In Rhodesia the suicide rate was higher in the Europeans than in the Africans. In Singapore the highest suicide rate was for Chinese, lower for Indians, and least for Malay. In Zambia, Europeans were found to have higher rates than Africans. It is difficult to generalize on the basis of this diversity of findings. However, we tentatively offer the following generalizations: Africans tend to have lower suicide rates than non-Africans, and persons of more privileged socioeconomic standing have higher suicide rates than less privileged persons.

MANIA

Symptoms of mania may include elation, expansiveness, grandiosity, excessive activity, speeded thought processes, loudness, loquaciousness, poor judgment, excessive spending or giving away of money, foolish business ventures, flight of ideas, distractibility, psychomotor agitation, paranoid ideation, lessened sleep requirement, irritability, anger, inexhaustability, and sometimes violence.

The classical conceptualization of bipolar disorder is of rather long periods of normality between manic and depressive episodes. However, research reveals that manic episodes are often preceded and/or followed by depressive episodes, that depressive episodes are frequently preceded and/or followed by manic episodes, and that manic-depressives are often far from well between episodes.

Winokur, Clayton, and Reich (1969) studied the immediate course for 100 patients hospitalized for mania. About half of the manic episodes were preceded by a depressive period that was an average of 3.7 months duration. The episode of mania lasted an average of 54 days. Over half of the manic episodes were followed by a depressive episode. Winokur et al also studied 33 episodes of depression in bipolar disorder. Fifteen of 33 patients had manic episodes prior to and 9 had manic episodes following the depression. Winokur et al followed up 28 bipolar patients for 2 years after discharge. Eleven percent were found to be chronically ill, 18% had partial remission without episodes, 46% were well with episodes, and 145 were well in every way. Harrow, Goldberg, Grossman, and Meltzer (1990) followed up 73 manic patients 1.7 years after hospitalization. At that time 42% of the patients had had a full manic syndrome during the previous year, 13% had a full depressive syndrome, and 53% had a full manic and/or full depression syndrome. Only 34% had no manic symptoms; 34%, no depressive symptoms; and 21%, neither manic nor depressive symptoms. At the time of follow-up, 32% of the patients were given an overall outcome rating of poor; 38%, moderate impairment; and 30%, good. Harrow et al concluded that "many hospitalized manic patients have a severe, recurrent, and pernicious disorder; and in routine clinical practice, lithium is an effective prophylaxis for fewer than the 70% to 80% of manic patients previously reported."

There is a tendency for the well intervals in manic-depressive patients to become progressively shorter. There is a great variability from patient to patient in regard to the pattern of the frequency and duration of manic and depressive occurrences. They could last from days to years, although weeks and months are the rule. Clinicians have commented upon the similarity of behavior and ideation from depressive episode to depressive episode and from manic episode to manic episode in individual patients (Cutler & Post, 1982).

It is common for a manic to exhibit considerable antisocial behavior. It is also common for them to use alcohol excessively during both their depressive and their manic episodes. The former is thought to have the immediate function of relieving depression, with the latter decreasing arousal and activity. Research support for this clinical opinion exists, although it seems to indicate excessive alcohol intake is more common during the manic episodes.

Research has borne out the classical opinion that bipolars patients are ambitious, hardworking individuals. One study demonstrated that bipolar depressives had a greater drive toward success and achievement and were more aggressive than depressed patients and controls. (Matyssek & Feil, 1983). Being extroverted, driven, work-oriented, obsessed, and having a cyclothymic or a dysthymic temperament all appear to be precursors of bipolar disorder (Akiskal, Hirshfeld, & Yerevanian, 1983). Persons with unipolar disorder are found to be of introverted premorbid personality.

Many manic-depressives are hypomanic between actual episodes; that is, they are very energetic, enthusiastic, and self-confident—but not to the point of mania. In fact, many relatively normal non-manic-depressive persons could be described as hypomanic. Hypomanics are often highly successful individuals.

Research has demonstrated that relatives of bipolar depressed patients had more educational and occupational achievement than did relatives of unipolar depressed persons, even though the two groups of depressed persons did not differ in achievement. This difference was not dependent upon whether or not the relative had bipolar illness (Coryell et al., 1989). Such findings add to the already rather strongly established association of bipolar illness and high achievement.

The lifetime chance of having bipolar illness differs in various investigations in various places. However, the stated figures are generally around 1% in Britain and Europe and somewhat less in the United States (Mendlewicz, 1988). Numerous studies have examined the concordance rates of monozygotic and dizygotic twins with regard to manic-depressive illness. It is apparent that the chances of a bipolar diagnosis are several times greater for monozygotic twins than for dizygotic twins (Mendlewicz, 1988).

There is evidence of a linkage between manic-depressive illness and genetic markers. Linkage refers to the proximity of two genes on the same chromosome, with one of the genes being established and the other suspected. Research has demonstrated the appearance beyond chance expectation of both color blindness and manic depressive illness in family members (Mendlewicz, Fleiss, & Fieve, 1972; Reich, Clayton, & Winokur, 1969).

There is some evidence that Jews are especially inclined to bipolar illness. The reasons for this are not clear, although genetics is a possibility. Also, it must be borne in mind that the stereotype of the Jewish personality, like the profile of the manic-depressive personality, is that of a hard-working, intelligent, ambitious, and successful person.

Mania occasionally develops after a head injury or stroke. Because this is an uncommon occurrence, most of the articles in the literature are of a case study nature. However, one study was based on 11 patients (Starkstein, Pearlson, Boston, & Robinson, 1987). Since five of the patients had a prior history of depression and five had a family history of mood disorder, it would appear that these patients had a predisposition to mood disorder. Eight of the patients had limbic area lesions, and nine had right hemisphere involvement. The authors suggested that these two areas may be of etiological importance.

TREATMENT

DEPRESSION

In Table 5.1 the major categories of psychologically oriented therapy are succinctly described. The three most fundamental categories are the psychodynamic, the behavioral, and the cognitive approaches. Loosely associated with these theoretical approaches are corresponding theories regarding etiology and corresponding techniques. In brief, dynamically oriented approaches purport to modify intrapsychic structure and functioning; behavioral-oriented approaches purport to modify behavior that causes and sustains depression; and cognitive approaches hope to change maladaptive beliefs about oneself and the environment. Most mental health professionals of various theoretical orientations believe that depressed persons should be given appreciable support, encouragement, and the warmth and positive regard of the therapist. Research has demonstrated the efficacy of cognitive therapy; however, the reasons for this are not certain at this time. It is not known whether the benefits accrue from the improved thought patterns or from other ingredients such as the therapist–patient relationship or other nonspecifics. Also, the fundamental assumption of Beck that depression is caused by faulty thought patterns has not been definitively established. It could be that the negative thoughts and attitudes are a function of depression. It is generally recognized that pessimism, guilt, and poor self-concept are common components of the depressive syndrome. The two categories of drugs that have been used most over the past quarter of a century are tricyclic antidepressants and MAO inhibitors, the former category being dominant.

Table 5.2 contains a listing of drugs commonly used in mood disorder therapy. Any different effects within this category of drugs probably are of function of their relative degree of effect upon the neurotransmitters norepinephrine, serotonin, acetylcholine, and histamine. These drugs differ in

TABLE 5.1 Therapy

Approach	Theory	Process	Procedure
Biological	Biochemical imbalance	Restoration of normal physiological processes	Pharmacotherapy and/or somatic therapies
Dynamic	Anger directed against the self following real or symbolic loss	Insight into unconscious conflict and cathartic discharge of affect	1. Supportive: Amelioration of aggravating unconscious conflicts 2. Depth: Resolution of unconscious conflicts.
Behavioral: Affective	Anxiety inhibits potentially gratifying behaviors	Reduction of conditioned anxiety	Systematic desensitization or alternative counter-conditioning procedures
Operant	Deficit in self-reinforcement or excess self-punishment	Increase occurrence of reinforcement (decrease punishment)	1. Direct contingency management by therapist 2. Skills training
Self-Control	Deficit in self-reinforcement or excess punishment	Increase administration of self-reinforcement (decrease self-punishment)	Skills training in (a) self-monitoring; (b) self-evaluation; and)c) self-reinforcement
Cognitive	Maladaptive beliefs and distorted information processing	Change beliefs and alter information processing distortions	1. Cognitive therapy: Inductive reasoning, empirical examination of beliefs, training in (a)self-monitoring; (b) cognitive hypothesis testing; and (c) cognitive restructuring 2. RET: Deductive reasoning and persuasion

Source: Hollon, S. D., & Beck, A. T. (1979). Cognitive therapy for depression. In P. C. Kendall & S. D. Hollon (Eds.), *Cognitive behavioral interventions: Theory, research and procedures*. (p. 156). New York: Academic Press.

TABLE 5.2   Commonly prescribed antidepressant drugs

CATEGORY	GENERIC NAME	BRAND/TRADE NAME
TRICYCLIC AND CLOSELY RELATED ANTIDEPRESSANTS	Amitriptyline	Elavil, Endep
	Amoxapine	Asendin
	Clomipramine	Anafranil
	Desipramine	Norpramin
	Doxepin	Sinequan
	Imipramine	Janimine, Tofranil
	Maprotiline	Ludiomil
	Nortriptyline	Pamelor
	Protripyline	Vivactil
	Trimipramine	Surmontil
MAO INHIBITORS	Isocarboxazid	Marplan
	Phenelzine	Nardil
	Tranylcypromine	Parnate
OTHER	Bupropion	Wellbutrin
	Fluoxetine	Prozac
	Trazodone	Desyrel

degree of sedation, with amitriptyline providing the greatest amount of sedation. For some patients this is an undesirable side effect. On the other hand, many patients with insomnia profit from taking the entire daily dosage before going to bed. It is common for the psychiatrist to start with a low dosage and increase it every week for 3 or 4 weeks. It often takes a couple of weeks for the patient's depression to respond to the drug, but if there is no change by 4 weeks it appears that the drug is probably not going to be effective. Side effects include dry mouth, thirst, constipation, urinary hesitance, orthostatic hypotension (rapid drop in blood pressure upon standing up), increased blood pressure, cardiac irregularities, sweating, tremor, delirium, nausea, speech blockage, weight gain, and impotence. With some patients the tricyclic antidepressants can be gradually discontinued after a stable period without depression. However, some patients have to be on these drugs for an almost indefinite period, although perhaps at a lower dosage. Research indicates that these drugs have prophylactic value in preventing or reducing the magnitude of depressive episodes.

In a review of the literature on the efficacy of tricyclic antidepressants (Bielski & Friedel, 1976), it was pointed out that the variables that most consistently predicted favorable response were psychomotor retardation, anorexia, weight loss, middle and late night insomnia, and higher socioeconomic class. The variables that most consistently predicted unfavorable response were delusions, multiple prior episodes, and neurotic, hypochondriacal, and hysterical traits. It thus appears that the features of endogenous depression are associated with positive response to the tricyclic antidepressants.

Research has indicated that tricyclic antidepressant drug plasma levels of different patients differ considerably with the same dosage. It has been suggested that the great individual differences in regard to outcome may be in part a function of the greatly differing plasma levels. A task force of the American Psychiatric Association (1985) reviewed the studies that have been carried out on tricyclic plasma levels and concluded that monitoring of plasma level of patients certainly has feasibility, in regard to both obtaining and maintaining optimal use of the drug in ordinary clinical situations, and in especially close monitoring plasma levels in patients who have high medical risks.

The common side effects of the tricyclic antidepressants are peripheral disturbances such as dry mouth, blurred vision, constipation, postural hypotension, and various idiosyncratic reactions. However, Meador-Woodruff's (1990) review of the literature shows that psychiatric side effects are more common than is generally realized. The most common of these is delirium similar to delirium from other causes and including disorientation, confusion, altered level of consciousness, memory impairment, concentration difficulty, and altered sleep patterns. In addition to delirium, other psychiatric manifestations such as psychosis, mania, agitation, and depersonalization can occur. These psychiatric side effects appear to be a function of the anticholinergic properties of the tricyclics. Meador-Woodruff maintained that from 5% to 10% of tricyclic-treated patients exhibit psychiatric side effects.

MAO inhibitors are given when tricyclic antidepressants are not effective. Tricyclic drugs are ordinarily first given, for four reasons: They are thought to be more effective; they cannot be given immediately upon cessation of MAO inhibitor administration because of the side effects, but the MAO inhibitors can be given immediately upon cessation of the tricyclics; MAO inhibitors are believed to have more side effects; dietary precautions have to be taken with MAO inhibitor administration.

Patients for whom MAO inhibitors are prescribed are usually started on a relatively small dosage with once-a-week increments. With too high a dose patients may appear intoxicated and exhibit ataxia, confusion, and sometimes euphoria. Sedation and overstimulation are both common, and various MAO inhibitors differ in degree of activation. Side effects include dizziness, orthostatic hypotension, sexual impotence, inability to have orgasm, insomnia, muscle cramps, urinary hesitancy, constipation, and dry mouth. A number of foods, including beer, red wine, aged cheeses, dry sausage, Italian green beans, brewer's yeast, smoked fish, and liver, should be avoided. The consumption of such food while taking MAO inhibitors may result in severe headaches, dangerously high blood pressure, and possibly even a stroke. These symptoms may also be produced by a number of drugs that include decongestants, Demerol®, and local anesthetics. It is apparent that the psychiatrist must coordinate the patient's total drug regimen. The length of time patients should remain on medication is basically the same as with tricyclic antidepressants.

Fluoxetine (Prozac®) is a very promising, relatively new antidepressant that is related to neither the tricyclic antidepressants nor the MAO inhibitors. Its antidepressant action is presumed to be a function of it strongly blocking the uptake of serotonin and therefore increasing the amount of the neurotransmitter available. It does not have sedative and anticholinergic (dry mouth, blurring of vision, urinary difficulty, constipation) effects. A limitation of this drug is that in some patients it increases anxiety, nervousness, and insomnia. Since most depressed people tend to have these symptoms, an increase is obviously undesirable. The popular media has focused on a few patients taking fluoxetine who have exhibited violent or suicidal behavior. However, there is no hard evidence that those incidents were caused by fluoxetine.

In electroconvulsive therapy (ECT) a tonic-clonic seizure is electrically produced through electrodes placed on the head. The seizure is essentially the same as that experienced by the epileptic except that precautionary measures are taken to prevent brain damage, bone fractures, great patient fear, and other undesirable effects. ECT is typically given three times a week for about 3 weeks. Research has demonstrated ECT to be superior to tricyclic antidepressants, MAO inhibitors, simulated ECT, and placebo for severe depression. ECT has the disadvantage of producing memory impairment lasting for a few weeks after treatment. There is also the possibility of permanent brain damage in some patients (Templer, Hartlage & Cannon, 1992). The decision to administer ECT should not be made until more conservative methods have been employed and the patient is informed of the risk.

Not all depressed patients respond favorably to ECT. In view of this fact and in light of the risks of ECT, the prediction of the sort of patient who will and will not respond favorably is a matter of great practical importance. A great deal of research has been carried out, but the prediction of successful response to ECT has been fairly disappointing. A number of studies investigating biological factors have found that EEG, autonomic reactivity, calcium metabolism, the dexamethasone suppression test, and other endocrine variables, produce rather discouraging predictive ability. The clinical variables of weight loss, early morning wakening, and somatic delusions seem to be the most consistent predictions of favorable response, but these variables provide a large margin of error (Scott, 1989). However, on the basis of the clinical variables that were statistically significant, one could perhaps infer that endogenous depression predicts favorable outcome.

Mania

In contrast to other disorders in which a large array of drugs and other treatment modalities are employed, lithium carbonate (usually referred to as lithium) is clearly the treatment most indicated for mania and manic depression. Although lithium was used by Dr. Cade in Australia in 1950 and was being used in Europe by 1960, it was not approved for use in the United States until 1970. Lithium can best be described as a mood stabilizer. Lithium is of clearly demonstrated efficacy in the treatment of mania. Bipolar patients are typically put on lithium on a more or less permanent basis for prophylactic purposes. Some authorities contend that lithium maintenance treatment does not obliterate the manic or depressive episodes but greatly reduces their severity.

The modes of action of lithium are not clearly understood. However, it does have effects on neurotransmitters, electrolytes, and neuroendocrine systems. Although lithium is clearly superior to tricyclic antidepressants in preventing manic episodes in manic-depressives, the research findings are equivocal with the comparison of lithium and tricyclic antidepressants in preventing depressive episodes in patients with this diagnosis. Tricyclic antidepressants are superior to lithium in preventing depressive episodes in unipolar depressives (Prien et al., 1984).

Side effects are, unfortunately, a major consideration in lithium treatments. These include gastrointestinal distress, tremor, muscular weakness and rigidity, excessive thirst, and excessive urination. Perhaps the most serious concerns are hypothyroidism and the potential for damage to the kidneys. There is a rather narrow range of appropriate lithium blood levels. With too low a level, the lithium will not work, and with too high a level toxicity will occur. Patients must have their lithium blood levels assessed on a regular basis.

Before lithium, antipsychotic drugs and ECT were the treatments most often used for mania. ECT should not be used in conjunction with lithium. However, lithium is not infrequently combined with an antipsychotic drug, especially in patients who are exhibiting both affective disorder and thought disorder. Sometimes lithium and tricyclic antidepressants are used concurrently. The general consensus of mental health clinicians is that psychotherapy is not productive when a patient is in a full-blown manic episode.

Other medications may be used when lithium is ineffective or cannot be used because of the side effects. The most important of these are two anticonvulsants, carbamazepine (Tegretol®) and valproic acid (Depakene®, or Depakotre®). These may be effective when the disorder has reached the rapid cycling phase and lithium is no longer useful.

AT HIGHER RISK FOR INSOMNIA

Anxious Persons

Depressed Persons

Persons Experiencing Pain

Persons with Breathing Problems

Persons with Cardiovascular Problems

Females

Older Persons

Persons Experiencing Stress

Persons with Brain Disorders

Persons with Posttraumatic Stress Disorder

SIX

Sleep Disorders

When one considers that humans spend about a third of their lives sleeping or attempting to sleep, there has not been a tremendous amount of research in this domain. The amount of research also appears small when one considers the percentage of the population that has sleep problems. Childhood autism and multiple personality are rare disorders in comparison to insomnia, but there have been a number of books written on the former two topics. Nevertheless, in the past 20 years we have learned a lot about sleep and sleep disorders, and there is now a good accumulation of established facts and tentative generalizations.

INSOMNIA

Millions of persons suffer considerable genuine distress each year from insomnia, yet many noninsomniacs, including some mental health professionals, take complaints of sleep disturbances lightly. Research indicates that insomniacs overestimate the length of time needed to get to sleep. Nevertheless, research is equally firm in showing that insomniacs take longer to get to sleep and have more frequent awakenings. Many insomniacs seem to be bothered by intrusive thoughts as they attempt to get to sleep. Persistent inability to sleep causes anxiety to be associated with the sleep situation, which produces a vicious cycle of insomnia. Sleep difficulty can be caused by physical problems such as pain. It is a common symptom of depression and a common component of anxiety.

In order to determine the prevalence of sleep disorders, 1,006 representative households in the Los Angeles metropolitan area were surveyed. It was found that 52.1% of the adults in those households had some sort of sleep disorder. The specific prevalences were 42.5% for insomnia, 11.2% for nightmares, 7.1% for excessive sleep, 5.3% for sleeptalking, and 2.5% for sleepwalking. These conditions were frequently chronic and started early in life. Insomnia was found to be much more prevalent in women than in men, 60.5% and 39.4%, respectively. Insomnia is more common in persons over the age of 50 and in persons of lower educational and socioeconomic status. Insomnia, nightmares, and excessive sleep were associated with more physical and more mental health problems (Bixler, Kales, Soldatos, Kales, & Healey, 1979).

In a study of insomniacs with a mean age of 48, it was found that the sleep difficulty began before age 40 in about two thirds of the patients. Three quarters of the patients reported that the onset of insomnia was associated with stressful life events, such as interpersonal relationship problems, loss of a significant other, change in education or work status, or health factors. The mean duration of the insomnia was 14 years. It is apparent that insomniacs tend to be anxious, depressed, and generally maladjusted persons, often with physical health problems, and greatly frustrated by their inability to sleep well.

Research indicates that insomniacs are more physically aroused at night. They have faster heartbeats and higher body temperature. Some sleep researchers believe that the brain has an arousal system and a sleep system and that for sleep to occur the latter must override the former. If such does not occur, insomnia ensues (Hauri, 1980). Sleep and sleep difficulty apparently are familial variables. One study found family resemblance for self-reported amount of sleep obtained, amount of sleep needed, and amount of sleep needed minus amount of sleep obtained (Ayers, Ruff, & Templer, 1979).

There are a variety of medical disorders that produce or contribute to insomnia because of pain, itching, breathing difficulty, and fear of death. These disorders include asthma and other chronic obstructive lung diseases, angina, cardiac dysrhythmias, hypertension, peptic ulcers, genitourinary conditions, blood disorders, skin disorders, metabolic disorders, and malnutrition (Williams, 1988).

Abnormal or atypical sleep patterns are found in a number of neurological disorders (Lugaresi, Cirignotta, Mondini, Montagna, & Zucconi, 1988). Epileptics characteristically display increased wakefulness after sleep onset and nocturnal awakenings. Rapid eye movement (REM) sleep is decreased in lesions associated with cerebrovascular disease. In Parkinson's disease there is a reduction in total sleep time, an increase in number of awakenings and wakefulness after sleep onset, and reduced REM sleep. In Alzheimer's disease, multiinfarct dementia, and most dementias, there is a decrease in total sleep time and decrease in various EEG indices of sleep quality. One might reason that if persons with documented brain disorder frequently have sleep difficulties, then many persons who have sleep difficulties may have these difficulties caused or aggravated by more subtle brain abnormalities.

Consistent with the fact that insomnia is frequently associated with neurological disorders is the well-established fact that the quantity and quality of sleep declines with age and a large portion of our elderly population is bothered by insomnia (Vitiello & Prinz, 1988).

Relaxation techniques, change of life-style, stress management, counseling, and instructions (such as to retire at the same time every night in a dark, quiet and comfortable place) benefit many insomniacs. It is often said by mental health professionals that insomnia is a symptom and that the underlying disorder should be treated. The ideal goal is to enable the patient to have a good sleep every night without the use of drugs. However, drugs are sometimes needed, especially if the insomnia and/or underlying disorder are severe and chronic. Barbiturates and related sedative drugs have been used for insomnia for decades. However, the research showing the greater benefits and fewer risks of the benzodiazepines is rather impressive. Roth, Roehers, and Zorick (1988) summed up this research as follows:

> The benzodiazepines are regarded as the drugs of choice for symptomatic treatment of insomnia according to the consensus conference. The benzodiazepines are preferred for several reasons. First, the margin of safety is relatively wide compared to all other sedative hypnotics. Second, tolerance to their hypnotic effects does not develop as rapidly as with other sedative hypnotics. Numerous studies have shown that benzodiazepines remain effective for at least four weeks of repeated nightly administration. Finally, physical dependence does not readily develop to benzodiazepines. (p. 375)

The treatment of insomnia is often a broad-spectrum approach that begins after a thorough investigation of all of the possible causes. The clinician should inquire into the drinking habits of the patient. It is very common for persons to make their insomnia worse by the consumption of alcohol, which reduces REM sleep in addition to producing physiological dependence. The use of prescribed drugs, over-the-counter drugs, and street drugs should be asked about. The patient's entire medical condition and history should be assessed. Psychological, psychiatric, and social problems and current life stressors may prove to be of considerable importance.

Tricyclic antidepressants, especially those with stronger sedative effects, taken before going to bed are also quite effective. It is likely that tricyclic antidepressants' efficacy with insomnia in depressed persons is a function of both the sedative effects and the less direct effects from the amelioration of depression. In one study using imipramine, a tricyclic antidepressant with low sedative properties, and trimipramine, a more sedating tricyclic, the two drugs did equally well for the depression, but the more sedating drug was superior for the insomnia (Kupfer, Spiker, Coble, & McPartland, 1978).

NARCOLEPSY

Narcolepsy can be classified into two types, idiopathic and symptomatic (Karacan & Howell, 1988). The former is of unknown etiology, and the latter is associated with some diseases. Symptomatic narcolepsy often occurs in association with brain concussions, encephalitis, and tumors of the mesodiencephalic region. Although narcolepsy is usually thought of as an adult disorder, about one third of patients are first diagnosed in adolescence or childhood.

Yoss and Daly (1957) published their four criteria for the diagnoses of narcolepsy. They are daytime sleep attacks, cataplexy, sleep paralysis, and hypnagogic hallucinations. They are often referred to as the "narcoleptic tetrad." The term *sleep attack* may be somewhat misleading insofar as it may imply to some that the patient is completely alert and suddenly falls asleep. The truth is that the patient is usually sleepy before falling asleep. The patient then falls asleep in circumstances in which most people do not fall asleep, such as after lunch or while watching television. Patients with more serious cases of narcolepsy may fall asleep while walking, driving, playing a sport, teaching, or even in sexual intercourse (Karacan & Howell, 1988). Cataplexy consists of muscular weakness and hypotonia and is often triggered by some sort of emotion. It lasts from a few seconds to a few minutes. It occurs in about two thirds of narcolepsy patients and is more common in idiopathic than symptomatic narcolepsy. Sleep paralysis is similar to cataplexy but is not triggered by emotion; it lasts for several minutes, and hallucinations may occur. It typically occurs about two or three times a month. Sleep paralysis occurs in about a third of narcolepsy patients. It should be pointed out that sleep paralysis is not confined to narcolepsy patients and probably occurs in about 4% or 5% of the general population. Hypnogogic hallucinations are auditory or somatosensory, are dreamlike in nature, and occur in a state of clouded consciousness. They occur in about a third of narcolepsy patients and produce a great deal of anxiety. A disproportionate number of narcolepsy cases are associated with headache, diabetes, obesity, and low blood pressure. Narcoleptic patients tend to have a lower than normal brain blood flow. Also, related to brain functioning is the disproportionate number of extrapyramidal symptoms and oculopupillary changes.

Narcolepsy patients do not tend to have serious psychopathology. However, a number of studies converge to the generalization that they tend to be depressed (Reynolds, Christiansen, Taska, Colde, & Kupfer, 1983). Also, narcolepsy patients tend to have adjustment problems in regard to social life and family life (Walsh, McMahan, Sexton, & Smitson, 1982). However, cause-and-effect relationships have not yet been disentangled with respect to either the depression or the adjustment problems.

The treatment of narcolepsy is symptomatic, with the highest priority usually given to reducing sleepiness and sleep attacks during the day. Psychomotor stimulants are ordinarily used. The main drugs of choice are permoline, methylphenidate (Ritalin®), and amphetamines, in that order (Roth et al., 1988). Tricyclic antidepressants have also been reported effective. However, there has been a dearth of tightly controlled double-blind studies that assess the efficacy and comparative efficacy of drugs for treating narcolepsy.

NIGHTMARE DISORDER

In nightmare disorder there are recurring frightening dreams that are typically vivid and extended. There is often a recurrence of a similar theme. They occur primarily during REM sleep, which tends to be more common during the end of the night. The anxiety is experienced as more cognitive than somatic, probably because the REM-related loss of muscle tone inhibits body movement. After awakening, the patient becomes immediately responsive and alert and is able to give a detailed description of the nightmare both then and in the morning. It is often difficult to return to sleep after such a dream. The disorder is more common in females. Over half of the cases start before the age of 10 and two thirds before the age of 20. Children frequently outgrow the disorder. Nightmare disorder is more likely to be associated with psychopathology in adults.

Research indicates that there is a strong affective component in nightmares. In adults, anxiety is the most common affect. Anger is the second most common, followed by surprise (Ware, 1988). There is reason to believe that anxiety from daytime experiences forms the content of nightmares. This is vividly observed in children and adults who have nightmares pertaining to traumatic experiences as one symptom of posttraumatic stress disorder. Most children have at least one nightmare while growing up.

Nightmares are rather common in victims of torture (Peterson et al., 1985). They are also common in U.S. Vietnam War veterans. One study found that dreams with military themes occurred 47% of the time in veterans with posttraumatic stress disorder but in only 3% of the time in veterans without posttraumatic stress disorder. In one study it was found that in 10 of 12 Cambodian concentration camp survivors suffering from posttraumatic stress disorder tricyclic antidepressants apparently caused a reduction or complete cessation of nightmares (Boehnlein, Kinzle, Ben, & Fleck, 1985). Success has also been reported with behavioral treatment in both children and adults (Fleming, 1986). In a study following the 1989 San Francisco Bay area earthquake, persons in that area were having twice as many nightmares as control persons in Arizona, and in a 3-week period 40% of the Californians but only 5% of the Arizona subjects had nightmares with earthquake content (Wood, Bootzin, Rosenhan, Nolen-Hoeksema, & Jourden, 1992).

NIGHT TERRORS

In night terror disorder, also known as "pavor nocturnus," the person suddenly wakes up with a panicky scream. The patient abruptly sits up in bed and looks extremely anxious, with dilated pupils, profuse perspiration, rapid breathing, and a rapid pulse. The patient tells of fragmentary horrible dream images but is virtually impossible to comfort. There is usually morning amnesia for the incident. These incidents are more likely to occur when the person is fatigued or under stress.

Night terror disorders occur most often in children between the ages of 2 and 12. Between 1% and 4% of children at some time have the disorder, and a much greater proportion of children experience isolated episodes. Ordinarily, the disorder remits spontaneously before or at puberty. When the disorder begins in adulthood, it ordinarily begins in the 20s or 30s. It is more common in males.

The majority of cases of night terror disorders are not serious enough to necessitate treatment. However, reassurance that the disorder is not serious can be helpful. More severe cases often benefit from the antianxiety drug diazepam (Valium®). The mechanisms of the apparent efficacy of diazepam are not known. However, Valium suppresses Stage 4 sleep, the stage in which night terrors usually occur.

In adults, night terrors tend to occur in persons who have high levels of anxiety in addition to depression, obsessive-compulsive, and phobic tendencies. In one study a third of night terror patients had major life events that preceded this problem (Kaleset al., 1980). Night terrors occur during deep sleep, not during REM sleep.

SLEEPWALKING DISORDER

In sleepwalking the person gets out of bed, walks around, and engages in various minor activities and either returns to bed or wakes up during the episode. In either case the person has little or no memory for what had transpired. The activities that could occur include dressing, opening doors, eating, and going to the bathroom. The person has a blank stare and can be awakened only with great difficulty. The assertion that the sleepwalker never hurts himself or herself is a myth. Sleepwalking is more likely to occur if the person is tired. It can range from nightly to infrequently occurring. Most sleepwalkers are male. The disorder usually begins between the ages of 6 and 12 and usually lasts for several years. It occasionally persists into adulthood. One percent to 6% of children have the disorder at some time.

Sleepwalking occurs at least once in approximately 15% of all children between the ages of 5 and 12. It is more common in males and far more common in children than adults.

Sleepwalking appears to have a genetic predisposition in that the concordance rate is six times higher in identical twins than in fraternal twins. The disorder, at least in children, does not appear to be highly associated with other psychopathology. Psychological disturbance seems to be more common in adult sleepwalkers.

BRUXISM

Bruxism consists of grinding the teeth during sleep. Patients with this disorder tend to have considerable anxiety and depression. Also, bruxism often occurs in conjunction with stressful events during the day and in persons anticipating stressful events (Ware, & Rugh, 1988). Bruxism, as one might imagine, results in dental problems. However, there are teeth-protecting appliances that can be placed in the mouth of the patient before going to bed. Bruxism occurs in persons of varying ages but is most common in childhood and adolescence. About 15% of children 3–17 years of age have a history of bruxism.

SLEEP ROCKING (HEAD BANGING)

Sleep rocking consists of rhythmical movements of a child's head and body. Onset is usually at about 6 months. It may occur in any stage of sleep. It varies in severity from cases where the parents should be told that there is nothing to worry about to cases in which there is injury and intervention is imperative. This is a fairly rare disorder. The etiology is not known.

SLEEP APNEA

In sleep apnea, as the name implies, the patient merely stops breathing. Guilleminault, Eldridge, and Dement (1972) defined apnea as a cessation of air exchange at the nose and mouth lasting at least 10 seconds. They proposed that for the diagnosis of the sleep apnea syndrome the patient must have at least 30 episodes of apnea during the night. Sleep apnea is more common in persons over the age of 60, in men, and in persons who are obese (Guilleminault & Dement, 1988). The two most common symptoms of sleep apnea are disturbed nocturnal sleep and excessive daytime sleepiness. Other symptoms may include fatigue, deficits of memory and judgment, suspiciousness, anxiety, depression, and morning headaches and nausea. Aggravating factors include alcohol intake, partial sleep deprivation, allergies, shift work, smoking, atmospheric contaminants, central nervous system depressants, and high altitude. Treatment includes weight reduction programs, medroxyprogesterone (a respiratory stimulant), tricyclic antidepressants, and surgery of the upper airway.

NOCTURNAL MYCLONUS

In nocturnal myoclonus there are repetitive movements of the legs during sleep, especially extension of the big toe with partial flexion of the ankle, knee, and hips. Persons so afflicted often do not know that they have this condition. It can occur in any stage of sleep. There is little basis to estimate the prevalence in the general population. However, it seems to be more common in the elderly, and there is evidence that up to a third or more of elderly persons have this condition (Moore & Gurakar, 1988). Nocturnal myoclonus is not associated with serious psychopathology. However, there is a study in which nocturnal myoclonus patients were found to be higher on the Hypochondriasis and Hysteria scales of the MMPI.

RESTLESS LEGS SYNDROME

In restless legs syndrome, patients usually have symmetrical creeping sensations in the lower legs between the knee and the ankle. The sensations are not experienced as being on the skin but at a deeper level, such as the bones. The name of this syndrome comes from the fact that patients are unable to remain still, and they often pace the floor, take a walk, stand, sit on the edge of the bed, or lie in bed kicking their legs. The majority of persons with restless legs syndrome also have nocturnal myoclonus. Women often develop this condition during pregnancy. The etiology is not known. However, a disproportionate number of patients have anemia and other nutritional deficiencies.

AT HIGHER RISK FOR DISSOCIATIVE DISORDER

Persons Who Act Out

Schizophrenics

Brain Disordered Persons

Persons in Stressful Circumstances

Epileptics

Persons With Many Somatic Complaints

Persons Sexually Abused as Children

Persons Physically Abused as Children

Persons with Somatoform Disorders

SEVEN

Dissociative Disorders

The dissociative disorders are difficult to define. In general, they are conditions in which the smooth and orderly functioning of identity, memory, and orientation is interrupted, but the interruption appears not to be due to a brain disorder or secondary to a psychosis.

TYPES OF DISSOCIATIVE DISORDERS

MULTIPLE PERSONALITY DISORDER

In multiple personality disorder the patient exhibits two or more personalities. The transition from one personality to another is usually sudden, but it occasionally takes a matter of hours or days. The transition is thought to be triggered by stress; in therapeutic situations, by hypnosis. The personalities are usually aware of the other personalities. It is common for the personalities to be radically different, for example, one being very reserved and proper and the other being flamboyant and impulsive.

PSYCHOGENIC FUGUE

In psychogenic fugue the patient travels to a new locality and is unable to recall his or her new identity. There may be perplexity and disorientation, but this diagnosis cannot be made if there is a demonstrable brain disorder. In addition, the patient's behavior is more purposeful and less confused than in organically based amnesia. The new personality is usually more outgoing and antisocial than the original personality. Violent behavior sometimes occurs. Depression is common.

PSYCHOGENIC AMNESIA

In psychogenic amnesia there is usually an inability to remember all events in a certain period of time such as the first few hours after a highly disturbing event. In some cases there is amnesia for only some of this period. The most uncommon type of amnesia is generalized amnesia, in which the patient is unable to remember anything about his or her entire life.

DEPERSONALIZATION DISORDER

In depersonalization disorder the patient has feelings of unreality about himself or herself and the world. The experience is often described by the patient as like being in a dream. These symptoms are reported as ego-dystonic, as not being in full control of one's behavior. The onset is usually sudden, but the remission is generally gradual. Many normal persons occasionally have depersonalization experiences, and this disorder does not merit extended discussion in this chapter.

HISTORICAL BACKGROUND AND PREVALENCE

The first person to employ the word *disassociation* was Pierre Janet, a contemporary of Sigmund Freud. Janet maintained that memories become dissociated from other memories and are blocked from consciousness to somehow produce conversion disorder. Fahy (1988) traced the development of the concept of dissociation and its role in multiple personality disorder postulated in the 19th and early part of the 20th century. In 1890, William James spoke of a plurality of selves in the normal individual and said that these selves could undergo derangements that could result in multiple personality. The widely read book *Three Faces of Eve* by Thigpen and Cleckley (1957) popularized the disorder. In this famous case history, Eve White was conservative and conventional, Eve Black was flamboyant and seductive, and Jane was a third personality who knew about both Eve White and Eve Black.

In the 1895 classical "Studies in Hysteria" by Freud and Breuer all of the cases were women with multiple personality and most of them had been sexually abused as children. Freud and Breuer maintained that the multiple personality was caused by the sexual molestation. Freud later stated that the sexual molestation did not really happen. Fahy (1988) offered his opinion that the sexual acts actually did occur but were denied by Freud because his patients were in his own social circle. Fahy maintained that 1980 was a benchmark year because the diagnosis of multiple personality was incorporated into the third edition of the *Diagnostic and Statistical Manual of Mental Disorders* of the American Psychiatric Association and because of several other important publications in that year. Graves (1980) counted only 47 reported cases of multiple personality from 1901 to 1969. However, he counted 50 cases either reported in the literature or known to him personally from 1971 through 1980 which amounts to a total of 97 cases from 1901 through 1980. Coons (1986) estimated that 6,000 cases had been diagnosed in North America by 1986. Thus there seems to be no doubt that there has been a dramatic increase in the number of multiple personality diagnoses being made in the past decade or so.

The ratios of female to male multiple personality patients have ranged from 4:1 to 9:1. Ross, Norton, and Wozney (1989) compared 28 male and 207 female multiple personality patients over a number of variables. The similarities in regard to symptoms, history, and demographics were much more pronounced than were the differences. However, the women were more likely to have been prescribed antidepressants, antianxiety drugs, and sedatives. The men engaged in more antisocial behavior. Twenty-nine percent of the men, compared to 10% of the women, had been convicted of crimes.

ASSOCIATED FEATURES

If one adapts the traditional viewpoint that multiple personality is a rare disorder, the similarity of facts for two studies (Ross, Norton, & Wozney, 1989; Putnam, Guroff, Silberman, Barbara, & Post, 1986) seem to legislate against the possibility of one or the other having very atypical patients or very atypical patient selection. Table 7.1 displays features of multiple personality found in these studies. The Ross, Norton, and Wozney (1989) study also found that the vast majority of these patients were victims of childhood sexual abuse and childhood physical abuse and had attempted suicide. The patients had been in mental health treatment a mean of over 6 years prior to diagnosis. Most patients had between two and four prior diagnoses.

A number of studies have demonstrated different personalities of multiple personality patients having different EEGs and other physiological recordings. This would seem to argue for the deeply ingrained nature of the various personalities in multiple personality. Thigpen and Cleckley (1954), using their famous patient "Eve," found different EEGs with different muscle tension and alpha background in different personalities. Also working with "Eve" were Condon, Daston, and Pacoe (1969), who reported three types of lateral eye movement across the three personalities.

TABLE 7.1   Two large series of multiple personality patients

ITEM	Ross (N = 236)	Putnam (N = 100)
Mean age in years	30.8	35.8
Years in mental health system prior to diagnosis	6.7	6.8
Other psychiatric diagnoses	2.7	3.6
Mean number of personalities	15.7	13.3
Percentage of:		
Males	12.3	8.0
Childhood sexual abuse	79.2	83.0
Childhood physical abuse	74.9	75.0
Suicide attempts	72.0	71.0
Child personality	86.0	85.0
Personality of opposite sex	62.6	53.0
Amnesia between personalities	94.9	98.0

Source: From Ross, Norton, and Wozney (1989), *Canadian Journal of Psychiatry*, *34*(5), pp. 413–418. Copyright 1989 by the *Canadian Journal of Psychiatry*. Used with permission.

ETIOLOGY

Psychodynamic explanations have dominated the field. One sort of explanation, especially for amnesia, is that unpleasant memories are forgotten as a sort of defense or protective mechanism. Consistent with this notion is the fact that amnesia frequently begins after some traumatic event such as a battlefield experience or civilian catastrophe. Psychoanalytically favored explanations are often employed, especially for multiple personality. Such explanations usually say in effect that a wish or urge that is repressed and unconscious in one personality becomes conscious and manifest with another personality (e.g., the proper Eve White becoming the improper Eve Black).

It seems to the present authors that etiological clues can be obtained from the fact that the dissociative disorders are often associated with trauma, especially childhood sexual and physical abuse; and by observing the similarities of the dissociative disorders with other disorders, especially (1) schizophrenia, (2) the somatoform and personality disorders, and (3) brain disorders.

TRAUMATIC EXPERIENCES

In one study it was found that 68% of the multiple personality disorder patients suffered from sexual abuse, 60% from physical abuse, 22% from neglect, 20% from abandonment, and 10% from emotional abuse; 4% had witnessed an accidental death. The authors noted that physical abuse was not confined to beating but included burning with cigarettes or scalding water and cutting. It was reported that major trauma continued to occur after the development of multiple personality and that 24% were raped as adults (Coons, Bowman, & Milstein, 1988).

Coons, Bowman, Pellow, and Schneider (1989) found that 100% of their atypical dissociative patients and 82% of their patients with psychogenic amnesia reported sexual, physical, or psychological abuse as children. About half experienced trauma in adulthood. Bliss (1984) reported that 60% of multiple personality patients had been sexually abused and that 40% had been physically abused. Saltzman and Solomon (1982) reported six cases of multiple personality patients who had been sexually abused as children. Putman, Gurof, Silberman, Barban and Post (1986) found that 97% of multiple personality disorder patients had been abused as children. Eighty-three percent had been sexually abused, primarily incestuous. Seventy-five percent had been physically abused. Sixty-eight percent had been both physically and sexually abused.

It has been contended that dissociation is on a continuum ranging from the pedestrian dissociation that normal people experience at one end to multiple personality at the other end. An example of the former, given by Spiegel and Cardena (1991), is that of driving a car and maintaining a conversation at the same time. Psychological scales of this continuum of dissociation have been developed, and in one study it was found that college students' scores on such a scale correlated with history of stressful or abusive early experiences (Sanders, McRoberts, & Tollefson, 1989). In a study with psychologically disturbed adolescents it was found that dissociation score was positively correlated with physical abuse, sexual abuse, psychological abuse, neglect, and negative home atmosphere (Sanders & Giolas, 1991).

In research with 236 persons with multiple personality diagnosis it was found that 19% had worked as prostitutes and 89% had been victims of childhood physical or sexual abuse or both (Ross, Norton, et al., 1989). Ross, Anderson, Heber and Norton (1990) related these findings to the high incidence of childhood sexual abuse of both prostitutes and multiple personality patients. Ross et al. (1990) went on to describe their study with 20 persons with multiple personality, 20 prostitutes, and 20 exotic dancers. Seven of the exotic dancers and one of the prostitutes met the criteria for multiple personality. Thirteen of the multiple personality disorder patients, five exotic dancers, and seven prostitutes met the criteria for psychogenic amnesia. Psychogenic fugue criteria were met by five of the multiple personality patients but none of the exotic dancers and prostitutes. Depersonalization disorder criteria were met by 13 of the multiple personality disorder patients, 4 of the exotic dancers, and 3 of the prostitutes. It is apparent that both the exotic dancers and the prostitutes exhibited considerable dissociative manifestations, although, as expected, fewer than that in subjects selected on the basis of their multiple personality diagnosis. All three groups had been extensively physically and sexually abused, but more of this occurred in the multiple personality subjects. Fifteen of the multiple personality subjects, 10 of the exotic dancers, and 8 of the prostitutes had been physically abused. The respective numbers for sexual abuse were 16, 13, and 11. The respective years of duration were 15, 4, and 4 for physical abuse and 13, 3, and 2 for sexual abuse.

SCHIZOPHRENIA

Schizophrenia and dissociative disorder patients share a tenuous grasp on the reality that the rest of us perceive, even though the dissociative disorders are not classified as psychoses. Also, schizophrenic patients (see Chapter 2) are troubled by an uncertain sense of identity, that is, are they male or female, heterosexual or homosexual, a child or an adult, a good person or an evil person? The authors have had a number of schizophrenic patients tell them that they often feel as if they are two persons. Fuguelike states and memory difficulty are reported in schizophrenics (Akhtar & Brenner, 1979). In the above-reported study by Solomon and Solomon (1982), the highest mean score on an MMPI scale of ten multiple personality patients was on the Schizophrenia Scale. In a more recent study (Coons et al., 1988), the highest MMPI score was also on the Schizophrenia Scale.

A high proportion of patients who have received a multiple personality diagnosis have had one or more Schneiderian first-rank symptoms of schizophrenia. As indicated in Chapter 2, these Schneiderian symptoms are regarded by many clinicians as being pathognomonic of schizophrenia.

Kluft (1987a) interviewed 30 consecutive multiple personality disorder patients and found that all 30 had one or more first-rank symptoms, with a mean of 3.6 symptoms per patient. The first-rank symptoms more likely to be present were voices arguing, voices commenting on one's action, influences playing on the body (somatic passivity), thought withdrawal, thoughts ascribed to others (thought insertion), made feelings, and made volitional acts.

In another study by Kluft (1987b), 30 multiple personality patients had a mean of 3.4 Schneiderian first-rank symptoms. In a series of 20 multiple personality patients of Ross, Heber, Norton, and Anderson (1989) there were a mean 6.6 symptoms; and this was actually greater than the mean of 4.4 for the schizophrenic patients of Ross et al. In the research of Ross, Anderson, Heber, and Norton (1990) 20 persons with multiple personality had a mean of 6.6 first-rank symptoms of schizophrenia.

In the research of Coons, Bowman, and Milstein (1988), 72% of multiple personality disorder patients had auditory hallucinations, 16% had visual hallucinations, and 34% had self-mutilating behavior. Twenty-four percent of their patients had a previous diagnosis of schizophrenia.

It is common for multiple personality disorder patients to claim extrasensory perception. In one group of 22 patients there was a mean of 5.5 different extrasensory phenomena, including mental telepathy, telekinesis, clairvoyance, and seeing ghosts.

The Ross, Norton, and Wozney (1989) study also described various kinds of alter personalities in their subjects. It is our opinion that some of the sorts of personalities are so far from reality (e.g., a demon or dead relative) that schizophrenia should at least be suspected. The persecutor alter personalities sometimes instruct the individual to harm himself and/or other persons. As is stated in Chapter 2, command hallucinations often occur in schizophrenia, and the clinician should take heed when such phenomena are reported by the schizophrenic patient.

Research of Armstrong and Loewenstein (1990) determined the Rorschach responses of 14 dissociative disorder patients who had both multiple personality and psychogenic amnesia. The Rorschach responses were those usually given by persons who have a distortion of reality and inaccurate perception of others. Unusual thought processes, such as the image of a girl with two bodies but one vagina, were brought out by the Rorschach.

A fairly common symptom of multiple personality is that of imaginary companions in childhood. Multiple personality patients are more likely to have had imaginary companions in childhood than are patients with schizophrenia, panic disorder, depression, and eating disorders. Although childhood imaginary companions are frequently seen in normal children, the phenomenon is more likely to persist into late adolescence or even adulthood in multiple personality patients (Ross, Norton, et al., 1989).

Malenbaum and Russell (1987) reported on an 11-year-old boy who had received both a diagnosis of schizophrenia and a multiple personality diagnosis. He heard three voices—loud, medium, and soft. All three voices instructed him to kill himself. He would ask questions such as "What would happen if I drink bleach?" He once put a rope around his neck. Beginning at age 4, he spent much time in his room talking to imaginary voices. He began to have definite auditory hallucinations at age 6. About a year and a half before admission the voices began to get louder and increasingly gave command hallucinations to harm himself. It was found that the boy's mother had had similar experiences. At age 3 or 4 she began hearing seven different voices after her father left and her stepfather began sexually abusing her.

In a review of 12 cases of multiple personality in children from 4 to 12 years of age, four of the patients had auditory hallucinations and one had possible auditory hallucinations (Vincent & Pickering, 1988).

PERSONALITY AND SOMATOFORM DISORDERS

The dissociative disorders have in common with the somatoform disorders, and with at least the antisocial form of personality disorder, the employment of some sort of deception or distortion of the truth. In one study the second highest MMPI scale score of 10 multiple personality patients was on the Psychopathic Deviate Scale (Solomon & Solomon, 1982). The Psychopathic Deviate Scale also had the second highest score in another study (Coons et al., 1988). In research of Coons, Bowman, and Milstein (1988), 32% of their multiple personality disorder patients—28% of the women and three (75%) of the four men—had a history of legal difficulties. One of the men had been incarcerated in a state penitentiary several times for armed robbery. Another man had engaged in many violent rapes, which he maintained had occurred after his primary personality picked up women in a bar and his assaultive alter emerged. He also engaged in armed robbery to support a drug habit. The third male was an adolescent who engaged in assault and battery, firesetting, shoplifting, and vandalism. Twenty-eight percent had a drug abuse or dependence diagnosis history, and 24% had an alcohol abuse or dependence history. Family history was also consistent with criminality and antisocial behavior. Thirty-six percent of the fathers, 10% of the mothers, and 10% of the siblings had drinking problems.

Heavy alcohol use may predispose one to psychogenic fugue. The fugue usually follows stress, such as marital quarrels, personal rejections, military conflict, or natural disaster. In one study with 37 subjects, fugue patients identified their behavior as being the result of attempted flight from justice, domestic stress, vocational stress, mental hospitalization, or working (Berrington, Liddell, & Foulds, 1956). Since these fugues occur in stressful circumstances and often bring about removal from such circumstances, a reasonable question is whether fugue symptoms have the function, either deliberately or without conscious deliberation, of bringing the afflicted one to a more favorable environment.

The American Psychiatric Association's (1968) *Diagnostic and Statistical Manual*, second edition, placed the dissociative disorders under hysterical neuroses. Furthermore, in one investigation, 8 of 10 multiple personality patients met the diagnostic criteria for hysteria, and 6 had conversion symptoms (Coons, 1984). In another study, 13 of 14 multiple personality patients had conversion symptoms (Bliss, 1980). As pointed out in Chapter 8, it has been recognized for a number of decades that persons with conversion disorder and hysteria tend to be unreliable informants and frequently have antisocial tendencies. Since our knowledge of dissociative disorders is largely dependent upon self-report of persons who may not be remarkably reliable informants, we cannot have overwhelming confidence in the apparent knowledge we have of the individual patients and the disorders.

Multiple personality is very often accompanied by numerous somatic complaints and problems. Among the more common of these are headache, unexplained pain, gastrointestinal disturbances, palpitations, parasthesias, analgesias, anesthesia, and paralysis (Bliss, 1984; Coons & Milstein, 1986; Kluft, 1986; Putnam et al., 1986; Ross, Heber, et al., 1989). Ross, Heber, et al. (1989) found that their 20 multiple personality disorder patients had more somatic symptoms than their 20 eating disorder, 20 panic disorder, and 20 schizophrenic patients. Seven of the multiple personality patients but only one of the eating disorder patients, two of the panic disorder patients, and none of the schizophrenic patients met the criteria for somatization disorder.

Watson and Tilleskijar (1983) found that in 29 patients with a hysteria diagnosis, 20 received a dissociative disorder diagnosis, and that 10 of these patients also had a conversion disorder diagnosis.

Dissociation and hypnosis are two phenomena that are positively correlated. Multiple personality patients obtain high scores on their ability to be hypnotized (Bliss, 1984; Fahy, 1988; Putnam et al., 1986). Hypnosis serves to bring out the alter personalities in psychotherapy, and can produce aspects of multiple personality disorder in normal subjects (Harriman, 1942). Kampman (1976) found that 7% of normal subjects were able to obtain an age regression alter personality under hypnosis. And using all good hypnotic subjects, Kampman found that 43 of 78 subjects were capable of age regression under hypnosis. Thus, we see that people who are suggestible and/or are adept at playing roles are the sort of people who have multiple personality diagnoses, and that there is some sort of unintentional or intentional distortion of the truth as rigorous thinkers perceive the truth.

BRAIN DISORDERS

Amnesia can be produced by brain injury, epilepsy, migraine headaches, cerebrovascular accidents, degenerative brain conditions, alcohol, and drugs (Coons, 1984). There is a report of 6% of epileptics generally, and 78% of temporal lobe epileptics manifesting fugue (Feindel & Penfield, 1954). If documented brain conditions can produce dissociative phenomena, one must wonder if at least some cases of dissociative disorder considered to be of psychogenic origin may have brain disorder etiology.

Mesulam (1981) found that of 12 patients with both temporal lobe epilepsy and dissociative states 7 had multiple personality and 5 had the delusion of diabolical or supernatural possession. There have been several other reports of temporal lobe epilepsy in multiple personality disorder patients (Benson,

Miller, & Signer, 1986). In a study of 50 multiple personality patients in which there were EEGs on 30, 16 were normal, 6 showed apparent medication effects, and 7 were definitely abnormal. Three of the patients had histories of grand mal seizures, and two had histories of temporal lobe seizures (Coons, et al., 1988). Twenty-eight of the 50 patients had headaches. Thirteen of the patients maintained that their headaches occurred in the transition from one personality to another. Eleven described their headaches as disabling.

FORMULATION AND TREATMENT

It is the opinion of the present authors that multiple personality and probably the other dissociative disorders do not constitute an independent diagnosis. Rather, they form a part of a more fundamental and pervasive diagnostic category, most frequently in one of three domains schizophrenia, brain disorder, and antisocial/somatoform/malingering. We tend to believe that a dissociative disorder diagnosis alone means that an important diagnosis has been missed. We are, however, willing to entertain a less radical position—a distinction between primary dissociative disorder, which is a relatively "pure" form of the disorder, and secondary dissociative disorder, which results from an underlying, more pervasive disorder.

Most of the treatment reported in the literature is dynamically oriented psychotherapy and/or hypnosis. Although good outcome has been reported, controlled research is apparently lacking. It is our opinion that a broad-spectrum intervention that treats the pervasive underlying disorder is probably the best approach.

AT HIGHER RISK FOR SOMATOFORM DISORDERS

Females

Lower Socioeconomic Status Persons

Below Average IQ Persons

Blacks

Persons Who Act Out

Persons in Frail Health

Persons Experiencing Stress

EIGHT

Somatoform Disorders

In somatoform disorders there are physical symptoms, suggesting a physical disorder but with no confirmation from medical tests and examinations.

CONVERSION DISORDER

In conversion disorder the patient usually loses or has impairment of a function of the body. An example of a classic conversion disorder is that of "glove anesthesia," in which the anesthesia (lack of sensation) is in the area of the hand and wrist on which a glove would fit. However, the actual anatomical nerve distribution to the arm and hand does not conform to this glove notion.

Textbooks of psychiatry and abnormal psychology tend to stress those conversion symptoms that are most dramatic, such as blindness and paralysis. In Table 8.1 (Watson and Buranen, 1979), the percentage of textbooks that mentioned such symptoms was compared to the actual percentage in two groups of patients. It is apparent that the more mundane types of symptoms, such as fainting and headache, are more common than the dramatic, classical symptoms.

Females have about twice the incidence of conversion disorders of males (Stefansson, Messina, & Meyerowitz, 1976). The reasons for the sex differences are not clear, although as Stefansson et al. (1976) have suggested, our society considers being ill to be unmanly, but accidents and drinking are acceptable male characteristics. The peak age for occurrence of the disorder was found to be 25 for females and 30 for males. It is more common among

TABLE 8.1   Frequencies with which conversion symptoms are mentioned in textbooks and frequencies of their appearance in two psychiatric samples

SYMPTOMS	% of Texts Mentioning Symptoms	% of Patients Manifesting Symptoms	
		Watson-Buranen	Woodruff et al
Paralysis	100	8	12
Anesthesia	94	38	32
BlindnessDeafness	94	0	20
Deafness	72	0	4
Mutism	61	0	0
Tunnel vision	55	0	0
Convulsions	55	12	20
Paresthesia	50	25	28
Tics	50	2	0
Nonheadache pain/hyperesthesia	39	58	88
Selective motor loss	39	10	0
Miscellaneous visual	39	0	0
Tremor	39	10	0
Aphasia	33	2	44
Contracture	33	2	0
Analgesia	28	10	0
Aphonia	28	0	0
Night blindness	22	0	0
Coughing	22	0	0
Vomiting	22	5	32
Appendicitis	22	0	0
Nausea	22	5	80
Fainting	22	22	56
Headache	17	32	80
Blurred vision	17	12	64
Ataxia/unusual gait	17	15	0
Globus hystericus	17	2	28
Tuberculosis	17	0	0
Speech disturbances	17	0	0
Dizziness	17	22	84

Source: Watson, C. G., & Buranen, C. (1979). The frequencies of conversion reaction symptoms. *Journal of Abnormal Psychology, 88*, pp. 210.

lower socioeconomic status persons, less educated persons, and blacks. One study presented limited evidence suggesting a disproportionate number of conversion disorder patients are youngest siblings (Stephens & Kamp, 1962).

First-degree female relatives of conversion disorder patients have a high incidence of conversion disorders. First-degree male relatives have a high incidence of alcoholism and antisocial personality (Woerner & Guze, 1968). However, genetics does not appear to be a direct determinant of hysteria since there is no difference in the concordance rate of fraternal and identical twins (Slater, 1961).

The frequent presence of acting out behavior and antisocial features in persons with conversion disorders has long been recognized and has research support (Guze, Woodruff, & Clayton, 1971). Consistent with such a relationship are findings mentioned above regarding male relatives of conversion disorders patients having antisocial features.

It has also been found that a disproportionate number of persons with conversion disorder have schizophrenia (Lewis & Berman, 1965). In spite of the classical description of the conversion disorder patient having *la belle indifference* (an attitude of indifference), the bulk of the evidence indicates that depression exists in many, perhaps most, persons with conversion disorders (Templer & Lester, 1974).

The article of Lecompte and Clara (1987) focused upon the variety and extent of psychiatric disorders in 100 conversion disorder patients. They found that 87% of their patients met the criteria for one or more additional psychiatric diagnoses. Forty-five percent of the patients had an affective disorder; 36%, a personality disorder; 19%, a substance abuse disorder; 16%, an anxiety disorder; 5%, a dissociative disorder; 2%, a schizophrenic diagnosis; and 1%, a paranoid disorder. The large number of mood disorder diagnoses is consistent with the previous literature on the various somatoform diagnoses, and the substantial number of personality disorder and substance abuse diagnoses is consistent with the antisocial behavior that has long been reported in patients with somatoform disorder. The fact that 87% of their patients had other psychiatric diagnoses led Lecompte and Clara to agree with the earlier assertion of Ford and Folks (1985) that conversion is a symptom rather than a disorder.

Sexual maladjustment has frequently been ascribed to the conversion disorder female patient in the clinical literature (Templer & Lester, 1974). However, one study showed women with conversion disorders to have no more sexual problems than did women in a control group (Roy, 1981a). Perhaps a balanced perspective is that the clinician should be alert to the possibility of sexual problems but should not assume such.

ETIOLOGY

The etiology of conversion disorders is not completely known. Dynamically oriented clinicians maintain that the symptoms have both primary gain and secondary gain. The former refers to the supposed advantage of having an intrapsychic conflict converted to the somatic realm. We believe that the secondary gain is a more plausible explanation. This position is that the symptom serves a function in the environment (e.g., to avoid work, to avoid sex with one's spouse, to avoid being returned to the battlefront, or to gain attention, affection, or financial compensation). Actually, this viewpoint fits learning and cognitive models of behavior at least as well as psychodynamic ones.

Consistent with such a secondary gain type of formulation is the large amount of evidence for a frequent association of conversion disorders and antisocial tendencies. Sometimes it seems that there is a thin line of distinction between the malingerer (one who is lying about a symptom) and the conversion disorder patient whose disorder manipulates the environment.

The demographic variables show that members of society with less status and power—namely, females, blacks, and low socioeconomic status persons—are more prone to conversion disorders. It appears that women in the Arab world are especially prone to conversion disorders. A possible generalization is that those persons who are lacking in the more effective resources for extracting what they need from the environment resort to conversion symptoms.

There is likely a biological substrate for conversion disorder. Frail health and unfavorable biological endowment predisposes one to conversion disorders. Slater (1961) found that in discordant twins the one with conversion disorder tended to have a lower birth weight and poor health and was more likely to be left-handed or ambidextrous.

Conversion disorders frequently are present along with an actual documented physical disorder. In one study (Stefansson et al., 1976), 56% and in another study (Whitlock, 1967), 62.5% of conversion disorder patients had accompanying diagnoses of a bona fide medical disorder. It is not rare for epileptics to have both documented seizures and hysterical seizures (Ramani, Quesnez, Olson, & Gummit, 1980). If one copes successfully with his or her environment through illness, then illness may be positively reinforced.

A reasonable synthesis of the etiological evidence would seem to point to a combination of health problems, underprivileged position in society and undersocialization or acting out tendencies being conducive to the development of conversion disorders.

It is possible that more persons than is ordinarily realized are diagnosed as having conversion disorder but actually have physical illness. In one study, patients so diagnosed were followed up 9 years later, and it was found that 60% had either died or developed signs of physical illness, especially of the central nervous system, during this time (Slater & Glithero, 1965). In another study it was found that 63% of patients given a conversion disorder diagnosis were found to have a brain disorder (Whitlock, 1967).

Epidemics of conversion symptoms have been reported. Olczak, Donner-stein, Hershberger, and Kahn (1971) studied an outbreak of stomach cramps, convulsion-like manifestations, and tremors in 52% of adolescents in a camp for culturally deprived high school students. A greater proportion of girls were affected. Moss and McEvedy (1955) reported on an epidemic of overbreathing and fainting in a girls' high school and found that those girls who had the symptoms had higher scores on the Extraversion and Neuroticism scales of the Maudley Personality Inventory, as Eysenck would have predicted.

In a very interesting study Kriechman (1987) reported 12 cases in which a child or adolescent manifested a somatoform disorder shortly after a sibling had manifested a somatoform disorder. The symptoms of the siblings were either the same or very similar. Their female relatives had a high rate of soma-tization and histrionic personality diagnoses, and their male relatives had considerable alcohol abuse and other indicators of antisocial or socially unstable behavior.

Behavioral techniques are often employed in the treatment of conversion disorder and other somatoform disorders. If at least some cases of somatoform disorders have etiology that fits with learning principles, then it would seem reasonable that treatment based on learning theory might be effective. If a symptom has been reinforced by getting attention from other persons or not having to work, then it would seem that changing behavior-reinforcement relationships would result in reduction of the symptoms.

SOMATIZATION DISORDER

Somatization disorder used to be referred to as hysteria or Briquet's Syndrome. Whereas a conversion disorder ordinarily involves a single dysfunctioning, somatization disorder involves a number of diverse somatic symptoms, which may include a conversion disorder symptom. Among the more common symptoms are gastrointestinal complaints, menstrual and other gynecological irregu-larities, pain, cardiovascular symptoms, pulmonary symptoms, dizziness, sexual maladjustment, and headaches. It is a predominantly female disorder.

The nature of persons with somatization disorder can be further understood by a study in which 20 somatization disorder patients were compared to 20 patients with a hysterical personality diagnosis (Kaminsky & Slavney, 1983). The similarities of these two groups of patients were more salient than the differences. Both tended to have unstable childhoods and poor relationships with their mothers and fathers. Both groups tended to have had unhappy marriages and a history of sexual maladjustment. Substance abuse was common in both. The similar history of these two groups of patients is consistent with the clinical lore of hysterical personality features in patients with the diagnosis of hysteria. There were, however, a couple of significant differences on psychological tests and interview material. The somatization disorder patients had higher neuroticism and more obsessive tendencies.

Patients with somatization disorder tend to be dramatic not only in their description of their symptoms but generally dramatic and very talkative. As is the case with conversion disorder patients, they are not reliable informants and are prone to acting out behavior. Often the personality disorder diagnosis of histrionic personality, formerly called hysterical personality (see Chapter 13, "Personality Disorders") applies to them.

HYPOCHONDRIASIS

In a study with 512 British hypochondriacal patients (Kenyon, 1964) it was found that the three most common parts of the body involved were head and neck, abdomen, and chest, in that order. By bodily system the musculoskeletal, gastrointestinal, and central nervous systems predominated. Sixteen percent had unilateral symptoms, and of these 73% were left-sided. The most commonly associated psychiatric symptoms were depression, anxiety, tiredness, and weakness.

The layperson's stereotype of elderly persons includes greater hypochondriacal manifestations. There are published studies that show elderly persons to be more hypochondriacal. However, there have been studies that have not confirmed this stereotype (Barsky, Frank, Clerary, Wyshak, & Klerman, 1991). It is common knowledge that older persons are less healthy and vigorous than younger persons. However, it is often difficult to determine whether the greater somatic concern of any person is a function of hypochondriasis or actual medical problems.

Hypochondriasis seems to be more common in lower socioeconomic classes. In fact, it has been found that in general lower-social-status psychiatric patients are more likely to express preoccupation about somatic functioning. It was found that in Israel persons of Oriental extraction were more likely to be hypochondriacal than were persons of European origins (Hes, 1968). In Israel persons of European extraction ordinarily have more advantageous social and economic position. Hypochondriasis is a frequent concomitant of depression and anxiety disorders. Hypochondriasis seems to be more frequently associated with depression in non-Western cultures.

There is some research evidence that hypochondriacs are more closely attuned to internal sensations than are nonhypochondriacs. Tyrer, Lee, and Alexander (1980) found that hypochondriasis-diagnosed patients were able to gauge their heart rate more accurately than were patients with phobia or generalized anxiety disorder while being shown stressful and calming movies.

SOMATOFORM PAIN DISORDER

The majority of patients in pain clinics have some sort of physical abnormality, but their pain complaints are often out of proportion to the abnormality. The most consistent finding in personality research on pain patients is that they are depressed and anxious. It is both likely and understandable that depression and anxiety results from the pain. However, a vicious circle frequently ensues in which the depression and anxiety bring the pain more into focus and make it less endurable.

One study found different reactions to pain in four different ethnic American groups (old American, Jewish, Irish, and Italian). The Jewish and Italian patients were much more emotional and expressive in response to pain, more likely to cry, to groan and moan, to complain about pain, and to maintain that it was unbearable. The Old American and Irish demonstrated less expressive behaviors.

In addition to ethnic differences, personality factors account for expressiveness of pain. Extroverts are more expressive than are introverts, but the latter can tolerate more pain (Lynn & Eysenck, 1961). Men can tolerate more pain than women can, at least in experimental situations. With increasing age, tolerance to cutaneous pain increases and tolerance to deep pain decreases (Woodrow, Friedman, Siegelaub & Collen, 1972).

Students of introductory psychology and biology are told that when a stimulus activates the pain receptors a neural message is sent to the brain and is interpreted as pain. This is basically correct. However, the situation is not that simple. To account for the complexities of pain, Melzack and Wall (1965) proposed the gate control theory. Basically, this theory is that the dorsal horns of the spinal cord act as a "gate" to increase or decrease the flow of neural transmission to the brain. The gating is controlled both by peripheral stimulation and by cortical influence associated with such factors as anxiety or attitudes or expectations. The gate theory appears to be able to explain prolonged pain which persists long after the original source of stimulation has been removed. Melzack and Wall suggest that the efficacy of acupuncture, a Chinese method of pain relief through sticking needles into precisely selected parts of the body, is a function of the stimulation from the needles closing the gate to the target pain transmission. The gate control theory is also consistent with observations regarding phantom limb pain (e.g., a person feeling intense pain in his or her foot months or years after the leg was amputated below the knee). This is experienced by about a third of amputees. The gate theory also appears to mesh with referred pain (e.g., a heart condition causing pain in the shoulder).

The entire social and psychological context of the pain determines the degree to which one will express pain and tolerate pain. It is well known that some persons maintain their religious convictions and that some soldiers deny information to the enemy in spite of extreme torture. Beecher (1959) noted that soldiers wounded in battle in World War II required morphine much less than did men with similar wounds in civilian life. The Plains Indians of North America formerly engaged in self-torture as part of religious ceremonies. Athletes are often not aware of the seriousness of injuries until after the game. Both boxers and street fighters usually react minimally to injury inflicted on them during a fight.

As reviewed by Chaturvedi and Michael (1986), chronic pain is frequently found in psychiatric patients. In fact, some studies have reported that as many as half of psychiatric patients have pain as a major presenting complaint. Pain is especially common in patients with depression and anxiety. It is less frequently seen in schizophrenics. Chaturvedi and Michael reported the findings of their own study in which 14% of psychiatric outpatients reported chronic pain. Forty-three percent of these patients had a dysthymic disorder; 20%, anxiety states; and 20%, somatoform disorders. In comparison to non-pain psychiatric patients the target patients were more likely to be middle-aged, female, having an anxiety disorder, and having a dysthymic disorder. The pain patients were significantly less likely to have schizophrenia or mania.

Pain clinics typically use a broad-spectrum approach that includes pain-relieving drugs, counseling, electrophysiological stimulation, and behavioral techniques, including biofeedback, hypnosis, and psychotherapy. Nevertheless, pain, like death, is an inherently negative entity. It is too much to expect persons with intractable pain to be "happy" about their situation.

The sorts of behavioral interventions for pain can be divided into three categories: a respondent conditioning model, an operant conditioning model, and a cognitive-behavioral model (Turk & Rudy, 1990).

In the respondent model there is classical conditioning, in which anxiety becomes associated with the stimuli and circumstances surrounding pain. Our bodies have built-in protective mechanisms in which such behaviors as limping and avoidance are adaptive insofar as they prevent further tissue damage, promote healing, and decrease pain. However, the patient avoids an increasing array of situations. Furthermore, these situations become conditioned stimuli, and anxiety becomes the conditioned response. And the anxiety intensifies the pain. Thus, there is a vicious circle (Philips, 1987). The evidence for this theoretical formulation is equivocal. Nevertheless, there has been clinical work and research based upon these concepts. Such intervention has used general relaxation and biofeedback. It does appear that some pain patients are helped by these strategies. However, they are certainly not a panacea, and the research evidence is mixed (Keefe & Gil, 1986; Turner & Chapman, 1982). Biofeedback probably should be used with other modalities rather than constituting the sole intervention process (Turk & Rudy, 1990).

The operant conditioning model of pain focuses more upon pain behavior than upon pain experience. Some of the reinforcers of the expression of pain are attention from significant others and medical personnel, rest, drugs, and financial compensation. And experimental research buttressed the contention that expression of pain is to some extent a function of social reinforcers. For example, patients with more solicitous spouses reported more pain than did patients with nonsolicitous spouses (Block, Kremer, & Gaylor, 1980). Fordyce (1978) has advocated a broad-spectrum approach that includes extinction of pain-related behavior such as asking for drugs, increasing physical activity to increase strength and endurance and flexibility, working to quota rather than to pain levels, and more generally positive reinforcement for activity. We have no doubt that it is possible for operant programs to reduce pain expression and other pain behavior; we have no doubt that is possible for athletic coaches and Marine drill sergeants to reduce pain behavior. Yet we believe that the job is less than half done if the patient continues to suffer. On the other hand, for the manipulative and attention-seeking person who greatly exaggerates or even feigns pain, nothing could be better than this sort of operant approach.

A number of studies have found that pain patients tend to have low self-efficacy and to feel helpless about their situation. And pain patients with more self-efficacy were found to have better outcome following pain intervention. More important than support for the assumptions of cognitive-behavioral rationale is the fact that research has demonstrated its efficacy (Corey, Etlin, & Miller, 1987).

DYSMORPHOBIA

In dysmorphobia there is a preoccupation with imagined bodily defects or an exaggeration of the extent of the defect. These usually involve facial features or skin imperfections, but any part of the body may be involved. This disorder is more common in adolescents and young adults.

There has not been a great deal written about dysmorphobia. However, there is sufficient information in the literature to know that a substantial percentage of these patients are psychotic (Hardy, 1982). Depression is common in dysmorphobic patients (Hardy & Cotterill, 1982). Dysmorphobic patients tend to have generally low self-concepts, a finding that should not viewed as surprising since their body image is almost by definition a negative one.

CONCLUSION

We maintain that there are four themes that tend to run through the somatoform disorders. Those persons who are at high risk for somatoform disorders tend to be socially disadvantaged, to have inadequate coping resources, to have a history of health problems, and to exhibit antisocial conduct. The greater any one of these themes, the greater the risk of somatoform disorder. The more themes that are present, the greater the risk of somatoform disorders.

PART III

DISORDERS OF SELF-CONTROL

AT HIGHER RISK FOR IMPULSE DISORDERS

Alcoholics

Persons Who Act Out

Mood Disordered Persons

High Risk Takers

Stimulus Seekers

Extraverts

Youthful Persons

NINE

Disorders of Impulse Control

In impulse disorders the patient has a strong impulse to engage in a given behavior. This impulse is often accompanied by a feeling of tension, which is released upon the commission of the act. The act is ego-syntonic and pleasurable or gratifying. The four most common sorts of disturbances recognized by the diagnostic nomenclature are pyromania, pathological gambling, kleptomania, and trichotillomania.

PYROMANIA

In pyromania the person feels an irresistible impulse to set fires and to watch them, enjoying the process. Although such behavior is considered impulse disorder behavior, there is often considerable preparation and planning for the fire in addition to elimination of the evidence. One basis for identification of the perpetrator is his repeatedly being seen at various fires.

Most pyromaniacs are children, adolescents, or young adults with a peak age of about 17 years. The overwhelming preponderance of pyromaniacs are male. Stewart and Culver (1982) stated that their boy/girl ratio of 14:1 was actually lower than ratios reported by other researchers. They cited ratios of 29:1 and 19:1. Stewart and Culver went on to say that such high gender ratios also are found with adults, and they cited ratios of 78:1 and 26:1.

Most pyromaniacs engage in other antisocial behavior, often of an aggressive sort. In fact, one study found few differences between violent adolescents who were and were not firesetters. Both groups had high rates of robbery, assault, use of weapons, and sexual assault. Both groups had a high incidence (over 90%) of minor neurological abnormalities, and both groups had a high incidence (over 80%) of head injuries. Both groups had mean IQs in the mid-80s. However, the firestarters had significantly more placements and were more likely to have been in a residential psychiatric treatment facility (Ritvo, Shanok, & Lewis, 1983).

The literature abounds with descriptions of impulsivity, disobedience, aggressiveness, fighting, destructiveness, and scant regard for the property of others in pyromaniacs. The study of Heath, Hardesty, Goldfine, and Walker (1983) provided even more credibility to the contention that children who set fires are strongly antisocial. Heath et al. found that 63% of the pyromaniacs, but only 19% of the control children, met the criteria for conduct disorder, the diagnosis that is most similar to that of the adult psychopathic personality diagnosis.

A larger than chance proportion of pyromaniacs exhibit psychotic symptoms and/or alcoholism. The majority of pyromaniacs are below average in intelligence, although the range of IQ is considerable. One study (Lewis & Yarnell, 1951) reported that about 70% of adult pyromaniacs were of below normal intelligence. Childhood offenders also tend to have low IQs (Ritvo et al., 1983).

Some authors have divided children who set fires into preadolescent and adolescent and have found that the former tend to be more psychiatrically disturbed and emotionally deprived. The latter are more apt to engage in firesetting as a group activity (Mavromatis & Lion, 1977).

Firesetters tend to come from broken and often chaotic homes. They have a history of having been physically abused, and they are often witnesses to other violence in the home. Both the fathers and the mothers tend to have a history of antisocial behavior and alcoholism. Some sort of psychiatric history is common in the parents.

The classical psychodynamic explanation is that pyromania is a function of psychosexual maladjustment (Marshall & Barbaree, 1984). Setting fires and sexual activitation do seem to have some common properties, such as excitement, warmth, mystery, escalation and deescalation of activity, danger, and risk of being caught. Although it is not possible to muster research support for psychosexual dynamics in the typical case of pyromania, some cases show an unmistakable psychosexual element. In one case a man had a history of frequently masturbating to orgasm in the presence of fires or with the fantasy of fires. He became sexually aroused by seeing a lit match. He was able to have sexual intercourse only if he was watching a fire (Lande, 1980).

Other psychodynamics conjectured in the clinical literature include hostility toward authority, retaliation toward significant others, and self-destructive drive. It should, however, be borne in mind that the criteria for pyromania state that if the firesetting is a function of some sort of personal gain or advantage, such as defrauding an insurance company or concealing a crime, it is not classified as pyromania.

It is the opinion of the present authors that pyromania is a reflection of various types of psychopathology and motivations. Pyromania is a symptom that can be part of various syndromes. Different persons have pyromania for different reasons. However, the clinical and research literature does seem to indicate a couple of unifying threads—a thread of strong and very overt antisocial behavior and a thread of inadequacy. The pyromania is ordinarily one of a number of antisocial activities. The second thread, that of inadequacy, is often interwoven with such disadvantages as low IQ, neurological abnormality, psychiatric problems, and a disturbed home life.

In one study it was found that in a 200-day period 14 patients accounted for 17 fires and 16 admissions to a psychiatric hospital (Geller, 1984). It is apparent that a number of these patients were psychotic, as evidenced by command hallucinations, irrational thinking, and poor judgment. It is also apparent that these psychotic patients had been living in the sort of setting (e.g., group homes) where schizophrenics and other highly disturbed people live in a more protective environment than the rest of us in the community and yet a less protective one than a state hospital. Geller suggested that these fires are often a cry for help and an attempt to return to a more protective environment.

PATHOLOGICAL GAMBLING

In pathological gambling there is a chronic progressive pattern of behavior in which the gambler becomes more and more anxious and frantic on account of his or her losses so that the amount of money gambled increases in a futile attempt to win back the money lost.

EPIDEMIOLOGY

It is difficult to accurately assess the prevalence of pathological gambling in the United States. However, most authorities contend that it is increasing (Lesieur & Rosenthal, 1991). A national survey in 1974 seemed to indicate that 0.77% of the general population of the United States are pathological gamblers. Surveys carried out between 1984 and 1988 in Ohio, New Jersey, Pennsylvania, Maryland, and New York provide prevalence rates ranging from 1.4% to 3.4% for compulsive gamblers (Culleton, 1985; Sommers, 1988; Volberg & Steadman, 1988, 1989).

Pathological gamblers tend to be male, with estimates ranging from 60% to 80%. There are some indications that the proportion of female gamblers is rising (Wolkowitz, Roy, & Doran, 1985). A disproportionate number of pathological gamblers appear to be under the age of 35, of lower income, black or Hispanic, and Catholics (Lesieur & Blume, 1991).

Gender differences were found in the clinical histories of pathological gambling patients in a study conducted at a private psychiatric hospital that specializes in problem gambling and problem drinking. Eighty-two percent of females and 24% of males were abused as children. Fifty percent of the females and 15% of the males had a history of suicide attempts. Fifty percent of females and 9% of males reported having a compulsive-gambler mother. Forty-two percent of the males and 8% of the females reported a history of criminal arrest (Ciarrochi & Richardson, 1989).

DESCRIPTION OF PROBLEM BEHAVIOR

Custer (1984) presented his formulation in regard to the phases that compulsive gamblers go through in becoming progressively worse. Petty gambling usually begins in early adolescence, and substantial gambling ordinarily begins at about age 17 for males and 25 for females. In the first stage of becoming a compulsive gambler, the "winning stage," the person is usually successful and is buoyed up by the success to even greater self-confidence, but his wagers are not yet foolish bets and he has not begun to splurge and squander. This phase may last for months to several years and usually ends with a substantially large win. Next comes the "losing phase," in which the betting escalates in magnitude and in imprudence. The person then begin to "chase," that is, to bet progressively larger amounts in attempting to gain back the money lost. A sense of urgency prevails in which the search for money intensifies and may involve the cashing in of bonds, the cashing in of insurance policies, and borrowing through legal channels. As legal resources are exhausted, the compulsive gambler turns to illegal sources such as bookies and loan sharks and often pleads with relatives and friends to bail him out. In the "desperation phase" the gambler may resort to criminal activities, such as writing bad checks and cheating other, more naive gamblers. Family and employment are neglected. Finally, their entire world collapses as they lose their jobs and significant others and are faced with legal difficulties. Depression ensues, and sometimes suicide occurs.

CONSEQUENCES OF PATHOLOGICAL GAMBLING

It should not be surprising that pathological gambling is harmful not only to the gambler but to his or her family. In a study in which the control group were women with nongambling husbands, the wives of pathological gamblers tended to have depression, suicidal problems, and a high rate of disorders that have traditionally been regarded as having a psychosomatic component (Lorenz & Yaffee, 1988). Research shows that children of pathological gamblers have an array of disturbances that may include depression, loneliness, anger, guilt, feeling abandoned, psychosomatic illness, drug abuse, overeating, and having gambling problems themselves (Jacobs, 1989).

The control of one's gambling problem does not mean that life is completely back to normal. One cannot completely erase the harm brought to other persons and the suffering of the afflicted individual. Neither do one's debts disappear. The mean in debt status of pathological gamblers was found to be $53,350 in one treatment center (Division of Alcoholism, 1988), $54,662 in a second (Blackman, Simone, & Thomas, 1986), and $92,000 in a third (Politzer, Morrow, & Leavey, 1985). A group of female Gamblers Anonymous members were found to have a debt of $14,979 (Lesieur, 1988a).

ASSOCIATED CHARACTERISTICS OF PATHOLOGICAL GAMBLERS

There are three features that are often associated with pathological gambling. They are substance abuse, antisocial behavior, and mood disorder.

Substance Abuse

A high rate of substance abuse and pathological gambling is almost common knowledge in both fields, especially the latter. Custer and Custer (1978) found that 8% of Gamblers Anonymous members were alcoholic, and another 2% were addicted to other drugs. Linden, Pope, and Jonas (1986) reported 52% alcohol or substance abuse with Gamblers Anonymous members. Lesieur (1988a) found that 52% of the 50 female Gamblers Anonymous members had abused alcohol and/or drugs at some point in their lives. Ramirez, McCormick, Russo, and Taber (1983) found that 39% of pathological gamblers in a Veterans Administration hospital met alcohol and/or drug abuse criteria within a year of admission, and 47% met the criteria at some point in their lives.

In addition to the studies that show high substance abuse rates in pathological gamblers, some studies have assessed the extent of gambling problems in substance abusers. One study reported that 17% of alcoholics had "gambling difficulties" (Haberman, 1969). In another study with alcohol and drug dependency inpatients, 9% were given a pathological gambler diagnosis, and an additional 10% showed signs of problematic gambling. The authors reported that 5% of patients abusing only alcohol, 12% of patients abusing a combination of drugs and alcohol, and 18% abusing only drugs, showed clear signs of pathological gambling. In research administering a psychometric instrument, the South Oaks Gambling Screen, to alcohol and substance abuse patients, 14% scored in the pathological gambling range, and an additional 14% showed signs of pathological gambling (Lesieur & Heineman, 1988).

A number of reports suggest that pathological gamblers tend to have a diversity of addictions or addictive-like behaviors. Adkins, Rugle, and Taber (1985) maintained that 14% had heterosexual addictive patterns. Lesieur (1988b) said that 24% of his interviewees were compulsive overspenders; 20%, compulsive overeaters; and 12%, sexually addicted. Jacobs (1988) maintained that compulsive gamblers, compulsive overeaters, and alcoholics have common characteristics.

Antisocial Behavior

Most crimes committed by the pathological gambler are those in which one can acquire money in a short period of time (Lesieur & Rosenthal, 1991). Most of these crimes do not involve actual violence, but 21% of the male prison inmates and 15% of the female prison inmates in the Lesieur and Rosenthal study had committed armed robbery.

The description of the compulsive gambler has some resemblance to that of the antisocial (psychopathic) personality insofar as both have poor impulse control, the use of manipulation and dishonesty, extraversion, and apparent inability to profit from experience. Tharp, Matzman, Syndulko, and Ziskind (1980) found a lower level of autonomic nervous system reactivity than characteristically found in normal individuals. As described in Chapter 13 "Personality Disorders" low autonomic reactivity in experimental situations has also been found with psychopaths.

Nevertheless, it is apparent that many gamblers do not fit the entire stereotype of the Cleckley conceptualization of psychopathy that includes low anxiety, low guilt, and insufficient concern about their behavior. Many gamblers better fit Eysenck's conceptualization of the psychopath as being an "extraverted neurotic."

Pathological gamblers were compared with control subjects on the MMPI and were found to have a higher Psychopathic Deviate Scale mean, indicating violation of the expectations of society; they scored higher on the Hypomania Scale, indicating an excess of poorly directed behavior; higher on the Psychasthenia Scale, indicating higher anxiety; and lower on the Social Introversion Scale, indicating extraversion (Graham & Lowenfeld, 1986; Moravek & Munley, 1983). The Edwards Personal Preference Schedule indicated that pathological gamblers are high on achievement, exhibitionism, dominance, heterosexuality, and endurance. It has been found that risk-taking in gambling is related to risk-taking in other arenas, such as cigarette smoking and risky driving. Gamblers tend to be "sensation seekers," that is, persons who attempt to increase sensory stimulation not only in laboratory research but in real-life situations such as parachuting, scuba diving, and volunteering for novel experiments (Zuckerman & Neeb, 1979).

Mood Disorder

The clinical impression based literature contains considerable reference to an association between pathological gambling and mood disorder. This impression is substantiated by one study in a special gambling treatment program in a Veterans Administration Hospital. Seventy-six percent of the patients were diagnosed as having major depressive disorder, 38% were diagnosed as having hypomanic disorder, and 26% were diagnosed as having both major depressive disorder and hypomanic disorder. Twelve percent of the subjects had made potentially lethal suicidal attempts (McCormick, Russo, Ramirez, & Taber, 1984).

Linden, Pope, and Jonas (1986) found that 72% of a Gamblers Anonymous group had experienced at least one major depressive episode. Fifty-two percent had recurrent major affective episodes. There was a 20% history of panic disorder, a disorder that is often associated with depression and responds well to tricyclic antidepressants. Ciarrochi and Richardson (1989) reported that an amazingly high 90% of their pathological gambling patients in a private psychiatric hospital had a mood disorder diagnosis.

A number of reports converge to show a high rate of suicide attempts in compulsive gamblers. Suicide attempt history was reported to be 12% by McCormick, Russo, Ramirez, and Taber (1984), 15% by Livingston (1974), and 24% by Custer and Custer (1978). McCormick et al. also found that another 6% mentally rehearsed a specific plan or made a suicidal gesture, 10% had occasional thoughts of wishing they were dead, 12% made preparations for a serious suicide attempt, 18% thought of a specific method of suicide, 22% frequently thought of suicide but chose no method, and only 20% apparently had no suicidal inclinations.

ETIOLOGY

Wolkowitz, Roy, and Doran (1985) pointed out that a variety of psychodynamic formulations have addressed compulsive gambling. Freud saw similarities between masturbation and compulsive gambling, both being irresistible impulses that are associated with both enormous pleasure and subsequent guilt. Other dynamic formulations include rebellion against parents, a mixture of genital and pregenital conflicts, and the need for omnipotence and special privilege.

Compulsive gambling has often been viewed within an operant behavior frame of reference (Marshall & Barbaree, 1984). Animal experimental research has demonstrated that variable schedules of reinforcement produce great resistance to extinction. In like fashion, the compulsive gambler is rewarded (by a win) in an irregular and inconsistent fashion. Perhaps the potential gambler who loses bets rather early in his life is more "lucky" than he realizes.

TREATMENT

Gamblers Anonymous is a self-help organization similar to Alcoholics Anonymous. Most large cities and many small cities throughout the world have Gamblers Anonymous programs. The members tell the group about their gambling difficulties and are given help in working out a plan of financial restitution. The member who feels a relapse approaching can obtain support from his fellow members. Associated with Gamblers Anonymous is Gam-Anon for teenage children. This, of course, has a parallel in Alonon for the spouses of alcoholics and Aloteen for the children of alcoholics. The 12 steps of Gamblers Anonymous are quite similar to the 12 steps of Alcoholics Anonymous.

The "bible" of Gamblers Anonymous is *Gamblers Anonymous*, often referred to as the "G.A. Big Book." It contains in a very readable and straightforward fashion the associations's history, organizational structure, the "12 steps" and "12 traditions," and a number of interesting personal stories and testimonials.

An array of psychological interventions for pathological gambling has been reported by mental health professionals. Dynamically oriented treatment, ordinarily tailored to the etiological perspective of the therapist, has been reported. Aversion therapy is sometimes employed (e.g., administering electric shocks to the patients in association with slides of betting shops, poker hands, and roulette wheels) (Saeger, 1970). Having patients keep records of gambling to obtain greater recognition of its negative effects has been employed (Cotler, 1971). "Paradoxical intention," specifically forcing the gambler to gamble even when he does not want to, has been reported to be beneficial (Victor & Krug, 1967).

If compulsive gambling is associated with mood disorder, one might wonder if lithium (see Chapter 5, "Mood Disorders") might be helpful for compulsive gamblers with notable affective disturbance. Moskowitz (1980) reported that three such patients improved after being placed on lithium. Needless to say, three cases cannot provide the confidence of well-controlled research. Nevertheless, the apparent improvement of these patients does generate some cautious encouragement. Thus, lithium treatment must be regarded, along with Gamblers Anonymous and the other psychologically oriented therapies, as showing promise but in need of well-controlled research before a definitive perspective can be obtained.

As is the situation with alcoholism, some clinicians maintain that the goal of controlled social behavior is a viable alternative to complete abstinence. Rankin (1982) reported on a compulsive gambler who agreed to gamble only on Friday and Saturday, to limit his weekly bets, to not reinvest his winnings, and to abide by some other restrictions. The patient decreased the amount of money he spent gambling, improved his marital relationship, and found a better job. We believe that, as is the situation with alcoholism, the last word regarding the controlled-versus-abstinence issue has not yet been heard.

KLEPTOMANIA

In kleptomania the person is unable to resist the impulse to steal that often arises very suddenly and while in stores. The person usually has no tremendous need for the object and steals for no apparent overwhelming motive.

EPIDEMIOLOGY

It is the general consensus of clinical opinion that kleptomaniacs tend to be female, but the evidence for such an opinion is less than overwhelming. Kleptomania is well distributed over all ages from children to the elderly and is seen in all socioeconomic strata.

It is very difficult to estimate the prevalence or incidence of kleptomania because most kleptomaniacs do not voluntarily enter treatment and because we don't know how much kleptomanic behavior goes undetected. The literature suggests that only a minority of shoplifters—15% (Yates, 1986) and 24% (Schlueter, O'Neal, & Hickey, 1989)—are kleptomaniacs. It stands to reason that precise figures can never be known because it is much more difficult to objectively assess motivation than to objectively assess behavior.

ETIOLOGY AND ASSOCIATED CHARACTERISTICS

There are a number of reports of kleptomania occurring after some sort of brain injury or abnormality has occurred (Goldman, 1991). A 71-year-old man began stealing after he developed dementia. A 25-year-old man with presenile dementia stole a variety of objects. A middle-aged woman began stealing after she developed a right parietal mass accompanied by apathy and depression. Nonsensical stealing occurred in a woman with narcolepsy. However, it would seem very unlikely that any specific sort of brain disorder would prove to directly cause kleptomania. A more plausible interpretation is that brain pathology reduces impulse control and judgment. It is our opinion that in all stealing the thief gains something. And there is no reason to believe that the common thief never has emotions that transcend the acquisition. Perhaps there is not a clear line of distinction between the two categories of stealing but rather a continuum of intrinsic versus external motivation. We suspect that the diagnosis of kleptomania is more likely to be given to persons of higher social status. The wife of the university president is more apt to be called a kleptomaniac and the university janitor a thief for stealing the same thing.

In a study with college students it was found that the students with a shoplifting history tended to have more abnormal MMPI scores than control college students. The scale that best differentiated the groups was the Psychopathic Deviate Scale, which reflects antisocial tendencies. One interesting study found differences between male and female shoplifters. The males manifested a higher rate of antisocial behavior and incarceration. The women were more likely to manifest a history of psychiatric care for depression and other disorders (Gibbens, Palmer, & Prince, 1971). Thus, it appears, at least in this research, that the females come closer to meeting the criteria of kleptomania and the males the criteria of ordinary thievery.

It is the formulation of the present authors that kleptomania and stealing in general are symptoms rather than syndromes. There is probably a diversity of underlying syndromes but that these are usually in the personality disorder realm.

TREATMENT

A variety of interventions have been employed that ordinarily parallel the clinician's etiological conceptualization. Dynamically oriented therapists deal with such matters as money representing ungratified oral needs, sibling rivalry in which the kleptomaniac is competing with a favored sibling for parental attention or gifts, and stealing as providing libidinized adventure and excitement.

Behavior therapy approaches, often with an aversive element, have been implemented. One patient was treated by being instructed to keep a record of her stealing and to hold her breath until it becomes "mildly painful" (Keutzer, 1972). One patient was punished by having the humiliation of returning the stolen article (Robertson & Meyer, 1976). Treatment for a 15-year-old girl with kleptomania included giving her electric shocks when she picked up a coin with a red light on but not giving a shock with a green light (Warmann, 1980).

Bulimics have an above average tendency toward kleptomania. McElroy, Keck, Pope, and Hudson (1989) reported that in 43 women who were successfully treated with antidepressant drugs for bulimia nervosa, three had kleptomania; both conditions improved concurrently. Unfortunately, the present authors know of no well-controlled research demonstrating the efficacy or lack of efficacy of any form of treatment for kleptomania.

TRICHOTILLOMANIA

In trichotillomania there is a frequent and irresistible impulse to pull out one's hair. The act temporarily relieves the feeling of tension. These actions produce not only patches of partial baldness but medical conditions of the scalp such as infections. Although in most patients the head is the only or primary area involved, other locations include eyebrows, eyelashes, beard, armpits, and pubic hair. It is common for the person to deny the problem and attempt to conceal the affected areas from other persons. Associated behavior may include head-banging, nail-biting, scratching, gnawing, and acts of self-mutilation.

EPIDEMIOLOGY

Trichotillomania is neither a common nor a rare disorder. Mannino and Delgado (1969) found 7 cases out of 1,368 patients seen at a mental health center. Onset is ordinarily in childhood, but adult onset, even in late middle age, has been reported. The disorder is more common in females. The etiology is not known, but there is limited evidence that it may be more common in persons with schizophrenia and mental retardation. Stress is believed by some clinicians to play a role.

CLINICAL IMPRESSIONS REGARDING ETIOLOGY

There have been a number of clinical reports about the etiology being a function of disturbed family relationships. Greenberg and Sarner (1965) maintained that 84% of the mothers were "highly pathological" and 87% of the fathers were "helpless and ineffectual." Mothers have been also described as ambivalent, double-binding, and aggressive; and the fathers have also been described as passive and rejecting. Various psychodynamic explanations have been given for this disorder, including disrupted psychosexual development, symbolic castration, self-hatred, mourning processes, loss of the mother, and separation (Krishnan, Davidson, & Guajardo, 1985).

Associated Psychopathology

A disproportionate number of patients with trichotillomania appear to have notable and often even serious psychopathology. In the Greenberg and Sarner (1965) study 10% of their patients were said to be schizophrenic and 37% were said to have borderline personality disorders. Sethi, Chaturvedi, Gupta, and Trivedi (1982) reported on a 22-year-old Hindu man in India who was very psychotic. He exhibited fearful behavior, illogical talking, muttering to himself, neglect of hygiene, auditory hallucinations, and delusions of persecution and reference. He plucked out his eyebrows to the extent that there was no hair left. After administration of antispychotic drugs he ceased the plucking, and his eyebrows grew back.

Several cases of trichotillomania in the retarded have been described in the literature. Barmann and Vitali (1982) described the case of a 5-year-old girl with a mental age of 16 months who would pull her hair while playing. They also described the case of a 9½-year-old girl with a mental age of 18 months who pulled her hair both during play and while eating. She began this activity at age 3 and developed bald spots and scalp infections. Their third case was that of a 3-year-old boy from moderately to severely retarded who began to pull his hair out when he was 1 year old and developed bald spots and scalp infections. Barrett and Shapiro (1980) reported on a 7-year-old girl who would pull her hair out and eat it. She also had tantrums and would engage in destructive and aggressive play. In a case reported by Litt (1980) a five-year-old mildly retarded boy began to pull his hair out when his grandfather grew irritable and confused and began to beat him. The boy became 50% bald. George, Brewerton, and Cochrane (1990) reported that three of five patients with bulimia also had trichotillomania. All three of these young women were as reluctant to talk about their trichotillomania as they were to talk about their bulimia. With all three bulimics, the trichotillomania preceded the bulimia.

Treatment

Krishnan, Davidson, and Guajardo (1985) reviewed the literature on behavioral treatment of trichotillomania. It appears that a variety of behavioral techniques used with a variety of populations and in a variety of settings are very effective. However, Krishnan et al. appropriately pointed out that most of these studies are not well controlled. Psychodynamically oriented treatment has also been employed, but with this too there are apparently no well-controlled studies. Trichotillomania has also been treated with psychotropic drugs that include tricyclic antidepressants, MAO inhibitors, and antipsychotic drugs. Since anxiety and depression are said to be common in persons with this disorder, it would appear that drugs that reduce these states would improve the condition. One of the most promising new treatments for trichotillomania is clomipramine, a tricyclic antidepressant drug that is very effective for obsessive-compulsive disorder patients. The rationale for its use in trichotillomania includes the fact that many patients with this disorder have obsessive-compulsive features.

AT HIGHER RISK FOR EATING DISORDERS

Anorexia and Bulimia

Females

Adolescents and Young Adults

Persons Who Act Out

Persons with Conflict with Parents

Persons with History of Obesity

Persons in Occupations Requiring Slenderness

Persons with Above Average IQ

Persons in Sports Requiring Slenderness

Persons in Developed Nations of the World

Whites

Persons with Anorexic or Bulimic Relatives

Homosexual Adolescent Males

Obesity

Lower Socioeconomic Status Persons

Persons with Low Metabolism Rates

Persons Obese as Children

Persons with Improper Diets

Persons Who Overeat

Persons with Obese Relatives

TEN

Eating Disorders

OBESITY

Obesity was divided by Stunkard (1983) into three degree classifications: mild (20%–40% overweight), moderate (41%–100% overweight), and severe (over 100% overweight). According to these criteria, 90.5% of obese persons are mildly obese, 9% are moderately obese, and 0.5% are severely obese.

Obesity is a serious detriment to one's physical health. Estimates of obese adult Americans range from 15% to 50%. Many clinicians maintain that overeating is caused by various psychodynamic factors. It is said that at least some obese persons have a strong oral fixation producing a sense of loneliness or depression, and that overeating is an attempt to fill the inner void. Some women are said to become or remain obese to avoid sexual activity. The senior author (D.I.T.) recalls an obesity treatment patient who said he liked being called "Big Jerry" and liked the sense of power and authority his great mass gave him. Although some of these dynamic factors could very well exist in some obese individuals, research evidence for a general obese personality is lacking.

It appears that a characteristic of some obese persons is their ability to eat very large amounts of food without experiencing the usual symptoms of distress that normal people feel when overeating (Castelnuovo-Tedesco & Scheibel, 1975). This observation may have a parallel with the contention of some clinicians and researchers that alcoholism-prone individuals are better able to consume large amounts of alcohol without becoming sick.

Seriously obese persons are preoccupied with their obesity, and they are disgusted and embarrassed by their bodies, which they regard as grotesque.

However, the vast majority are not psychotic or in any way seriously psychologically disturbed. Research does indicate that they tend to be mildly depressed and somewhat more impulsive than the average person. There are also a number of clinical reports of passive-dependent and passive-aggressive personality features. Also, research seems to indicate a high rate of childhood family instability, divorce, and parental loss.

When most people think of obesity, they think of adults. However, it is estimated that upward of 30% of young children and adolescents are obese (Foreyt, 1987). Obese children are at a greater risk for cardiovascular problems such as hypertension and for orthopedic difficulties. Most overweight children become overweight adults, with the associated health problems. If being overweight continues through childhood and adolescence, the odds are 28 to 1 against the person becoming a normal-weight adult (Stunkard & Burt, 1967). Obese children are unquestionably at a psychosocial disadvantage. Research indicates that children have negative attitudes toward children who are obese and use adjectives such as stupid, mean, lazy, and ugly to describe them (Sclafani, 1980). Adults also have such negative attitudes toward obese children. Poor self-concept in obese children and adolescents results from these attitudes.

The obese person is a member of a disadvantaged and even discriminated-against minority group. In one study children were asked to rank other children on the basis of drawings as to how much they might want such a person to be their friend. The mesomorphic child was ranked number 1, the one with leg braces second, the child in a wheelchair third, the child with an amputated hand fourth, the child with a disfigured face fifth, and the obese child last (Richardson, Hastorf, Goodman, & Dornbush, 1961). One study found that teachers wrote less favorable letters of recommendation for obese students. This was especially the case for obese female students (Canning & Mayer, 1967). In one experimental study mental health workers attributed more psychopathology to the obese models who were simulating the same sort of abnormality as the nonobese models (Young & Powell, 1985). Other research demonstrated that store personnel took longer to wait on obese than nonobese customers (Pauley, 1989).

Socioeconomic status is inversely related to obesity. Lower socioeconomic status women were found to be overrepresented in a 7 to 1 ratio. Lower status men were also overrepresented but not to the same extent as females. The explanation for these social status differences probably includes the relatively low cost of "filling" foods, lack of knowledge about nutrition, external locus of control, and learned helplessness.

Schacter (1971) has pointed out the similarities of obese humans and rats made hyperphagic by lesioning of the ventromedial nucleus of the hypothalamus. Both the obese human and the rat made obese from lesions in the ventromedial nucleus are finicky. If the rat's food is made less palatable by alteration with quinine, the obese rat actually eats less than the normal-weight rat. Experiments have demonstrated that obese humans will actually eat less than normal persons if the food is not palatable. Obese rats will work less hard for food than will normal rats. One study demonstrated that obese persons would eat more sandwiches than normal persons if the sandwiches were on the table but would eat fewer sandwiches if they had to go to the refrigerator to get them. Schachter maintained that the eating of obese persons is a function of external rather than internal factors. On international flights their eating is governed not by time since last meal (and associated internal cues) but by external factors such as time of day and amount of daylight.

Weight reduction programs ordinarily have a behavioral component to the diet structure in addition to a group support element. Those programs are usually effective in producing weight loss, with the typical loss in a 10- to 12-week program being 10 to 12 pounds. Great variability is found in follow-up studies a year or more later, with many patients having regained all of the weight they lost.

Hundreds of thousands of persons have participated in group-based programs for weight reduction, but only a minority of such groups have been led by physicians, nurses, psychologists, and other health professionals. Most groups are led by lay persons. The largest noncommercial group is Take Off Pounds Sensibly (TOPS). TOPS has weekly meetings that include group support and weigh-ins. The typical member is female, middle-aged, and lower middle class. The largest commercial group is Weight Watchers. Weight Watchers also uses weigh-ins and group support but in addition employs behavior modification, inspirational lectures from successful members, and carefully designed nutritional programs. The drop-out rates in these programs are very high. Nevertheless, there are many obese persons who have benefited from these cost-effective programs (Stunkard, 1983).

A study by Craighead, Stunkard, and O'Brien (1981) impressively demonstrated the efficacy and comparative efficacy of behavior modification in moderately obese persons who received various combinations of behavior modification, appetite-suppressant drugs, and no treatment. It is apparent that although drug treatment produced faster loss of weight, the behavior modification was most effective in producing a sustained weight loss.

The recalcitrance of the weight problem has resulted in some obese persons seeking medically risky radical procedures, such as lipectomy (surgical removal of fat), surgical decrease in size of stomach, or a surgical shortening of the small intestine to decrease the caloric absorption of food. Other treatments include exercise, total fasting under close medical supervision, and drugs—

usually psychomotor stimulants such as amphetamines, which suppress appetite but also have medical and psychological risks (see Chapter 12, "Drug Abuse"). Furthermore, weight is almost invariably gained back after discontinuation of the drug.

The difficulty many obese patients have in maintaining weight loss has led to the "set point theory" (Keesey, 1986), which postulates that the body will defend against change in some sort of set, or ideal, body weight for that individual. Consistent with the set point theory is the evidence that in adulthood fat cell numbers can be increased but not decreased (Krotkiewski et al., 1980). It was further found in a study with dieting obese women that after fat cell size decreased to normal, weight reduction ceased.

It should also be pointed out than in many overweight patients the obesity is caused at least in part by a low metabolic rate sometimes associated with endocrine disorders. Such individuals have the misfortune of attaining more weight than the average person with the same caloric consumption.

Wooley and Wooley (1984) asked the question "Should obesity be treated at all?" Their arguments were based upon the facts that obese and lean people do not invariably differ in the amount eaten, that mild to moderate obesity does not greatly reduce longevity, that weight reduction programs are not highly successful in keeping weight down an extended period of time, that some compliant obese persons suffer from chronic hunger while on a semistarvation diet, that such dieting is an emotional drain on the patient, and that repeated weight fluctuations may be harmful to one's health.

ANOREXIA NERVOSA

Anorexia nervosa is a disorder in which a person who is apparently otherwise physically healthy refuses to eat. Many anorexics have a history of obesity. With or without such a history, they are obsessed with the idea that they are too heavy. Anorexics appear to be unaware of their body hunger cues. Although anorexics are not classified as psychotic, such unrealistic thinking seems almost delusional. A number of clinical reports indicate that a not insignificant minority of anorexic patients display psychotic symptoms at some time in their illness. In a systematic study it was found that of 130 anorexic and bulimic patients, 17 (13%) had displayed psychotic manifestations (Hudson, Pope, & Jonars, 1984).

Some of the physical manifestations of anorexia nervosa include loss of the menstrual period; thinning hair; dry, flaking skin; constipation, languo (a downy growth of body hair); lowered blood pressure; lowered body temperature; lowered chloride and potassium levels (if vomiting); and lowered pulse rate. The mortality rate is about 15% (American Psychiatric Association, 1987). It is not uncommon for anorexia to be accompanied by compulsive stealing (Dally, 1969). Anorexics seem to be generally more inclined to acting out than the average person. It is common for anorexic patients to drink large quantities of caffeine-containing beverages, especially diet colas. Such beverages have few calories and suppress the appetite while increasing energy (Sours, 1983).

There seems to be a not clearly understood relationship between anorexia and obsessive-compulsive manifestations. In one study, 16 of 151 female obsessive-compulsives had past histories of anorexia nervosa (Noshirvani, Kasviskis, Marks, Tsakiris, & Montiero, 1991). Another study reported 33% of 51 bulimic patients to have met the criteria for obsessive-compulsive disorder at some time in their lives (Hudson, Pope, Yurgetin-Todd, Jonas, & Franken-burg, 1987). Anorexics certainly seem to be obsessed with their weight. And the high level of activity displayed by them could be viewed as compulsive behavior. In personality assessment studies by Wonderlich & Swift (1990) anorexics were repeatedly found to be obsessional, introverted, anxious, and neurotic.

Anorexia nervosa is primarily a disorder of adolescent and young women. It is more common in above-average social status. Anorexic patients tend to be above average in education (Willi & Grossman, 1983). Ninety-seven percent of anorexics are white. The low incidence of anorexia in nonwhite persons has been found not only in the United States but in Australia and South Africa.

The incidence of anorexia nervosa is not only higher in the privileged segments of society but is higher in more prosperous parts of the world, such as North America, Western Europe, and Australia. There appears to be a high prevalence of anorexia nervosa in occupations where a slim figure is stressed, such as ballet and fashion modeling (Szmulkler & Tantam, 1984).

It has been recognized for more than two decades that anorexia and bulimia tend to be familial disorders. With 32 pairs of anorexic nervosa twins, the concordance rate was 52% for the monozygotic twins and 11% for dizygotic twins (Garfinkel & Garner, 1982). In another study, with 11 sets of twins, the concordance rate for bulimia nervosa was 33% for monozygotic twins and 0% for dizygotic twins (Hsu, Chesler, & Santhouse, 1990). Bulimic twins were studied by Fichter and Noegel (1990), who found concordance rates of 83% and 27%, respectively.

It is a common clinical opinion that anorexia nervosa is increasing. One study confirmed this impression. It was found that in a region of Switzerland the incidence was 0.38 per 100,000 for 1956–58, 0.55 per 100,000 for 1963–65, and 1.12 per 100,000 for 1973–75 (Willi & Grossman, 1983).

Dynamically oriented psychologists contend that the anorexic is in effect rebelling against her mother in a childlike refusal to eat. It is a common clinical impression that until the onset of anorexia the patient was regarded as a very compliant youngster. Other posited psychodynamics include the rejection of adult status and rejection of sexuality by the maintenance of an emaciated body. Indeed the anorexic usually has a low or absent sex drive.

Treatment of anorexia nervosa ordinarily takes place in a hospital. Usually, both psychotherapy and behavior therapy are employed. Some psychotherapists place more emphasis upon unconscious factors and others upon the here-and-now issues relevant to the eating disorder. In the behavior therapy, positive reinforcement is given for eating. Anorexia nervosa is always regarded as a serious condition because it is often long-lasting and because of its damaging effects upon the body—sometimes ending in death.

A number of investigators have reported rapid weight gain with behavioral modification for anorexia nervosa (Wolf & Crowther, 1992). Typically, the patient is provided with such reinforcers as time out of her room, visitors, or television access. However, there is a scarcity of well-controlled research that determines the long-term effect. Systematic desensitization has been used to reduce the anorexic's great fear of obesity. In this the patient's hierarchy of food-related stimuli are determined, and she is asked to visualize them while under therapist-induced relaxation. Behavior modification strategies to improve the social skills of the patients so that they can feel more comfortable at a normal weight have been tried.

In one study, 100 anorexic females were followed up 4–8 years after first presentation. Forty-eight had good outcome as defined by normal or near-normal weight, regular menstruation, and psychosocial adjustment. In 30 the outcome was intermediate, in 20 it was poor, and 2 patients had died. About a quarter of anorexia nervosa patients have a chronic condition (Hsu, 1988). Less favorable outcome was predicted by longer duration of illness, older age of onset, bulimia, anxiety when eating with others, poor childhood social adjustment, and poor parental relationships (Hsu, Crisp, & Harding, 1979).

There has been one reported follow-up study with male anorexia nervosa patients. They were followed up a mean of 8 years since first presentation. The pattern of outcomes was rather similar to that found in female anorexia nervosa patients. Twelve (44%) had outcomes that were considered good, 8 (30%) had outcomes that were considered poor (weight more than 15% below normal and poor or no sexual activity), and 7 (26%) had intermediate outcomes (Burns & Crisp, 1984).

There have been several reports of anorexia nervosa patients tending to have a history of substantial medical illness. Dally (1969) found that 38 of 140 anorexia nervosa patients had childhood physical ill health, including asthma, tuberculosis, and congenital blindness. More recent investigators reported diabetes, Turner's syndrome, and urogenital abnormalities. In a controlled study it was found that an anorexia nervosa group did have a significantly greater history of serious illness than the two control groups, patients seen in a general medical practice and a group of schizophrenics (Patton, Wood, & Johnson-Sabine, 1986). However, the reason(s) for this relationship are not clear. It is not known if biological weakness causes both the anorexia nervosa and the medical illnesses or if there are psychosocial reasons for the association, such as the assumption of a patient role.

BULIMIA NERVOSA

Bulimia consists of binge eating followed by self-induced vomiting or purging with laxatives. Such can lead to potassium loss and other complications. Although bulimia is usually regarded as a disorder that one either has or doesn't have, it appears that a not inconsequential percentage of the general population has at least some elements of the disorder. In one survey of 369 consecutive women attending a British family planning clinic (and presumed not remarkably atypical of the general population of young women), 21% reported binge eating, 3% reported vomiting as a means to weight control, and 5% reported using laxatives for weight control (Cooper & Fairburn, 1983). The point prevalence of bulimia, using rather strict definitions, has been reported as about 1% (Fairburn & Beglin, 1991). Lifetime prevalence is thought to be less than 5%.

Bulimia is frequently associated with anorexia nervosa. About half of anorexics have bulimia (Hudson, Pope, Jonas, & Yungelun-Todd, 1983), and in one study about half of bulimics reported a past history of anorexia nervosa (Pyle, Mitchell, & Eckert, 1981).

In a study that exclusively used bulimic patients without an anorexic nervosa diagnosis, they were found to have characteristics similar to anorexia nervosa patients, including preoccupation with food and an exaggerated fear of becoming obese (Pyle, Mitchell, & Eckert, 1981). These patients were all female, primarily young, and tended to display drug abuse, stealing, and impulsive behavior generally.

Bulimic patients have been found to differ from anorexic patients in several respects. They tend to be heavier; to be more sexually active, to be more likely to menstruate regularly and to remain fertile, to be more extroverted, to more frequently engage in acting out behavior, to be more apt to have a history of obesity, to have an older age of onset, to be more depressed, to have higher suicidal risk, to have more self-mutilation, to have a higher frequency of obesity in their mothers, to be less likely to deny hunger, and to have a less favorable prognosis They also came from families with more marital discord and with parents more emotionally distant from their daughters (Garfinkel, Moldofsky, & Garner, 1980).

One study showed that bulimic women were less well adjusted than normal women in several areas of life. They were less well adjusted in work, social and leisure activity, family relations, marriage, and relationship to parents (Johnson & Bernt, 1983).

Although bulimia is regarded as primarily a disorder of young females, two surveys with college students showed about a tenth of students with bulimic behavior to be male (Halmi, Falk, & Schwartz, 1981). A large proportion of these students were dancers or gymnasts. In one study, in which three bulimic males were studied intensively, it was found that all three had poor impulse control, anxiety, depression, and guilt; had abnormal nonsuppression on the dexamethasone suppression test (DST) ordinarily found in endogenous depression, and had a family history of affective disorder (Gwirtsman, Roy-Byrne, Lerner, & Yager, 1984).

It appears that homosexual men are more likely to be bulimic than are heterosexual men (Carlat & Camargo, 1991). The incidence of bulimia in this population has been reported to range from 27% (Herzog, Dennis, Gordon, & Pepose, 1984), to 53% (Schneider & Agras, 1987), to 63% (Woodside, Garner, Rockert et al, 1990).

The incidence and prevalence of substance abuse in bulimic women are very high. Hatsukami, Eckert, Mitchell, and Pyle (1984) reported that 30% of 108 bulimic women in an outpatient clinic had a current or past diagnosis of alcohol or drug dependency. Mitchell, Hatsukani, Eckert, and Pyle (1985) found that in 275 bulimic women 34% had histories of drug- or alcohol-related problems, 23% had histories of alcohol abuse, and 18% had histories of treatment for prior chemical dependence.

As is the case with anorexia nervosa, there is evidence that bulimia is increasing. A survey of general-population American females showed bulimia life history rate of 17.7% for those ages 12–20, 10.3% for ages 21–30, 6.3% for ages 31–40, and 5.3% for ages 40–64. Because of the nature of life history indices one would expect more older women to report a positive history because of longer time at risk. Since the opposite was found, it does appear that the disorder is increasing.

MOOD AND BIOLOGICAL CORRELATES OF ANOREXIA AND BULIMIA

Anorexia and bulimia appear to be associated with mood disorders. Depression is common in both disorders, and there are suggestions of common neuroendocrine dysfunction in both depression and the eating disorders. Both anorexics and bulimics have been found to have the same abnormality on the dexamethasone suppression test as depressives (Hudson, Laffer, & Pope, 1982). Furthermore, there is a high prevalence of mood disorders in the relatives of anorexics and bulimics. (Hudson et al., 1984). Pyle, Mitchel, and Eckart (1981) found that 48% of bulimic patients had a first-degree relative with depression. Both bulimics and anorexics have responded to tricyclic anti-depressant drugs (Enas, Pope, & Levine, 1989; Mitchell et al., 1990). Bulimics have also responded favorably to MAO inhibitors (Walsh, Stewart, Rosse, Gladis, & Glassman, 1984).

In anorexic and bulimic patients, the highest mean is on the Depression (D) Scale, and the second highest mean is on the Psychopathic Deviate (Pd) Scale, the scale that most reflects impulsiveness and the propensity for acting out behaviors. It is here pointed out that alcoholics tend to have the highest Psychopathic Deviate Scale score and second highest on the Depression Scale. Alcoholics, like eating disorder patients, tend to be impulsive and depressed, without serious mental illness. Both alcoholism and the eating disorders can bring about poor health and an early death. Incidentally, there is a high rate of alcohol abuse in persons with anorexia and bulimia, and a disproportionate number of alcoholics have a history of eating disorder features (Lundholm, 1989; Peveler & Fairburn, 1990).

There seems to be a disproportionate number of anorexics who have some sort of brain abnormality. In addition to reports of a history of pregnancy and birth complications (Artmann, Grau, Adelmann, & Schleiffer, 1985; Bakan, Birmingham, & Goldner, 1991), ventricular enlargement has also been reported (Artmann el al., 1985; Krieg, Pirke, Lauer, & Backmund, 1988). Furthermore, there is evidence that brain abnormality is more common in chronic cases of anorexia (Dolan, Mitchel, & Wakeling, 1988). Nevertheless, the relatively high IQs of anorexics tend to legislate against the typical patient having considerable brain pathology.

At least one case of hypothalamic tumor has been misdiagnosed as anorexia nervosa (Heron & Johnston, 1976). Anorexia nervosa has in some cases been found to be associated with various types of hypothalamic-pituitary dysfunction that includes abnormal temperature regulation, a number of atypical hormonal findings, and defects in urinary concentration or dilution (Gold, Kaye, Robertson, & Ebert, 1983).

PICA

Pica is the persistent eating of a nonnutritive substance. Infants typically eat paint, plaster, string, hair, or cloth. Older children eat animal feces, sand, leaves, insects, or pebbles. Pica usually begins between 1 and 2 years of age. It ordinarily remits in early childhood but occasionally not until adolescence. Pica in adulthood is less common. The disorder is more common in mentally retarded persons. Its etiology is not known.

Danford and Huber (1982) found that 25.8% of 991 institutionalized mentally retarded adults displayed pica. Nonfood pica was found in 16.7%, food pica 5.4%, and a combination of food and nonfood pica in 3.7% of these retarded persons. Profoundly retarded persons were much more likely to manifest this behavior than persons retarded to a less extreme degree. Medical complications include lead intoxication, nutritional deficiencies, and gastrointestinal obstruction necessitating surgery.

McAlpine and Singh (1986) also determined the prevalence of pica in an institution for the retarded. Their prevalence of 9.2% of 607 retarded persons was lower than that reported by Danford and Huber (1982), and this was probably to a large extent a function of their more restricted definition of pica, which excluded food. The percentages of time during observational session that an object was used were clothes (30.5%); dirt, dust, or fluff off the floor (16.6%); toys (10.1%); paper (8.3%); grass (5.5%); metal, plastic, or concrete (4.6%); cigarettes and cigarette butts (4.6%); string (4%); buttons (4%); wood (2.7%); hair (2.7%); soil (2.7%); straw (2.7%); wire (2.7%); and feces (2.7%). The findings of Lofts, Schroeder, and Maier (1990) were quite similar to those of McAlpine and Singh (1986). Lofts et al. found that 15.5% of 806 institutionalized retarded adults displayed pica. The incidence of pica was positively associated with degree of retardation: 2.3% mildly, 10.4% moderately, 24.4% severely, and 62.5% profoundly retarded demonstrated pica.

Perhaps the sort of pica that has been distributed most widely geographically, temporally, and culturally, is geophagia—the eating of clay. German explorer Alexander von Humbolt found in his travels along the Orinoco River from 1799 to 1804 that Ottomac Indians ate clay dug from the river banks. The Ottomac Indian diet was chiefly fish and turtles, and during the two or three months of the year when the river was flooded so that they could not fish, they ate clay. The Indians then ate about a pound of clay a day. However, they ate small amounts during the rest of the year (Prince, 1989).

Hunter and deKleine (1984) reported Mayan Indians about 150 miles northeast of Guatemala City consumed clay as part of the Black Christ religious beliefs and practices. The clay at the famous Black Christ shrine was said to have supernatural properties and was said to cure a variety of illnesses, including leprosy, blindness, muteness, yellow fever, malaria, and mental illness.

Vermeer (1971) found geophagia to be very widespread in southeastern Ghana. In a survey he found that 46% of adult females reported regular clay consumption for prolonged periods, and they were more likely to eat such when they were pregnant. Fourteen percent of the adult males consumed clay with some degree of regularity. Clay was more commonly eaten in rural areas. Children consumed it to a lesser degree and parents often tried to discourage children from doing so. The Ghanians maintained that the clay tastes good and that it brings them good luck.

In the United States clay is more commonly consumed by pregnant women, very young children, the retarded, lower socioeconomic class persons, and by blacks, especially southern blacks (Feldman, 1986; Prince, 1989). The practice seems to have been brought over by slaves from Africa and now seems to be in a decline, although there are suggestions that some black women are replacing clay consumption with that of laundry starch.

The eating of clay and starch by pregnant black women in the United States has been reported, at least in the past, as quite high. Fifty-five percent of pregnant black obstetric patients in a Georgia hospital acknowledged eating dirt. In an Alabama survey 75% of pregnant women ate starch and 27% ate clay. In a Harlem hospital 66% reporting eating starch. In a rural Mississippi survey 41% ate starch and 27% ate clay (Prince, 1989; Feldman, 1986).

Geophagia seems to be most common in Africa and among people with African origins. Other parts of the world where it is more likely to be seen include Indonesia, Sumatra, Australia (among the Aborigines), Iran, Turkey, and India (Prince, 1989). It is apparent that geophagia is more likely to occur in economically less developed nations.

There is a long history of pica having been regarded as of malnutrition origin and/or being treated successfully by dietary supplements. As reviewed by Lofts, Schroeder, and Maier (1990), in 1000 A.D., pica was treated with iron supplementation. In 1831 pica was found to be associated with dietary deficiency. In 1868 a case of pica was reportedly cured by iron supplementation. In 1870 pica was associated with anemia. Bhalla, Khanna, Srivastava, Sur, and Bhalla (1982) maintained that zinc is needed for appropriate taste sensitivity and that taste sensitivity is altered in zinc deficiency. They found that zinc administration eliminated pica in nonretarded Asian Indian children.

Most impressive evidence that at least some cases of pica are caused by malnutrition and can be successfully treated by dietary supplementation was recently reported (Lofts, et al., 1990). Lofts et al. found that 54% of retarded persons with pica but only 7% of retarded controls without pica had serum zinc levels below the normal range. Pica behavior decreased greatly when zinc supplement was introduced and greatly increased when the supplement was discontinued. Reintroduction of zinc supplementation at a higher level brought pica behavior even lower than it was at the first introduction of zinc.

The etiology of pica seems to be determined by a variety of factors, biological, psychological, and cultural. However, at this point it may not be wise to view all pica as a disease that must be vigorously treated and eradicated. Geophagia may be harmless in some persons and could conceivably be beneficial to their health.

AT HIGHER RISK FOR ALCOHOLISM

Males

Persons with Family History

Persons Who Act Out

Native Americans

Black Americans

Hispanic Americans

Lower Socioeconomic Status Persons

Persons Hyperactive as Children

Anxious Persons

Depressed Persons

Homosexuals

Persons in Stressful Situations

Bartenders

Foodservice Workers

Entertainers

Persons with Alpha Rhythm Deficits

Persons with Attention Deficits

Police Officers

Physicians

ELEVEN

Alcoholism

There is no generally agreed upon definition of alcoholism. Yet, even by conservative definition, at least 3% of the population of the United States are alcoholics. Less than 5% of alcoholics are skid row alcoholics.

FACTS ABOUT ALCOHOL

The percentage of alcohol is drastically different in different beverages. Beer in the United States is about 4% alcohol. It tends to be somewhat higher in Canada and in the United Kingdom and other European countries (Turner, 1990). Wine typically has about 11% alcohol. Beverages made from distillation usually have about 40% alcohol. In this last category the word *proof*— meaning twice the alcohol percentage—is commonly employed.

The magnitude of the effect of alcohol is in proportion to the quantity consumed. Many people claim that different alcoholic beverages have different effects upon them that are independent of the amount of alcohol ingested. These claims are probably for the most part based upon psychological expectation, inaccurate subjective assessment, or hearsay. Nevertheless, it is possible that some minor effects may occur from the different "congeners," or impurities, that are in the various beverages. One can consume alcohol more rapidly by ingesting beverages with a higher percentage of alcohol.

During a 9-week strike of the Norwegian Wine and Spirit Monopoly (Hoverak, 1983), one could purchase beer but could not purchase spirits or wine. Reports of drunkenness and domestic quarrels decreased dramatically during the strike and increased dramatically when the strike was over.

173

The chief independent variable for determining reactions to alcohol is the brain-blood alcohol level. Table 11.1 displays the behavioral effects as a function of blood alcohol level. It is very unusual for blood level to be at around the 0.50 or 0.60 necessary for death. This is because the drinker ordinarily passes out before this point is reached. Although alcohol is a central nervous system depressant in some persons, sometimes it has stimulating properties. This may be because it releases the cortex from inhibitory control. Situational variables, such as mood of the occasion, personality of the subject, whether or not the subject is alone, and the sex of other people present, are extremely important determinants of behavior. In stimulating surroundings, the drinker may become extroverted and behave in a noisy, excited, or aggressive manner. In quiet surroundings, especially when alone, the drinker may become dull, sullen, or sleepy.

TOLERANCE, DEPENDENCE AND WITHDRAWAL

A relatively inexperienced drinker obtains more of an effect from a given amount of alcohol than does a person who drinks more frequently. With increased alcohol usage "tolerance" is produced; that is, a larger amount of alcohol is necessary to obtain the same effect. Some alcoholics can drink a quart of whiskey a day without showing signs of intoxication. In addition to "psychological dependence" there is "physiological dependence," which refers to the changes in the body that produce a need for alcohol. When alcohol is not available to a person dependent upon alcohol, "withdrawal" symptoms occur.

The early withdrawal symptoms are anxiety, depression, tremor, restlessness, insomnia, thirst, and loss of appetite. These symptoms occur in the first two days and reach their peak for about a day to a day and a half. Patients with coexisting anxiety disorder have withdrawal symptoms of greater severity (Johnston, Thevos, Randall, & Anton, 1991). When seizures (ordinarily tonic-clonic) occur, they do so between 12 hours and 2½ days. Delirium tremens can occur from a day to a week after cessation of drinking but are most likely to occur about 3 or 4 days after cessation. Most alcoholics who have suffered from the delirium tremens (DTs) describe it as a terrifying and anguishing experience. The afflicted individual often has visual and tactile hallucinations and may believe that animals such as rats or snakes are going to attack him or her. Other symptoms of DTs include profuse sweating, fever, and disorientation. DTs are a life-threatening condition.

PATTERNS OF DRINKING IN ALCOHOLICS

Some alcoholics are called "periodic" or "binge" drinkers and are capable of going weeks or months in between their usually severe drinking bouts that last

TABLE 11.1   Blood alcohol level and behavioral effects

Percent Blood Alcohol Level	Average Effect
.02	Reached after approximately one drink: light or moderate drinkers experience some pleasant feelings; e.g. sense of warmth and well being.
.04	Most people feel relaxed, energetic and happy. Time seems to pass quickly. skin may flush, and motor skills may be slightly impaired.
.05	More observable effects begin to occur, Individual may experience lightheadedness, giddiness, lowered inhibitions, and impaired judgement. Coordination may be slightly altered.
.06	Further impairment of judgement; individual's ability to make rational decisions concerning personal capabilities is affected; e.g., driving a car. May become a lover or fighter.
.08	Muscle coordination definitely impaired and reaction time increased; driving ability suspect. Heavy pulse and slow breathing. Sensory feelings of numbness in the cheeks, lips, and extremities occur.
.10	Clear deterioration of coordination and reaction time. Individual may stagger and speech may become fuzzy. Judgement and memory further affected (legally drunk, in most states).
.15	All individuals experience a definite impairment of balance and movement. Large increases in reaction time.
.20	Marked depression in motor and sensory capability; slurred speech, double vision, difficulty standing and walking may all be present. Decidedly intoxicated.
.30	Individual is confused or stuporous; unable to comprehend what is seen or heard. May lose consciousness ("passes out") at this level.
.40	Unusually unconscious. Alcohol has become deep anesthetic. Skin may be sweaty and clammy.
.45	Circulatory and respiration functions are depressed and can stop altogether.
.50	Near death.

Source: Corry, J. M., & Cimbolic, P. (1985). *Drugs: Facts, alternatives decisions.* Belmont, CA: Wadsworth.

from a period of days to weeks. The "continuous" alcoholics drink excessively every day. Some drink excessively only on weekends. Periodic alcoholics have been found to function at a somewhat higher psychosocial level than continuous alcoholics (Ashley et al., 1976). Periodic alcoholics tended to have higher-level occupations and are less likely to be unemployed or "skid row" alcoholics or without a fixed address. The health status of the periodic drinkers is better.

Jellinek's four types of alcoholism are widely cited. In "alpha alcoholism" the afflicted individual employs alcohol in an attempt to rid himself of some sort of unpleasant experience such as insomnia, anxiety, depression, or pain. According to Jellinek (1960) this sort of alcoholic does not exhibit loss of control, and his condition is not progressive. The chief feature of "beta alcoholism" is the presence of physical disorders such as cirrhosis of the liver. "Gamma alcoholism" is characterized by increased tolerance and physical dependency. Gamma alcoholism is probably the most common type in the United States, Canada, the British Isles, and the northern Europan countries. "Delta alcoholism" is characterized by increased tolerance and dependence and by almost continual drinking of small or moderate amounts of alcohol throughout the day—day after day.

The popular stereotype of every alcoholic "losing control" after the first drink and continuing to drink until he passes out is definitely not true. In a series of studies carried out by Mello and Mendelson (1972) in an experimental laboratory that resembled a hospital ward, alcoholics were given great access to alcohol, sometimes in unlimited quantities. Each alcoholic exhibited his characteristic pattern. The extreme drinking frenzy that one might have expected in these alcoholics, given the opportunity to drink, was not observed. In fact, not one of the alcoholics drank to "oblivion."

In alcohol idiosyncratic intoxication, also referred to as pathologic intoxication, a very small amount of alcohol has a great effect on the person, often with serious maladaptive behaviors such as belligerent and assaultive actions. This pathologic intoxication occurs shortly after the ingestion of alcohol, and it subsides within a few hours. Amnesia for the episode is common. Persons who have suffered head injuries and encephalitis are especially prone to the condition. There also have been reports of afflicted persons having epileptic-type EEG irregularity after receiving small amounts of alcohol.

PERSONALITY OF ALCOHOLICS

There have been a number of studies indicating that alcoholics tend to have high scores on the Psychopathic Deviate Scale and Depression Scale of the Minnesota Multiphasic Personality Inventory (MMPI); the former usually are higher than the latter. Practicing clinicians recognize that many alcoholics have low frustration tolerance and difficulty with impulse control. Thus, the elevation on the Psychopathic Deviate Scale, showing acting out behavior, is not surprising. However, the cause-and-effect relationship between depression and alcoholism is a controversial matter, with proponents for both possibilities—depression as a cause of alcoholism and alcoholism as a cause of depression. Probably both are correct. In one study it was found that alcoholic penitentiary inmates, who presumably were abstinent during incarceration, had higher scores on the MMPI Depression Scale than did nonalcoholic inmates (Templer, et al., 1978). On the other hand, experimental research has demonstrated that alcohol actually depresses the mood of alcoholics (Mello & Mendelson, 1970).

The importance of the subjective distress and the antisocial features of alcoholics was brought into clear focus by the factor analysis of Brooner, Templer, Svikis, Schmidt and Monopolis (1990) in which Factor 1 was called "Neuroticism." Its highest factor loadings were with the Neuroticism Scale of the Eysenck Personality Inventory, the Depression Scale of the MMPI, the Psychasthenia Scale (indicating anxiety and worry) of the MMPI, and female gender. Factor 2 was labeled "Essential Familial." Its highest factor loadings were with number of alcoholic first-degree relatives, essential (more severe) alcoholism, and the Psychopathic Deviate Scale of the MMPI. Brooner et al. recommended that both an alcoholic's subjective distress and his or her predisposition to antisocial behavior be considered in attempting to obtain a comprehensive perspective and treatment plan.

Jones (1971) followed up on individuals in middle age who had been intensively studied as high school students. Both in adolescence and in midlife the male alcoholics were impulsive, extraverted, displayed an apparent need to demonstrate their masculinity, and were rather insensitive to the nuances of interpersonal relationships. The female alcoholics, both in adolescence and in middle age, were introverted, highly sensitive to criticism, and had great difficulty in social adjustment.

CONSEQUENCES OF ALCOHOLISM AND ALCOHOL ABUSE

HANGOVER

The so-called hangover ordinarily occurs on the morning after the night of alcohol overindulgence. Headache is perhaps the most notable symptom and is thought to be caused by changes in brain fluids. Other symptoms include gastrointestinal distress, fatigue, and thirst. When we think of hangovers, we ordinarily think of people who feel miserable and look miserable. However, performance is also unfavorably affected. In one study U.S. Navy pilots flew simulated flights 15 hours after consuming a rather large amount of alcohol. The performance of the pilots was worse on all six measures of performance, significantly so on three of the measures, than that of the pilots in the control no-alcohol group. The authors attributed the poor performance to diminished ability to process information and to divide attention among two or more mental tasks. The authors expressed concern about the fact that some of the pilots were not aware of their performance decrements (Yesavage & Leirer, 1986).

BLACKOUTS

The "blackout," or inability to recall events that took place while intoxicated, has traditionally been regarded as almost pathognomonic of alcoholism. The occurrence and frequency of blackouts is associated with the severity of alcoholism.

ACCIDENTS

It is estimated that alcohol is involved in over 50% of fatal and 25% of nonfatal automobile accidents. It has been found that up to 40% of fatal industrial accidents, 69% of drownings, and 70% of fatal falls are alcohol-related. Even household accidents are more common in alcoholics than in the average person. Because of changes in bone tissue, bones are more readily fractured in alcoholics.

Although about three quarters of persons arrested for driving while intoxicated (DWI) could be diagnosed as alcoholic, they are an atypical group. In comparison to other alcohlics, DWI offenders are more antisocial, aggressive, and impulsive and are more likely to have a criminal history (Lucker, Kruzick, Holt, & Gold, 1991).

BRAIN PATHOLOGY

Research provides support for the contention that there are two different sorts of syndromes with different brain pathology. One is the Korsakoff's syndrome; the other is known as dementia associated with alcoholism (DAA). Korsakoff's disorder is associated primarily with memory impairment but without general loss of intellectual ability. Recent memory difficulty and "confabulation" (the nondeliberate filling in of memory gaps with false imformation) are salient in Korsakoff's disorder. In DAA there is a more general loss of intellectual abilities (Lishman, 1981; Wilkinson & Carlen, 1981). It has been suggested that the former disorder is associated with subcortical pathology as a function of thiamine deficiency and that the latter is associated with cortical atrophic changes (Victor & Laureno, 1978). However, some authors have contended that the two conditions are not always distinct and can coexist in the same patients (Wilkinson & Poulos, 1987).

Computerized tomography has demonstrated cerebral cortical atrophy (Gurling, Curtis, & Murray, 1991). Even in one study in which all of the alcoholics were under the age of 50 (mean, 42.4 years), mild to moderate cortical atrophy was found in 11 of 16 men who were compared to a normal control group. The degree of atrophy was positively associated with the length and severity of alcohol abuse and with neuropsychological test findings (Kroll, Seigel, O'Neill, & Edwards, 1980). However, all brain pathology in alcoholics cannot be presumed to be permanent since research has demonstrated a reversal of cortical atrophy after rather short-term abstinence from alcohol. Furthermore, on the Trailmaking Test, a commonly used neuropsychological test on which alcoholics characteristically display inferior performance, alcoholics abstinent for at least 1 year had almost identical performance to control men (Templer, Ruff, & Simpson, 1975).

ALCOHOLIC HALLUCINOSIS

In alcoholic hallucinosis the afflicted individual has a clear sensorium, in contrast to the disorientation seen in the psychotic states during DTs described above. Alcoholic hallucinosis is characterized by persistent auditory hallucinations (primarily voices) and usually occurs in alcoholics of many years duration. It is sometimes a withdrawal symptom and sometimes exhibited under the influence of alcohol.

VARIOUS PHYSICAL DISORDERS

Probably the best known of physical ailments associated with alcoholism is cirrhosis of the liver. The pathology involves scarring, hardening, and enlargement of the liver. The extended abdomen looks like that of a pregnant woman. The symptoms include sallowness of skin, vomiting of blood, and jaundice. Chronic alcoholism is the most common cause of cirrhosis, and 80% of cirrhosis deaths occur in alcohol abusers. Nevertheless, only a fairly small percentage of alcoholics are victims of cirrhosis. About a quarter of cirrhosis patients die within 5 years. Alcoholics are also at high risk for fatty liver, alcoholic hepatitis, and cancer of the liver. The signs and symptoms of fatty liver may include pain in the upper right quadrant of the abdomen, jaundice, and dark urine. The signs and symptoms of alcoholic hepatitis may include jaundice, fever, pain in the upper right abdomen, and chemistry findings suggestive of some sort of hepatic obstruction. Alcoholic hepatitis often follows fatty liver and often precedes cirrhosis.

Other health problems common in alcoholics are dyspnea on exertion, palpitations, night cough, chest pain, fatigue, edema, muscular atrophy, alcoholic pancreatitis, cancer of the pancreas, ulcers and irritation of the stomach, colds, pneumonia, tuberculosis, oral cancer, dietary deficiencies such as pellagra and anemia, poor dental hygiene, skin disease, and neuritis.

SEX LIFE

A large percentage of alcoholic men have sexual dysfunction. Whalley (1978) reported that 54% had sexual dysfunction in comparison to 28% in their control group. Fahrner (1987) found a 47% rate of loss of libido; 43%, erectile dysfunction; 43%, premature ejaculation; and 28%, delayed ejaculation. The patients reported that their sexual dysfunction was more common during high alcohol consumption periods. However, at follow-up 4 months after treatment, Fahrner did not find a significant decrease in the prevalence of sexual dysfunction. Also discouraging was the fact that the abstinent alcoholics did not show more improvement than alcoholics who were not abstinent. However, all of the patients had normal testosterone levels both before and after treatment. Farkas and Rosen (1976) showed men an erotic film following ingestion of varying amounts of alcohol. The penile plethysmograph (which measures increase in penis circumference) showed that the men who consumed alcohol had less sexual arousal than those who consumed only a beverage with taste indistinguishable from alcohol. The men who consumed larger amounts of alcohol had less arousal than the men who were administered smaller amounts. In one study it was found that testosterone levels were reduced in eight of nine alcoholics in 11 to 12 days of heavy drinking but returned to baseline levels after alcohol withdrawal (Mendelson & Mello, 1979).

CRIME

A substantial proportion of incarcerated convicted felons have a history of alcohol abuse. Over half of all men convicted of felonies are found to be alcoholics. With the exception of antisocial personality, alcoholism far exceeded any other psychiatric diagnosis. The plight of the intoxicated victim is probably less well known than the actions of the intoxicated perpetrator of crime. Wechsler, Thum, Demone and Dwinell (1972) found that of persons brought to an emergency service because of fights or assaults, 60% had positive breathalyzer readings. Thirty-three percent of those injured in fights or assaults while intoxicated were fighting with persons they knew, and 63% were injured by unknown persons. Of the 53 individuals who reported having been assaulted on the streets without a preceding argument or any sort of interaction. 64% had positive readings.

SUICIDE

Over one third of suicides are associated with the use of alcohol. There have been a number of reports indicating that the rate of suicide in alcoholics is very high. In one study, Templer (1974) found that of 11 alcoholics who had killed themselves after psychiatric hospitalization 10 had used guns. Nine of the 11 patients killed themselves within 1 month.

FETAL ALCOHOL SYNDROME

Heavy alcohol consumption by a woman during pregnancy produces fetal alcohol syndrome in the child. This syndrome includes mental retardation, pre- and postnatal growth retardation, distinctive abnormal facial features, and reduced head circumference.

EPIDEMIOLOGICAL FACTORS

AGE

Hospitalizations for alcoholism are most common from ages 30 to 60. It is not known why alcoholism tends to decrease in severity in old age, but in some alcoholics of long standing it ceases to be a problem. There are numerous clinical reports of severe alcoholics who, when they reach their 60s or 70s, are able to have a satisfying drink or two and then stop. However, there is evidence that from 5% to over 20% of elderly problem drinkers had started drinking over the age of 45 (Maletta, Pirozzolo, Thompson, & Mortimer, 1982).

RELIGION

It is sometimes difficult to separate the effect of religion from that of confounding variables such as ethnic background and socioeconomic status. Nevertheless, it is quite clear that some religions have a low prevalence of alcoholism. Moslems, whose religion forbids any use of alcohol, have a very low prevalence. The same generalization applies to some very fundamentalistic Protestant denominations such as those that flourish in the southern part of the United States. It makes sense that if someone is indoctrinated from childhood that he should "never touch a drop" he or she would be less likely to become an alcoholic, especially if one does not relinquish the religious values of his or her upbringing. The alcoholism rate is also low among Jews, who tend to use alcohol primarily in small quantities and who consume wine in the context of family life and religious observances. It is said that Jews abhor excessive drinking not only because it represents misuse of a substance used in a religious context but because impropriety would make already persecuted people even more vulnerable. The alcoholism prevalence of Jews has been increasing in recent years, especially among the more secular Jews who have rejected or ignored Jewish traditions.

OCCUPATION

Alcoholism prevalence is related to occupation. Among the occupations with a high prevalence of alcoholism are waiters, restaurants owners, liquor dealers, bartenders, longshoremen, stevedores, police officers, transportation workers, sailors, cooks, musicians, meat cutters, authors, editors, reporters, and bakers. Physicians, especially psychiatrists, have a high rate of alcoholism.

COUNTRY AND ETHNICITY

Precise comparisons of alcoholism rates in various countries is not possible because of the varying criteria and methods of reporting and even political factors. Asian nations, Arab countries, and Israel have low prevalences. The low alcoholism rate of the Chinese has been attributed to the fact that they view drinking as an activity that takes place almost exclusively with eating and for some limited medicinal purposes. Their culture discourages solitary drinking and excessive drinking. Their cultural toasting at dinner tables promotes social interaction and cements bonds of friendship. Although Asians and Asian Americans are thought of as having a low rate of alcohol abuse and alcoholism, this may not always be the case with Japanese and Japanese Americans. Their crime rates are very low, but when Japanese Americans do commit crimes it is often related to drinking and/or gambling.

Although all indices of alcoholism rates in various countries have distinct limitations, alcohol per capita consumption and deaths from cirrhosis of the liver are the two indices that are most often used. There is greater alcohol consumption and more cirrhosis of the liver in the Mediterranean countries than in the northern European countries. Authorities on alcoholism have traditionally taught that, although wine is customarily consumed with meals in Mediterranean countries, the alcoholism rates are lower than in the northern European countries. However, the high death rates from cirrhosis of the liver indicate that harmful effects do frequently occur in the Mediterranean countries. Incidentally, the lowest consumption of alcohol is in Albania, the only predominantly Moslem country in Europe.

Also pertaining to the matter of health is the difference in life expectancy between males and females. It was hypothesized by Templer, Griffin, and Hintze (in press) that there would be greater differences between life expectancy of females and life expectancy of males in countries that have more alcoholism. This hypothesis was based on the fact that the alcoholism rates are higher in men than in women. Even after statistically controlling for life expectancy, alcohol consumption and cirrhosis deaths are associated with greater longevity of females. It should be noted that there is less gender longevity difference in Moslem countries.

The alcoholism prevalence of Native Americans is generally regarded as very high. Alcoholism has been reported to exist in over half of Indians on some reservations. Drinking in American Indian children is not uncommon. In fact, a case of delirium tremens has been reported in a 9-year-old Indian boy (Sherwin & Mead, 1975). The precise reasons for excessive drinking by Native Americans are not known, but conjecture ranges from biological differences to deplorable social conditions, including poverty, discrimination, and the humiliation accorded to conquered people.

About three quarters of all Native American deaths can be traced to alcohol in some way. Five of the 10 major causes of death among Native Americans are alcohol-related accidents, cirrhosis of the liver, alcoholism, suicide, and homicide. The cirrhosis of the liver mortality rate is four times that of the U.S. national average. The suicide rate is one-and-a-half times the national average, and alcohol is a factor in 80% of Native American suicides. The homicide rate is three times the national average, and alcohol is a factor in 90% of all homicides. Alcohol-related accidents constitute the leading cause of death, with a mortality rate that is three times the U.S. average. The arrest rate for Native Americans over the age of 14 is 3 times that of blacks and 10 times that of whites. Alcohol is believed to be a factor in three quarters of all Native American crimes. However, it should be remembered that there are great individual differences among the almost 300 tribes or bands of Native Americans.

Sex

Male alcoholics greatly outnumber female alcoholics. The reasons for this are uncertain. However, both moderate drinking and excessive drinking have traditionally been more tolerated for males than for females. Nevertheless, the possibility of relevant biological difference should not be overlooked, especially in view of the evidence that hamster and chimpanzee males consume more alcohol than their female counterparts.

More recent research indicates that a given amount of alcohol has a greater effect in women than in men, even when body weight is controlled for (Frezza et al, 1990). This is apparently a function, at least in part, of males having a greater amount of a stomach enzyme that metabolizes alcohol so that less is absorbed into the blood stream. Women of equal weight get about 30% more ingested alcohol into the blood stream than do males. The lower amount of enzyme may also explain why alcoholic women are more prone to liver disorders than are alcoholic men.

In comparison to male alcoholics, female alcoholics are more likely to drink alone at home rather than in a public place, to have an older age of onset, to have less trouble with the law and less job loss, to be more depressed and make more suicide attempts, to have more hospitalizations for other sorts of mental disorder, and to suffer more medical consequences of excessive drinking (Schmidt, Klee, & Amens, 1990). Female alcoholics also have a better prognosis (Sanchez-Craig, Leigh, Spivak, & Lei, 1989; Sanchez-Craig, Spivak, & Davila, 1991).

An interesting study found an interaction between religion and sex in Northern Ireland. Among males, Catholics had a higher prevalence of drinking problems. However, among females, the Protestants had a higher prevalence (Blaney & Makenzie, 1980). The authors acknowledged they did not know the reasons for this phenomenon but suggested the possibility that greater differentiation in sex roles among Catholics could be a factor.

Sexual Preference

There is some evidence that gays have a greater incidence of drinking problems than do heterosexuals. In one study it was determined that 10% of adult homosexuals in Los Angeles are in crisis or danger stages of alcohol consumption and that an additional 21% drink excessively or are at a high risk of needing treatment (Fifield, 1975). In another study it was determined that 29% of male gays surveyed drank "more than they should" (Weinberg & Williams, 1974). This is close to the 30% of male homosexuals who exhibited excessive drinking or alcohol dependence reported by Saghir, Robins, Walbran, and Gentry (1970). Sagir and Robins (1971) found that 25% of homosexual women and 5% of heterosexual women had histories of excessive drinking. McKirnan and Peterson (1989) found that 23% of homosexual men and 16% of heterosexual men had drinking problems and that 23% of homosexual women and 8% of heterosexual women had drinking problems. The reasons for the apparently high incidence in gays are not clear. However, a life-style that frequently includes socialization in bars is an explanation sometimes given. The excessive drinking also may be related to the fact that homosexuals constitute a discriminated-against minority group that is too often rejected not only by society but by their own families.

ETIOLOGY

BIOLOGICAL CAUSATION

Schuckit, Goodwin, and Winokur (1972) reported on alcoholics and nonalcoholics who were raised by their biological parents and those raised by foster parents. The findings indicated that the most crucial determinant of becoming an alcoholic was having a biological parent who was alcoholic. Merely being reared by an alcoholic parent seemed to have little relevance. Consistent with a genetic formulation are the studies that have found genetic markers such as color blindness, phenylthiocarbamamide taste sensitivity, and blood groups to have an occurrence higher than expected by chance in the relatives of alcoholics (Hill, Goodwin, Cadoret, Osterland, & Doner, 1975). Furthermore, it is possible to determine degree of alcohol consumption in successive generations of rats by breeding.

The question of exactly what is inherited that predisposes one to alcoholism remains to be answered. However, some progress toward answering this questions seems to have been made in the area of alpha rhythm, the EEG 8-to-10 cycles-per-second rhythm that is most commonly observed when an individual is relaxed, with eyes closed. Alcoholics and relatives of alcoholics have been found to demonstrate less alpha rhythm than do nonalcoholics (Docter, Naitoh, & Smith, 1966). Since alpha activity is increased by alcohol administration in both alcoholics (Docter et al., 1966) and normal persons (Begleiter & Platz, 1972), it is conceivable that alcohol consumption in alcoholics is a (maladaptive) adaptive mechanism to increase alpha rhythm to a more normal level. In one study the biological sons of alcoholics showed greater alpha rhythm response to alcohol administration than did control subjects (Pollock et al., 1983).

Alcoholics have a high rate for attention deficit disorder as children and have a much higher number of children with the disorder than do control parents (Wood, Wender, & Reimherr, 1983). Tarter, McBride, Buonpane, and Schneider (1977) found a higher rate of attention deficit disorder in primary than in secondary alcoholics. Primary alcoholics were defined as those who began excessive drinking at an early age and in general displayed more symptoms of alcoholism. Different ethnic groups apparently have different physiological reactions to alcohol. Wolff (1978) found that Japanese, Korean, and Taiwanese American adults and infants exhibited vascular reactivity and mild symptoms of intoxication with doses of alcohol that produced no or minimal effect upon Caucasian adults and children. Possibly the low prevalence of alcoholism among Asians can be attributed to unpleasant effects from alcohol. Montiero, Klein, and Schuckit (1991) found that Jewish young men experienced more nausea, dizziness, and feelings of floating and clumsiness than did the young men who served as controls. Fenna, Schaefer, Mix, and Gilbert (1971) experimentally investigated the impressions of police that Canadian Eskimos and Indians take longer to "sober up" than do Caucasians while in jail. The rate of disappearance of alcohol from the blood was significantly slower for the Eskimos and Indians than for Caucasians.

ENVIRONMENTAL CAUSATION: STRESS

Stress is thought to be one possible cause of alcoholism. Clinical experience suggests that alcoholics are often abstinent or drink in moderation until stressful circumstances enter their lives. There have been experiments indicating that animals who are subjected to stress, such as crowding in cages, exhibit an increase in amount of alcohol consumption (Theissen & Rodgers, 1965).

TREATMENT

AVERSION CONDITIONING

Aversion conditioning for alcoholism is usually carried out with the use of an emetic (vomit-inducing) drug in association with alcohol ingestion. In a review of the topic, Elkins (1991) estimated that 35,000 alcoholics have received this treatment since the 1930s, with most current treatment taking place in private hospitals. These hospitals have rather consistently reported 1-year abstinence rates of about 60%. Elkins stated that more definitive efficacy research is needed, but he generally provided an encouraging perspective.

DISULFIRAM

Disulfiram (better known by its trade name, Anatabuse®) is a drug that causes a severely unpleasant reaction if combined with alcohol. It is given to motivated alcoholics who intend to be totally abstinent, and it is taken every day. If the person taking disulfiram should drink, he or she would experience flushing, a throbbing headache, throbbing in head and neck, respiratory difficulty, thirst, nausea, vomiting, palpitations, chest pain, abnormally low blood pressure, fainting, anxiety, weakness, blurred vision, and confusion. Death is possible. It is apparent that the decision to administer disulfiram should not be taken lightly. In fact, it is not used with patients in poor health or over 50 years of age. The users often carry cards to the effect that they are taking the drug. The chemical mechanisms involve the inhibition of the breakdown of acetaldehyde. Unfortunately, some patients decide they want to start drinking and stop taking the disulfiram. A few days after the discontinuation of disulfiram the ingestion of alcohol either no longer produces the aversive reaction or produces it to a lesser degree.

ALCOHOLICS ANONYMOUS

Alcoholics Anonymous, or AA as it is ordinarily called, was founded by "Bill W.," a stockbroker, and "Dr. Bob," a surgeon in Akron, Ohio, in 1935. It is based upon the "Twelve Steps" and the "Twelve Traditions." The steps are as follows:

1. We admit we are powerless over alcohol—that our lives have become unmanageable.
2. We believe that a power greater than ourselves can restore us to sanity.
3. We make a decision to turn our will and our lives over to the care of God as we understand Him.
4. We will make a searching and fearless moral inventory of ourselves.
5. We will admit to God, to ourselves, and to another human being, the exact nature of our wrongs.
6. We are entirely ready to have God remove all these defects of character.
7. We humbly ask Him to remove our shortcomings.
8. We will make a list of all persons we have harmed, and we will make amends to them all.
9. We will make direct amends to such people whenever possible, except when to do so would injure them or others.
10. We will continue to take a personal inventory and when we are wrong promptly admit it.
11. We will seek through prayer and meditation to improve our conscious contact with God as we understand Him, praying only for knowledge of His will for us and the power to carry that out.
12. Having had a spiritual awakening as the result of these steps, we will try to carry this message to other alcoholics, and to practice these principles in all our affairs.

It is apparent from the 12 steps that AA has an emphasis that is spiritual, with a basis in Christian-Judaic tradition. However, different AA members stress and interpret this spiritual focus in different ways, and some members contend that even an atheist or agnostic can belong to AA by viewing AA as their "higher power." It appears that group support provides a good part of the core of AA's psychotherapeutic ingredients. It is common for AA members to have a good portion of their lives taken up with AA with such activities as attending meetings and counseling other members who have consumed alcohol or feel an urge to do so. AA stresses that alcoholism is like a disease that can be arrested but never cured and that therefore complete abstinence is necessary. Great emphasis is placed upon the evils of alcohol, and members frequently recount their previous lives of disgust, degradation, and suffering. AA is often criticized for being authoritarian, dogmatic, simplistic, naive, antiintellectual, antipsychologist, and antipsychiatrist. However, if a treatment works, it should not necessarily be condemned because it is distasteful to some mental health professionals. Many alcoholics assert that psychologists and psychiatrists failed to help them but that AA has been effective. Nevertheless, animated testimonials should not be regarded as the most acceptable scientific evidence. One study showed 35% of members to be abstinent 1 year after entrance (Baekeland & Lundwall, 1975). This 35% figure is in the same range as most other alcoholic treatment programs.

In addition to AA there is Al-Anon, a predominantly female endeavor, to which the spouses of alcoholics belong. In addition to providing mutual support, great emphasis is placed upon the uncritical understanding of the alcoholic spouse. There also exists an Al-Ateen which is for teenagers of alcoholic parents. There are a number of self-help groups that are similar to or associated with AA. A number of them are composed of members with very specific occupation, religious, ethnic, or sexual preference characteristics.

Is Moderate Drinking Possible in Alcoholics?

The traditional viewpoint, and certainly the one strongly advocated by Alcoholics Anonymous, is that an alcoholic must maintain total abstinence because he or she can never drink socially or in moderation. In the past two decades this viewpoint has been challenged. There have been a number of reports in the literature that individuals who previously had drinking problems were able to drink in moderation (Pattison, Headley, Gleser, & Gottschalk, 1968), and in one review of 261 follow-up studies of alcoholism treatment, controlled drinking comprised 10% of treatment outcome, even though controlled drinking had not been a treatment goal (Emrick, 1975). Drew (1968) cited a diversity of sources, primarily official government statistics, regarding such things as hospital admissions, physical and mental complications of alcoholism, drunken driving, and other legal offenses that seem to indicate that the prevalence of alcoholism declines in late middle age. Animal experimentation upon the "alcohol-deprivation effect" (Sinclair & Senter, 1968) could also be viewed as casting doubt upon the wisdom of total abstinence, at least in some cases of alcoholism. It has been demonstrated that when rats were allowed unrestricted access to alcohol for 3 weeks or more and then deprived for a period of time, they consumed even higher amounts of alcohol when alcohol was again made available to them. A number of alcoholic patients report that each subsequent alcoholic episode following a period of abstinence is of greater severity.

Sanchez-Craig, Annis, Bornet, and MacDonald (1984) randomly assigned early stage problem drinkers to either an abstinence-oriented or a controlled-drinking cognitive-behavioral program. Both groups were taught to identify risk situations and existing competencies, to develop cognitive and behavioral coping, and to assess their progress objectively. The controlled-drinking group was also taught procedures for moderate drinking. Six months after treatment the patients averaged about 13 drinks per week, in contrast to the 51 drinks per week before treatment. This level of drinking was maintained at the 2-year follow-up. However, the drinking level and pattern were the same for the two groups. It was rather surprising that most persons in the abstinence group, as in the moderation group, developed moderate drinking. The two groups did not differ significantly in percentage of persons abstinent, percentage of persons drinking moderately, and percentage of persons drinking heavily. However, it should be noted that the patients were regarded as early problem drinkers rather than severe alcoholics. Fifty-one drinks a week, or an average of seven drinks a day, is considerably less than that consumed by many severe alcoholics. The findings might have been different if the subjects had more serious drinking problems.

Miller (1991) reviewed the reports of persons who had successfully controlled their drinking and formulated the following conclusion regarding which alcoholics were successful and which were unsuccessful in controlling drinking. Those who achieved greater success in controlling their drinking tended to be younger (under 40), had fewer life problems related to alcohol, had been drinking for less than 10 years, did not see themselves as alcoholics, and did not subscribe to the concept of alcoholism as a disease.

MEDICAL CONSIDERATIONS

Although there is wide variation in opinion regarding what psychologically and medically oriented treatments for alcoholism are best, there is no doubt that medical intervention is often necessary in severe acute intoxication and in the management of alcohol withdrawal. The immediate strategy when blood alcohol levels approach lethal magnitude is that of preventing respiratory depression. Artificial ventilation is used until sufficiently normal breathing is resumed. Physiological homeostasis is monitored, and other medical conditions are taken into account.

In medically supervised withdrawal a drug with sedative properties is used in progressively smaller doses to minimize withdrawal symptoms. Theoretically, alcohol can be used, and some alcoholics withdraw themselves with alcohol. However, most physicians prefer drugs that act less rapidly and therefore are more amenable to titration. Drugs in the antianxiety category or the sedative category are most frequently employed.

At least 135 different drugs and combinations of drugs have been used in the treatment of alcoholism withdrawal. Benzodiazepines (the most commonly used category of antianxiety drugs) are the drugs that are used most in the United States, and double blind studies indicate that they are the most effective. In Europe a greater variety of drugs are used for alcohol withdrawal, the most commonly used drug being carbamazepine, an anticonvulsant with chemical similarities to the tricyclic category of antidepressant drugs. One study compared carbamazepine to diazepam (Valium®), the benzodiazepine most often used in the United States and found both drugs to be of equal efficacy (Malcom, Ballenger, Sturgis, & Anton, 1989).

Although hospitalization has traditionally been considered imperative in alcoholism treatment, recent evidence challenges this position. Miller and Hester (1986) reviewed 26 relevant controlled studies and found that residential treatment provided no overall advantage over nonresidential treatment. Furthermore, they found no advantage of longer-stay over shorter-stay inpatient programs. Nevertheless, the authors did point out some evidence seeming to indicate that more severe and less socially stable alcoholics do better with hospitalization, whereas patients who have a lesser degree of alcoholism and are married and employed do better with outpatient treatment.

PROGNOSIS

Alcoholism has traditionally been regarded as not having a good prognosis. Vaillant and Milofsky (1982), however, have suggested a relatively encouraging long-term perspective with alcoholics. They studied the natural history of 110 male alcoholics who were 47 years of age at the time of the study. Forty-nine of the men had at some time achieved abstinence for at least a year. It is most interesting that those alcoholics with the severest drinking problems were more likely to have obtained the year's abstinence. The 18 men who had returned to problem-free drinking had had fewer previous symptoms of alcohol abuse. Those men who obtained abstinence relied upon what Vaillant and Milofsky called "substitutes"—Alcoholics Anonymous, religion, antianxiety drugs, marijuana, compulsive work or hobbies, compulsive gambling, compulsive eating, and chain smoking. The authors found that at the time of their study over half of their subjects were abstinent or had returned to social drinking. They stated: "Over the short term, alcohol dependence often resembles a remitting but progressive illness like multiple sclerosis; over the long term, among those who survive, alcoholism often resembles a self-limiting illness."

Gibbs and Flanagan (1977) reviewed 45 studies related to prognosis in alcoholics and found that the variables most often predictive of success were a higher Arithmetic Scale score on the Wechsler IQ test, steady work history, being married or cohabiting, stable marriage, higher-status occupation, fewer arrests, employment at time of admission, type of occupation, history of AA contact, and higher social class. Thus, we see that with alcoholism, as with other psychopathological conditions, patients with more assets and resources have a better prognosis.

AT HIGHER RISK FOR DRUG ABUSE

Males

Lower Socioeconomic Status Persons

Blacks

Hispanics

Persons Who Act Out

Persons with History of Arrests

Persons with Low Frustration Tolerance

Single or Divorced Persons

Persons from Broken Homes

Physicians

Nurses

Youthful Persons

Persons with Drug Abusing Friends or Relatives

Insomniacs

Persons Experiencing Physical Pain

TWELVE

Drug Abuse

It is common for psychoactive drugs to be categorized into three groups: central nervous system depressants, central nervous system stimulants, and hallucinogenic drugs. It should be borne in mind that central nervous system depressants do not necessarily cause emotional depression. They depress the central nervous system, and physiological processes in general, and usually decrease activity. Another caveat is that hallucinogenic drugs do not necessarily cause hallucinations, such as in schizophrenia, with grossly faulty reality appraisal. Rather, minor perceptual distortions, such as slightly changed perception of colors coming from lights, are more common.

The categorization of drugs into the customary three categories is somewhat arbitrary because many drugs have two or even three of these effects. Different drugs at different dosages at different times and circumstances affect different people in different ways. An example is alcohol, which is ordinarily classified as a central nervous system depressant. Alcohol can produce sleep, violent behavior, agitation, anxiety, emotional depression, and elation.

CENTRAL NERVOUS SYSTEM DEPRESSANTS

OPIATES

An opiate (also called opioid or narcotic) is any drug, either natural or synthetic, that has actions similar to those of morphine. These drugs are used medically to relieve pain, to treat coughs, and to treat diarrhea. All of the opiates relieve pain, produce at least mild euphoria, are addicting, and

193

decrease appetite, sex drive, and anger. The opiates can be divided into three categories: the naturally occurring alkaloids, including morphine and codeine; the "semisynthetic narcotics," derived from morphine and including heroin; and the "wholly synthetic narcotics." Opium comes from the poppy *(papaver somniferum)* seed. The opium alkaloid most commonly used for legitimate pain-relieving purposes is morphine. The most commonly used street opiate is heroin, which is derived from morphine. Although very similar to morphine, addicts report that it provides a more potent effect. Opium has been used for thousands of years. In previous centuries it had primarily been used in Asia, especially China. It was introduced to the United States on a large scale by Chinese laborers in the 1850s and 1870s. The increase in its use and addiction began with its medicinal use during the Civil War, and thousands of soldiers from both sides came home addicted. The first major legislation to limit the use of opiates was the Harrison Narcotics Act of 1914. The United States is currently thought to have over a million, possible 3 or 4 million heroin users. The heroin addict ordinarily resorts to a life of crime to support his or her habit; prostitution, shoplifting, and burglary are among the most common of such crimes.

The "rush" from an injection is almost immediate, reaches its peak in 5 minutes, and lasts from 4 to 6 hours. In addition to the euphoria, there is drowsiness, psychomotor retardation, slurred speech, nodding of the head, pupillary constriction, and ordinarily a decrease in sexual desire. After the effects subside, there are the "withdrawal" symptoms, which compel the addict to obtain another "fix." These symptoms include tearing of the eyes, nasal congestion, pupillary dilation, piloerection ("goose pimples"), sweating, diarrhea, yawning, hypertension, tachycardia (rapid heart beat), fever, and insomnia. Although narcotics addicts speak of withdrawal symptoms with dread, especially if the withdrawal is abrupt ("cold turkey"), many objective observers equate the degree and nature of withdrawal symptomatology to influenza.

In the minds of the average person every heroin user is an addict, and every addict is one until death. However, such is not the case. In one study (O'Donnell, Voss, Clayton, Slatin & Room, 1976) only 10% of heroin users had used it in the past month, and of those who used it more than 100 times in their lives, only 50% had used it in the past 2 years. Thirty-two percent of users had a history of using it almost every day, but only 1% of these users had taken heroin within the past 24 hours. It has been suggested by Johnson (1977) that blacks are much more likely than whites to have used heroin within their lifetime but not to be currently using it.

The preponderance of narcotics addicts are in the large cities. A disproportionate number of addicts are minorities, especially blacks and Hispanics. Three quarters are male. Most are in their teens and 20s. They tend to come from chaotic family lives and to have endured unhappy childhoods. Physicians are especially prone to narcotics addiction.

A number of studies have indicated a high degree of depression among opiate addicts (Rounsaville, Weissman, Crits-Cristoph, Wilber, & Kleber, 1982). It is likely that for some addicts the use of drugs is a maladaptive attempt to escape from the depression. In one study it was found that 15 (36%) of 45 addicts had a major depression. This depression appeared to be more than a short-term reaction to the detoxification or to stressful life events in that 12 of the 15 depressed addicts but only 2 of the 27 addicts without depression had an abnormal response to the biochemical indicator of endogenous depression, the dexamethasone suppression test (see Chapter 5). The authors maintained that the dexamethasone suppression test has potential for identifying depressed addicts and treating their depression (Dackis, Pottash, Gold, & Annitto, 1984).

The most widely used treatment for heroin addiction is methadone maintenance. This is not regarded as a "cure" or ideal treatment by anyone. In fact, methadone is itself a narcotic. However, the patient can function in society much better. Methadone produces less drowsiness or great euphoria so that the addict can hold a job. He/she does not have to engage in illegal activities to pay for the methadone, which is provided at the clinic two or three times a week. The need to have criminal associates is less pressing. Methadone tolerance develops more slowly than tolerance to morphine or heroin. Furthermore, the euphoriant effects of heroin are partially blocked when one is on methadone. Unfortunately, many methadone clients do not adhere faithfully to the regimen. Withdrawal symptoms in neonates whose mothers were addicted to methodone are more severe than in infants whose mothers were addicted to heroin, and later in childhood they have more neuropsychological defects and behavioral problems (Davis & Templer, 1988). Another treatment for heroin addiction is the opiate antagonist drug naltrexone. Some studies have shown it to be more effective than placebo and others have demonstrated no significant difference (San, Pomarol, Peri, Olle & Cami, 1991). Perhaps a reasonable generalization is that it may be helpful to some addicts but it is no "miracle" drug.

One hundred New York male narcotic addicts first admitted to the U.S. Public Health Hospital in 1952 were followed for 20 years. Although their mean age at admission was only 25, 23% had died within that 20-year period, mostly from unnatural causes. Of the remaining 77 addicts, 35 were abstinent, 25 were active narcotic addicts, and 17 were of uncertain status. Although the natural history of narcotics testing does not generate optimism, as with most antisocial behavioral patterns, improvement is often seen in middle age (Vaillant, 1973). Research in Stockholm County in Sweden in 1984 followed up 188 opiate addicts treated in 1971 and 1972. Their death rate was 18.3% in excess of general population deaths. Fifty-one percent of the causes of death were injury or poison, and 69% of these were ascribed to suicide or probable suicide (Engstrom, Adamsson, Allebeck, & Rydeberg, 1991).

Codeine is a naturally occurring alkaloid of opium. It has been used to alleviate mild to moderate pain and in cough syrup for over 100 years. There are a number of over-the-counter cold or cough relief preparations in addition to those limited to prescriptions. Some, usually adolescent "experimenters" will combine alcohol and codeine. However, the serious narcotic addict will not want to be bothered with codeine. Nevertheless, tolerance and withdrawal symptoms can occur, but the few addicted individuals are more likely to be involved with the drug for legitimate purposes of pain relief rather than for euphoria.

Of the wholly synthetic narcotics, the most commonly used are meperidine (Demerol®) and propoxyphene (Darvon®). Both are ordinarily referred to by their trade names.

Demerol is ordinarily used for moderately severe pain such as is experienced postoperatively. However, it also produces euphoria and is therefore illicitly used by drug abusers. It is also abused by medical and paramedical personnel because of their access to this drug. Demerol is often used by heroin addicts when heroin is not available. However, the euphoria is second rate compared to that of heroin. Also, Demerol can produce hallucinations, dizziness, nausea, vomiting, and sweating (Correy & Cimbolic, 1985).

Darvon is indicated for mild to moderate pain. It is often in drug preparations that contain aspirin. It is not often used by drug abusers. There are three reasons for this. One is that it is not available in injectable form. A second is the frightening side effects that can include psychosis. The third is the weak euphoric and analgesic properties. Darvon does not even do a very good job in reducing the withdrawal symptoms of heroin.

MARIJUANA

The principal psychoactive ingredient in marijuana, hashish, and related derivatives of the hemp plant *(Cannabis sativa)* is tetrahydrocannabinol (THC). Marijuana produces relaxation and euphoria similar to the effects of alcohol. Other effects include a slowed time sense (e.g., 5 minutes seeming like an hour), increased appetite, and subjective intensification of perceptions that can in some individuals produce a definite psychedelic effect. Side effects include paranoia and depression. There are great individual differences in respect to the type and degree of effects from marijuana. Also, the effects vary as a function of the setting. In the presence of friends and pleasant surroundings an individual may be relaxed or euphoric under the influence of marijuana, but in less secure surroundings he or she may be frightened and paranoid. Occasionally, hallucinations are produced.

Marijuana has symbolized conflicts in our society—conflicts between youths and older persons, liberal versus conservative elements, the forces of the establishment versus those who feel oppressed or in need of change. Because of the strong underlying emotions it is difficult to come to a balanced perspective with respect to health and safety hazards. Marijuana does sometimes contribute to automobile accidents, and researchers have produced evidence suggesting certain deleterious effects upon health. However, it would be inaccurate to place marijuana in the same category as heroin with respect to the damage to the individual and to society. Much has been written about the "amotivational syndrome," in which an individual is both outside the mainstream of achievement-oriented society and smokes very large quantities of marijuana. This amotivational syndrome has been observed not only in marijuana users in North America but in hashish users in the Middle East. However, it is difficult to say to whether the lack of motivation results from the marijuana smoking, the marijuana smoking results from the lack of motivation, or both are the results of a third factor. It is apparent that in regard to the amotivational syndrome and the health and safety hazards, more definitive research must be accumulated.

SEDATIVES: BARBITURATES

The drugs classified as sedatives are often divided into barbiturate and nonbarbiturate sedatives. The barbiturates are drugs that are derived from barbituric acid. In general, the barbiturates are the older sedatives, and they are not used as much as they used to be.

The short- and intermediate-acting barbiturates are those that are most often used and most often abused. They are ordinarily prescribed as sleeping medication. They have onset of action of from 15 to 40 minutes, with a duration of action of 6 hours. In general, there are two sorts of people who misuse these drugs: the street-type polydrug abusers who have an antisocial life-style and take the barbiturates to get "high" and the ordinary middle-class individuals, female more times than not, who are given prescriptions by their physicians for insomnia. The effects, the tolerance, and the withdrawal symptoms are similar to those of alcohol. Barbiturate overdose is often life threatening. Tolerance does not take long to develop. Unfortunately, the lethal dose remains the same. The principal mechanism in overdose is in the depressing of the respiratory centers of the brain.

In general, the nonbarbiturate sedatives are quite similar to the barbiturates with regard to the effects and the dangers, although the latter may be of slightly lower magnitude. Also, the actions of the nonbarbiturates may be somewhat more specific. The more commonly used of these drugs include methaqualone, glutethimide (Doriden®), ethchlorvynol (Placidyl®), methyprylon (Noludar®), and chloral hydrate.

Solvents (Volatile Hydrocarbons)

A number of organic solvents are sniffed to produce intoxication. These include paint, glue, gasoline, nail polish remover, cleaning fluid, lighter fluid, and industrial products. The initial effects are euphoric, somewhat similar to the effects of alcohol. However, with larger amounts of solvents inhaled, psychotic manifestation, confusion, disorientation, and a clouding of consciousness can occur. Solvent sniffing is most commonly seen in boys in their early teens. Inhalant users tend to come from the ranks of the poor, minorities, children, adolescents, and young adults. They tend to come from families with considerable disorganization; youngsters frequently living with only one parent or with no parent. They tend to do poorly in school.

Carlini-Cotrim and Carlini (1988) determined the extent, nature, and correlates of solvent abuse among low-socioeconomic-status youth ages 9–18 in São Paulo, Brazil. Twenty-four percent of these students reported lifetime use of solvents, and 5% had used them within the past 30 days. Solvent users were more likely than the non-solvent users to report the use of other street drugs and alcohol, poor performance in school, and heavy alcohol consumption by close relatives; they were male and employed. The authors attributed the association of solvent use and being employed to the stress of working precociously, having their own money, and enlargement of the social circle beyond home and school.

There are a number of clinical reports of solvent use producing brain damage. In controlled research it was found that 20 paint sniffers were significantly lower on neuropsychological tests, including those of memory, motor speed, auditory discrimination, and visuomotor functioning than were control youngsters. A significant inverse relationship between duration of paint sniffing and level of test performance was found (Tsushima & Towne, 1977).

CENTRAL NERVOUS SYSTEM STIMULANTS

Amphetamines

Amphetamines were first used in medical practice in the 1930s for the treatment of narcolepsy and parkinsonism. There was a mushrooming of medically prescribed use in the three following decades for a variety of purposes, most notably weight reduction. However, the bulk of the medical profession is now reluctant to prescribe amphetamines except for childhood hyperactivity and narcolepsy.

Amphetamines usually produce elation, talkativeness, increased self-esteem, increased activity, increased endurance, and increased sense of energy. However, when the amphetamine wears off in a few hours, the person "crashes." That is, he or she feels depressed, weak, lethargic, and irritable. Then there is the craving for more amphetamine. Furthermore, tolerance develops in the habitual users so that larger dosages are required to produce the desired effects. Frequent use of amphetamines sometimes leads to an "amphetamine psychosis," which has symptoms quite similar to those of paranoid schizophrenia. Amphetamine abusers have been found to be impulsive, hostile, manipulative, and self-centered, with an inflated sense of self worth (Leavitt, 1982).

COCAINE

Cocaine is extracted from the leaves of the coca plant, which is grown in South America, especially Peru, Boliva, and Colombia. When the Spanish conquered Peru, they forbade the consumption of coca, which was used extensively by the Inca Indians for religious and other purposes. However, when the Spaniards found that the Indians did not have the strength to toil for them without it, they reversed their policy. Coca leaves continue to be consumed by many Indians in the Andes Mountains. Since the proportion of cocaine in coca is very small, the Indians' use of it has been described as more comparable to North American coffee consumption than to illicit drug abuse. In 1858, cocaine was isolated as the active ingredient in coca. In the late 19th century cocaine was advocated for a variety of medical uses. Even Sigmund Freud wrote enthusiastically about its properties and used it himself.

The effects of amphetamine dependence and abuse and cocaine dependence and abuse can be very similar. In fact, there has been research that indicates experienced users of these two drugs are often unable to tell the difference between them. One difference is that the psychoactive effects last longer in amphetamine use.

The "rush" comes a few seconds after taking and consists of self-confidence, euphoria, and a generally very positive state of well-being. Severe intoxication, however, can include confusion, incoherent speech, anxiety and fear, paranoia, ideas of reference, auditory hallucinations, feeling insects on the skin (formication), stereotyped movements of the mouth and tongue, and bizarre behavior. Physiological signs are tachycardia, pupillary dilation, elevated blood pressure, perspiration or chills, nausea, and vomiting.

Cocaine is used in various sorts of coca preparations. Coca paste is made by extracting the coca from the leaf with organic solvents such as gasoline. It is usually smoked in a pipe or in a cigarette with tobacco or cannabis. Coca paste is primarily used in the Central American and South American countries where it is produced. Contamination by solvents in the extraction process is not uncommon and often results in medical and psychological problems.

A common form of cocaine used in the United States is cocaine hydrochloride powder, which is usually inhaled through the nostrils and then absorbed into the blood stream by the mucous membranes. Cocaine hydrochloride can also be injected. It is occasionally mixed with heroin and injected, and this combination, referred to as a "speedball," can be medically very hazardous.

Cocaine abuse pattern can be of two types, episodic and daily or almost daily. In the episodic type the usage is separated by 2 or more days of nonuse. A relatively extreme form of episodic use is "bingeing," which may consist of a continuous high dose use for a 48-hour period. Bingeing is ordinarily carried out with smoking or injection. Binges are followed by a very distasteful "crash", which may last several days. Symptoms of the crash include anxiety, tremulousness, insomnia, irritability, fatigue, agitation, and depression. When the crash lasts more than 24 hours, it is referred to as withdrawal.

The snorting of cocaine often results in irritation to the nostrils and nasal mucous membranes so that the user appears to have a cold. Poor appetite and undernourishment are often seen in frequent users. However, the harm to one's health is generally regarded as less than with abuse of other drugs such as heroin.

Cocaine frequently produces perceptual changes such as increased sensitivity to light and difficulty in focusing the eyes. Hallucinations accompanying intensified use are fairly common, visual, tactile, and olfactory hallucinations being the most common. Auditory and gustatory hallucinations are less common. Examples of visual hallucinations are spots of lights, stripes, and various geometric patterns but usually not complex entities such as people. A common tactile hallucination is that of insects on the skin. Paranoid ideation and even delusions sometimes occur.

In one study with 85 recreational cocaine users, 37 (44%) had experienced at one or more times some perceptual phenomena, mainly increased sensitivity to light, halos around bright lights, and difficulty in focusing the eyes (Siegel, 1978a). Thirteen subjects (15%) reported visual hallucinations, consisting principally of objects moving in the periphery of the visual field. "Something just went by the corner of my eye" was a typical response. However, the persons realized that the objects were not really there. With the eyes closed or with dim illumination they appeared like flashes of lights. Geometric patterns were also reported. Eleven subjects (13%) reported tactile hallucinations, including itching of the skin, foreign particles moving under the skin, insects moving on or under the skin, and the sensation of people brushing against the body. Six subjects (7%) reported olfactory hallucinations, the smells including smoke, gasoline, natural gas, feces, urine, and garbage. Three subjects (4%) reported auditory hallucinations, and three (4%) reported gustatory hallucinations.

Deaths from cocaine intoxication have been rapidly increasing all over the United States. The rates ordinarily cited should be regarded as conservative because there are probably many cocaine intoxication deaths that are not known about (Welti, 1987). The exact mechanisms of death are still uncertain. However, the cardiovascular and the respiratory systems apparently play a major role. Death is often preceded by high fever or convulsions or both. Intravenous injection is very dangerous because such administration quickly results in high blood levels. However, there are other modes of fatal administration (Welti, 1987). The contention of some persons that nasal use of cocaine never, or rarely, results in death is not true. Snorting cocaine does result in death, although it is definitely a less dangerous method. The free-base chunks of cocaine in alkaloid called "crack" on the street may even be more dangerous than IV injection. Death occasionally occurs when it is rubbed on the penis or in the vagina as an aphrodisiac. When sexually stimulated, the blood vessels beneath the mucosa become engorged and rapidly absorb the cocaine. "Body packers," the persons who smuggle cocaine by insertion of cocaine packets into the rectum or vagina or by swallowing the packages, are also at risk. The packages occasionally break and enable large amounts of the drug to be absorbed into the blood stream.

The MMPI scale that cocaine abausers are highest on is the Psychopathic Deviate (Pd) Scale, followed by the Hypomanic (Ma) Scale (Walfish, Massey, & Krone, 1990). This pattern is found very often in criminals, delinquents, and persons diagnosed as having antisocial (psychopathic) personality disorder. Cocaine abusers also tend to be high on the Depression (D) Scale. The Psychopathic Deviate and the Depression scales are the two MMPI scales that alcoholics also tend to be highest on.

Drug use by medical students is not a matter about which the medical profession is proud. Conrad, Hughes, Baldwin, Achenbach, and Sheehan (1989) surveyed 589 senior medical students in 13 different medical schools. They found that reported lifetime use was 36%, use in past year was 17%, and use in the past month was 6%. The reasons for taking cocaine were to experiment (60%), to "get high" (50%), to have a good time with friends (48%), to increase energy level (17%), and to stay awake (10%). Eighteen percent of the medical students said that they would probably be using cocaine 5 years from now.

Cocaine use during pregnancy, especially during the first trimester, causes deficits and abnormal behavior in the infant. The problems include low birth weight, difficulty organizing information, attention deficits, visual orientation difficulty, and aversive response to stimulation, including parental interaction. Although very little is known about the status of these children beyond the age of 3, hyperactivity seems to be one of the problems observed over that age. It has been suggested that cocaine's action in blocking norepinephrine and dopamine could hinder normal neuronal development.

CAFFEINE

There are at least two religious groups, the Seventh Day Adventists and the Church of Jesus Christ of the Latter Day Saints (Mormons), that recognize the effects of caffeine and strongly discourage its use. Caffeine is perhaps the most widely used drug in North America. Tea has about half as much caffeine content as coffee, and cola beverages have about a third the amount. Many people are not aware of the caffeine they consume in products other than coffee, tea, and cola. A number of soft drinks in addition to the colas contain caffeine. A number of over-the-counter medications (e.g., several aspirin-based pain medications) contain caffeine. Chocolate contains a drug (theobromine) very similar to caffeine. Both are classified as xanthines, which are naturally occurring stimulants found in the leaves of many plants.

Caffeine is clearly a central nervous system stimulant. Its users maintain that caffeine improves mood, promotes rapid and clear thinking, enhances mental activity, and decreases drowsiness, fatigue, and reaction time. Interference with sleep is perhaps the chief complaint. Research has demonstrated that caffeine does increase attention and endurance.

Caffeine intoxication can occur in some individuals with a dose as small as that contained in a couple of cups of coffee. The signs and symptoms include restlessness, nervousness, excitement, insomnia, flushed face, diuresis, and gastrointestinal distress. With very high levels of caffeine one might observe muscle twitching, tachycardia (rapid heartbeat), cardiac arrhythmia, periods of apparent inexhaustibility, and psychomotor agitation.

Veleber and Templer (1984) experimentally determined the effects of caffeine in normal persons. The subjects were administered one of three different dosages under double-blind conditions. Measures of anxiety, depression, and hostility were taken immediately before caffeine administration and an hour after the consumption. Significant increases were obtained with all three measures, anxiety, depression, and hostility. The authors suggested the possibility that if they had done the posttesting sooner than an hour later they might not have had an increase in depression, since it is well known that other central nervous system stimulants such as amphetamines produce an initial increase in mood and a later depression.

Research has related caffeine consumption to personality. Heavy users have been found more likely to be female, inactive in religion, less educated, smokers, depressed, and insecure. One study found that psychiatric patients who consumed more coffee tended to have personality disorder diagnoses. Their history often revealed impulsivity and failure and learning disabilities in school (Furlong, 1975). Another study showed that alcoholic psychiatric patients consumed more coffee than did nonalcoholic psychiatric patients (Ayers, Ruff, & Templer, 1976).

In a study by Edelstein, Keaton-Brasted, and Burg (1984), caffeine use was prohibited in a psychiatric hospital. This was conducted in two stages, the first being withdrawal from the wards and the second being withdrawal from the canteen and from sources outside the hospital. Ten patients each were selected for three problem areas: enuresis at night, insomnia, and violent behavior necessitating restraints. There was remarkable improvement in each of the three areas.

Nicotine

The active ingredient of tobacco is *nicotine,* and it appears that nicotine withdrawal symptoms occur when smokers attempt to abstain from smoking. These symptoms include anxiety, sleep difficulty, irritability, headache, concentration difficulty, anger, frustration, restlessness, fatigue, craving to smoke, increased appetite, and weight gain.

Eysenck (1965) has been a major contributor to the literature on smoking and personality, with his concepts of extroversion and neuroticism ranking as the most consistently related dimensions of smokers and ex-smokers. Wiggins (1968) reviewed this literature and found that the two main dimensions differentiating smokers are higher extroversion and higher neuroticism than for nonsmokers. Seven of 10 studies found smokers to be more impulsive, and 3 of 4 studies showed greater orality among smokers and that all significant relationships seen in the studies indicated that smokers were more "antisocial," as defined by measures of rebelliousness, belligerence, misconduct, etc.

If smokers tend to be more neurotic, impulsive, and distress-prone, then it is reasonable to suggest that smokers smoke more during periods of distress than in relatively calm periods. Research indicates that women exhibit more anxiety, irritability, and depression during the premenstrual and menstrual portions of the menstrual cycle. The research of Steinberg and Cherek (1989) found that female cigarette smokers increased number of cigarettes, number of puffs, and time spent inhaling during the menstrual phase.

In general, most treatment modalities for smoking are either aversive techniques, hypnosis-based, group support–oriented, or some combination of the three. The aversion techniques include electric shock and having the client smoke so rapidly that it becomes unpleasant.

Success rates from professional services should ideally be compared not only to no-treatment control groups but to the results obtained solely from the patient's own effort. Schachter (1982) presented intriguing and provocative evidence from a longitudinal study that persons who quit smoking based entirely on their own efforts actually reported more success than those persons who attended formal treatment programs. Subsequent research basically replicated findings of Schachter (Rzewnicki & Forgays, 1987). Schachter suggested that formal treatment programs for smoking cessation may be ineffective or even detrimental. However, alternative explanations have been given (Cohen et al., 1989)

A relatively new drug treatment appears to have encouraging research support. Glassman, Jackson, Walsh, Roose, and Rosenfeld (1984) reported that clonidine, a widely used hypertensive drug, was more effective than either placebo or benzodiazepines in reducing withdrawal symptoms of smoking cessation. Covey and Glassman (1991) reviewed nine different double-blind studies that compared clonidine with placebo, and they inferred that clonidine was more effective. They also noted a trend for this drug to be more effective for female than for male smokers.

Another pharmacological treatment is nicotine replacement therapy, usually through nicotine gum. In general it facilitates short-term abstinence but does less well on a long-term basis (Clarke, 1991). One review of the literature found that nicotine gum and placebo produce abstinence rates of 23% and 13%, respectively, at 1 year. Nicotine gum, unfortunately, has side effects such as nausea, hiccups, belching, and jaw ache. The more recently developed nicotine patch that delivers a steady dose of nicotine through the skin avoids these side effects and therefore shows promise.

HALLUCINOGENIC DRUGS

LSD

The so-called hallucinogenic or psychedelic drugs produce an altered state of consciousness. The most commonly used of these drugs, lysergic acid diethylamine, is a derivative of the fungus ergot of rye. It is most often referred to as LSD or its street name "acid." The LSD trip typically lasts for 6 to 12 hours. There are distortions of body image, perceptual illusions, various visual experiences such as lights and geometric patterns, and synesthesia (hearing colors or seeing sound). There is frequently euphoria, although during the so-called bad trip there can be terrible anxiety and panic, with fear of death or losing one's mind. Frequently, there is also transcendental or spiritual experiences, and such effects provide part of the rationale for LSD's therapeutically fostering insight in a variety of conditions ranging from alcoholism to schizophrenia. There are reports of "flashbacks" of the LSD experience that are said to occur sometimes a number of months or even years after taking the drug. The fact that about a fifth to a quarter of persons from nonpsychiatric populations who had used LSD reported flashbacks would legislate against the contention that flashbacks do not really exist but are merely hallucinations in persons who have schizophrenia.

OTHER HALLUCINOGENIC DRUGS

Peyote is a cactus that originated in northern Mexico and has psychedelic properties. The most important active ingredient is mescaline. Mescaline is the first psychedelic that has been synthesized. The Indians used peyote to enhance spirituality and self-understanding. The Spaniards who colonized the New World regarded peyote as having diabolic properties and attempted, sometimes in a very brutal fashion, to stamp out its use among the Indians. However, after the U.S. Civil War, peyote use spread to the western states and to over 50 different tribes. Its ceremonial use became, and still is today, often a blend of Christian and traditional Indian elements. Users of peyote report an enriching and transcended spiritual experience. Sometimes visions such as of Jesus and the Great Spirit are reported. Increases in dimensionality, in vividness and variation of perception of size, and in appreciation of color may occur. Out-of-body experiences are common, as are auditory hallucinations, most notably voices.

There are several dozen psychoactive mushrooms with psilocybin and related chemicals as the psychedelic ingredients. For hundreds of years, Native Americans in Central America and as far south as Chile used these mushrooms for ceremonial purposes. It was not until the 1950s that Caucasians began using them on a sporadic basis. The effects of psilocybin are rather similar to those of LSD and mescaline. However, psilocybin has a shorter duration and is believed to provide an experience that is warmer, less forceful, more likely to foster communications with other people, and less likely to produce "bad trips."

Most hallucinogenic abusers are polydrug users, who often were introduced to the drug by friends who suggested that they "experiment" with the drug. Many people take it once or twice and find it very unpleasant and never use it again. Those who do use it do so in more of a sporadic than an everyday fashion, so dependence is not as large an issue as with other drugs, such as the narcotics, sedatives, and alcohol. The effects of the hallucinogenic drugs are so mind-altering that it would be very difficult for a person to use it on a daily basis and maintain a job and more generally the semblance of adequate social functioning. However, both dependence and tolerance do occur.

Phencylidine (PCP)

Used briefly in 1963 as a surgical anesthetic and postoperative analgesic, phencylidine was discontinued for these uses because of its undesirable psychological effects. Although it was effective as an anesthetic, about a third of patients experienced agitation, excitement, and disorientation during the recovery period. It began to appear on the street in the late 1960s. It can be regarded as a cross between a sedative and a psychedelic drug (Grinspoon & Bakalar, 1980), although it also has stimulant properties. It affects different people in markedly different ways at different times. It is easy and cheap to synthesize. It is commonly contained in or substituted for other more expensive street drugs (drug pushers are frequently dishonest with their customers.) The effects of PCP, which is usually smoked but may be snorted, injected, swallowed, and even applied rectally and in eye drops, are felt in 5 minutes and last for several hours. The peak is usually experienced within a half hour. It takes a day or two before all of the acute effects are dissipated. Occasionally, the effects last for several days, and there is some evidence of a recirculation in the body. Psychological dependence does develop and monkeys will self-administer it and develop withdrawal symptoms.

Low dosages frequently produce giddiness and euphoric feelings similar to those produced by alcohol. Flushing, sweating, increased blood pressure and heart rate, ataxia, diplopia (double vision), agitation, and anxiety are other effects. In high dosages, catatonia, violence, convulsions, and respiratory depression and cardiac arrest may occur. PCP sometimes produces psychosis with schizophrenia-like properties. In fact, PCP administered to schizophrenics exacerbates the symptoms. This may be a function of the fact that it is known to produce a dopamine release. Psychosis is more common in chronic users but has been known to occur following a single administration. The violence toward persons and property that PCP is infamous for ordinarily occurs when the person is psychotic.

There are no known antagonists for PCP, so the medical condition has to be treated symptomatically. Tactile and auditory contact with the patient should be kept to a minimum. All external stimuli should be reduced, and ideally the patient should be placed in a dark and soundproof room. He or she should be observed closely. Some persons under the influence of PCP become extraordinarily violent, strong, and impervious to pain. Their breaking handcuffs, proceeding to attack after being shot, and requiring numerous officers to restrain them have often been reported.

A difficult-to-comprehend phenomenon is that PCP users continue to use it in spite of its negative effects. In one study of 31 users (Siegel, 1978b), the subjects reported negative experiences every time they used it but positve experiences only 60% of the time. The positive effects included heightened sensitivity to outside stimuli (97% of users), stimulation (92%), dissociation (88%), mood elevation (61%), inebriation (55%), tranquilization or relaxation (55%), and euphoria (8%). The negative experiences included restlessness (76%), perceptual disturbances (75%), disorientation (63%), anxiety (61%), paranoia (34%), hyperexcitability (27%), confusion (25%), and irritability (22%).

Chronic PCP users tend to be very impulsive individuals who suffer from depression, anxiety, irritability, confusional states, and not infrequently psychosis. Neurological problems include memory difficulty, losing items, speech disturbances, visual disturbances, concentration difficulty, ataxia, increased deep tendon reflexes, diminished coordination, repetitive movements, and nystagmus. Neuropsychological testing has confirmed the deficits based upon clinical reports. However, one study provided limited encouragement of at least partial recovery in that neuropsychological test performance improved after PCP abstinence was obtained (Cosgrove, 1986).

CONCLUSION

Why do people take drugs? We maintain that there are basically two fundamental reasons: (1) for increase in positive subjective state and decrease in negative subjective state and (2) to produce optimal level of central nervous system activation. Both heroin and cocaine produce euphoria and reduce bodily and psychological pain. We propose that, all other things being equal, a person with excessive CNS arousal would prefer heroin, and the person with CNS arousal deficit would prefer cocaine.

PART IV

DISORDERS OF INTERPERSONAL MALADJUSTMENT

AT HIGHER RISK FOR PERSONALITY DISORDERS

Children Who Act Out

Persons with Brain Disorders

Alcoholics

Drug Abusers

Persons with Lower Socioeconomic Status

Children of Mothers with Prenatal Difficulties

Persons with Perinatal Difficulties

Persons with Abnormal EEG

Children from Broken Homes

Persons with Family Histories of Personality Disorders

THIRTEEN

Personality Disorders

P ersonality disorder diagnoses are made when the principal problem of the individual is an enduring personality trait that is maladaptive and/or harmful to others. When psychologists and psychiatrists employ the term *personality disorder* without qualification, they ordinarily imply pronounced antisocial tendencies. However, not all of the personality disorders involve extensive acting out behavior.

The personality disorders certainly are not discrete entities. It is often quite arbitrary what personality disorder category a person is assigned to because of the overlap of characteristics. In fact, the creation and designation of personality disorders also have been quite arbitrary rather than reflecting any scheme of nature or universally agreed upon nomenclature.

Personality disorders diagnoses differ markedly by sex. Males are more likely to be given an antisocial or paranoid personality diagnosis. Females are more likely to be given a histrionic, borderline or dependent personality diagnosis. Such differences seem understandable in that women in most cultures have been expected to be emotional and dependent, just as men have been expected to be independent, aggressive and prepared for self-defense.

ANTISOCIAL (PSYCHOPATHIC) PERSONALITY

The personality disorder that has been written about and observed the most for decades throughout the world is that of the antisocial personality, otherwise known as the psychopathic or sociopathic personality. Cleckley's (1964) con-

211

ceptualization of psychopathy is probably best known. He described the following characteristics of the psychopath.

Psychopathic Characteristics

Persistent Lying

The psychopath is an inveterate user of the lie, usually for the purpose of gaining some advantage, such as to con someone out of money or to get out of trouble. However, sometimes the lying seems to be without strong motivation or purpose. The psychopath has little respect for the truth.

Irresponsible Sex Life

The psychopath is a hedonically oriented individual who will take risks and hurt others and sometimes eventually himself for thrills and pleasure, including sex, alcohol, and drugs. He or she tends to have little commitment or emotional attachment to sex partners.

Incapacity for Love

Psychopaths may use the word *love* but not mean it as most people do. Their interpersonal relationships are shallow and lacking in loyalty and emotional depth. They use both significant others and strangers for their own advantage.

No Life Plan

Frequently psychopaths live only for the thrills of the moment without any life plan. Their goals are short-term. They have low frustration tolerance and are unwilling to postpone immediate gratification.

Charm

The psychopath is a charmer. He or she usually is an extravert with a pleasant smile and manner and creates a good first impression. He or she seems sincerely genuine in his like for the other person and interested in that person's welfare. In short, the psychopath is a successful manipulator and con artist. Psychopaths are often successful salespersons. Many clinicians contend they tend to be good-looking.

Low Level of Anxiety

The psychopath seems to have too low a level of anxiety for his own welfare. He will therefore engage in risk-taking behavior and fail to see danger ahead and the consequences of his behavior.

No Guilt or Shame

The psychopath may feign guilt but really feel little or no remorse for the actions committed and little genuine feeling for the person hurt.

Does Not Learn from Experience

The psychopath does not seem to profit from punishment or from mistakes. Or possibly he needs more "hard knocks" than the average person to learn appropriate behavior. It is generally recognized that the psychopath's antisocial behavior lessens somewhat in middle age.

Lacks Insight

The psychopath tends to blame his or her problems on other people, circumstances, and bad luck. He seems unable to grasp how he/she is different from other people and how his/her behavior is regarded as objectionable by others.

Does Not Respond to Kindness

Students and young professionals in correctional institutions not infrequently bestow overwhelming kindness on psychopaths in an effort to reform them. They will claim great gratitude but steal from, lie to, and manipulate these kind persons, just as they have done with their parents, their spouses, and many other people.

The British use the term *psychopath* more freely, with a broader array of antisocial behavior, even with considerable anxiety present. In fact, the famous British psychologist Hans Eysenck refers to the psychopath as an "extroverted neurotic." He views the psychopath as emotionally and autonomically unstable, like other neurotics, but slow to condition and learn from his experience, like other extroverts.

It is the opinion of the present authors that even though the entity of psychopath is more deserving of a diagnostic category than persons with other personality disorders, the typical criminal seen in prison or jail has other characteristics interspersed with psychopathic features. We probably see more "pure psychopaths" outside of institutions (e.g., lying about the used car he is attempting to sell us or to the wealthy person he or she intends to marry for money).

PREVALENCE FACTORS

Persons given a diagnosis of antisocial personality tend to be youthful. However, it is generally felt that there is a partial "burnout" of the most flagrant psychopathic behavior rather than a fundamental change of personality with middle age. The antisocial personality diagnosis is given to many more men than women across national, socioeconomic, and age lines. Being a member of a disadvantaged racial group, urban as contrasted to rural residence, and low socioeconomic status are associated with having an antisocial personality diagnosis.

ETIOLOGY

One methodological problem with research on psychopaths is that it is invariably conducted with persons who are incarcerated or at least have been dealt with in some way by the judicial system. Such means of procuring subjects, therefore, excludes the smoothly functioning psychopaths who don't get caught or who engage in activities that are exploitative or parasitic but not necessarily illegal. Furthermore, in the quest for research subjects, anyone who is caught in unlawful activity may be included, without careful regard for some of the classic subtle personality features such as charm and glibness.

Biological Etiology

Genetics.   There is no doubt that psychopathic behavior is observed in the relatives of psychopaths. Needless to say, common environment may account for some of this trend. However, there is some evidence of a genetic influence. Persons with antisocial personality diagnosis tend to have fathers who have alcoholism or antisocial personalities, even when the person was not reared with the father (Robins, 1975).

In research of Crowe (1974) 52 adult adoptees born to women in a reformatory were compared to control adoptees selected from the state index of adoption by being the nearest entry to that of the proband and matched for age, sex, and race. The children of the reformatory women had a significantly higher rate of antisocial personality than did the control subjects.

Brain Abnormalities.   A number of studies (Hare, 1970) have consistently demonstrated that a substantial proportion of psychopaths, perhaps in the neighborhood of half, have abnormal EEGs, in contrast to 10% or 15% in the general population. The most common sort of abnormality is that of slow waves. Hare pointed out that this slow-wave activity resembled that found in children and is therefore congruent with the childlike emotionality and impulsivity of the psychopath.

Further evidence of brain pathology or dysfunctioning in psychopaths is the research that indicates that individuals with personality disorders, especially psychopathic, hysterical, and antisocial types, were more likely than normal persons to have mixed handedness (Standage, 1983). Persons with mixed handedness are more likely to have brain dysfunction, such as the sort often associated with learning disabilities and childhood hyperactivity.

A number of clinicians and researchers have noted the similarity of the behavior of psychopaths to that of animals and humans with lesions of the frontal lobe and functionally associated subcortical structures, especially the septum and hippocampus. The research of Altman, Brunner, and Bayer (1973) meshes with this contention. They administered a number of neuropsychological tasks to a group of psychopaths, a group of psychiatric patients, and a college student control group. Relative to both control groups, the psychopaths exhibited test performance similar to that observed with frontal lobe lesion patients. That is, they did poorly on the tasks that tap cognitive flexibility and perseverance. However, more recent research has been unable to differentiate psychopathic prison inmates from nonpsychopathic prison inmates on the basis of neuropsychological tests (Hart, Forth, & Hare, 1990). It could be that the neuropsychological and neurological deficits may be more a characteristic of criminals than psychopaths per se.

Autonomic Nervous System Stability. The autonomic nervous system of psychopaths seems to be more stable than that of nonpsychopaths, perhaps especially in electrical skin conductance. Psychopaths demonstrate fewer spontaneous electrodermal responses and have lower resting levels of skin conductance (which indicates a lower level of autonomic arousal) (Hare, 1970). This lesser autonomic responsivity of psychopaths could be viewed as congruent with their low anxiety, low guilt, social facility, "cool" attitude, and ability to feel or display no discomfort while lying.

Conditioning. Psychopaths tend to do poorly on tasks of conditioned fear response (Hare, 1970). This difficulty in avoiding a noxious stimulus in a laboratory situation seems congruent with the psychopath's well-known inability to mend their ways with punishment. It is also consistent with Eysenck's theoretical formulation mentioned above.

Sensation Seeking. Perhaps related to both autonomic nervous system stability and speed of conditioning is the sensation-seeking propensity that psychopaths tend to have. There have been studies that found psychopaths to be high on sensation seeking on the four scales of the Zuckerman Sensation-Seeking Scale. These are the Thrill and Adventure-Seeking Scale, the Experience-Seeking Scale, the Disinhibition Scale, and the Boredom Susceptibility Scale. In research of Emmons and Webb (1974) psychopaths scored higher than did nonpsychopaths on the Experience-Seeking Scale, the Disinhibition Scale, and the Boredom Susceptibility Scale.

Fairweather (1953) determined the learning rates of psychopaths in an experimental situation with three sorts of conditions: certain reward, uncertain reward, and no reward. The psychopaths learned best when the reward was uncertain. Quay (1965) interpreted the results in terms of psychopaths liking the heightened stimulation that goes with the uncertainty.

Psychosocial Etiology

The greater prevalence of antisocial personality diagnoses among males and among blacks is probably a function, at least in part, of social forces. Society permits more acting out by males. And the impoverished environment that blacks disproportionately live in is more conducive to crime. Furthermore, as alluded to above, some of the criteria of psychopathy (e.g., fighting) make it more likely that persons of lower socioeconomic status and males would be so diagnosed. On the other hand, lower socioeconomic environments are more likely to produce family and general social instability that could lead to antisocial behavior.

A considerable amount of clinical literature states that psychopaths tend to come from homes that are lacking in emotional warmth and/or provide inconsistent discipline. Research has consistently demonstrated that psychopaths tend to have suffered the loss of a parent, especially by separation and especially the father, in childhood (Hare, 1970).

PROGNOSIS

Clinical lore is that psychopaths do not respond well to psychotherapy or to any form of treatment. They tend to be as dishonest and manipulative with their therapists as with other persons they relate to. It seems that the best prognostic indication is age itself. Middle age, perhaps because of decrease in energy and sexual drives and perhaps because of finally learning from years of punishment, tends to bring with it a reduction in antisocial behavior.

BORDERLINE PERSONALITY DISORDER

The personality disorder that has been written about the second most often is probably that of borderline personality. This disorder has been an especially "hot" topic for the past decade or so. Persons so diagnosed are impulsive, emotionally labile and unstable, and tend to engage in disruptive behavior that is harmful to themselves, to others, and to their interpersonal relationships. They have uncertainty and ambivalence about their identity, their life goals, and their relationships with significant others and other persons they interact with. They tend to be chronically dissatisfied with life. Some conceptualize this disorder as a level of personality organization rather than as a specific personality disorder.

It is very common for persons diagnosed with borderline personality to have an additional diagnosis that can be clearly thought of as a psychiatric one (Fiester, 1990). This may especially be the case with mood disorder. Point prevalence rates (rates at a given point in time of people who have the disorder) have been reported from 24% to 74% for major depressive disorder, 4% to 20% for bipolar disorder, 3% to 14% for dysthymic disorder, and 7% to 11% for atypical bipolar disorder.

Persons who have borderline personality disorder have a disproportionate number of anxiety disorder diagnoses. And the reported prevalence of personality disorder with anxiety disorder has been from 20% to 62%, with borderline personality disorder being one of the more common diagnoses (Reich, 1987; Reich, Noyes, & Troughton, 1987). Akiskal (1981) found that if a patient has both a personality disorder and a phobia, the probability is .60 that there will be a depressive disorder.

Some research indicates that borderlines tend to be abnormal or atypical on biological measures. The length of time from onset of sleep to onset of rapid eye movement (REM) sleep is unusually short. Borderline patients have exhibited the same abnormal finding on the dexamethasone suppression test that endogenously depressed patients do. That is, when administered the synthetic cortisol called dexamethasone suppression of cortisol production does not occur. Borderline personality patients tend to have the same sort of abnormal pursuit eye movements as do schizophrenics. Thus, it is seen that just as borderline patients often resemble depressives and schizophrenics clinically, they resemble them biologically as well.

An array of studies show borderline patients to be high on the Depression, Psychopathic Deviate, Psychasthenia (anxiety), and Schizophrenia scales of the MMPI (Gandolfo, Templer, Cappelletty, & Cannon, 1991). Gandolfo et al. administered the MMPI to three groups of patients: borderlines, schizophrenics, and depressives. The other two groups were chosen because the concept of borderline personality has historical roots in and clinical resemblance to them. It was found that all three groups had high scores on the MMPI and that on most of the scales the two groups could not be differentiated. The authors noted that on the 10 regular MMPI clinical scales the borderline patients were highest on 4 and second highest on 4 others. Gandolfo et al. stated: "The maladaptive behavior cannot be denied. However, the magnitude of the subjective distress, and the pervasiveness and intensity and duration of life dissatisfaction, raises the question of whether an Axis I diagnosis would be more appropriate" (p. 788).

Borderlines tend to come from pathological families and to have had an unhappy childhood. Chronic brutalization, either with physical violence or verbal abuse, is common, Early parental loss is also common. The parents of borderlines tend not to be consistently warm, nurturing, or empathic. Often the parents do not permit their children to become independent (Masterson, Lulow, & Costello, 1982; Stone, 1986).

Research indicates that a disproportionate number of borderline personality patients have brain dysfunctioning or damage. In one study, 35 (38%) of 91 borderline patients had neurological dysfunction that included 25 (27%) patients with minimal brain dysfunctioning or learning disability and 10 (11%) with trauma or encephalitis or epilepsy. In this study the males were significantly more likely to have neurological dysfunctioning and females more likely to have affective disorder. Many borderline patients have the residual effects of childhood attention deficit disorder that includes impulsivity, irritability, poor frustration tolerance, aggressive outbursts, temper tantrums, anger, substance abuse, emotional lability and concentration difficulty (Johnson, 1991). It has been reported that borderline patients with attention deficit-hyperactivity disorder respond favorably to the psychomotor stimulant methylphenidate (Ritalin®), which is the drug most often given to children with attention deficit hyperactivity–disorder (Wender, Reimherr, & Wood, 1981). Johnson (1991) recommended:

> When the client has a history of MBD, head injury, or other neurological impairment, it is helpful to be able to say, "You know, your MBD (head injury, epilepsy) seems to have the effect of making you fly off the handle easily" (or "get distracted," "say things you're sorry about," "look for excitement all the time"). Once the therapist has helped the client identify a biological basis for weak impulse control or stimulus-seeking needs, he or she can address therapeutic issues surrounding this information. (p. 168)

Antipsychotic drugs have been found to be effective in borderline personality disorder. They have been reported as useful for helping to stabilize reality testing in diminished cognitive dysfunction. They have apparently been useful for reducing impulsivity, depression, hypersensitivity to rejection, anger, hostility, and paranoid or schizotypal features (Cowdry, 1987; Cowdry & Gardner, 1988; Ellison & Adler, 1990; Serban & Siegal, 1984; Soloff et al., 1986). In one study Cowdry and Gardner (1988) found that the MAO inhibitor tranylcypromine was effective with borderline patients in reducing suicidality, anxiety, rejection, sensitivity, anger, and impulsivity. Carbamazepine (Tegretol®) is a drug with both anticonvulsant and mood-stabilizing properties that has been used for an increasing array of problems and conditions in the last decade or so. Cowdry, Pickar, and Davies (1985) found modest positive effects in controlling impulsivity in borderline patients but noted that a few patients with prior depressive episodes experienced a recurrence of depressive symptoms.

There has been a long-standing disagreement about whether treatment of borderlines should be insight-oriented or oriented toward emotional and environmental support. The former orientation is based upon the assumption that the disorder is a product of malformed psychic structure and that a reconstruction of personality is needed. The latter is often based upon the assumption that the borderline is unable to soothe himself or herself and that a nurturant therapist is needed to provide the comfort and stability that was lacking in childhood (Chessick, 1982; Johnson, 1991; Waldringer, 1987). As we view the situation, there is insufficient evidence to support one position over the other. It is possible that some borderline patients should have insight-oriented therapy; some, supportive therapy; and some, no psychologically oriented therapy.

In one study, borderlines who had been given psychotherapy for intervals ranging from 3 months to 5 years were followed up from 2 to 10 years later. Twenty-two percent were said to be dramatically improved and even functioning better than in their premorbid state. Thirty-seven percent were described as having modest gains, and 41% were neither better nor worse (Kernberg, 1984). Since there was no control group, it is difficult to say whether the changes were a function of the psychotherapy or spontaneous remission or age. An age factor can certainly not be ruled out. We remind our readers that psychopaths, drug addicts, alcoholics and schizophrenics often improve or "burn out" with age.

There have been at least two follow-up studies with borderline patients, and the outcome was found to be quite variable, although a bit better than would have been predicted on the basis of the widely held belief among mental health clinicians that the characterological features of borderlines are deeply rooted and entrenched. In one of the studies it was found that slightly more than half of the borderline patients were rated good or recovered, with follow-ups averaging 15 years postdischarge. About a fifth were rated "poor" or "marginal," and about a third of the former patients were given intermediate ratings (McGlashan, 1986).

SCHIZOTYPAL PERSONALITY DISORDER

Persons diagnosed with schizotypal personality disorder may exhibit eccentricity, strange appearance. awkward interpersonal relationships, paranoid ideation, delusions of reference, unusual word usage, digressive discourse, and inappropriate or constricted affect. However, they do not present with these patterns to the extent of warranting a schizophrenic diagnosis.

There is a greater than chance proportion of schizophrenic relatives in schizotypical personality disorder. Those with schizotypal personality disorder, but not those with other personality disorder diagnoses, have the same impaired eye tracking that schizophrenics have (Siever, 1990). Schizotypical personality disorder has responded favorably to antipsychotic drugs. These have reduced ideas of reference, anxiety, depression, depersonalization, anger, hostility, and somatization (Ellison & Adler, 1990).

There are two ways of viewing the schizophrenic like characteristics, the disproportionate number of schizophrenic relatives, and the schizophrenic-like biochemical abnormalities of schizotypical patients. One point of view is that both disorders are on a continuum of severity, rather than being distinct and separate entities. Proponents of this point of view speak of a "schizophrenic spectrum." The other point of view is that schizotypal personality patients have a mild case of schizophrenia and should receive a schizophrenic diagnosis rather than a personality disorder diagnosis.

PARANOID PERSONALITY DISORDER

Persons with paranoid personality are unreasonably suspicious, unfriendly and not warm in interpersonal relationships, oversensitive to slights and minor injustices, hypervigilant, and attributing blame to others. Research indicates that a disproportionate number of paranoid personality disorder persons are found in the relatives of schizophrenics (Fiester, 1990).

PASSIVE–AGGRESSIVE PERSONALITY DISORDER

Persons with a passive–aggressive personality engage in such behaviors in a wide array of life situations, perhaps most at work, school, and in the family. Behaviors that may be exibited include procrastination, dawdling, stubbornness, making "mistakes," intentional inefficiency, "losing" things, complaining, criticizing others, negative reaction to constructive criticism, and dislike of authority.

Persons with passive–aggressive personalities are often people who are inadequate in one or more ways and are extremely talented in few or no domains. We tend to think of them as "little people" regardless of their size. They have feelings of inferiority and are often jealous of persons who are more endowed than they and tend to pick on persons they have authority over or perceive as their inferiors.

McCann (1988) provided a good review of various theoretical conceptualizations of the passive–aggressive personality. Psychoanalytic formulation has included the contention of oral-sadistic fixation at the biting state, resulting in caustic comments in addition to other contentions related to masochistic and passive–dependent needs and to guilt. Behavioral formulation proposes that the passive–aggressive person has not learned more adaptive behavior for expressing anger. The interpersonal perspectives hold that passive–aggressive behavior can be understood in terms of relationship dimensions, such as quarrelsome versus agreeable affiliation, and the dimension of submissiveness versus dominance. Social learning theory stresses history of reinforcement, with specific events and processes such as contradictory parental attitudes. Biologically based conceptualization stresses deeply ingrained biological processes that could lead to the insecurity and irritability observed in passive–aggressive persons.

HISTRIONIC PERSONALITY DISORDER

Histrionic personality individuals are ordinarily emotionally labile, talkative, dramatic, wanting to be the center of attention, impulsive, and extraverted, with low frustration tolerance.

NARCISSISTIC PERSONALITY DISORDER

In persons with a narcissistic personality diagnosis we often see selfishness and an attitude of entitlement, of wanting to be treated in a special way and wanting other people to shower them with compliments. They often have inflated opinions of their self-worth, but underlying such is often insecurity and doubting of one's positive attributes. Research that compared military male inpatients with narcissistic personality diagnoses to those with other personality disorder diagnoses found that the former were more apt to have sexually abused children, to have undergone a divorce or separation, and to have been admitted because of unruly conduct (Leetz, Martino-Saltzman, & Gormley, 1991). Male college students were found to be more narcissistic than female college students (Narayan, 1990). Asian-American college women were found to have lower narcissism scores than Caucasian-American women (Smith, 1990). Smith attributed this to traditional Asian values antithetical to narcissism, including modesty, respect for authority, and valuing relationships over individualism.

OBSESSIVE–COMPULSIVE PERSONALITY DISORDER

Individuals with obsessive–compulsive personality disorder tend to be perfectionistic, rigid, work-oriented, demanding of themselves for extremely high quality and quantity of work, indecisive, unemotional, self-controlled, parsimonious, introverted, rule-oriented, and conscientious. White, well-educated, employed males are at greater risk for obsessive-compulsive personality disorder (Nestadt, Romanski, Brown, & Chahal, 1991). The obsessive-compulsive personality disorder is frequently present in persons with obsessive-compulsive anxiety disorder (Pollak, 1987). Garamoni and Schwartz (1986) pointed out the similarities of the obsessive-compulsive personality and the Type A (heart attack-prone) personality, which is characterized by high drive, devotion to work, emotional constriction, and perseverence. Garamoni and Schwartz suggested that the Type A behavior pattern may be esentially one of compulsive achievement that is a subtype of the obsessive-compulsive personality.

AVOIDANT PERSONALITY DISORDER

Individuals with avoidant personality disorder would like to be with other persons more than they are but are too shy to do so. They typically are insecure persons with feelings of inferiority, who fear being rejected or criticized by others and are fearful that other persons might have a low opinion of them. Research using the MMPI found avoidant personality patients to have more anxiety, depression, and introversion than do patients with other personality disorder diagnoses (Schotte et al., 1991). In fact, the literature consistently shows much similarity between patients given an avoidant personality disorder diagnosis and those given a social phobia diagnosis (Mattick & Newman, 1991). Patients who received group systematic desensitization, behavioral rehearsal, and self-image work obtained significantly lower scores on an instrument measuring fear of negative evaluation (Renneberg, Goldstein, Phillips, & Chambless, 1990).

DEPENDENT PERSONALITY DISORDER

In dependent personality there is a strong need to be with other persons, to be well thought of by other persons, and to conform to the requests of other persons in order to gain approval and security and to avoid being alone. Dependent personalities are generally passive individuals who fear abandonment and who like others to tell them what to do. Reich, Noyes, and Trougton (1987) cited literature based on clinical impressions contending that anxiety disorder patients have dependent personality disorder features. On three different criteria for this disorder, Reich et al. found that a disproportionate number of panic disorder patients have dependent personalities. Cause-and-effect relationships could not be inferred with confidence. The authors suggested that dependent personality may predispose one to anxiety disorder. They also cited a prospective study by Nystrom and Lyndegard (1975) that found persons with dependent personality features tended to later develop anxiety disorder. Consistent with an association of dependency and insecurity is the study with college students by Overholser (1992), who found that scores on a dependency scale were correlated with depression, loneliness, self-criticism, and lower levels of self-esteem. Head, Baker, and Williamson (1991) found that persons diagnosed as having dependent personality disorder tended to have families of origin that were high in control and low in self-expressiveness.

SCHIZOID PERSONALITY DISORDER

Persons with schizoid personality feel little need or desire to be around other people. They express little emotion and tend to be regarded as odd or eccentric but not to the same degree as persons with schizotypical personality or schizophrenia. Several studies have focused upon the similarities of the schizoid personality and the avoidant personality (Overholser, 1989). In one study, schizoid and hysterical patients were compared. One might expect differences because hysterical persons have traditionally been regarded as extraverted and emotionally expressive. The differences found showed schizoids as more likely to be single, childless, and living alone (Studt, 1986).

CONCLUSIONS

The exact prevalence of the various personality disorders is most difficult to specify because there is frequently no clear line of distinction between personality disorder and normalcy. Most persons contain at least some characteristics of some of the personality disorders. Most persons have some degree of suspiciousness; indeed, gross gullibility would be a liability. Most persons have some need for order and other indications of compulsivity. Almost everyone manipulates other people. Furthermore, the line of distinction between the personality disorders and the other disorders is not clear, and as was pointed out above, the distinctions among the various personality disorders are not clear. The present authors are not pleased with the inclusion of schizotypal personality, which seems to be the description of a mild case of schizophrenia.

It appears that paranoid, antisocial, and compulsive personalities are more often diagnosed in males. Such sex differences are probably a function, at least in part, of social sex role expectations. Males are expected to be more independent, assertive, prepared to defend themselves, and capable of containing emotions. Females are expected to be more dependent, passive, expressive of feelings, and conforming.

Personality disorder features can probably best be understood as an interaction of biological endowment and learning to cope with one's environment.

Gender is only one of a large number of contributing variables. A person who is constitutionally disposed to anxiety would be more apt to cope with his or her environment by compulsive ordering. A beautiful woman would be more likely to receive positive reinforcement for histrionic or narcissistic behavior than an ugly woman.

In some cases the environment one is reared in and lives in would appear to strongly determine personality disorder characteristics. Very rigid and strict religious or parental upbringing may foster compulsive behavior. A very threatening environment, such as a high-crime neighborhood, may foster suspiciousness. Relentless oppression by powerful forces may produce passive-aggressive behavior. Avoidance of others may in some cases be traced back to a history of being abused or excessively criticized by others.

AT HIGHER RISK FOR SEXUAL DISORDERS

Paraphilias

Persons Who Act Out

Males

Persons Under the Age of 40

Persons of Lower Socioeconomic Status

Alcoholics

Persons with High Sex Drives

Persons with Frontal Lobe Disinhibition

Persons Who Have Been Sexually Abused

Inadequacies

Persons with Inadequate Knowledge

Persons Who were Rape Victims

Persons Molested as Children

Depressed Persons

Anxious Persons

Persons with Marital Conflicts

Elderly Persons

Persons in Poor Health

Alcoholics

Drug Abusers

Diabetics

Persons Taking Antipsychotic Drugs

Persons Taking Antidepressant Drugs

Persons Taking Antihypertensive Drugs

Persons with Low Self-Concept

Persons Receiving Chemotherapy for Cancer

FOURTEEN

Sexual Disorders

THE KINSEY STUDY

Alfred Kinsey and his associates in the 1940s, conducted bold and pioneering research on the sex lives of Americans that helped us to understand both normal and abnormal sexual behaviors. His 12,000 subjects were not selected on a random or representative basis and were a motley assortment of people ranging from college fraternity and sorority members to YMCA and YWCA employees. All of the figures and percentages given by Kinsey should, therefore, probably not be regarded as precise. Rather, they should be thought of as "ballpark" figures that provide useful estimates in a domain previously shrouded in ignorance.

FREQUENCY OF SOCIALLY UNACCEPTABLE SEXUAL BEHAVIOR

Kinsey found that sexual behavior regarded as sinful or deviant and, in fact, illegal sexual behavior was much more common that most people had realized. For example, Kinsey reported that about a third of all men and one fifth of all women had one or more homosexual experiences. He reported that 9 of 10 men and 6 of 10 women had masturbated. His data indicated extramarital intercourse for half the men and a quarter of the women.

FREQUENCY OF SEXUAL BEHAVIOR AS A FUNCTION OF AGE

Kinsey found that the peak of sex outlet and apparently sex drive is greatest in the teens for males and in the 30s for females. Thus, male sexual drive peaks at an earlier age than muscular strength and athletic and various physical abilities and also before the complete development of secondary sexual characteristics, such as facial and body hair.

Sex in Childhood

Freud maintained that children are sexually inactive during the so-called latency period, which roughly corresponds to the grade-school years. Kinsey found that children of all ages are more active than Freud and most other people had realized. Masturbation, homosexual activity, and heterosexual activity that sometimes includes coitus are all rather common in childhood.

Male-Female Differences

In addition to finding the sexual drive peak at different ages for the two sexes, Kinsey discovered a difference with respect to stimuli producing sexual arousal. He found that females were aroused primarily by direct tactile stimulation, such as kissing, caressing, and fondling of the genitalia and breasts. However, he found males to be aroused by a larger array of stimuli, especially those of a psychic or nontactile sort. Males were much more likely to be aroused by looking at naked females or pictures of naked females, reading sexual material, having sexual fantasies, and listening to talk about sex. Kinsey contended that such differences are a function of fundamental biological factors, a contention that may or may not be correct. Also, Kinsey's generalizations may not be as accurate now as they were in his time.

Socioeconomic Status

Kinsey found that sexual behavior and attitude differed as a function of socioeconomic status. People of lower social status had sexual intercourse at an earlier age and engaged in more premarital sex. However, they masturbated less, were less likely to engage in sexual behavior other than intercourse (such as fellatio, cunnlingus, and deep kissing), were less likely to employ a variety of positions in sexual intercourse, and were less tolerant of nudity.

SEXUAL PARAPHILIAS

In understanding the sexual paraphilias (also called perversions or deviations) it is helpful to bear in mind that many of the behaviors considered deviant or perverted are often manifest in couples regarded as normal. Biting and scratching often occurs in the lovemaking of persons not classified as masochists or sadists. Most men who go to strip shows and topless bars and most women who go to male strip shows could not be diagnosed as voyeurs. Gebhard, Gagnon, Pomeroy, and Christenson (1965) contended that virtually all men have voyeuristic tendencies and that the real difference between the average man and the peeper is in the willingness to assume risks.

Another fact to consider is that most sexual paraphilias are predominantly male. It is not certain whether this is because cultural forces place greater restrictions on females than on males or because of what Kinsey regarded as the inherent tendency for males to be aroused by a greater variety of stimuli.

Exhibitionism

Exhibitionism is one of the most common sex offenses in the United States, Canada, and Europe. Exhibitionism may almost invariably occur in a public place such as a street, park, or public building. The exhibitionist obtains greater gratification if the woman displays a strong emotional response such as fear. He tends to be disappointed if she seems indifferent. In exhibitionism the victim is almost always a stranger. The exhibitionist does not pursue sexual intercourse or later contact.

Exhibitionism is most common in the 20s. In the vast majority of cases the exhibitionist is from pubescence to age 35. Most exhibitionists over the age of 21 are married, although there is often considerable marital disharmony. Forgac and Michaels (1982) inferred from the literature two types of exhibitionists: the classically described timid, neurotic type and an antisocial type. Jorgac and Michaels then administered psychological tests to both the classical exhibitionist without any other criminal involvement and the antisocial type with other criminal involvement. The antisocial types did indeed exhibit test profiles more characteristic of antisocial individuals. They also had a lower level of education than the classical exhibitionist.

Jones and Frei (1979) viewed exhibitionism as having a biological basis in the context of a phylogenetic perspective. They pointed out display behavior as observed in nonhuman primate males. The squirrel monkey displays the erect penis both in situations of courting and of aggression. These facts are especially noteworthy because psychological discussion of exhibitionism has stressed both the sexual and aggressive aspects.

Exhibitionism is often viewed as an almost exclusively male deviation. Female strippers, however, are obviously exhibiting their bodies. Wagner (1974) described some possible differences between female strippers and exhibitionists. He contended that stripping is a continuous routine behavior, in contrast to male exhibiting, which is sporadic and impulsive. The stripper experience is said to be from mildly excited to bored detachment, in contrast to the exhibitionist's great state of excitement. Strippers strive for positive attention and attraction from the audience, whereas the exhibitionist's actions have more of a hostile element.

It is difficult to form generalizations about the victims of exhibitionism since it appears that only a minority of women report the incident to the police. In a survey of college females, 32% reported having been the victim of an exhibitionist. Of these women, 57% were exposed before the age of 20. In general, it appears that most victims are minors or of college age at the time of the action (Cox & MacMahon, 1975). Most victims report negative reactions, especially fear and disgust. However, most women do not report it as extremely traumatic, and it appears that such victimization ordinarily does not produce serious mental health or psychosexual adjustment difficulties.

VOYEURISM

Voyeurism is sexual gratification in viewing others in a state of undress, the viewing being an end in itself rather than foreplay or a prelude to a sexual act. Ordinarily, the voyeur watches females he does not know well. Sometimes voyeurism is associated with triolism—sex involving three, for example, a husband who enjoys viewing another man having sex with his wife. The so-called peeping Tom causes much consternation in the neighborhood by his peering through bedroom windows. However, most voyeurs are not dangerous persons. Voyeurs are typically young men of low socioeconomic status who are socially inept and generally prone to minor criminality (Smith, 1976).

PEDOPHILIA

Child molestation is much more common than most people realize. Surveys of nonclinical populations reveal that as high as 1 in 3 girls and 1 in 10 boys are molested. Jaffe, Dynneson, and ten Bensel (1975) analyzed 291 cases of sexual molestation of children under the age of 16 in Minneapolis. The mean age of the child was 10.7 years, and the mean age of the molester was 28. Eighty-eight percent of the victims were girls. All of the molesters were male. Forty-five percent of the acts consisted of indecent exposure. Thirty-nine percent consisted of "indecent liberties" (physical advances, genital manipulation, obscene language, etc.). Six percent of the acts were rape, 3% nonforced sexual intercourse, 2% sodomy (oral or anal sex), and 4% "other." One half of the offenses occurred in the five summer months of May through September. One half of the offenses occurred between 2 p.m. and 6 p.m. The authors found that 54% of the offenders were strangers but pointed out that most previous investigators have reported that the majority of the offenders had previously known the children.

The research of Erikson, Walbek, and Seely (1988) found more serious and invasive sex acts than did the Jaffee et al. (1975) study. Erikson et al. reported 21% vaginal contact, 2% anal contact, and 24% oral sex with 259 molested girls. They reported 17% anal contact and 43% oral sex for 102 molested boys. Erickson, et al. also commented that their findings do not support the contention of some previous authors that injury is very uncommon and that the vast preponderance of molestation involves only looking and touching.

In regard to the sex of the child molester, most molesters are heterosexual, an intermediate number are homosexual, and the fewest are bisexual. Research indicates that heterosexual pedophiles are more likely to be married and to have more masculine interests than do homosexual pedophiles.

One study (Groth & Birmbaum, 1978) divided their child molesters into "fixated" and "regressed." The former never developed a sexual relationship with adults, wherein the latter "regressed" from such a relationship. All regressed offenders, whether they molested boys or girls, had heterosexual adult relationships. There is considerable research indicating that pedophiles tend to be or at least to feel socially inadequate. Psychological tests have pointed to their being passive, weak, dependent, and inadequate in relating to adult females; they have feelings of inferiority and of being unable to compete with other men and are anxious, insecure, and timid. One study using video-tape found pedophiles to be socially inadequate in terms of such behaviors as loudness and inflection of voice, eye contact, and facial expression (Barlow, Abel, Blanchard, Bristow, & Young, 1977).

Research indicates that the verbal report of sexual arousal and measured penile tumescence in response to nude pictures of adult females have a rather similar pattern in both pedophiles and normal men. Normal men tend to be aroused by nude female pictures as young as 6 years of age. Perhaps the differences between pedophilic and normal men are more in the realm of behavior than psychodynamics. Pedophilics molest children, and normal men do not. Moreover, the acting out tends to transcend the matter of molestation. Pedophiles tend to be more inclined to criminality outside the sexual realm; to exhibit more deviant behavior, attitudes, and life-styles; and to be more inclined to alcohol abuse than normal men (Langevin, Handy, Russon, & Day, 1985).

There are times when the child initiates the sexual relationship with the molester. This does not occur as often as pedophiles say it happens, but it is not a rare occurrence. In the research of Gebhard, Gagnon, Pomeroy, and Christenson (1965), according to the offender the child encouraged the advances 48% of the time, were passive 37% of the time, and resisted 15% of the time; but according to the child's account of the situation, the respective percentages were 16%, 8%, and 75%. The fact that the child very often returns to the molester—60% of the cases reported by Swanson (1968)—could be viewed as consistent with the reports of voluntary participation. On the other hand, pedophiles use varying degrees and kinds of coercion, including threats, promises, gifts, and taking advantage of the emotional needs of the child.

Mental health professionals have traditionally viewed the molestation of boys by older females as rare. However, there is now evidence that such may not be the case. One survey found that 2.9% of college males had been heterosexually molested before the age of puberty (Fritz, Stoll, & Wagner, 1981). In another study (Petrovich & Templer, 1984) it was found that 49 (59%) of 83 rapists in a penitentiary had been molested by at least one female at least 4 years older than themselves.

The serendipitous findings of Petrovich and Templer (1984) were extended by the investigation of Condy, Templer, Brown, and Veaco (1987). These researchers found that history of molestation by older females is not confined to incarcerated rapists. Sixteen percent of college men, 46% of convicted rapists, 37% of child molesters, and 47% of non–sex offender inmates reported boyhood heterosexual molestation. The mean age of both college men and prison men at the time of the molestation was about 12½ years. Most of the molesting women were friends of the family, neighbors, or baby-sitters. In contrast to the male molestation of children, sexual intercourse took place in a clear majority of instances. Most of the men did not view their experiences in a negative fashion. However, men were more likely to view the experience as negative if it was with their mother or other close relative or if they were forced into the sex acts. The study revealed that the heterosexual molestation of boys was somewhat more common in lower-socioeconomic status persons. In the study by Condy et al., the information provided by female inmates and college students substantiated the findings with male subjects. The prison women reported a much higher incidence of molesting boys than did the college women.

All children are not at equal risk of being molested. There is a higher incidence among children from economically underprivileged families. Families of molested children frequently receive public assistance and frequently are single-parent families.

INCEST

Incest exists at all socioeconomic levels but is more common among the economically deprived. Father-daughter incest is most often reported to legal authorities. The father who has incestual relations with his daughter tends to come from a background of economic and emotional deprivation. He often left home at a very young age. It has been suggested that this absence of a parent figure at an early age brings about deemphasis of the special value of the parent-child relationship in the male who becomes an incestuous father. The father frequently has a poor employment history. Psychopathic and paranoid features are common. Some fathers are psychotic or retarded. Many are alcoholic, and incestuous acts are frequently committed under the influence of alcohol. The incestuous father is often described as hypersexual, sometimes with a "pathological obsession with sex" (Gebhard et al., 1965). It is common for him to have a dominant, even tyrannical role in the family. Kirkland and Bauer (1982) found incestuous fathers to be anxious and socially alienated individuals with a propensity for acting out behavior.

In a survey of 796 undergraduates at six New England colleges and universities, 15% of the females and 10% of the males reported sexual experience with a sibling (Finkelhor, 1980). Seventy-four percent of the experiences reported were heterosexual, 16% between brothers, and 10% between sisters. The preponderance of the experiences were between the ages of 7 and 12, with a median of 10 years. Fondling and touching of the genitals were the most common activities. One fourth of the experiences were described as exploitive either because force was used or because of a large age discrepancy between the partners. Thirty percent of the respondents said their experiences were of a positive sort, 30% said they had been negative, and 40% did not feel strongly either way. The experience was more likely to be perceived negatively if coercion or a large age discrepancy was involved.

Herman, Russell, and Trocki (1986) conducted research to determine the long-term effects of incestuous abuse in childhood on a nonclinical sample of women in the community. The preponderance of the women said they were upset by the incestuous experiences at the time they occurred. Thirty-five percent said they had been extremely upset; 20%, very upset; and 26%, somewhat upset. Eleven percent said they had not been very upset, and 8% said they were not at all upset at the time. About half of these women said that this abuse had from substantial to great impact on their adult lives. The sorts of impact they stated most frequently were negative feelings about men or sex or themselves, generalized anxiety and distrust, difficulties in forming or maintaining intimate relationships, and sexual problems. Lasting harm was more likely to have been reported if the abuse had been forceful or violent; if it involved vaginal, anal, or oral penetration; if it had extended over a long period of time; or if the perpetrator had been a father or stepfather. However, 22% of the women reported not being aware of any long-lasting effects, and 27% reported only slight residual effects.

Incest between mother and child, especially between mother and son, is regarded as being the least common and most intensely taboo form of heterosexual incest. One study assessed 26 cases of women in the Dallas court system who had engaged in incestuous behavior with their children (McCarty, 1986). In five of these cases the woman was an accomplice. In nine cases the women were co-defendants with a male as the other co-defendant. In 12 of the cases the woman was an independent co-defendant. The gender of the victims was rather evenly divided, with at least two of the women molesting both boys and girls. The molested daughters ranged from 2 to 15 years of age, with a mean age of 6.4 years. The sons ranged from 4 to 17, with a mean of 9.6 years. Most of the women tended to describe their childhood as "rough" or "horrible," and 17 of them were sexually victimized as children. Their own marriages were problem-filled, and eight (31%) of the women were married before the age of 16. Three of the women had histories of prostitution. One woman said she engaged in sex orgies. The majority of the women engaged in a wide array of sexual behaviors with numerous sex partners and were said by the author to use "poor judgment" in the selection of sex partners. Nine (36%) of the women had serious problems with alcohol or drugs. A disproportionate number of the women were of borderline intelligence. Although this study does not confirm the clinical impression of some authors that most incestuous mothers are psychotic, it is apparent that the mothers in this study were not well adjusted.

FETISHISM

Fetishism is sexual excitement or activity in connection with an inanimate object, often some sort of clothing or personal apparel. Tables 14.1 and 14.2 describe types of fetishes and typical objects of fetish behavior documented in a study by Chalkley and Powell (1983). The patients ranged in age from 12 to 59 years, with a median of 28 years. Thirty-eight (81%) of the males were heterosexual. The one woman was a lesbian. Only 3 of the 48 patients had psychotic diagnoses.

Fetishes can be readily conceptualized in a learning therapy frame of reference. Such is exactly what Rachman (1966) did in his experiment in which a pair of women's boots (conditioned stimulus) was coupled with a picture of a nude woman (unconditioned stimulus). After sufficient pairings, the boots alone were capable of producing sexual arousal as measured by the penile phethysmograph. However, it is apparent from Table 14.2 that all objects do not have equal fetish capacity. Some categories of objects have greater pre-potency than others.

TRANSVESTITISM

One study evaluated the characteristics of 136 American and 86 Australian transvestites (Buhrich & Beaumont, 1981). The findings were remarkably

TABLE 14.1 Numbers of patients with different types of fetish, listing individual fetishes which occurred more than once

TYPES OF FETISH	NO OF PATIENTS
Parts of the body:	11(22.9%)
Legs 3	
Clothes:	28(58.3%)
Clothes (including baby's clothes 1, "mod" clothes 1, but otherwise unspecified) 11	
Knickers, panties, men's pants 10	
Underwear 7	
Stockings 5	
Mackintoshes and raincoats 4	
Suspenders and suspender belts 3	
Dresses 2	
Skirts 2	
Corsets, girdles 2	
Slips 2	
Soft materials and fabrics:	3(6.3%)
Silk 2	
Clothes made of soft materials and fabrics:	4(8.3%)
Nylon knickers and panties 2	
Footwear:	7(14.6%)
Shoes 3	
High-heeled shoes 2	
Boots 2	
Leather and leather items:	5(10.4%)
Leather jackets 2	
Rubber and rubber items:	11(22.9%)
Rubber macs 6	
Rubber tubes and enemas 4	
Rubber 3	
Other objects:	7(4.2%)
Handkerchiefs 2	
Other	2(4.2%)

Reproduced by permission of the Royal College of Psychiatrists from: Chalkley, A. J., & Powell, B. E. (1983). Clinical description of forty eight cases of sexual fetishism. *British Journal of Psychiatry*, 142, p. 293.

similar for the transvestites in the two countries. All were male. Almost half of these men started cross-dressing before puberty, and in the vast majority cross-dressing was well established by late adolescence. Intense fetishism was usually present during adolescence but then waned. In almost a quarter of the subjects the fetishism ceased. The fetishism was frequently associated with

TABLE 14.2 Numbers of patients with different types of fetish-related behaviour, disregarding behaviour which only occurred once among the sample. (Where particular types of fetish recur in connection with a particular kind of behaviour, these are specified)

FETISH RELATED BEHAVIOUR	NO. OF PATIENTS

Seeing someone dressed in:
   Clothes 6
   Rubber and rubber items 4
	11(22.9%)

Gazing at:
   Footwear 2
   Legs 2
	6(12.5%)

Fondling:	4(8.3%)
Sucking:	2(4.2%)

Inserting up rectum:
   Rubber items 4
   Footwear 2
	6(12.5%)

Following:	2(4.2%)
Stealing: Clothes 12	18(37.5%)
Hoarding: Clothes 3	6(12.5%)

Wearing:
   Clothes 14
   Rubber and rubber items 5
   Footwear 4
   Leather and leather items 3
	21(43.8%)

Rolling in:	2(4.2%)
Burning:	2(4.2%)
Cutting or snipping:	2(4.2%)

Reproduced by permission of the Royal College of Psychiatrists from: Chalkley, A. J., & Powell, B. E. (1983). Clinical description of forty eight cases of sexual fetishism. *British Journal of Psychiatry*, 142, p. 293.

fantasies of being bound. Buhrich and Beaumont divided the transvestites into two groups. The "nuclear transvestites" were satisfied with cross-dressing; the "marginal transvestites" had a stronger feminine identification, desired feminization by hormones or surgery, and had a stronger interest in a homosexual direction. Transvestitism in women is less common. In an article describing three such cases, some common properties became apparent (Stoller, 1982). All three took intense sexual pleasure in dressing in male clothing, had normal female anatomy and physiology, had been very masculine since childhood, and had engaged in homosexual relations. In all three women there was no effort to change their sex, and in only one was there effort to pass as a male.

SADISM AND MASOCHISM

Spengler (1977) pointed out that the study of sadomasochistic behavior is difficult because those persons who practice it tend to be quite secretive with respect to their behavior. Spengler also recommended caution with respect to the methodology of his own study in West Germany. His subjects were contacted in two ways: questionnaires in response to contact advertisements used by sadomasochists to seek partners (44%) and questionnaires distributed to members by cooperating sadomasochistic clubs (56%). The response rate was 27% for the ads, 29% for the club members, and 28% for the total. Of the 244 men who participated, 30% were exclusively heterosexual, 38% exclusively homosexual, and 31% bisexual. All respondents were male. In regard to sadomasochistic practices, 60% included a cane, 66% a whip, 60% bonds, 26% anal manipulations, 27% torture apparatus, 9% nipple torture, 6% needles, 7% clothespins or clamps, 7% glowing objects, and 4% knives or razor blades. The more extreme and dangerous practices were much less frequent than the "classical" elements of beating and bondage. Fetishistic practices were very often associated with the sadomasochistic acts, the most common being leather (50% of the men), boots (50%), jeans (19%), and uniforms (16%). In terms of role preference, 13% of the men were exclusively active, 19% versatile but mainly active, 29% versatile, 22% versatile but mainly passive, and 16% exclusively passive. Sexual preference was not related to role preference. In regard to the methods of seeking a partner, 64% used contact ads; 36%, friends; 25%, pubs; 23%, special bars; 21%, partners; 20%, clubs; 13%, prostitution; and 8%, parties. Most of the men had been aware of their sadomasochistic tendencies in their adolescence or youth. Seven percent reported this to be 10 years or younger; 10%, age 11–13; 25% age 14–16; 15%, age 17–19; 20%, age 20–24; 12%, age 25–29; and 11%, 30 years or older. Their most common reactions to their first experience were "I wanted to do it again" (69%), "I was troubled" (40%), "I was glad" (24%), "I thought it was normal" (23%), "I felt happy" (22%), and "I was afraid for the future" (21%). In regard to their current frequency of sadomasochistic behavior in the past year, 15% did not engage in such activity; 20%, 1–3 times; 28%, 4–6 times; 19%, 7–24 times; and 18%, more often. Thus, the typical subject engages in this behavior about twice a month. The homosexual men engaged in this behavior more frequently than did the heterosexual men. In regard to number of sex partners in the past year, 5% reported no partners; 11%, one partner; 25%, 2–3 partners; 21%, 4–5 partners; 15%, 6–10 partners; and 23%, more than 10 partners. Sexual preference was strongly related to number of sex partners. One percent of the heterosexual men, 25% of the bisexual men, and 38% of the homosexual men had had more than 10 partners.

EROTIC PIERCING

Erotic piercing is done to the nipples, scrotum, perineum, and the glans and shaft of the penis. Gold, silver, or stainless steel rings or studs up to 2 cm in diameter are placed into the holes. In one study (Buhrich, 1983), those persons who put notices in a magazine devoted to erotic piercing were contacted, and information was obtained from 6 females and 154 males. One of the females reported being bisexual, and two were interested in tattoos. Forty-nine percent of the men reported being homosexual or bisexual; 44% reported sadomasochism; 41%, tattoos; 18%, bondage and/or discipline; and 10%, fetishism. Buhrich advised making inferences with caution because of his sampling procedures. However, he suggested that erotic piercing is a predominantly male phenomenon that is associated with homosexuality, sadomasochism, bondage, fetishism, and tattoos.

NECROPHILIA

Necrophilia is sex with dead bodies. It is regarded as rare. In a review, Templer and Eberhardt (1980) located 17 cases in the English- and German-language professional journals. One of the necrophiliacs was a woman, and the other 16 were men. The acts included fondling of genitalia and breasts, sexual intercourse, and oral and anal sex. Most of the acts took place in funeral homes and cemeteries. Templer and Eberhardt concluded, not surprisingly, that the necrophilic is a severely disturbed person; psychosis, brain pathology, mental retardation, or alcoholism is frequently involved.

BESTIALITY

Kinsey, Pomeroy, and Martin (1948) found that 8% of the male population had had sexual experience with animals. Among boys raised on farms, 77% obtained orgasm through animal contact sometime after the onset of adolescence. There is a dearth of research literature on the topic.

FROTTAGE

Frottage consists of obtaining sexual pleasure from rubbing or pressing against another person, usually in a crowded place. Little is known about the type of men who engage in this behavior or its etiology.

Obscene Phone Calls

Obscene phone calls constitute one of the more common sex crimes. This can be grasped by the number of women who are victimized in their lifetime. The survey of Herold, Mantle, and Zematis (1979) found that 61% of the female Canadian college students they surveyed had received obscene phone calls.

In what may be the only research based on a study of obscene phone callers, Freund, Sher, and Hucker (1983) found that of 86 men initially presenting with exhibitionism 11 were later found to also be obscene phone callers. The authors conceptualized obscene phone calls as logically related to exhibitionism, voyeurism, and toucherism, which they referred to collectively as the "courtship disorders" which they differentiated from their other two major categories, rape and pedophilia.

Rape

The consensus of opinion in the clinical literature is that rapists have more than sexual motivation. Aggressive and power motives are two that are stressed most often. The aggression involved is vividly demonstrated by the fact that the rape victim is frequently beaten and humiliated in various ways such as being subjected to anal intercourse. Among the more common physical injuries encountered in rape victims are trauma to the head and neck, extremities, external genitalia, the perineum, the urethra, the vagina, the cervix, and the uterus. The nature of these injuries can include bruises, hemorrhages, concussions, stab wounds, and fractures. To add to this unpleasant picture is the possibility of venereal disease, other sexually transmitted disease, and pregnancy.

Many rapists are said to harbor considerable hostility toward women. However, among other rapists the act can be viewed as one component in a pervasively predatory and opportunistic life-style. In general, rapists tend to be impulsive young men with low frustration tolerance. The average IQ of convicted rapists is lower than that of other penitentiary inmates, even lower than that of other violent criminals (Templer, 1977). Research indicates that about 50% of convicted rapists were under the influence of alcohol at the time of the rape. Rape occurs more frequently in the summer and less frequently in the winter (Michael & Zumpe, 1983). Needless to say, rape has a devastating effect upon the victim, who frequently suffers from depression, anxiety, marital stress, and sexual adjustment problems.

Although most persons dichotomize men into a small minority of rapists and a vast majority of nonrapists, evidence indicates that a broad spectrum of sexually coercive behavior is quite pervasive. In one study of 201 college men, 43% had held a woman's hand, 53% had kissed a woman, and 37% had touched a woman's genital area against her will. The degree of sexually coercive behavior was related to personality measures of irresponsibility, lack of a social conscience, and a value orientation legitimizing aggression, particularly against women (Rapaport & Burkhart, 1984).

Although men sometimes joke about being raped by women, such cases have been reported, although they are very uncommon (Sarrel & Masters, 1982). Erection and ejaculation apparently can occur even in emotional states such as fear. It should be noted that a parallel situation exists when women are raped that it is not uncommon for them to lubricate and not rare for them to have orgasms even though they viewed the event as traumatic. We can will our sexual behavior more than we can will our sexual physiology. The raped men later experienced emotional and sexual difficulties.

It is much more common for males to be raped by other males than by females. Groth and Burgess (1980) reported upon 22 cases of such rape. The victims at the time of the attack were engaging in some type of solitary activity, such as hitchhiking (8 of the 22 cases), swimming, or hiking. The victims had a mean of 17½ years of age. The act most commonly performed was anal intercourse. Most of the offenders had a prior conviction for some sort of sexual assault. Their ascribed motivation included conquest and control, revenge and humiliation, and sadism and degradation. The victims felt the experience to be emotionally very upsetting with a long-lasting impact upon their lives. It is of interest to note that the youthfulness of the victims is congruent with the common observation in prisons and jails that smooth-skinned adolescents are especially vulnerable to sexual assault. Goyer and Eddleman (1984) reported on 13 Navy and Marine Corps men who were raped either on a ship or on shore. They ranged from 18 to 31 years of age, with a mean age of 21.2 years. Two of the victims had been previously assaulted. Eleven of the victims were heterosexual, one bisexual, and one heterosexual before but homosexual after the assault. The men reported experiencing depression, anxiety, fear, anger, disturbances in peer relationships, and sexual maladjustment.

Some of the dimensions of rape of females by other females were described in 20 cases in Massachusetts (Cochran & Drucker, 1984). For the 17 cases for which gender was available, 13 of the victims were female and 4 male. The rapists were from 13 to 32 years of age; 11 (55%) were from 17 to 24 years old. Eleven of the rapists were single, four were married, two were divorced or separated, and three were of unknown marital status. The victims tended to be somewhat younger. Eight were below the age of 17, five were from 17 to 24, and one was between 25 and 32. In five cases the victim was a stranger, in six cases an acquaintance, in one case a friend, in one case a family member, and in seven cases not specified. The limited number of cases and the limited information regarding these cases prohibit confident generalization. However, at least in the small-scale study in Massachusetts, the typical case is that of one young woman raping another young woman.

PROSTITUTION

Although prostitution is not ordinarily classified as a deviation, it is placed in this chapter because it is illegal and frequently associated with a maladaptive and injurious life-style and patterns of behavior. Many prostitutes are drug addicts. Some are beaten and financially taken advantage of by their "pimps." Some are beaten, robbed or killed, by their "tricks" (customers). Some of the tricks are beaten, robbed, and killed.

Most prostitutes come from low socioeconomic backgrounds and disorganized family life. A disproportionate number of them experienced incest or other molestation. Davis (1971) provided a detailed study of the background of 30 prostitutes. They had sexual intercourse for the first time from 7 to 18 years of age, with a mean of 13.6 years. With two of the women first intercourse was by rape at age 7 and age 9. Three other women reported sexual intercourse with brothers, fathers, or stepfathers before the age of 13. Nineteen of the 30 women had sexual intercourse by the age of 13. Twenty-eight of the 30 women did not like their first sexual experience and did it to please the male and/or because of social conformity. Great family instability was present for 24 of the 30 women. This instability included drunkenness, violence, and absentee parents. Conditions within the family were brought to the attention of the authorities. Eighteen of the 30 women spent 1 year or more under the age of 12 living away from home, such as in foster homes or with relatives. Twenty-eight of the women reported that they were regarded as "troublemakers" or "slow learners" or in some way not living up to adult expectations. Twenty-three of the women reported having been sentenced to a juvenile home or training school as adolescents for truancy, incorrigibility, or sex delinquency. These women found that social pressure encouraged their promiscuity. There was a "drift" or "slide" from prostitution that began at a mean of 17.3 years of age. The experience of a pick-up was often exciting, and the prostitution enhanced their peer status in addition to being lucrative.

In another study it was found that adolescent prostitutes with a mean age of 17 years displayed more depression, anxiety, deviant life-style, and alienation, less favorable self-concept, and more negative attitude toward men, than did nonprostitute delinquent girl control subjects and normal girl control subjects. The authors also found that 28 (65%) of the 43 prostitutes were in special education classes, and they suggested that this represented subnormal intelligence, neuropsychological deficit, cultural disadvantage, or some combination of these factors (Gibson-Ainyette, Templer, Brown, & Veaco, 1988).

DIGRESSION TO ADOLESCENT SEX OFFENDERS

There is increasing evidence in recent years that an appreciable proportion of sex offenders are adolescents (Davis & Leitenberg, 1987). About 20% of all rapes and about 30% to 50% of child sexual abuse involve adolescent offender. Furthermore, about 50% of adult offenders report that their first crime occurred during adolescence. The cut-off age for determining adolescence was 18 or 19 in most of these studies.

The victim in these offenses tends to be a younger child. In one study 62% of the victims were under the age of 12, and 44% were under the age of 7 (Fehrenbach, Smith, Monastersky, & Deisher, 1986). In another report, 46% of the victims were under the age of 10; 19%, from 10 to 19, and 25%, 20 years old or older (Deisher, Wenet, Paperny, Clark, & Fehrenbach, 1982). Most studies show that roughly 80% of the victims are female. The literature indicates that in a distinct majority of the cases the victim and offender knew each other, with the relationship ordinarily being that of friend, acquaintance, or relative. Adolescent sex offenders are less likely to use weapons than are adult offenders. Intoxication is also less likely than in adult offenders. The literature generally indicates that about 95% of the offenders are male. A disproportionate number of offenders have a low IQ and a history of learning difficulties, repeating a grade, and school expulsion. Many of the offenders themselves were victimized at an earlier age.

TREATMENT OF THE PARAPHILIAS

There is some evidence that the administration of an androgen-depleting steroid, medroxyprogesterone acetate, is helpful in a variety of male sex offenders (Money et al., 1975) Its efficacy is probably a function of a reduction in sex drive. Some men so treated are able to be maintained in the community, leading normal lives, including their sex lives, although at a reduced frequency of intercourse. The hormonal effects are not permanent, and titration to the desired hormonal and sex drive appears possible.

Castration as a punishment and treatment for sex offenders has been carried out in Germany, Norway, Finland, Estonia, Iceland, Latvia, Sweden, Switzerland, the Netherlands, and Greenland. It is of interest that castration tends to be a phenomenon of Protestant, especially Lutheran, rather than Catholic countries. Heim and Hursch (1979) reviewed the literature on recidivism of sex offenders in European countries after castration and inferred considerable reduction in recidivism rates. Reported side effects included reduced sex drive in regard to normal in addition to paraphilic sex, depression, the feeling of having been maimed, loss of facial and body hair, weight loss, a more female fat distribution, hot flashes, softer skin and a more effeminate face, and lessened muscularity. On the other hand, a substantial percentage of the castrated men cited primarily positive changes that included feeling calmer.

Behavioral techniques have been employed for a variety of sexual deviations. Aversive conditioning is frequently used, electric shock being the aversive stimulus most often used (e.g., paired with a picture of a naked child presented to a pedophile). In aversion relief therapy, an aversive stimulus is presented while the patient is doing or thinking about the activity to be eliminated, with the cessation of the problem behavior or thought coinciding with the cessation of the aversive presentation. An example is the application of electric shock to a pedophile with the presentation of a slide of a naked little girl. The shock terminates when the slide terminates. The termination may coincide with the slide of a naked adult female. Shame aversion therapy has been used with exhibitionism, pedophilia, transvestism, and obscene phone calls.

TRANSSEXUALISM

Transsexualism is ordinarily classified as a gender identity disorder rather than a paraphilia. Transsexuals feel an incongruity between their anatomical sex and their psychological orientation, a dilemma that they often describe as being trapped in the wrong body. Prevalence has been estimated as 1 in 100,000 for male transsexuals and 1 in 130,000 for female transsexuals (Pauly, 1974). However, there is a large preponderance of male transsexuals seeking treatment. Dressing in the clothing of the opposite sex is common in transsexuals, although most transvestites are not transsexuals. Most authorities regard transsexualism and transvestitism as two separate syndromes.

Black female transsexuals (those women desiring to be men) seem to be underrepresented. However, there is some evidence to suggest that those few black female transsexuals frequently have a serious psychological disturbance such as schizophrenia (Lothstein & Roback, 1984). Lothstein and Roback suggested that the matrifocal aspect of black subculture permits appropriate levels of assertiveness of females without compromising their femininity, so black females may be "inoculated" against severe gender identity pathology. They suggested that therefore serious psychopathology such as schizophrenia ordinarily must be present to produce black female transsexuality.

Hoenig and Kenna (1979) found that 48% of a group of transsexuals clearly had EEG abnormalities, and another 24% had borderline abnormalities. A disproportionate number of abnormalities were in the temporal lobes. The authors related their findings to a great amount of clinical literature that reports temporal lobe abnormalities in a variety of sexual deviations. Nevertheless, the significance of these EEG abnormalities is unclear, especially since they apparently do not occur in all transsexuals.

Research indicates that transsexuals tend to be less well adjusted than the average person, with depression, anxiety, and low self-esteem being common (Derogatis, Meyer, & Vazquez, 1978). Verschoer and Poortinga (1988) compared the past and present psychosocial characteristics of 68 male and 55 female Dutch transsexuals in hormonal treatment. The females more frequently had displayed cross-gender behavior during childhood than did the males. In contrast to the males, females more often married a person of their anatomical sex. They were also found more likely to have a stable relationship with a person of their anatomical sex. The females reported having had a better relationship in their parental home. The difference between the 21% of males and the 33% of females who had been under psychiatric care was not statistically significant. Nineteen percent of both the males and females had attempted suicide at least once, thus supporting other research evidence that transsexuals tend to be less happy than nontranssexuals.

There is a divergence of opinion as to what percentage of transsexuals should have sex reassignment surgery. However, it is generally agreed that this radical procedure should be done only after counseling and thorough exploration of the personality of the person seeking surgery. In general, the operation is more likely to be indicated if the candidate conforms to the classic description of the transsexual. When other conditions such as schizophrenia are present, clinicians are less likely to recommend surgery. It is recommended that surgery be postponed until a trial period of living in a cross-gender role has been completed. During this period the transsexual assumes the dress of the opposite sex. The transsexual man is placed on estrogens, which result in breast growth, softer skin texture, diminished muscular strength, feminine distribution of subcutaneous fat, and diminished body hair. The transsexual women receive testosterone injections, which increase facial and body hair, deepen the voice, suppress menstruation, and enlarge the clitoris.

The male transsexual has his penis and testicles removed, and an artificial vagina is constructed. The female transsexual undergoes a bilateral mastectomy and often a hysterectomy and ovariectomy as well. Attempts have been made to construct an artificial penis, but these have not been very successful.

A number of studies have investigated the adjustment and mental health changes of transsexuals who underwent sex-reassignment surgery (Hunt & Hampson, 1980). In general most subjects showed a modest improvement in subjective state, interpersonal functioning, sexual satisfaction, and adjustment to society. The majority of the subjects were glad they had the surgery. However, for those who are not pleased there can be no turning back.

SEXUAL DYSFUNCTION

Just as Kinsey and associates were pioneers in regard to investigating sexual behavior through interviewing, Masters and Johnson (1970) were pioneers in investigation through direct observation. They started a laboratory in St. Louis in 1954 for the purpose of determining physiological and behavioral functioning. Much of the material in this section is based on their observations.

HYPOACTIVE SEXUAL DESIRE

The incidence of low sex drive or desire is difficult to specify. First of all, different persons have different opinions about how low desire has to be for classification as abnormal. Also, optimal sex desire is relative to that of one's partner. Furthermore, one may have very low sex desire with respect to one partner or situation but not in regard to another partner or situation. Nevertheless, various authors have provided estimates ranging from 1% to 38% in males and from 31% to 49% in females (Seagraves & Seagraves, 1991). The etiology is often not known. However, since we do know that persons in poor health tend to have low sexual interest, medical problems should be ruled out. It also should be borne in mind that low sexual interest is often a symptom of depression. When such is the case, treatment of the depression may bring about an increase in sexual desire.

PREMATURE EJACULATION

Premature ejaculation is one of the most common sources of sexual distress for heterosexual couples. Prevalence of premature ejaculation in general population males range as high as 38% (Spector & Carey, 1990). It is especially common in young males. Kinsey found an inverse relationship between age and speed of ejaculation. Although Kinsey regarded fast ejaculation as physiologically superior, the sex partner becomes most frustrated when when the man consistently ejaculates before she has an orgasm. One study found that premature ejaculators and normal control men did not differ in rate of sexual arousal. However, premature ejaculators ejaculated at a lower level of sexual arousal. Also, the premature ejaculators engaged in sexual intercourse less frequently. An inverse relationship between speed of ejaculation and period of abstinence from intercourse was found (Spiess, Geer, & O'Donohue, 1984). Thus, more frequent intercourse may be helpful for some couples.

Godpodinoff (1989) distinguished between primary and secondary premature ejaculation. In his study the men with primary premature ejaculation had had such from the beginning of their sex lives. They reported fear of failure, limitation of sexual excitement by such measures as use of multiple condoms or local anaesthetic, younger age (38.3), longer interval from onset to medical consultation (17.0 years), and no demonstrable organic cause. The men with secondary premature ejaculation had a mean age of 51.6 years, an onset that typically began after some degree of erectile difficulty, a duration of only 14 months, and either a relationship problem or an organic problem such as cardiovascular disease or alcoholism. Godpodinoff maintained that secondary premature ejaculation patients should be referred either for psychotherapy or for treatment for their medical condition. He stated that primary ejaculation patients are best treated with behavioral techniques.

Masters and Johnson's treatment includes the "squeeze" technique, in which control is taught by having the female partner squeeze the man's penis as the point of ejaculation is approaching in order to postpone the process.

IMPOTENCE

In impotence the male is unable to obtain an erection. Impotence can be classified as primary or secondary. In primary impotence the man has never been able to obtain an erection. In secondary impotence, there is a history of having been potent. Secondary impotence is much more common. A man could be impotent in one circumstance or with one sex partner but potent under other conditions. Many men are occasionally unable to perform, for examples, when anxious or under the influence of alcohol; and such occasional failure is not to be labeled impotence. Impotence is frequently of psychological origin. In some cases this is thought to be associated with deep-seated attitudes toward oneself, toward sex, toward women, or toward one's sex partner. In other cases, the impotence can be explained in terms of principles of learning. A common occurrence is for a man to be impotent on one occasion because of stressful circumstances and, because of an association of anxiety with the approach of sex, is consequently unable to perform. Clinical impression is that impotent men have considerable anxiety, and research has demonstrated that men so afflicted score much higher on psychological tests of anxiety than do control men (Munjack, Oziel, Kanno, Whipple, & Leonard, 1981). However, it is not clear whether high anxiety is a cause or an effect or both.

The Masters and Johnson therapeutic procedure for psychogenic impotence is to instruct the patient and his partner to caress but to have no expectation of intercourse, which should not be attempted until an unquestionably strong state of readiness is obtained. The set of not expecting intercourse reduces the anxiety and thereby facilitates an erection.

An estimated 10% or 15% of impotence is primarily a function of biological causes (Kolodny, Masters, & Johnson, 1979). Among the more numerous physical conditions that produce impotence are old age, diabetes, and the effects of alcoholism. The common occurrence of impotence in diabetics is due to the decreased peripheral circulation. The most common dysfunctions encountered in male diabetics are erectile dysfunction and reduced libido. Diabetic women do not appear to experience a significant a degree of sexual dysfunction.

Some studies show that impotent men have lower testosterone level than do normal men, and other studies show no difference (Schwartz, Kolodny, & Masters, 1980). A reasonable inference is that although testosterone level can sometimes be a factor, insufficient testosterone is not a cause of impotence in the preponderance of affected men. Testosterone therapy appears to be effective in increasing sexual interest, but it seems to have little or no effect on erectile functioning (O'Carroll & Bancroft, 1984).

Penile prostheses are sometimes employed when impotence does not respond to other treatments. The candidates for such are usually men with irreversible medical causes such as diabetes. There are two types of devices. In one a fixed rod is inserted into the penis. A problem here is that the penis is always semierect. The firmness is less than optimal for sexual intercourse. And the rod-inserted penis is too firm for comfort, in addition to causing social embarrassment. In the alternative procedure an inflatable prosthetic device is inserted and inflation is carried out when intercourse is desired. The penis is flaccid when not inflated. The surgery for this prosthesis is somewhat more complicated. However, patients seem more satisfied with the results than when a stiff rod is implanted. Nevertheless, 40% of patients receiving the inflatable implant experience some malfunction after several years so as to require corrective surgery (Tiefer, Moss, & Melman, 1991).

A quite recent and promising development is that of intracavernous (within the inflatable spaces of the penis that become filled with blood during erection) injections. In one study 11 impotent men obtained an erection upon the injection of phenoxybenzamine or papaverine but did not obtain an erection after saline injection (the control procedure). The mechanisms of the drug action are not clear, but it has been suggested to be a function of the drugs' adrenergic blocking and/or smooth muscle relaxant actions. It has been found that impotent men can give themselves injections. This technique seems especially helpful for men whose impotence is a function of their medical condition and therefore not expected to respond to psychologically oriented interventions (Brindley, 1983).

With vasoconstrictor injection an erection is usually evident within 15 minutes and lasts from 1 to 4 hours. One of the more common side effects was priapism, the failure of the erection to subside. However, with a perfection of treatment techniques this problem is less common than when it was first introduced. One study treated 82 consecutively admitted patients, most of whom reported great success both in terms of sexual functioning and in terms of their marital and general psychological satisfaction. The most common side effects were bruising (26%), nodule development (21%), abnormal liver function tests (7%), and pain (5%). However, there was a 35% dropout rate (Althof et al., 1987). In a 1-year follow-up study with 42 men and their 26 partners, 84% of the injections were producing satisfactory erections. Treatment resulted in improvement in quality of erection, sexual satisfaction, frequency of intercourse, and coital orgasm (Althof et al., 1991). The dropout rate was 59%. The more common side effects were fibrotic nodules (26%), abnormal liver function values (30%), and bruising (19%).

Althof et al., (1989) addressed the logical question: if intracavernosal injection is so good for impotence, why do almost half of the men drop out of treatment? There appear to be a number of reasons, among them the pain and side effects. Other reasons include aversion to injection and the fact that there is a less than 100% success rate. It is obvious that one's sex life has less of a spontaneous nature and more of a mechanical or treatment emphasis for both the patients and their partners. Most of the dropouts occurred during the early treatment period. Althof et al. recommended that clinicians devote extra care in this very important phase of the treatment. They maintained that it is important that the patient experience success at this time and that the clinician should give ample dosage rather than being too preoccupied with the possibility of side effects. And since a substantial percentage of the patients drop out even before the dosing begins, it is very important that adequate explanation and reassurance be given.

Perhaps more promising than all of the mechanical and injection devices and procedures are the more recently developed vacuum constriction instruments for producing an "assisted erection." These are relatively safe, noninvasive, and economical (Witherington, 1991). In one study, 91% of the men and 73% of their female partners rated the treatment as either "moderately satisfying" or "extremely satisfying" (Villeneuve, Corcos, & Carmel, 1991). In another study at the time of 1-year follow-up, 87% of the men reported obtaining erection sufficient for intercourse, and the dropout rate was only 20% (Turner et al., 1991).

INHIBITED MALE ORGASM

Inhibited male orgasm is the opposite of premature ejaculation. That is, the man is unable to ejaculate or able to do so only after an inordinate time. It is a much less frequent complaint than premature ejaculation, except in elderly men. In fact, in many elderly men it should be regarded as a fact of life. They and their wives should be counseled to focus upon the enjoyment of the sex act and not concern themselves with whether or not ejaculation occurs. In youthful and middle-aged men, inhibited male orgasm is often regarded as resulting from various psychic factors that have apparently not been clearly defined by research. Sometimes the cause can be a problem such as excessive alcohol or drug use or physical disturbances such as prostate disorder, injury and degenerative disease of the spinal cord, sympathetic ganglia damage, or lesions of the genitourinary system. A number of drugs can produce inhibited male orgasm. The antipsychotic drugs are among the most notable in this regard, with thioridazine (Mellaril®) perhaps being the biggest offender. Retarded ejaculation is a fairly common side effect of the tricyclic antidepressants. The MAO inhibitor antidepressants also have been reported to cause such. A number of antihypertensive drugs have caused retarded ejaculation. Heroin and methadone can retard or delay ejaculation. The exact physiological mechanisms that bring about retarded ejaculation are not known, but different mechanisms for the various categories of drugs have been suggested. Anticholinergic effects are a frequently advanced explanation. It is of interest to note than thioridazine has been occasionally used for the treatment of premature ejaculation.

In the treatment of inhibited male orgasm, Masters and Johnson first have the wife manually stimulate the husband to ejaculation. After ejaculation has been successfully accomplished, the treatment moves into the state where the wife continues to manually stimulate the male but inserts his penis into her vagina shortly before ejaculation. The period of time from intromission to ejaculation is gradually extended to the point where normal intercourse can be achieved without the wife's manual stimulation.

INHIBITED FEMALE ORGASM

Inhibited female orgasm is the term for the older term *frigidity*, a word with scornful connotations toward the affected woman, that fortunately is no longer used. Infrequent orgasm or complete inability to experience such is the most common dysfunctioning of females. Various surveys have determined that over 5% of the female population is nonorgasmic. The etiology is ordinarily considered psychological, with negative attitudes and unfortunate experience conjectured as being the culprits. Masters and Johnson begin the treatment of inhibited female orgasm with what they call "sensate focus." That is, the husband and wife explore and stimulate her body to discover the touches and the touched areas that provide pleasure. The greater the relaxation and enjoyment in a situation with no demands, the more sex become less performance-oriented. Female orgasm is more likely to take place when no attempt is made to force it or to think in terms of success or failure.

VAGINISMUS

Vaginismus is the spastic contraction of the vaginal opening before attempted penetration so that intercourse is impossible or almost impossible. Such occurs in women fearful of sex, sometimes because of transmitted parental or religious attitudes, sometimes because of traumatic experiences such as rape.

O'Sullivan (1979) reported that 23 Irish women with vaginismus constituted 42% of women referred to him for sexual dysfunctioning during the period under consideration. Seventy percent of women with vaginismus, in contrast to 18% of women with other sexual dysfunctions, recalled their father as a threatening figure, capable of generating fear throughout their early years. O'Sullivan maintained that vaginismus results from early experience with a threatening and sometimes physically abusive father and that this is responsible for the acute anxiety these women experience when vaginal penetration is attempted with their husbands.

The first step used by Masters and Johnson in the treatment of vaginismus is to demonstrate its existence and nature to the wife and to the husband, who is also present. First the gynecologist and then the husband attempts to insert a finger into the vagina and observe the prohibitive contraction of the vagina. Then a small dilator is inserted into the woman's vagina so that she can experience vaginal penetration with minimal discomfort. Then, in a gradual fashion, increasingly larger dilators are employed so that anxiety and vaginal contraction are no longer associated with penetration. When the woman is able to feel comfortable about penetration, sexual intercourse is resumed.

DYSPAREUNIA

Dyspareunia means painful coitus. Such could result from physical causes such as infection or structural defect. In regard to the former, the infection could be in the vagina, cervix, uterus, ovaries, fallopian tubes, or rectum. A structural defect causing pain could involve bruised segments of the hymenal ring or other problems in the vaginal outlet, the clitoris, or the vaginal barrel; traumatic laceration of uterine support; surgical sequelae; cancer; or the aging process. However, some of the same attitude, information, and experience factors that contribute to vaginismus and organic dysfunctioning can produce painful coitus. And if a woman is not satisfactorily aroused to produce adequate vaginal lubrication, pain is likely to result. Although we tend to think of dyspareunia as an exclusively female problem, it occasionally occurs in men as a result of irritation, injury, or anatomical anomaly. The treatment of dyspareunia, in both females and males, is the treatment of its cause.

HOMOSEXUAL SEXUAL DYSFUNCTIONING

Paff (1985) did a survey of 10 psychotherapists in southern California regarding the sexual problems of their homosexual patients and divided these problems into three types: desire phase disorder, arousal phase disorder, and orgasm phase disorder. The number of gay men who had these categories of disorders were 5%, 23%, and 30%, respectively. Forty-two percent of the gay men reported no disorder. At least 80% of the desire phase problems involved penetrating or being penetrated anally. The genesis of desire problems often involved negative attitudes toward their own homosexuality, negative attitudes toward the assumption of a feminine role, the pain involved in anal intercourse, and difficulty in penetrating or being penetrated. Paff maintained that primary impotence, that is, never having obtained an erection, is almost nonexistent among gay men. Erectile difficulty is common in gay men, and Paff contended that this is often based upon attitudes toward sex and homosexuality. Premature ejaculation is apparently much less common than with heterosexual men. Retarded ejaculation is much more common in gay men. It was the opinion of Paff that this should be treated as it is with heterosexual men, that is, encouraging relaxation and focusing on the pleasure rather than attempting to force ejaculation to occur. Less appears in the literature about sexual dysfunctioning in lesbians.

FOLLOW-UP ASSESSMENT OF TREATMENT EFFICACY

Follow-up after treatment for sexual dysfunction usually shows a mixture of sustained success, virtual failure, and success that is not sustained. Masters and Johnson and many other sex therapists extensively prescribe masturbation for nonorgasmic women, with the assumption that ability to achieve orgasm by masturbation is transferred to the sexual intercourse situation. It is very common for women to be given a regimen of masturbatory exercises to do at home, and at times this is in conjunction with all-women group therapy directed toward the eventual goal of coital orgasm. Most of the success rates reported are quite encouraging. Wallace and Barbach (1974) reported that 87% of the women studied were successful in obtaining orgasm with their sex partners. Ersner-Hershfield and Kopel (1979) reported an 82% success rate. However, Wakefield (1987) suggested that these rates could be spuriously inflated by such procedures as including women who only rarely could achieve orgasm as being nonorgasmic before treatment. Wakefield reanalyzed the Ersner-Hershfield and Kopel data in a more stringent fashion and concluded that only 47%, instead of 87%, were no longer nonorgasmic with their sex partners; only 20% if orgasm by vibrator was discounted.

CHROMOSOMAL AND HORMONAL ABNORMALITIES

Most of the paraphilias and sexual dysfunctions that we have considered are ordinarily regarded as primarily psychogenic. However, there are developmental abnormalities that are entirely of biologic origin, although it is apparent that these can result in both deficient sexual functioning and psychosocial maladjustment.

At conception the X or Y chromosome carried by the sperm cell is added to the X chromosome within the ovum to determine the genetic sex of the fetus. Since there are 44 other chromosomes a 46 XY chromosome pattern is seen in the normal male and a 46 XX pattern in the normal female. At 6 weeks gestation the male and female are anatomically indistinguishable. In a normal male fetus there will be sufficient testosterone for the development of male anatomy. In the normal female there is a low level of testosterone, so female anatomy is developed. In addition to the normal differentiation of sexual anatomy, there is a differential effect upon the brain and the pituitary gland, which affects both development and behavior. In abnormalities, there is a breakdown in this developmental process of chromosomal and hormonal development.

In Klinefelter's syndrome there is an extra X chromosome that results in a 47 XXY pattern. Such occurs in 1 of every 500 male births. Childhood sexual and other development appear normal although there is an above-average incidence of mental retardation. In adolescence small undeveloped testes, infertility, and low sex drive are present. There is an above-average representation of Klinefelter's syndrome in men in prisons and psychiatric hospitals. However, such men are ordinarily passive and lacking in ambition but with minor proclivity to sudden outbursts of aggression. Testosterone replacement therapy produces more normal secondary sexual characteristics, sex drive, and behavior.

Turner's Syndrome

In Turner's syndrome there is a single X chromosome and no Y chromosome. Such occurs in 1 of every 2,500 female births. These women are typically short and do not evidence normal sexual development at puberty. Some development does occur if estrogen is administred. Women with Turner's syndrome are sterile.

ADRENOGENITAL SYNDROME

In cases of insufficient cortisol in the adrenal cortex there is a buildup of other adrenal hormones that are usually masculinizing. If this happens during fetal development of genetic females, the effect can vary from mild clitoral hypertrophy to the formation of apparent male genitals. Needless to say, this may lead to maladjustment if the child is raised as the "wrong sex," the "right sex," or with uncertainty and confusion. Fortunately, cortisone can partially reverse this syndrome. The limited research on treated andrenogenital females shows an above-average rate of homosexual orientation. The andrenogenital syndrome in males leads to precocious puberty, sometimes in the preschool years, with adult genital stature and secondary sexual characteristics. Hormone therapy at an early age can prevent this syndrome.

TESTICULAR FEMINIZATION SYNDROME

Testicular feminization syndrome is a rare condition in which the genetic male fetus has normal testosterone production but the normal male genitals are not produced because the fetal tissue is insensitive to the testosterone. The infant, child, and adult strongly resemble normal females' as do the interests and sex drives of these male pseudohermaphrodites. They often have undescended testes and are ordinarily reared as girls.

Money and Normal (1987) found that of 24 male hermaphrodites assigned as and reared as males, at adulthood 20 were neither homosexual nor bisexual nor obtaining sex reassignment to live as females. This was in spite or neonatal ambivalence in assigning the sex, cosmetic inadequacy in masculine genital appearance, sitting posture for urination, and feminizing ($N = 9$) instead of virilizing ($N = 11$) at puberty. Money and Normal discussed these findings in terms of regarding chromosomes and testes as of great importance both by nature and by society. However, apparently all 20 of these men were not happy. Some joined the ranks of the suicidal; others suffered depression or drug addiction; some became dependent poor.

HIGH RISK PERSONS FOR DELUSIONAL DISORDERS

Middle Aged Persons

Immigrants

Lower Socioeconomic Status Persons

Africans

FIFTEEN

Delusional (Paranoid) Disorders

In delusional disorder the patient has a delusion or delusions but does not have the looseness of associations, hallucinations, bizarre behavior, or bizarre ideas of the schizophrenic. Ordinarily, the delusion is of a paranoid nature. At times the paranoid delusion may appear as unrealistic as the delusions of paranoid schizophrenics. In milder forms of paranoia, the patient may seek to protect himself by means of retaliation, such as filing a grievance or complaint or spreading gossip or rumors. While paranoia has been the primary focus in discussion of delusional disorder, other types of content may occur. In the erotomania type, the patient has the delusion that he or she is loved by a very famous or important person. In the grandiose type, there is the delusion of great talent or religious or political conversion or great scientific discovery. In the jealous type, there is the delusion that one's spouse or lover is unfaithful. In the somatic type, there is the delusion of some sort of medical disorder or defective or deformed body part.

Although Emil Kraepelin focused most of his writing on nomenclature on schizophrenia and bipolar illness, he contended that there is a third so-called functional psychosis called paranoia. A number of other diagnostic labels have been given to this condition over the years, including paranoid disorder, paranoid state, paranoid condition, paranoid reaction, paranoid disorder, reactive paranoid psychosis, and delusional disorder (Kendler, 1984).

Some authorities have questioned the legitimacy of a delusional disorder diagnosis, saying that it is a category of schizophrenia. However, most of the evidence indicates that this condition deserves a category of its own. In

255

delusional disorder there is ordinarily not a prominent thought disorder, no actually bizarre behavior, no hallucinations, and no marked decline in psychosocial functioning, and the age of onset is higher than in schizophrenia. It is more likely to appear in midlife. Furthermore, the rate of schizophrenia in relatives is closer to that for nonschizophrenic persons than to the rate in schizophrenia (Watt, Hall, Olley, Hunter, & Gardiner, 1980; Winokur, 1977).

Winokur (1986) found that 9 (32%) of 29 delusional disorder patients had paranoid relatives and that this was significantly higher than for the control patients who had only one (3%) paranoid relative. The paranoid manifestations included suspiciousness, jealousy, secretiveness, and delusions. The delusional patients also had significantly more paranoid relatives than did paranoid schizophrenics. Not a single one of the groups of paranoid schizophrenic relatives had a paranoid relative.

A number of different studies converge to the generalization that paranoid disorders are more common in immigrants than in indigenous psychiatric patients. Explanations have included discrimination, language barriers, disappointments in regard to the new country, and residual effects and bitter feelings about past colonial rule in their home countries (Ndetei, 1986).

There are also reasons to believe that cultural factors in the home countries could contribute to the manifested psychopathology. Table 15.1 displays the mode of injury feared as a function of cultural groups. Ndetei (1986) inferred that black immigrants (Africans, Jamaicans, other Caribbean people) had more paranoid features and were more likely to fear evil spirits, witchcraft, and magic. These findings are consistent with the previous literature. Kiev (1964) found fundamental symptoms of the acceptance of the existence of ghosts and spirits of the dead not only in West Indian immigrants in London but in normal control West Indians living in their home country. Tewfik and Okasha (1965) found the same paranoid pattern in West Indian psychiatric patients living in London and in their home country. All of the above findings are consistent with the literature indicating that in Africa there is a widespread belief in witchcraft and magic (Lambo, 1962) and that paranoid disorder is common in Africa (Lambo, 1955; Ndetei & Singh, 1982). It appears that African slaves brought belief of witchcraft and magic to the West Indies and that they were passed down from generation to generation (Ransford, 1972).

A number of different authors have reported and described delusional disorders often occurring after head injury. Sabhesan and Natarajan (1988) found that 14% of their head-injured patients and 23% of their closed injury patients manifested delusional disorders on a neurosurgical ward in India. The head-injured patients who had a history of alcohol abuse and those who had a more severe injury as defined by posttraumatic amnesia were significantly more likely to have developed delusional disorder. Sixty-five percent of the de-

TABLE 15.1   Mode of injury

Cultural(n)	Poison	Evil Spirits	Witch-craft	Magic	Electricity Radiation	FPhysical Attack	Not Speci-fied
English (94)	4	0	1	0	4	13	9
Black African (53)	9	6	4	1	0	2	12
Jamaican (137)	18	2	9	7	2	19	11
Continental European (72)	3	1	1	1	2	3	7
English speaking non-European(37)	0	0	0	0	0	2	4
Indian (90)	6	0	0	0	2	4	6
Middle Eastern (33)	0	0	1	1	2	1	2
Far Eastern (15)	0	0	0	0	1	0	2
Caribbean (62)	7	0	1	2	3	4	19
X^2 (df = 8) P	25.08 0.005	Y	Y	Y	6.64 NS	19.92 0.02	28.37 0.001

Source: *Acta Psychiatr Scand* 1985: 72: 38–39. © 1985 Munkagaard International Publishers Ltd., Copenhagen, Denmark.

lusions were of a persecutory nature; 18%, delusions of infidelity; 12%, affect-laden; and 6%, delusions of reference. Seventy-four percent of the patients developed their delusions during the period of posttraumatic amnesia and 26% following such.

There have been clinical reports and uncontrolled studies indicating that antipsychotic drugs, lithium, and tricyclic antidepressants are effective in delusional disorder (Kendler, 1984). However, it does not appear that any double-blind studies have been reported in the literature. The absence of such ideally controlled research is probably to a large extent a function of the small number of persons who receive this diagnosis.

Opjordsmoen (1988) followed up 41 Norwegian delusional disorder patients from 22 to 39 years after treatment and found fairly good outcome. The delusions had faded in 61% of the cases, were unchanged in 17%, and in another 17% were more prominent. Recovery was reported in 37% of the cases, mild defect in 32%, moderate impairment in 22%, and severe impairment in 22%. Opjordsmoen divided his delusional disorder patients into two groups: those who had precipitating factors and those who did not. The former had a much better outcome, with more employment time, more social contact, a higher percentage of children, and fewer hospitalizations since discharge.

Although the present authors regard psychosis, and certainly schizophrenia, as of basically biological origin, we are willing to concede the possibility of some delusional states as being of basically psychogenic origin. In schizophrenia there is a disturbance in the processing and sorting of information that differs in a qualitative fashion from the thinking of normal persons. However, we tend to view the delusional disorder patient as having thinking that differs from that of the normal person in degree rather than in kind. An analogy of such variance in degree of thinking can be made with that of a religious sect that believes the world is going to end on a specific day in the near future. Hundreds of millions of persons in the world believe that there will be some dramatic end of the world such as a Judgment Day. Certainly, they are not all psychotic. Different persons interpret the relevant scripture in different ways. The persons belonging to the religious sect receive reinforcement of their beliefs from fellow members and shun input from outsiders. The destruction of the earth from a nuclear war or some sort of intrusion of an extraterrestrial sort cannot be completely ruled out. Nevertheless, the members of the religious sect, most of whom are probably not psychotic in other ways, obviously had a false belief, as evidenced by the fact that the predicted last day passed and the world did not end. Perhaps a more mundane example would be that of different persons having vastly different opinions about the outcome of a football game. All of us, in arriving at our opinions and predictions, attempt to place optimal weights upon all known factors. However, we have limited knowledge of, selective attention to, and less than optimal skills in assigning probabilities to these factors and thus may assign disproportionate importance to some factors in interpreting phenomena or making predictions. This is the context we propose for the conceptualization of delusional disorders.

HIGH RISK PERSONS FOR FACTITIOUS DISORDERS

Antisocial Persons

Liars

Males

Persons in Trouble with the Law

Persons with Personality Disorder Diagnoses

Depressed Persons

Persons in Health Care Fields

SIXTEEN

Factitious Disorders

MUNCHAUSEN"S SYNDROME

Asher (1951) was an English physician who coined the term Munchausen's syndrome, which has also been called factitious disorder with physical symptoms, although the latter term is a bit broader. Baron von Munchausen was an 18th-century German adventurer, world traveler, and colorful character who was a legend for the fantastic stories that he fabricated. Asher maintained that in the Munchausen syndrome patients gave dramatic and untruthful medical histories, including apparent acute illness, that were made up of falsehoods. These patients had previously deceived physicians.

In Munchausen's syndrome, the patient fabricates physical symptoms with no apparent motive except to adopt the patient role. Some patients actually afflict physical harm on themselves such as producing abscesses by injecting saliva under their skin. Some patients exacerbate a persisting physical condition, for example, accepting a penicillin injection when they have a known history of unfavorable reaction to penicillin. There are frequently multiple hospitalizations, presentation with a dramatic flair, pathological lying, demanding attention, and noncompliance with the hospital routine.

Munchausen's disorder probably encompasses a rather heterogeneous group of persons and a rather heterogeneous group of symptoms. The distinctions have been made between prototypical Munchausen's versus nonprototypical Munchausen's, wandering versus nonwandering, and episodic versus chronic (Sutherland & Rodin, 1990). Asher (1951) posited three types, based upon somatic symptomology: the acute abdomen type, the hemorrhagic type, and the neurological type.

Overholser (1990) provided rules of thumb for differential diagnosis of factitious disorder with physical symptoms versus malingering. The factitious disorder patient is more likely to inflict actual tissue damage upon himself or herself than is the malingerer. The malingerer patient is more likely to be seen in an outpatient setting, and the factitious disorder patient is more likely to be seen on an inpatient basis. The factitious disorder patient is more likely to be discharged against medical advice. In the malingerer the problem is more likely to be transient and situational. After the malingerer has obtained his goal or has been detected, the malingering symptom or syndrome is no longer used, although it can be reused at a later date. Factitious disorder with physical symptoms is more likely to be a chronic condition. The malingerer is more likely to receive medications, but the factitious disorder patient is more likely to receive surgery. The malingerer is more likely to be agreeable and cooperative. The factitious disorder patient is more inclined to be belligerent and uncooperative. The factitious disorder patient is apparently willing to tolerate more pain.

EPIDEMIOLOGY

Although one study found that 7 of 10 Munchausen's syndrome patients were female (Sutherland & Rodin, 1990), the majority are male. This male predominance is difficult to understand in view of the facts that in most Western countries females go to physicians more often and that it is more socially acceptable for females to exhibit a sick role. Also, the overwhelming preponderance of persons with somatization disorder (hysteria) are females. And somatization disorder and Munchausen's syndrome both often involve a myriad of symptoms. The prevalence and incidence of this disorder are difficult to estimate. There are several reports of about 1% of persons arriving in medical settings warranting such a diagnosis. Other authorities say that the disorder is less common than that, and some even say that it is rare. The different estimates and opinions are probably a function of definition. The classical Munchausen presentation, with geographical wandering and extremely fantastic and absurd tall tales, is probably much less common than the more broadly conceptualized fictitious disorder with symptoms of current diagnostic nomenclature.

Sutherland and Rodin (1990) reported that three of their factitious patients were employed in health care fields—one in nursing, one in social work, and one in family counseling. They maintained that this situation is congruent with several previous reports of factitious disorder patients commonly having backgrounds in medically related fields or caring professions. This phenomenon is understandable. If one knows the symptoms, one is better able to feign the disorder. Also consistent is the accumulation of reports of a substantial number of these persons actually having a history of considerable physical illness. Often the Munchausen syndrome follows or is superimposed upon a genuine medical problem. Grunberger, Weiner, Silverman, Taylor, and Gordon (1988) found that 5 of 10 patients with factitious hypoglycemia had a history of insulin-dependent diabetes. Factitious dermatological disorders are often preceded by bona fide dermatological disorders. And factitious fever from tampering with the thermometer has followed brief febrile illness (Aduan, Fauci, Dale, Herzberg, & Wolff, 1979). In Chapter 8, "Somatoform Disorders" it is seen that in both conversion disorder and hysteria it is common for such to have been superimposed upon a confirmed medical disorder. Furthermore, dual diagnoses of Munchausen's syndrome and somatoform disorder are reported in the literature (Adrian et al., 1979). Both the factitious disorders and the somatoform disorders involve distortion of the truth regarding a medical condition. Both categories of disorder are associated with strong character disorder features.

Earle and Folks (1986) reported on a patient who was not helped by psychotherapy but was successfully treated by antidepressant drugs. One article reported nonsuppression on the dexamethasone suppression test (DST) in two Munchausen syndrome patients with major depression (Evans, Hsiao, & Nemeroff, 1984). Since such nonsuppression is classically associated with endogenous depression, the authors suggested depression in Munchausen syndrome may be more uncommon than the previous literature has implied. Evans et al. suggested that depression in Munchausen syndrome may sometimes be overlooked because the physical and psychiatric symptoms of the syndrome are so complex.

Pankratz and Lezak (1987) reported on five Munchausen syndrome patients with brain dysfunction. One was a 34-year-old woman who had right-sided weakness in association with lateralized dysfunction of cranial nerves II, VI, VII, XI, and XII. Her EEG had repeated runs of slow theta and polymorphic delta over the left posterior temporal area. The CT scan showed slowed marked enlargement (indicating atrophy) of the left lateral ventricle, which was thought to have resulted from a prior injury. Neuropsychological testing revealed visuoconceptual problems. Patient 2, who had at least 53 emergency room visits and 106 hospitalizations in a 21-year period, scored in the impaired range on visuospatial tasks. Patient 3 had had a head injury about 25 years previously, and the report described a 4-inch healed cranial scar on the left frontal area close to the coronal suture. Neuropsychological testing showed difficulty in abstract reasoning and in visuospatial organization. Patient 4 also had difficulty in visuospatial capacities and in retrieval of new learning. However, Pankratz and Lezak were apparently cautious in not inferring cause-and-effect relationships.

Asher (1951) himself suggested possible motives of persons with Munchausen's syndrome. Patients may have a desire to be the center of interest and attention. Even if they are suffering from the Walter Mitty syndrome, instead of playing the dramatic part of the surgeon, they submit to the equally dramatic role of the patient. Patients may bear a grudge against doctors and hospitals, which is satisfied by frustrating or deceiving them. Patients may be seeking drugs. Patients may also be seeking to get free board and lodgings for the night, despite the risk of investigations and treatment. Patients may even be trying to escape from the police.

Even though, by definition, factitious disorders have no apparent motive, there has been a good deal of speculation about motives. Suggested motivations of the assumption of a medically sick role have included masochism, anger toward others directed against oneself, suicidal tendencies, viewing medical personnel as comforting parent figures, and attempts to outsmart and fool the doctors (Overholser, 1990; Schoenfeld, Margolin, & Baum, 1987). Although most of the above motives have a more or less psychodynamic flavor, an operant frame of reference also seems plausible. A rat may not know why it turns left in a maze; and a pigeon may not know why it pecks a key, but both receive positive reinforcement. Perhaps methodical behavioral accounts of factitious disorders can help us understand the complex organization of stimuli and responses.

MUNCHAUSEN'S SYNDROME BY PROXY

Munchausen syndrome by proxy (MSBP) was first described by Meadow (1977). Rosenberg (1987) did an excellent job of describing this syndrome, in which children become the unwilling patients and victims of this type of aberrant adult behavior. A parent (usually the mother) will parade children to physicians with stories of varied illnesses, all factitious. The parent lies to both the physician and the child about the child's health in order to obtain extensive and often extreme forms of medical care, which are seen as malignant only after the fact. The parent may describe symptoms for which they themselves have a history. The parents find a great sense of purpose, safety, and satisfaction in helping their children obtain medical treatment for nonexistent or exaggerated problems, which the parent may have created or enhanced. These parents are usually familiar with medical terminology and hospital methods and practices, and they may be overly friendly with hospital staff. Such parents are often critical with third persons about the care the child is receiving and the fact that the problem cannot be easily diagnosed. The parent may insist that she is the "only one" for whom the child will eat, drink, or swallow medicines.

In some children, the diagnostic possibilities become rarer with time.

Despite multiple subspecialty consultations an unreserved organic diagnosis rarely is made. Doctors often think they are seeing never-before-described diseases. When symptoms and signs appear to be consistent with a particular diagnosis, the "disease" may be refractory to conventional therapy for no apparent reason.

Rosenberg (1987) did a rather exhaustive review of the literature on MSBP from 1966 to 1987 and located 117 cases. Forty-six percent of the children were male, and 45% were females; in 9% of the cases the sex was not specified. The mean time from the onset of the apparent symptoms to diagnosis was 40 months. Rosenberg made the distinction between the symptoms being "simulated" or "produced." An example that Rosenberg gave of simulation was that of a mother placing her menstrual blood in the child's urine and telling the doctor the child had been urinating blood. An example of produced illness is that of the mother placing feces in the child's intravenous line. Information on simulation or production of the symptoms was available for 72 of the 117 cases. In 25% of these 72 cases there was simulation; in 50% of the cases there was production; and in 25% of the cases there was both simulation and production. The actions of the mothers constituted child abuse by any standards. In fact, 10 (0.9%) of the victims died. Of the 107 survivors at least 8% had long-term morbidity that was defined as pain or illness that caused permanent disfigurement or permanent impairment of function. An incidental but very distressing finding is that of the 117 victims there were 10 deaths of siblings that occurred in unusual circumstances.

Rosenberg (1987) was unable to find much firm material about the perpetrators except that they were all mothers. In terms of employment, 27% of the mothers were nurses or nursing assistants. We wish to point out that, as stated above, a disproportionate number of Munchausen's syndrome patients work in health care fields. There was only one mother who was described as probably psychotic. Furthermore, in a number of reports the authors emphatically said the mother was not psychotic. Twenty-four percent had Munchausen's syndrome features themselves. Twelve of the mothers were said to have been suicidal, but for a large percentage of the mothers there was no indication one way or the other about suicidal inclinations. However, a substantial percentage of the women were said to have personality disorders, hysterical personality disorder being the one most often diagnosed. Borderline personality, narcissistic personality, and unspecified personality disorder were other diagnoses. Personality disorder diagnoses certainly seem reasonable in view of the dishonesty and antisocial behavior of these mothers. However, the reader must bear in mind that most of the citations were in pediatric or other nonpsychiatric medical journals. The psychiatric profile of the perpetrators was not a major focus of these articles. Nevertheless, our "clinical intuition" is that with such irrational and bizarre behavior a diagnosis of schizophrenia should at least be considered in some of these women.

GANSER'S SYNDROME

Ganser's syndrome, also called factitious disorder with physical symptoms, consists of feigning or intentional production of mental disorder. As is the case with Munchausen's syndrome, the only apparent motive is to assume the patient role. There is often a variety of manifested symptoms, such as auditory and visual hallucinations, memory impairment, and suicidal inclinations. Often suspicion is aroused by a far less than perfect concordance with the usual psychiatric disorders.

Ganser's syndrome will be 100 years old this decade. In 1897, Ganser described two prisoners who had brief psychotic episodes that included clouded consciousness, hallucinations, sensory changes of a hysterical sort, subsequent amnesia, and characteristic answers to questions. These answers were often *vorbeirenden* (German for "approximate answers"). As an example, if asked how many legs a horse has, the patient may say five. Foolish answers were also said by Ganser to be common in the syndrome.

Perhaps a disorder can be better understood by the various disorders involved in differential diagnosis. Difficult differential diagnosis involving Ganser's syndrome has involved consideration of dementia, malingering, schizophrenia, schizophreniform disorder, brief reactive psychosis, epilepsy, and hysteria (Carney, Chary, & Robotis, 1987).

It is common for Ganser's syndrome patients to use psychotropic or street drugs to alter their psychological state (Cosgray & Fawley, 1989). Some use psychomotor stimulants such as amphetamines, cocaine, or caffeine to produce insomnia. Some use psychedelic drugs to alter their reality appraisal and perceptual experiences. Some Ganser's syndrome patients use narcotics to produce euphoria. Alcohol or other central nervous system drugs are sometimes used to produce drowsiness.

There does not appear to be any controlled research on the efficacy of any sort of treatment for Ganser's syndrome. Cosgray and Fawley (1989) recommended confrontation and documentation in which the facts that prove patient falsification are firmly and objectively pointed out. Incidentally, the present authors say that would seem to be a logical plan in view of the fact that so many patients with character disorders are "thick-skinned." They often are better changed by confrontation and force than by kindness. It is apparent that most factitious disorder patients have strong character disorder features. However, extreme confrontation may not be indicated in very fragile personalities, such as is the case with schizophrenics and depressives. Other interventions that have been employed include insight-oriented psychotherapy, antianxiety drugs, and antipsychotic drugs.

CONCLUSION

Unfortunately, there is a paucity of research on Ganser's syndrome and Munchausen's syndrome. However, it appears that patients with factitious disorder resemble those with the personality, somatoform, and dissociative disorders insofar as they tend to be irresponsible persons who distort the truth and act out. In factitious disorder there is said to be no apparent motive. Nevertheless, the assumption of psychology is that behavior can be explained in terms of the laws of nature. At present it is best to view the factitious disorders as disorders of unknown etiology.

CONCLUSION

Throughout this book the epidemiological nature of the psychopathological syndromes has been stressed. Epidemiological facts are important if they contribute to the understanding of the syndrome and permit hypotheses about its etiology, possible treatment and even prevention.

On the basis of etiological factors, five salient generalizations can be offered.

1. Persons of lower socioeconomic status are at higher risk of developing most of the psychological disorders. This is probably a function of a number of factors such as inadequate opportunities for success in life, insufficient health care, inadequate nutrition, and maladaptive life-style. It would therefore appear that the less privileged segments of society are in need of better health care and resources and public health education so that the risk of psychological problems is reduced and so that appropriate interventions can be employed when problems do become manifest.

2. It is apparent that in the majority of psychological syndromes there is a disproportionate number of patients who have some sort of brain abnormality. We saw in Chapter 1 that brain tumors and other brain conditions can produce a wide array of psychological symptoms and can even simulate so called "functional" disorders such as schizophrenia and bipolar disorder. It would seem that brain researchers in the years ahead will provide us with a greater understanding of psychopathology. A practical consideration is that mental health clinicians should diligently investigate the possibility of brain or other medical disorders before assuming psychogenic etiology. An additional practical implication is that a modest degree of prevention of impact and chemical brain damage is possible through the prevention of motor vehicle and other accidents, malnutrition, deleterious prenatal and perinatal events, and industrial and agricultural neurotoxicity.

3. It is apparent that a number of psychological syndromes have an uneven proportion of males and females. In general, males predominate in acting out

behavior, and females are more prone to subjective distress. There are some indications that these discrepancies are being somewhat reduced as sex role expectations are becoming less disparate. We hope, however, that both unhappiness and antisocial behaviors are reduced in both sexes.

4. Many of the psychological disorders are familial, and there likely are both genetic and interpersonal etiological factors. One certainly cannot change his or her genetic endowment, but the prospective parents can at least be told the magnitude of risks, which in some disorders, such as Huntington's chorea, are very high.

5. Both research and common sense tell us that life events and circumstances can cause, precipitate, or aggravate psychological problems. Life can be difficult, people can be cruel, and the world can be harsh. There is no way to cushion ourselves from every conceivable onslaught or bit of bad luck. However, increased knowledge about the effects of life events can help in partial fortification against these effects. Hopefully, our society and other societies can launch an attack upon the social, economic, and political conditions that produce excessive stress, but such is beyond the scope of this book.

It is difficult to say whether biological (primarily psychotropic drugs) or psychologically based intervention does the most good for the greatest number of people. We maintain that it depends upon the nature of the disorder or problem. To the extent that a condition is biologically based, endogenous, serious, and pervasive and involves impaired reality appraisal, the biologically oriented treatments are better. To the extent that a condition is caused by life events, is stimulus-specific, nonpsychotic, and heavily involving interpersonal relationships, psychologically based interventions are superior. All other factors being equal, psychological interventions should be favored over biological interventions because of the potential side effects of the latter. There can, however, be no doubt that almost all psychological conditions, whether originating from primarily biological or primarily psychological factors, have both components, maintaining and aggravating the situations. We are pragmatists in that there are no categories of treatment that we prefer on a theoretical basis. We are for anything that works. We do, however, demand research evidence of efficacy.

The perspective on psychopathology proposed by the present authors is definitely not a "sugar-coated" one. It is a perspective in which much psychopathology and its persistence is heavily determined by the constrictions of one's biology. It is a perspective in which there is considerable determination by past life events that, unfortunately, like all of history, cannot be totally obliterated, either by thinking and talking about them or by attempting not to think or talk about them. It is a perspective in which all people are not created as equal but dealt different degrees of disadvantage by heredity and by environment. It is an epidemiological perspective in which one can never completely escape his or her "roots"—gender, sexual orientation, race, ethnicity, nationality, religion, and significant others. It is a perspective in which many disorders must be viewed as chronic, or long-term, or recurring, such as medical disorders like arthritis or essential hypertension. It is a perspective in which all human suffering can never be completely understood. It is a perspective in which we must do what we can with the clinical tools and procedures at our disposal while moving methodically forward in researching syndromes of psychopathology.

REFERENCES

Abramowicz, H. K., & Richardson, S. A. (1975). Epidemiology of severe mental retardation in children: Community studies. *American Journal of Mental Deficiency, 80*(1), 18–39.

Adkins, B. J., Rugle, L. J., & Taber, J. I. (1985, May). *A note on sexual addiction among compulsive gamblers.* Paper presented at the First National Conference on Gambling Behavior, National Council on Compulsive Gambling, New York.

Aduan, R. P., Fauci, A. S., Dale, D. C., Herzberg, J. H., & Wolff, S. M. (1979). Factitious fever and self-induced infection: A report of 32 cases and review of the literature. *Annals of Internal Medicine, 90*(2), 230–242.

Agras, S., Sylvester, D., & Oliveau, D. (1969). The epidemiology of common fears and phobias. *Comprehensive Psychiatry, 10*(2), 151–156.

Akhtar, S., & Brenner, I. (1979). Differential diagnosis of fugue-like states. *Journal of Clinical Psychiatry, 40*(9), 381–385.

Akiskal, H. S. (1981). Subaffective disorders: Dysthmic, cyclothymic, and bipolar II disorders in the "borderline" realm. *Psychiatric Clinics of North America, 4,* 25–46.

Akiskal, H. S., Hirschfeld, M. A., & Yerevanian, B. (1983). The relationship of personality to affective disorders. *Archives of General Psychiatry, 40,* 801–809.

Albala, A. A., Greden, J. F., Tarika, J., & Carroll, B. J. (1981). Changes in serial dexamethasone suppression tests among unipolar depressives receiving electroconvulsive treatment. *Biological Psychiatry, 16*(6), 551–560.

Allgulander, C., & Lavori, P. W. (1991). Excess mortality among 3302 patients with "pure" anxiety neurosis. *Archives of General Psychiatry, 48,* 599–602.

Althof, S. E., Althof, L. A., Turner, S. B., Risen, C. B., Bodner, D., Kursh, E. D., & Resnick, M. I. (1991). Sexual, psychological and marital impact of self-injection of papaverine and phentolamine; A long-term prosepctive study. *Journal of Sex and Marital Therapy, 17*(2), 101–112.

Althof, S., Turner, L., Levine, S., Risen, C., Bodner, D., & Resnick, M. (1987).

Intracavernosal injection in the treatment of impotence: A prospective study of sexual psychological and marital functioning. *Journal of Sex and Marital Therapy, 13,* 155–176.

Althof, S. E., Turner, L. A., Levine, S. B., Risen, C., Kursh, E., Bodner, D., & Resnick, M. (1989). Why do so many people drop out from auto-injection therapy for impotence? *Journal of Sex and Marital therapy, 15*(2), 121–129.

Altman, J., Brunner, R. L., & Bayer, S. A. (1973). The hippocampus and behavioral maturation. *Behavioral Biology, 8*(5), 557–596.

American Psychiatric Association. (1987). Diagnostic and statistical manual of mental disorders (DMS-III-R) (3rd ed., rev.). Washington, DC: Author.

American Psychiatric Association, Committee on Nomenclature and Statistics. (1968). Diagnostic and statistical manual of mental disorders. (DMS-II) (2nd ed.). Washington, DC: American Psychiatric Association.

American Psychiatric Association, Task Force on the Use of Laboratory Tests in Psychiatry. (1985). Tricyclic antidepressants—blood level measurements and clinical outcome: An APA task force report. *American Journal of Psychiatry, 142*(2), 155–185.

Amies, P. I., Gelder, M.G., & Shaw, P.M. (1983). Social phobia: A comparative clinical study. *British Journal of Psychiatry, 142,* 174–179.

Anderson, L., Dancis, J., & Alpert, M. (1978). Behavioral contingencies and self-mutilation in Lesch-Nyhan disease. *Journal of Consulting and Clinical Psychology, 46*(3), 529–536.

Andreasen, N. C., Olsen, S. A., Dennert, J. W., & Smith, M. R. (1982). Ventricular enlargement in schizophrenia: Relationship to positive and negative symptoms. *American Journal of Psychiatry, 139*(3), 297–301.

Armstrong, J. G., & Loewenstein, R. J. (1990). Characteristics of patients with multiple personality and dissociative disorders on psychological testing. *Journal of Nervous and Mental Disease, 178*(7), 448–454.

Artmann, H., Grau, H., Adelmann, M., & Schleiffer, R. (1985). Reversible and non-reversible enlargement of cerebrospinal fluid spaces in anorexia nervosa. *Neuroradiology, 27*(4), 304–312.

Asher, R. (1951). Munchausen's syndrome. *Lancet, 260,* 339–341.

Ashley, M. J., Olin, J. S., le Riche, W. H., Kornaczewski, A., Schmidt, W., & Rankin, J. G. (1976). "Continuous" and "intermittent" alcoholics: A comparison of demographic, sociological, and physical disease characteristics in relation to the pattern of drinking. *Addictive Diseases, 2*(3), 515–532.

Ayers, J., Ruff C. F., & Templer D. I. (1976). Alcoholism, cigarette smoking, coffee drinking and extraversion. *Journal of Studies on Alcohol, 37*(7), 983–985.

Ayers, J. L., Ruff, C. F., & Templer, D. I. (1979). Reported sleep: Needed minus obtained sleep, family resemblance, and age. *Perceptual and Motor Skills, 49,* 213–214.

Ayers, J. L., Templer, D. I., Ruff, C. F., & Barthlow, V. L. (1978). Trail Making

Test improvement in abstinent alcoholics. *Journal of Studies on Alcohol, 39*(9), 1627–1629.

Baekeland, F., & Lundwall, L. (1975). Dropping out of treatment: A critical review. *Psychological Bulletin, 82*(5), 738–783.

Baird, P. A., & Sadovnick, A. D. (1985). Mental retardation in over half-a-million consecutive livebirths: an epidemiological study. *American Journal of Mental Deficiency, 89*(4), 323–330.

Bakan, R., Birmingham, C. L., & Goldner, E. M. (1991). Chronicity in anorexia nervosa: Pregnancy and birth complications as risk factors. *International Journal of Eating Disorders, 10*(6), 631–645.

Baldessarini, R. J., & Davis, J. M. (1980). What is the best maintenance dose of neuroleptics in schizophrenia? *Psychiatry Research, 3*(2), 115–122.

Ball, R. A., & Clare, A. W. (1990). Symptoms and social adjustment in Jewish depressives. *British Journal of Psychiatry, 156,* 379–383.

Ball, T. S., Hendricksen, H., & Clayton, J. (1974). A special feeding technique for chronic regurgitation. *American Journal of Mental Deficiency, 78*(4), 486–493.

Ban, T. A., Lehmann, H. E., & Deutsch, M. (1977). Negative findings with megavitamins in schizophrenic patients. Preliminary report. *Communications in Psychopharmacology, 1*(2), 119–122.

Banner, C. N., & Meadows, W. M. (1983). Examination of the effectiveness of various treatment techniques for reducing tension. *British Journal of Psychology, 22*(3), 183–193.

Barlow, D. H., Abel. G. G., Blanchard, E. B., Bristow, A. R., & Young, L. D. (1977). A heterosexual skills behavior check list for males. *Behavior Therapy, 8,* 229–239.

Barlow, D. H., & Waddell, M. T. (1985). Agoraphobia. In D. H. Barlow (Ed.), *Clinical handbook of psychological disorders: A step-by-step treatment manual.* New York: Guilford Press.

Barmann, B. C., & Vitali, D. L. (1982). Facial screening to eliminate trichotillomania in developmentally disabled persons. *Behavior Therapy, 13*(5), 735–742.

Barrett, R. P., & Shapiro, E. S. (1980). Treatment of stereotyped hair-pulling with overcorrection: A case study with long term follow-up. *Journal of Behavior Therapy and Experimental Psychiatry, 11*(4), 317–320.

Barsky, A. J., Frank, C. B., Cleary, P. D., Wyshak, G., & Klerman, G. L. (1991). The relation between hypochondriasis and age. *American Journal of Psychiatry, 148*(7), 923–928.

Bateson, G., Jackson, D. D., Haley, J., & Weakland, J. (1956). Toward a theory of schizophrenia. *Behavioral Science, 1,* 251–264.

Beaumont, J. G., & Dimond, S. J. (1973). Brain disconnection and schizophrenia. *British Journal of Psychiatry, 123*(577), 661–662.

Becker, J. V., Skinner, L. J., Abel, G. G., & Cichon, J. (1986). Level of postassault sexual functioning in rape and incest victims. *Archives of Sexual behavior, 15*(1), 37–49.

Beech, H. R., Ciesielski, K. T., & Gordon, P. K. (1983). Further observations of evoked potentials in obsessional patients. *British Journal of Psychiatry, 142,* 605–609.

Beecher, H. K. (1959). Generalizations from pain of various types and diverse origins. *Science, 130,* 267–268.

Begleiter, H., & Platz, A. (1972). The effects of alcohol on the central nervous system in humans. In B. Kissin & H. Begleiter (Eds.), *The biology of alcoholism.* (pp. 308–316.). New York: Plenum Press.

Benedict, R. H. (1989). The effectiveness of cognitive remediation strategies for victims of traumatic head injury: A review of the literature. *Clinical Psychology Review, 9*(5), 605–626.

Benkelfat, C., Murphy, D. L., Zohar, J., Hill, J. L., Grover, G., & Insel, T. (1989). Clomipramine in obsessive-compulsive disorder. *Archives of General Psychiatry, 46,* 23–28.

Benson, D. F., Miller, B. L., & Signer, S. F. (1986). Dual personality associated witth epilepsy. *Archives of Neurology, 43*(5), 471–474.

Berg, R., Franzen, M., & Wedding, D. (1987). *Screening for brain impairment: A manual for mental health practice.* New York: Springer Publishing Co.

Berrington, W. P., Liddell, D. W., & Foulds, G. A. (1956). A re-evaluation of the fugue. *Journal of Mental Science, 102,* 280–286.

Besdine, R. W., Brody, J. A., & Butler, R. N. (1980). Senility reconsidered: Treatment possibilities for mental impairment in the elderly. *Journal of the American Medical Association, 244*(3), 259–263.

Bhalla, J. N., Khanna, P. K., Srivastava, J. R., Sur, B. K., & Bhalla, M. (1982). Serum zinc level in pica. *Indian Pediatrics, 20*(9), 667–670.

Bielski, R. J., & Friedel, R. O. (1976). Prediction of tricyclic antidepressant response: A critical review. *Archives of General Psychiatry, 33*(12), 1479–1489.

Bigler, E. D. (1988). Frontal lobe damage and neuropsychological assessment. *Archives of Clinical Neuropsychology, 3*(3), 279–297.

Binder, R. L. (1983). Neurologically silent brain tumors in psychiatric hospital admissions: Three cases and a review. *Journal of Clinical Psychiatry, 44,* 94–97.

Bixler, E. O., Kales, A., Soldatos, C. R., Kales, J. D., & Healey, S. (1979). Prevalence of sleep disorders in the Los Angeles metropolitan area. *American Journal of Psychiatry, 136*(10), 1257–1262.

Black, D. W. (1984). Mental changes resulting from subdural haematoma. *British Journal of Psychiatry, 145*(3), 200–203.

Blackman, S., Simone, R. V., & Thoms, D. R. (1986). Treatment of gamblers [Letter to the editor]. *Hospital and Community Psychiatry, 37*(4), 404.

Blaney, R., & McKenzie, G. (1980). The prevalence of problem drinking in Northern Ireland: A population study. *International Journal of Epidemiology, 9*(2), 159–166.

Blazer, D., George, L. K., Landerman, R., Pennybacker, M., Melville, M. L., Woodbury, M., Manton, K. G., Jordan, K., & Locke, B. (1986). Psychiatric disorders. A rural/urban comparison. *Archives of General Psychiatry, 43*(12), 1142.

Bliss, E. L. (1980). Multiple personalities: A report of 14 cases with implications for schizophrenia and hysteria. *Archives of Genral Psychiatry, 37*(12), 1388–1397.

Bliss, E. L. (1984). Spontanteous self-hypnosis in multiple personality disorder. *Psychiatric Clinics of North America, 7*(1), 135–148.

Block, A. R., Kremer, E., & Gaylor, M. (1980). Behavioral treatment of chronic pain: Variables affecting treatment efficacy. *Pain, 8*(3), 367–375.

Boehnlein, J. K., Kinzle, J. D., Ben, R., & Fleck, J. (1985). One-year follow-up study of posttraumatic stress disorder among survivors of the Cambodian concentration camps. *American Journal of Psychiatry, 138*, 601–607.

Bregman, J. D., Dykens, E., Watson, M., Ort, S. I., & Leckman, J. F. (1987). Fragile-X syndrome: Variability of phenotypic expression. *Journal of the American Academy of Child and Adolescent Psychiatry, 26*(4), 463–471.

Bridges, P. K., Goktepe, E. O., & Maratos, J. (1973). A comparative review of patients with obsessional neurosis and with depression treated by psychosurgery. *British Journal of Psychiatry, 123*(577), 663–674.

Brindley, G. (1983). Cavernosal alpha-blockade: A new technique for investigating and treating erectile impotence. *British Journal of Psychiatry, 143*, 332–337.

Brooks, D. N., & McKinlay, W. W. (1983). Personality and behavioral change after severe blunt head injury: A relative's view. *Journal of Neurology, Neurosurgery and Psychiatry, 46*(4), 336–344.

Brooks, N., Campsie, L., Symington, C., & Beattie, A. (1987). The effects of severe head injury on patient and relative within seven years of injury. *Journal of Head Trauma Rehabilitation, 2*(3), 1–13.

Brooner, R. K., Templer, D. I., Svikis, D. S., Schmidt, C., & Monopolis, S. (1990). Dimensions of alcoholism: A multivariate analysis. *Journal of Studies on Alcohol, 51*(1), 77–81.

Brown, D. R., Eaton, W. W., & Sussman, L. (1990). Racial differences in prevalence of phobic disorders. *Journal of Nervous and Mental Disease, 178*(7), 434–441.

Bruening, S. E., Davis, V. J., & Poling, A. D. (1982). Pharmacotherapy with the mentally retarded: Implications for clinical psychologists. *Clinical Psychology Review, 2*, 79–114.

Buchsbaum, M. S. (1990). Frontal lobes, basal ganglia, tenporal lobes—three sites for schizophrenia. *Schizophrenia Bulletin, 16*(3), 377–389.

Buhrich, N. (1983). The association of erotic piercing with homosexuality, sadomasochism, bondage, fetishism and tattoos. *Archives of Sexual Behavior, 12*(2), 167–171.

Buhrich, N., & Beaumont, T. (1981). Comparison of transvestism in Australia. *Archives of Sexual Behavior, 10*(3), 269–279.

Burns, T., & Crisp, A. H. (1984). Outcome of anorexia nervosa in males. *British Journal of Psychiatry, 145,* 319–325.

Butler, R. N. (1984). Senile dementia: Reversible and irreversible. *Counseling Psychologist, 12*(2), 75–79.

Canning, H., & Mayer, J. (1967). Obesity: An influence on high school performance? *American Journal of Clinical Nutrition. 20*(4), 352–354.

Carlat, D. J., & Camargo, C. A., Jr. (1991). Review of bulimia in males. *American Journal of Psychiatry, 148*(7), 831–843.

Carlini-Cotrim, B., & Carlini, E. A. (1988). The use of solvents and other drugs among children and adolescents from a low socioeconomic background: A study in Sao-Paolo, Brazil. *International Journal of The Addictions, 23*(11), 1145–1156.

Carney, M. W., Chary, T. K., & Robotis, P. (1987). Ganser syndrome and its management. *British Journal of Psychiatry, 151,* 697–700.

Carpenter, W. T., Strauss, J. S., & Bartko, J. J. (1974). Use of signs and symptoms for the identification of schizophrenic patients: 1. *Schizophrenia Bulletin, 11*(Winter), 37–49.

Castlenuovo-Tedesco, P., & Schiebel, D. (1975). Studies of superobesity: 1. Psychological characteristics of superobese patients. *International Journal of Psychiatric Medicine, 6*(4), 465–480.

Caveness, W. F., Meirowsky, A. M., Rish, B. L., Mohr, J., Dillon, J., & Weiss, G. (1979). The nature of posttraumatic epilepsy. *Journal of Neurosurgery, 50,* 545–553.

Chalkley, A. J., & Powell, G. E. (1983). The clinical description of forty-eight cases of sexual fetishism. *British Journal of Psychiatry, 142,* 292–295.

Charlesworth, B. G. (1991). *Negative emotion and clinical variables as predictors of relapse of schizophrenics residents in board and care homes.* Unpublished doctoral dissertation, California School of Professional Psychology, Fresno, CA.

Chaturvedi, S. K., & Michael, A. (1986). Chronic pain in a psychiatric clinic. *Journal of Psychosomatic Research, 30*(3), 347–354.

Chessick, R. D. (1982). Intensive psychotherapy of a borderline patient. *Archives of General Psychiatry, 39*(4), 413–419.

Ciarrocchi, J., & Richardson, R. (1989). Profile of compulsive gamblers in treatment: Update and comparisons. *Journal of Gambling Behavior, 5,* 53–65.

Clarke, A. D. B., Clark, A. M., & Reiman, S. (1958). Cognitive and social changes in the feeble-minded: Three further studies. *British Journal of Psychology, 49,* 144–157.

Clarke, P. B. S. (1991). Nicotinic receptor blockade therapy and smoking cessation. *British Journal of Addiction, 86,* 501–505.

Cleckley, H. M. (1964). *The mask of sanity: An attempt to clarify some issues about the so-called psychopathic personality.* St. Louis: C. V. Mosby.

Clementz, B. A., & Sweeney, J. A. (1990). Is eye movement dysfunction a biological marker for schizophrenia? A methodological review. *Psychological Bulletin, 108,* 77–92.

Cochrane, D., & Drucker, L. A. (1984). *Women who rape.* Boston: Massachusetts Trial Court, Office of the Commissioner of Probation.

Cohen, D., & Eisdorfer, C. (1988). Depression in family members caring for a relative with Alzheimer's disease. *Journal of the American Geriatric Society, 36*(10), 885–889.

Cohen, S., Lichtenstein, E., Prochaaska, J. O., Rossi, J. S., Gritz, E. R., Carr, C. R., Orleans, C. T., Schoenbach, V. J., Biener, L., Abrahms, D., Di-Clemente, C., Curray, S., Marlatt, G. A., Cummings, K. M., Emont, S. L., Giovino, G., & Ossip-Klein, D. (1989). Debunking myths about self-quitting. *American Psychologist, 44*(11), 1355–1365.

Condon, W. S., Ogston, W. D., & Pacoe, L. V. (1969). Three faces of Eve revisited: A study of transient microstrabismus. *Journal of Abnormal Psychology, 74*(5), 618–620.

Condy, S. R., Templer, D. I., Brown, R., & Veaco, L. (1987). Parameters of sexual contact of boys with women. *Archives of Sexual Behavior, 16*(5), 379–394.

Conrad, S., Hughes, P., Baldwin, D. C., Achenbach, K. E., & Sheehan, D. V. (1989). Cocaine use by senior medical students. *American Journal of Psychiatry, 146*(3), 382–383.

Coons, P. M. (1984). The differential diagnosis of multiple personality disorder: A comprehensive review. *Psychiatric Clinics of North America, 7*(2),51–67.

Coons, P. M. (1986). Child abuse and multiple personality disorder: Review of the literature and suggestions for treatment. *Child Abuse and Neglect, 10,* 455–462.

Coons, P. M., Bowman, E. S., & Milstein, V. (1988). Multiple personality disorder. A clinical investigation of 50 cases.*Journal of Nervous and Mental Disease, 176*(9), 519–527.

Coons, P. M., Bowman, E. S., Pellow, T. A., & Schneider, P. (1989). Post-traumatic aspects of the treatment of sexual abuse and incest. *Psychiatric Clinics of North America, 12*(2), 325–335.

Coons, P. M., & Milstein, V. (1986). Psychosexual disturbances in multiple personality: Etiology and treatment. *Journal of Clinical Psychiatry, 47*(3), 106–110.

Cooper, P., & Fairburn, C. G. (1983). Binge-eating and self-induced vomiting in the community. A preliminary study. *British Journal of Psychiatry, 142,* 139–144.

Corbett, J., & Harris, R. (1977). Progressive disintegrative psychosis of childhood. *Journal of Child Psychology and Psychiatry, 18*(3), 211–219.

Corey, D. T., Etlin, D., & Miller, P. C. (1987). A home-based pain management and rehabilitation programme: And evaluation. *Pain, 29*(2), 219–229.

Corry, J. M., & Cimbolic, P. (1985). *Drugs: Facts, alternatives, decisions.* Belmont, CA: Wadsworth Publishing Co.

Coryell, W., Endicott, J., Keller, M., Andreasen, N., Grove, W., Hirschfeld, R. M. A., & Scheftner, W. (1989). Bipolar affective disorder and high achivement: A familial association. *American Journal of Psychiatry, 146*(8), 983–988.

Cosgray, R. E., & Fawley, R. W. (1989). Could it be Ganser's syndrome? *Archives of Psychiatric Nursing, 3*(4), 241–245.

Cosgrove, J. (1986). *Changes in neuropsychological functioning associated with declining use of phencyclidines.* Unpublished doctoral dissertation, California School of Professional Psychology, Fresno, CA.

Cotler, S. B. (1971). The use of different behavioral techniques in treating a case of compulsive gambling. *Behavior Therapy, 2,* 579–584.

Covey, L. S., & Glassman, A. H. (1991). A meta-analysis of double-blind placebo-controlled trials of clonidine for smoking cessation. *British Journal of Addiction, 86,* 991–998.

Cowdry, R. W. (1987). Psychopharmacology of borderline personality disorder: A review. Symposium: The borderline patient (12987, Boston, Massachusetts). *Journal of Clinical Psychiatry., 48*(Suppl), 15-22.

Cowdry, R. W., & Gardner, D. L. (1988). Pharmacotherapy of borderline personality disorder: Alprazolam, carbamazepine, trifluoperazine and tranylcypromine. *Archives of General Psychiatry, 45*(2), 111–119.

Cowdry, R. W., Pickar, D., & Davies, R. (1985). Symptoms and EEG findings in the borderline syndrome. *International Journal of Psychiatry in Medicine, 15*(3), 210–211.

Cox, D. J., & MacMahon B. (1975). Incidence of male exhibitionism in the United States as reported by victimized female college students. *National Journal of Law and Psychiatry, 1,* 453–457.

Coyne, J. C., Kessler, R. C., Tal, M., Turnbull, J., Wortman, C. B., & Greden, J. (1987). Living with a depressed person. *Journal of Consulting and Clinical Psychology, 55*(3), 347–352.

Craighead, L. W., Stunkard, A. J., & O'Brien, R. M. (1981). Behavior therapy and pharmacotherapy for obesity. *Archives of General Psychiatry, 38*(7), 763–768.

Crowe, R. C., Pauls, D. L., Slymen, D. J., & Noyes, R. (1980). A family study of anxiety neurosis. Morbidity risk in families of patients with and without mitral valve prolapse. *Archives of General Psychiatry, 37*(1), 77–79.

Crowe, R. R. (1974). An adoption study of antisocial personality. *Archives of General Psychiatry, 31*, 785–791.

Crowe, R. R., Noyes, R., Pauls, D. L., & Slymen, D. (1983). A family study of panic disorder. *Archives of General Psychiatry, 40*(10), 1065–1069.

Crowe, R. R., Pauls, D. L., Venkatesh, A., Van Valkenberg, C., Noyes, R. J., & Martins, J. B. (1979). Exercise and anxiety neurosis: Comparison of patients with and without mitral valve prolapse. *Archives of General Psychiatry, 36*(6), 652–653.

Crowell, B. A., Blazer G. D., & Landerman, R. (1986). Psychosocial risk factors and urban/rural differences in the prevalence of major depression. *British Journal of Psychiatry, 146*, 307–314.

Culleton, R. P. (1985). *A survey of pathological gamblers in the state of Ohio..* Philadelphia: Transition Planning Associates.

Custer, R. L. (1984). Profile of the pathologic gambler. *Journal of Clinical Psychiatry, 45*(12, pt. 2), 35–38.

Custer, R. L., & Custer, L. F. (1978, December). *Characteristics of the recovering compulsive gambler: A survey of 150 members of gamblers anonymous.* Paper presented at fourth Annual Conference on Gambling, Reno, NV.

Cutler, N. R., & Post, R. M. (1982). Life course of illness in untreated manic-depressive patients. *Comprehensive Psychiatry, 23*(2), 101–114.

Dackis, C. A., Pottash, A. L. C., Gold, M. S., & Annitto, W. (1984). The dexamethasone suppression test for major depression among opiate addicts. *American Journal of Psychiatry, 141*(6), 810–811.

Dally, P. (1969). *Anorexia nervosa.* New York: Grune and Stratton.

Danford, D. E., & Huber, A. M. (1982). Pica among mentally retarded adults. *American Journal of Mental Deficiency, 87*(2), 141–146.

Davis, D. D., & Templer, D. I. (1988). Neurobehavioral functioning in children exposed to narcotics in utero. *Addictive Behaviors, 13*, 275–283.

Davis, G. E., & Leitenberg, H. (1987). Adolescent sex offenders. *Psychological Bulletin, 101*(3), 417–427.

Davis, N. J. (1971). The prostitute: Developing a deviant identity. In J. Henslin (Ed.), *Studies in the sociology of sex.* (pp. 297–324). New York: Appleton-Century-Crofts.

Davison, K. (1983). Schizophrenia-like psychoses associated with organic cerebral disorders: A review. *Psychiatric Developments, 1*, 1–34.

Davison, K., & Bagley, C. R. (1969). Schizophrenia-like psychoses assoicated with organic disorders of the central nervous system. In R. N. Herrington (Ed.), *Current problems in neuropsychiatry* (pp. 113–184.). Ashford, UK: Headley.

Day, R., Nielson, J. A., Korten, A., Ernberg, G., Dube, K. C., Gebhart, J., Jablensky, A., Leon, C., Marsella, A., Olatawura, M., [et al.]. (1987). Stressful life events preceding the acute onset of schizophrenia: A cross-national study from the World Health Organization. *Culture, Medicine and Psychiatry, 11*(2), 123–205.

Deisher, R. W., Wenet, G. A., Paperny, D. M., Clark, T. F., & Fehrenbach, P. A. (1982). Adolescent sexual offense behavior: The role of the physician. *Journal of Adolescent Health Care, 2,* 279–286.

Delgado-Escuerta, A., Mattson, R., King, L., Goldensohn, E. S., Speigel, H., Madsen, J., Crandall, P., Dreifuss, F., & Porter, R. J. (1981). The nature of aggression during epileptic seizures. *New England Journal of Medicine, 305,* 711–716.

DeLisi, L. E., Dauphinais, I. D., & Hauser, P. (1989). Gender differences in the brain: are they relevant or the pathogenesis of schizophrenia? *Comprehensive Psychiatry, 30*(3), 197–208.

Derogatis, L. R., Meyer, J. K., & Vazquez, N. (1978). A psychological profile of the transsexual: 1. The male. *Journal of Nervous and Mental Disease, 166,* 234–254.

DiLorenzo, T. M., & Ollendick, T. H. (1986) Punishment, In J. L. Matson & T. M. DiLorenzo (Eds.), *Punishment and its alternatives: A new perspective for behavior modification* (pp. 49–78). New York: Spring Publishing Co.

Division of Alcoholism. (1988). *Report on pathological gambling in New Jersey.* Trenton, NJ: Author.

Docter, R. F., Naitoh, P., & Smith, J. C. (1966). Electroencephalographic changes and vigilance behavior during experimentally induced intoxication with alcoholic subjects. *Psychosomatic Medicine, 28,* 605–615.

Dohrenwend, B. P., Levav, I., Shrout, P. E., Link, B. G., Skodol, A. E., & Martin, L. M. (1987). Life stress and psychopathology: Progress on research begun with Barbara Snell Dohrenwend. *American Journal of Community Psychology., 15* (6), 677–715.

Dolan, R. J., Mitchell, J., & Wakeling, A. (1988). Structural brain changes in patients with anorexia nervosa. *Psychological Medicine, 18*(2), 349–353.

Drew, L. R. (1968). Alcoholism as a self-limiting disease. *Quarterly Journal of Studies on Alcohol, 29*(4), 956–967.

Earle, J. R., & Folks, D. G. (1986). Factitious disorder and coexisting depression: A report of successful psychiatric consultation and case management. *General Hospital Psychiatry, 8*(6), 448–450.

Eaton, W. W. (1985). Epidemiology of schizophrenia. *Epidemiology Review, 7,* 105–126.

Edelstein, B. A., Keaton-Brasted, C., & Burg, M. M. (1984). Effects of caffeine withdrawal on nocturnal enuresis, insomnia, and behavior restraints. *Journal of Counsulting and Clinical Psychology, 52*(5), 857–862.

Egeland, J. A., & Hostetter, A. M. (1983). Amish study, I: Affective disorders among the Amish, 1976–1980. *American Journal of Psychiatry, 140*(1), 56–61.

Elkins, R. L. (1991). An appraisal of chemical aversion (emetic therapy) approaches to alcoholism treatment. *Behavioral Research Therapy, 29*(5), 387–413.

Ellison, J. M., & Adler, D. A. (1990). A strategy for the pharmacotherapy of personality disorders. *New Directions for Mental Health Services, 47*, 43–63.

Emery, V. O., & Oxman, T. E. (1992). Update on the dementia spectrum of depression. *American Journal of Psychiatry, 149*(3), 305–317.

Emmelkamp, P. M. G. (1990). Anxiety and fear. In A. Belleck, M. Hersen, & A. Kazdin (Eds.). *The International handbook of behavior modification and therapy* (pp. 283–305). New York: Plenum.

Emmons, T. D., & Webb, W. W. (1974). Subjective correlates of emotional responsivity and stimulation seeking in psychopaths, normals and acting-out neurotics. *Journal of Consulting and Clinical Psychology, 42*(4), 620.

Emrick, C. D. (1975). A review of psychologically oriented treatment of alcoholism: 2. The relative effectiveness of different treatment approaches and the effectiveness of treatment versus no treatment. *Journal of Studies on Alcohol, 36*, 88–108.

Enas, G. G., Pope, H. G., & Levine, L. R. (1989). Fluoxetine in bulimia nervosa: Double-blind study. In *New research program and abstracts*. Washington, DC: American Psychiatric Association.

Engstrom, A., Adamsson, C., Allebeck, P., & Rydeberg, U. (1991). Mortality in patients with substance abuse: A follow-up in Stockholm County, 1973–1984. *International Journal of Addiction, 26*(1), 91–106.

Erickson, W. D., Walbek, N. H., & Seely, R. K. (1988). Behavior patterns of child molesters. *Archives of Sexual Behavior, 17*(1), 77–86.

Ersner-Hershfield, R., & Kopel, S. (1979). Group treatment of pre-orgasmic women: Evaluation of partner involvement and spacing of sessions. *Journal of Consulting and Clinical Psychology, 47*, 750–759.

Evans, D. L., Hasiao, J. K., & Nemeroff, C. B. (1984). Munchausen syndrome, depression, and the dexamethasone suppression test. *American Journal of Psychiatry, 141*(4), 570–571. Eysenck, H. J. (1965). *Smoking, health and personality*. New York: Basic Books.

Eysenck, H. J. (1979). The conditioniing model of neurosis. *Behavioral and Brain Sciences, 2*, 155–199.

Fahrner, E.-M. (1987). Sexual dysfunction in male alcohol addicts: Prevalence and treatment. *Archives of Sexual Behavior, 16*(3), 247–257.

Fahy, T. A. (1988). The diagnosis of multiple personality disorder: A critical review. *Journal of Psychiatry, 153*, 597–606.

Fairburn, C. G., & Beglin, S. J. (1991). Studies of the epidemiology of bulimia nervosa. *American Journal of Psychiatry, 147*(4), 401–408.

Fairweather, R. J. (1953). *The effect of selected incentive conditions on the performance of psychopathic, neurotic, and normal criminals in a serial rote learning situation*. Unpublished doctoral dissertation, University of Illinois.

Faris, R. E. L., & Dunham, H. W. (1939). *Mental disorders in urban areas.* Chicago: University of Chicago Press.

Farkas, G. M., & Rosen, R. C. (1976). Effect of alcohol on elicited male sexual response. *Journal of Studies on Alcohol, 37*(3), 265–272.

Farmer, V. (1988). Broken heartland. *Psychology Today, 20*(4), 54–62.

Fehrenbach, P. A., Smith, W., Monastersky, C., & Deisher, R. W. (1986). Adolescent sexual offenders: Offenders and offense characteristics. *American Journal of Orthopsychiatry, 56,* 225–233.

Feindel, W., & Penfield, W. (1954). Localization of discharge in temporal lobe automatism. *A.M.A. Archives of Neurology and Psychiatry, 72,* 605–630.

Feldman, M. D. (1983). Nausea and vomiting. In M. H. Sleisenger & J. S. Fordtran (Eds.), *Gastrointestinal disease: Pathophysiology, diagnosis, management* (3rd ed.). Philadelphia: W. B. Saunders.

Feldman, M. D. (1986). Pica: Current perspectives. *Psychosomatics, 27,* 519–523.

Fenna, D., Schaefer, O., Mix, L., & Gilbert, J. A. (1971). Ethanol metabolism in various racial groups. *Canadian Medical Association Journal, 105*(5), 472–475.

Fichter, M. M., & Noegel, R. (1990). Concordance for bulimia nervosa in twins. *International Journal of Eating Disorders, 9,* 255–263.

Fiester, S. J. (1990). Comorbidity of personality disorders: Two for the price of three. *New Directions for Mental Health Services, 47,* 103–115.

Fifield, L. (1975). *On my way to nowhere: Alienated, isolated, drunk.* Los Angeles: Gay Community Services Center and Department of Health Services.

Finkelhor, D. (1980). Sex among siblings: A survey on prevalence, variety, and effects. *Archives of Sexual Behavior, 9*(3), 171–192.

Fishbach, M., & Hull, J. T. (1982). Mental retardation in the province of Manitoba: Towards establishing a data base for community planning. *Canadian Mental Health, 30,* 16–19.

Fleming, J. (1986). The successful use of imagery to treat nightmares associated with posttraumatic stress disorder. *Sleep Research, 15,* 80.

Flor-Henry. P. (1969). Psychosis and temporal lobe epilepsy: A controlled investigation. *Epilepsia, 10,* 363–395.

Ford, C. V., & Folks, D. G. (1985). Conversion disorder: An overview. *Psychosomatics, 26*(5), 371–374, 380–383.

Fordyce, W. E. (1978). Evaluating and managing chronic pain. *Geriatrics, 33*(1), 59–62.

Foreyt, J. P. (1987). Issues in the assessment and treatment of obesity. *Journal of Consulting and Clinical Psychology, 55*(5), 677–684.

Forgac, G. E., & Michaels, E. (1982). Personality characteristics of two types of male exhibitionists. *Journal of Abnormal Psychology, 91*(4), 287–293.

Forssman, H., & Akesson, H. O. (1970). Mortality of the mentally deficient: A study of 12,903 institutionalized subjects. *Journal of Mental Deficiency Research, 14,* 276–296.

Foss, G., & Peterson, S. L. (1981). Social-interpersonal skills relevant to job tenure for mentally retarded adults. *Mental Retardation, 19*(3), 103–106.

Freund, K., Scher, H., & Hucker, S. (1983). The courtship disorders. *Archives of Sexual Behavior, 12*(5), 369–379.

Frezza, M., diPadova, C., Pozzato, G., Terpin, M., Baraona, E., & Lieber, C. (1990). High blood alcohol levels in women: The role of decreased gastric alcohol dehydrogenase activity in first-pass metabolism. *New England Journal of Medicine, 322*(2), 95–99.

Fritz, G. S., Stoll, K., & Wagner, N. N. (1981). A comparison of males and females who were sexually molested as children. *Journal of Sex and Marital Therapy, 7*(1), 54–59.

Furlong, F. W. (1975). Possible psychiatric significance of excessive coffee consumption. *Canadian Psychiatric Association Journal, 20,* 577–582.

Gandolfo, R. L., Templer, D. I., Cappelletty, G. G., & Cannon, W. G. (1991). Borderline, depressive and schizophrenic discrimination by MMPI. *Journal of Clinical Psychology, 47*(6), 783–789.

Garamoni, G. L., & Schwartz, R. M. (1986). Type A behavior pattern and compulsive personality: Toward a psychodynamic-behavioral integration. *Clinical Psychology Review, 6*(4), 311–336.

Garfinkel, P. E., & Garner, D. M. (1982). *Anorexia nervosa: A multidimensional perspective.* New York: Brunner/Mazel.

Garfinkel, P. E., Moldofsky, H., & Garner, D. M. (1980). The heterogeneity of anorexia nervosa. Bulimia as a distinct subgroup. *Archives of General Psychiatry, 37*(9), 1036–1040.

Garvey, M., Noyes, R. J., Anderson, D., & Cook, B. (1991). Examination of comorbid anxiety in psychiatric inpatients. *Comperhensive Psychiatry, 32*(4), 277–282.

Gath, A., & Gumley, D. (1986). Behaviour problems in retarded children with special reference to Down's syndrome. *British Journal of Psychiatry, 149,* 156–161.

Gebhard, P. H., Gagnon, J. H., Pomeroy, W. B., & Christenson, C. V. (1965). *Sex offenders: An analysis of type.* New York: Harper & Row.

Gelfand, D. M., & Teti, D. H. (1990). The effects of maternal depression on children. *Clinical Psychology Review, 10*(3), 329–353.

Geller, J. (1984). Arson: an unforeseen sequela of deinstitutionalization. *American Journal of Psychiatry, 141*(4), 504–508.

George, M. S., Brewerton, T. D., & Cochrane, C. (1990). Trichotillomania (hair pulling). *New England Journal of Medicine, 322*(7), 470–472.

Gibbens, T. C., Palmer, C., & Prince, J. (1971). Mental health aspects of shoplifting. *British Medical Journal, 3*(775), 612–615.

Gibbons, J. S., Horn, S. H., Powell, J. M., & Gibbons, J. L. (1984). Schizophrenia patients and their families: A survey in a psychiatric service based on a DGH unit. *British Journal of Psychiatry, 144,* 70–77.

Gibbs, L., & Flanagan, J. (1977). Prognostic indicators of alcoholism treatment outcomes. *International Journal of Addiction, 12*(8), 1097–1141.

Gibson-Ainyelte, I., Templer, D. I., Brown R., & Veaco, L. (1988). Variables associated with adolescent prostitutes. *Archives of Sexual Behavior, 17,* 431–438.

Glassman, A. H., Jackson, W. K., Walsh, B. T., Roose, S. P., & Rosenfeld, B. (1984). Cigarette craving, smoking withdrawal and clonidine. *Science, 226*(4676), 864–866.

Godpodinoff, M. L. (1989). Premature ejaculation: Clinical subgroups and etiology. *Journal of Sex and Marital Therapy, 15*(2), 130–134.

Gold, P. W., Kaye, W., Robertson, G. L., & Ebert, M. (1983). Abnormalities in plasma and cerebrospinal-fluid arginine vasopressin in patients with anorexia nervosa. *New England Journal of Medicine, 308*(19), 1117–1123.

Goldman, M. J. (1991). Kleptomania: Making sense of the nonsensical. *American Journal of Psychiatry, 148*(8), 986–996.

Goldstein, P. C., & Nelson, D. (1984). Cognitive, psychotic or educational impairment in schizophrenia? [Letter to the editor]. *American Journal of Psychiatry, 141*(11), 1489.

Golwyn, D. H. (1988). Cocaine abuse treated with phenelzine. *International Journal of the Addictions, 23*(9), 897–905.

Goodwin, D. W. (1986). *Anxiety.* New York: Oxford University Press.

Gottesman, I. I. (1991). *Schizophrenia genesis: The origins of madness.* New York: Freeman.

Gottesman, I. I., & Bertelsen, A. (1989). Confirming unexpressed genotypes for schizophrenia. Risk in the offspring of Fischer's Danish identical and fraternal discordant twins. *Archives of General Psychiatry, 46,* 867–872.

Gourash, L., & Puig-Antich, J. (1986). Medical and biologic aspects of adolescent depression. *Seminars in Adolescent Medicine, 2*(4), 299–310.

Goyer, P. F., & Eddleman, H. C. (1984). Same-sex rape of nonincarcerated men. *American Journal of Psychiatry, 141*(4), 576–579.

Graham, J. R., & Lowenfeld, B. H. (1986). Personality dimensions of the pathological gambler. *Journal of Gambling Behavior, 2,* 58–66.

Graves, G. B. (1980). Multiple personality: 165 years after Mary Reynolds. *Journal of Nervous and Mental Disease, 168,* 577–596.

Gray, B. A., & Jones, B. E. (1987). Psychotherapy and black women: A survey. *Journal of the National Medical Association, 79*(2), 177–181.

Gray, J. A. (1985). The neuropsychology of anxiety. *Issues in Mental Health Nursing, 7*(1–4), 210–228.

Green, M. A., & Berlin, M. A. (1987). Five psychosocial variables related to the existence of posttraumatic stress disorder symptoms. *Journal of Clinical Psychology, 43*(6), 643–649.

Green, M. F., Satz, P., Gaier, D. J., Ganzell, S., & Kharabi, F. (1989). Minor physical anomalies in schizophrenia. *Schizophrenia Bulletin, 15*(1), 91–99.

Green, M. F., Satz, P., Smith, C., & Nelson, L. (1989). Is there atypical handedness in schizophrenia? *Journal of Abnormal Psychology, 98*(1), 57–61.

Greenberg, H. R., & Sarner, C. A. (1965). Trichotillomania: symptom and syndrome. *Archives of general Psychiatry, 12*, 482–489.

Grinspoon, L., & Bakalar, J. B. (1980). An alternative to the amobarbitol interview [letter to the editor]. *American Journal of Psychiatry, 137*(5), 635.

Groth, A. N., & Birnbaum, H. J. (1978). Adult sexual orientation and attraction to underage persons. *Archives of Sexual Behavior, 7*(3), 175–181.

Groth, A. N., & Burgess, A. W. (1980). Male rape: Offenders and victims. *American Journal of Psychaitry, 137*, 806–810.

Gruenberg, E. M. (1964). Epidemiology. In H. A. Stevens & R. Heber (Eds.), *Mental retardation: A review of research* (pp. 259–306). Chicago: University of Chicago Press.

Grunberger, G., Weiner, J. L., Silverman, R., Taylor, S., & Gordon, P. (1988). Factitious hypoglycemia due to surreptitious administration of insulin. Diagnosis, treatment and long-term follow-up. *Annals of Internal Medicine, 108*(2), 252–257.

Grunewald, K. (1975). Blind, deaf and physically handicapped mentally retarded. An epidemiological study as a base for action. *Proceedings of the 3rd Congress of the International Association for the Scientific Study of Mental Deficiency, 1*, 349–352.

Gruzelier, J., & Hammond, N. (1976). Schizophrenia: A dominant hemisphere temporal-limbic disorder? *Research Communications in Psychology, Psychiatry and Behavior, 1*(1), 33–72.

Guidice, M. A., & Berchou, R. C. (1987). Post-traumatic epilepsy following head injury. *Brain Injury, 1*(1), 61–64.

Guilleminault, C., & Dement, W. C. (1988). Sleep apnea syndromes and related sleep disroders. In R. L. Williams, I. Kaeacan, & C. A. Moore (Eds.), *Sleep disorders: Diagnosis and treatment* (2nd ed.; pp. 47–72). New York: John Wiley & Sons.

Guilleminault, C., Eldridge, F. L., & Dement, W. C. (1972). Insomnia, narcolepsy and sleep apneas. *Bulletin Physio-Pathologique Respiratoire, 8*, 1127–1138.

Gunn, J., & Bonn, J. (1971). Criminality and violence in epileptic prisoners. *British Journal of Psychiatry, 118*, 337–343.

Gurling, H. M., Curtis, D., & Murray, R. M. (1991). Psychological deficit from excessive alcohol consumption: Evidence from a co-twin control study. *British Journal of Addiction, 86*(2), 151–155.

Guze, S. B., Woodruff, R. A., & Clayton, P. J. (1971). A study of conversion symptoms in psychiatric outpatients. *American Journal of Psychiatry, 128*(5), 643–646.

Gwirtsman, H. E., Roy-Byrne, P., Lerner, L., & Yager, J. (1984). Bulimia in men: Report of three cases with neuroendocrine findings. *Journal of Clinical Psychiatry, 45*(2), 78–81.

Haberman, P. W. (1969). Drinking and other self-indulgences: Complements or counter-attractions? *International Journal of the Addictions, 4,* 61–77.

Hafner, J., & Marks, I. (1976). Exposure in vivo of agoraphobics: Contributions of diazepam, group exposure and anxiety evocation. *Psychological Medicine, 6*(1), 71–88.

Hagberg, B., & Kyllerman, M. (1983). Epidemiology of mental retardation—a Swedish survey. *Brain Development, 5*(5), 441–449.

Hagerman, R. I., McBogg, P. A., & Hagerman, P. J. (1983). Fragile X syndrome: History, diagnosis and treatment. *Developmental and Behavioral Pediatrics, 4*(2), 122–130.

Halmi, K. A., Falk, J. R., & Schwartz, E. (1981). Binge-eating and vomiting: A survey of a college population. *Psychological Medicine, 11*(4), 697–706.

Hamera, E. K., Peterson, K. A., Handley, S. M., Plumlee, A. A., & Frank-Ragan, E. (1991). Patient self-regulation and functioning in schizophrenia. *Hospital and Community Psychiatry, 42*(6), 630–631.

Hardy, G. E. (1982). Body image disturbance in dysmorphophobia. *British Journal of Psychiatry, 141,* 181–185.

Hardy, G. E., & Cotterill, J. A. (1982). A study of depression and obsessionality by dysmorphophobic and psoriatic patients. *British Journal of Psychiatry, 140,* 19–22.

Hare, R. D. (1970). *Psychopathy: Theory and research.* New York: John Wiley & Sons.

Harriman, P. L. (1942). The experimental induction of multiple personality. *Psychiatry, 5,* 179–186.

Harris, E. L., Noyes, R. J., Crowe, R. R., & Chaudhry, D. R. (1983). Family study of agoraphobia. Report of a pilot study. *Archives of General Psychiatry, 40*(10), 1061–1064.

Harrow, M., Goldberg, J. F., Grossman, L. S., & Meltzer, H. Y. (1990). Outcome in manic disorders. A naturalistic follow-up study. *Archives of General Psychiatry, 47,* 665–671.

Hart, S. D., Forth, A. E., & Hare, R. D. (1990). Performance of criminal psychopaths on selected neuropsychological tests. *Journal of Abnormal Psychology, 99*(4), 374–379.

Hartlage, L. C. (1981). Clinical application of neuropsychological data. *School Psychology Review, 10*(3), 362–366.

Hartlage, L. C., & Telzrow, C. F. (1986). *Neruropsychological assessment and intervention with children and adolescents.* Sarasota, FL: Professional Resource Exchange.

Hatsukami, D., Eckert, E., Mitchell, J. E., & Pyle, R. (1984). Affective disorder and substance abuse in women with bulimia. *Psychological Medicine, 14,* 701–704.

Hauri, P. (1980). *Current concepts: The sleep disorders.* Kalamazoo, MI: UpJohn Co.

Head, S., Baker, J. D., & Williamson, D. A. (1991). Family environment characteristics and dependent personality disorder. *Journal of Personality Disorders, 5*(3), 256–263.

Heath, G. A., Hardesty, V. A., Goldfine, P. E., & Walker, A. M. (1983). Childhood firesetting: An empirical study. *Journal of the American Academy of Child Psychiatry, 22,* 370–374.

Hecht, H., Von Zussen D., & Wittchen, H. (1990). Anxiety and depression in a community sample: The influence of comorbidity on social functioning. *Journal of Affective Disorders, 18,* 137–144.

Heide, F. J., & Borkovec, T. D. (1984). Relaxation-induced anxiety: Mechanisms and theoretical implications. *Behaviour Research and Therapy, 22*(1), 1–12.

Heim, N., & Hursch, C. J. (1979). Castration for sex offenders: Treatment or punishment? A review and critique of recent European literature. *Archives of Sexual Behavior, 8,* 281–303.

Herbst, D. S., & Baird, P. A. (1983). Nonspecific mental retardation in British Columbia as ascertained through a registry. *American Journal of Mental Deficiency, 87*(5), 506–513.

Herbst, D. S., & Miller, J. R. (1980). Nonspecific X-linked mental retardation 2. The frequency in British Columbia. *American Journal of Medical Genetics, 7*(4), 461–469.

Herman, J., Russell, D., & Trocki, K. (1986). Long-term effects of incestuous abuse in childhood. *American Journal of Psychiatry, 143*(10), 1293–1296.

Hermann, B. P., & Whiteman, S. (1984). Behavioral and personality correlates of epilepsy: A review, methodological critique, and conceptual model. *Psychological Bulletin, 95*(3), 451–497.

Herold, E. S., Mantle, D., & Zemitis, O. (1979). A study of sexual offenses against females. *Adolescence, 14*(53), 65–72.

Heron, G. B., & Johnston, D. A. (1976). Hypothalmic tumor presenting as anorexia nervosa. *American Journal of Psychiatry, 133*(5), 580–582.

Herzog, D. B., Dennis, K. N., Gordon, C., & Pepose, M. (1984). Sexual conflict and eating disorders in 27 males. *American Journal of Psychiatry, 141*(8), 989–992.

Hes, J. P. (1968). Hypochondriacal complaints in Jewish psychiatric patients. *Israeli Annals of Psychiatry and Related Disciplines, 6*(2), 134–142.

Heston, L. L. (1966). Psychiatric disorders in foster home reared children of schizophrenic mothers. *British Journal of Psychiatry, 112*, 819–825.

Hilbert, R. A. (1984). The acultural dimensions of chronic pain: Flawed reality construction and the problem of meaning. *Social Problems, 31*(4), 365–378.

Hill, B. K., Bruininks, R. H., & Lakin, K. C. (1983). Characteristics of mentally retarded people in residential facilities. *Health and Social Work, 8*(2), 85–95.

Hill, S. Y., Goodwin, D. W., Cadoret, R., Osterland, C. K., & Doner, S. M. (1975). Association and linkage between alcoholism and eleven serological markers. *Journal of Studies on Alcohol, 36*(7), 981–992.

Hoch, P., & Polatin, P. (1949). Pseudoneurotic forms of schizophrenia. *Psychiatric Quarterly, 23*, 248–276.

Hoenig, J., & Kenna, J. C. (1979). EEG abnormalitites and transsexualism. *British Jounral of Psychiatry, 134*, 293–300.

Hoffer, A., Osmond, H., & Smythies, J. (1954). Schizophrenic: New approach: Results of a year's research. *Journal of Mental Science, 100*, 29–45.

Holden, K., Mellits, E., & Freeman, J. (1982). Neonatal seizures: 1. Correlation of prenatal and perinatal events with outcomes. *Pediatrics, 70*(2), 165–176.

Hollon, S. D., & Beck, A. T. (1979). Cognitive therapy for depression. In P. C. Kendall & S. D. Hollon (Eds.), *Cognitive behavioral interventions: Theory, research and procedures* (pp. 153–203). New York: Academic Press.

Horowitz, M., & Wilner, N. (1976). Stress films, emotion, and cognitive response. *Archives of General Psychiatry, 33*(11), 1339–1344.

Horwitz, W. A., Kestenbaum, C., & Person, E. (1964, May 4–8). *Identical twin-"idiot savants"-calendar calculators.* 120th Annual Meeting of the American Psychiatric Association.

Hoverak, O. (1983). The 1978 strike at the Norwegian Wine and Spirit Monopoly. *British Journal of Addicition, 78*(1), 51–66.

Hsu, G. L. K., Chesler, B. E., & Santhouse, R. (1990). Bulimia nervosa in eleven sets of twins: A clinical report. *International Journal of Eating Disorders, 9*(3), 275–282.

Hsu, L. K. (1988). The outcome of anorexia nervosa: A reappraisal. *Psychological Medicine, 18*(4), 807–812.

Hsu, L. K., Crisp, A. H., & Harding, B. (1979). Outcome of anorexia nervosa. *Lancet, 1*(8107), 61–65.

Hudson, J. I., Laffer, P. S., & Pope, H. G., Jr. (1982). Bulimia related to affective disorder by family history and response to the dexamethasone suppression test. *American Journal of Psychiatry, 137*, 695–697.

Hudson, J. L., Pope, H. G. Jr, Jonas, J. M., & Yurgelun-Todd, D. (1983). Family history study of anorexia nervosa and bulimia. *British Journal of Psychiatry, 142*, 133–138.

Hudson, J. I., Pope, H. I. Jr., & Jonas, J. M. (1984). Psychosis in anorexia nervosa and bulimia. *British Journal of Psychiatry, 145*, 420–423.

Hudson, J. L., Pope, H. G. Jr, Yurgelun-Todd, D., Jonas, J. M., & Frankenburg, F. R. (1987). A controlled study of lifetime prevalence of affective and other psychiatric disorders in bulimic outpatients. *American Journal of Psychiatry*, *144*(10), 1283–1287.

Hunt, D. D., & Hampson, J. L. (1980). Follow-up of 17 biologic male transsexuals after sex-reassignment surgery. *American Journal of Psychiatry*, *137*(4), 432–438.

Hunter, J., & de Kleine, R. (1984). Geophagy in Central America. *The Geographical review*, *74*, 157–169.

Hurt, S. W., Schnurr, P. P., Severino, S. K., Freemna, E. W., Gise, L. H., Rivera-Tovar, A., & Steege, J. F. (1992). Late luteal phase dysphoric disorder in 670 women evaluated for premenstrual complaints. *American Journal of Psychiatry*, *149*(4), 525–530.

Insel, T. R., Murphy, D. L., Cohen, R. M., Alterman, I., Kilts, C., & Linnoila, M. (1983). Obsessive-compulsive disorder. A double-blind trial of clomipramine and clorgyline. *Archives of General Psychiatry*, *40*(6), 605–612.

Itil, T. M., Simeon, J., & Coffin, C. (1976). Qualitative and quantitative EEG in psychotic children. *Diseases of the Nervous System*, *5*, 247–252

Jablonski, S. (1991). *Jablonski's dictionary of syndromes and eponomic diseases. (2nd ed.)*. Malabar, FL.: Krieger.

Jacobs, D. F. (1988). Evidence of a common dissociative-like reaction among addicts. *Journal of Gambling Behavior*, *4*, 27–37.

Jacobs, D. F. (1989). Children of problem gamblers. *Journal of Gambling Behavior*, *5*, 261–268.

Jaffe, A. C., Dynneson, L., & ten Bensel, R. W. (1975). Sexual abuse of children: An epidemiologic study. *American Journal of Diseases of Children*, *129*, 689–692.

Jarrett, D. B., Coble, P. A., & Kupfer, D. J. (1983). Reduced cortisol latency in depressive illness. *Archives of General Psychiatry*, *40*, 506–511.

Jellinek, E. M. (1960). *The disease concept of alcoholism*. New Haven, CT: College & University Press.

Jeste, D. V., & Lohr, J. B. (1989). Hippocampal pathologic findings in schizophrenia: A morphometric study. *Archives of General Psychiatry*, *46*(11), 1019–1024.

Johansson, J., & Ost, L. G. (1982). Self-control procedures in biofeedback: A review of temperature biofeedback in the treatment of migraine. *Biofeedback and Self-Regulation*, *7*(4), 435–442.

Johnson, B. D. (1977). The race, class and irreversibility hypotheses: Myths and research about heroin. In J. D. Rittenhouse (Ed.), *The epidemiology of heroin and other narcotics*. (pp. 51–60). Rockville, MD: National Institute on Drug Abuse. (NIDA Research Monograph 16).

Johnson, C., & Bernt, D. J. (1983). Preliminary investigation of bulimia and life adjustment. *American Journal of Psychiatry, 140*(6), 774–777.

Johnson, H. C. (1991). Borderline clients: Practice implications of recent research. *Social Work, 36*(2), 166–173.

Johnston, A. L., Thevos, A. K., Randall, C. L., & Anton, R. F. (1991). Increased severity of alcohol withdrawal in in-patient alcoholics with a co-existing anxiety diagnosis. *British Journal of Addiction, 86*, 719–725.

Johnstone, E., Crow, T., Johnson, A., & MacMillan, J. (1986). The Northwick Park Study of first episodes of schizophrenia. 1. *British Journal of Psychiatry, 148*, 115–120.

Jones, B. M. (1971). Verbal and spatial intelligence in short and long term alcoholics. *Journal of Nervous and Mental Disease, 153*(2), 292–297.

Jones, I. H., & Frei, D. (1979). Exhibitionism—a biological hypothesis. *British Journal of Medical Psychology, 52*, 63–70.

Jones, J. C., & Barlow, D. H. (1990). The etiology of posttraumatic stress disorder. *Clinical Psychology Review, 10*(3), 299–328.

Jones, L. A. (1979). Census-based prevalence estimates for mental retardation. *Mental Retardation, 17*(4), 199–201.

Kales, A., Soldatos, C. R., Caldwell, A. B., Charney, D. S., Kales, J. D., Markel, D., & Cadieux, R. (1980). Nightmares: Clinical characterisitics and personality patterns. *American Journal of Psychiatry, 137*(10), 1197–1201.

Kaminsky, M. J., & Slavney, P. R. (1983). Hysterical and obsessional features in patients with Briquet's syndrome (somatization disorder). *Psychological Medicine, 13*(1), 111–120.

Kampman, R. (1976). Hypnotically induced multiple personality: An experimental study. *Experimental Hypnosis, 3*, 215–227.

Kanner, L. (1972). *Child psychiatry.* Springfield, IL: Charles C. Thomas.

Karacan, D. J., & Howell, J. W. (1988). Narcolepsy. In R. L. Williams, I. Karacan, & C. A. Moore (Eds.), *Sleep disorders: Diagnosis and treatment* (2nd ed.; pp. 87–105.). New York: John Wiley & Sons.

Karno, M., Golding, J. M., Sorenson, S. B., & Burnam, M. A. (1988). The epidemiology of obsessive-compusive disorder in five US communitities. *Archives of General Psychiatry, 45*(12), 1094–1099.

Kashani, J. H., Husain, A., Shekim, W. O., Hodges, K. K., Cytryn, L., & McKnew, D. H. (1981). Current perspectives on childhood depression: An overview. *American Journal of Psychiatry, 138*, 143–153.

Kasper, S., Rogers, S. L. B., Yancey, A., Schulz, P. M., Skwerer, R. G., & Rosenthal, N. E. (1989). Phototherapy in individuals with and without subsyndromal seasonal affective disorder. *Archives of General Psychiatry, 46*, 837–844.

Kaufman, D. M. (1985). *Clinical neurology for psychiatrists* (2nd ed. Orlando, FL: Grune & Stratton.

Kay, D. W. K. (1977). The epidemiology of brain deficit in the elderly. In C. Eisdorfer & R. O. Friedel (Eds.), *The cognitively and emotionally impaired elderly.* (pp. 11–26). Chicago: Year Book Medical Publishers, Inc.

Kay, D. W., Britton, P. G., Bergman, K., & Foster, E. M. (1977). Cognitive function and length of survival in elderly subjects living at home. *Australian and New Zealand Journal of Psychiatry, 11*(2), 113–117.

Kayton, L., & Borge, G. F. (1967). Birth order and the obsessive-compulsive character. *Archives of General Psychiatry, 17*(6), 751–754.

Keck, P. E., Cohen, B. M., Baldessarini, R. J., & McElroy, S. L. (1989). Time course of antipsychotic effects of neuroleptic drugs. *American Journal of Psychiatry, 146*(10), 1289–1292.

Keefe, F. J., & Gil, K. M. (1986). Behavioral concepts in the analysis of chronic pain syndromes. *Journal of Consulting and Clinical Psychology, 54*(6), 776–783.

Keesey, R. E. (1986). A set-point theory of obesity. In K. D. Brownell & J. P. Foreyt (Eds.), *Handbook of eating disorders: Physiology, psychology, and treatment of obesity, anorexia nervosa and bulimia* (pp. 63–87.). New York: Basic Books.

Kendler, K. S. (1984). Paranoia (delusional disorder): A valid psychiatric entity? *Trends in Neurosciences, 7,* 14–17.

Kendler, K. S., Neale, M. C., Kessler, R. C., Heath, A. C., & Eaves, L. J. (1992a). Generalized anxiety disorder in women: A population-based twin study. *Archives of General Psychiatry, 49,* 267–272.

Kendler, K. S., Neale, M. C., Kessler, R. C., Heath, A. C. & Eaves, L. J. (1992b). A population-based twin study of major depression in women. *Archives of General Psychiatry, 49,* 257–266.

Kenyon, F. E. (1964). Hypochondriasis: A clinical study. *British Journal of Psychiatry, 110*(467), 478–488.

Kenyon, F. E. (1976). Hypochondriacal states. *British Journal of Psychiatry, 129*(1), 1–4.

Kernberg, O. F. (1984). *Severe personality disorders: Psychotherapeutic strategies.* New Haven: Yale University Press.

Kettl, P. A., & Marks, I. M. (1986). Neurological factors in obsessive-compulsive disorder. Two case reports and a review of the literature. *British Journal of Psychiatry, 149,* 315–319.

Kety, S. S., Rosenthal, D., Wender, P. H., & Schulsinger, F. (1968). The types and prevalences of mental illness in the biological and adoptive families of adopted schizophrenics. In D. Rosenthal & S. S. Kety (Eds.), *The transmission of schizophrenia.* Oxford: Pergamon Press.

Keutzer, C. S. (1972). Kleptomania: A direct approach to treatment. *British Journal of Medical Psychology, 45*(2), 159–163.

Kiev, A. (1964). *Magic, faith, and healing: Studies in primitive psychiatry.* New York: Free Press of Glencoe.

Kinsey, A. C., Pomeroy, W. B., & Martin, C. E. (1948). *Sexual behavior in the human male.* Philadelphia: W. B. Saunders.

Kinsey, A. C., Pomeroy, W. B., Martin, C. E., & Gebhard, P. H. (1953). *Sexual behavior in the human female.* Philadelphia: W. B. Saunders.

Kirkland, K. D., & Bauer, C. A. (1982). MMPI traits of incestous fathers. *Journal of Clinical Psychology, 38*(3), 645–649.

Kivela, S., Pahkala, K., & Laippala, P. (1991). A one-year prognosis of dysthymic disorder and major depression in old age. *International Journal of Geriatric Psychiatry, 6*(2), 81–87.

Klerman, G. L. (1980). Overview of affective disorders. in H. I. Kaplan, (Ed.), *Comprehensive textbook of psychiatry.* (3rd. ed.; Vol. 2, pp. 1305–1319). Baltimore: Williams and Wlkins.

Kluft, R. P. (1987a). First-rank symptoms as a diagnosis clue to multiple personality disorder. *American Journal of Psychiatry, 144*(3), 293–298.

Kluft, R. P. (1987b). An update on multiple personality disorder. *Hospital and Community Psychiatry, 38*(4), 363–373.

Kluft, R. P. (1986). The prevalence of multiple personality. *American Journal of Psychiatry, 143*(6), 802–803.

Ko, G. N., Elsworth, J. D., Roth, R. H., Rifkin, B. G., Leigh, H., & Redmond, D. E., Jr. (1983). Panic-Induced elevation of plasma MHPG levels in phobic-anxious patients. *Archives of Genral Psychiatry, 40*(4), 425–430.

Kodman, F. J. (1963). Educational status of hard-of-hearing children in the classroom. *Journal of Speech and Hearing Disorders, 28*(3), 297–299.

Kogeorgos, J., Fonagy, P., & Scott, D. F. (1982). Psychiatric symptom patterns of chronic epileptics attending a neurological clinic: A controlled investigation. *British Journal of Psychiatry, 140,* 236–243.

Kolodny, R. C., Masters, W. H., & Johnson, V. E. (1979). *Textbook of sexual medicine.* Boston: Little Brown & Co.

Kriechman, A. M. (1987). Siblings with somatoform disorders in childhood and adolescence. *Journal of the American Academy of Child and Adolescent Psychiatry, 26*(2), 226–231.

Krieg, J. C., Pirke, K. M., Lauer, C., & Backmund, F. R. G. (1988). Endocrine, metabolism and cranial computed tomography findings in anorexia nervosa. *Biological Psychiatry, 23*(4), 377–387.

Kringlen, E. (1965). Obsessional neurotics. A long-term follow-up. *British Journal of Psychiatry, 111*(477), 709–722.

Krishnan, K. R., Davidson, J. R., & Guajardo, C. (1985). Trichotillomania—a review. *Comprehensive Psychiatry, 26*(2), 123–128.

Kroll, P., Seigel, R., O'Neill, B., & Edwards, R. P. (1980). Cerebral cortical atrophy in alcoholic men. *Journal of Clinical Psychiatry, 41*(12, pt. 1), 417–421.

Krotkiewski, M., Garellick, G., Sjostrom, L., Persson, G., Bjuro, T., & Sullivan, L. (1980). Fat cell number, resting metabolic rate, mean heart rate and insulin elevation while seeing and smelling food as predictors of slimming. *Metabolism, 29*(11), 1003–1012.

Kupfer, D. J., Spiker, D. G., Coble, P., & McPartland, R. J. (1978). Amitriptyline and EEG sleep in depressed patients. 1. Drug effects. *Sleep, 1,* 149–159.

Kushlick, A., & Cox, G. R. (1973). The epidemiology of mental handicap. *Developmental Medicine and Child Neurology, 15,* 748–759.

Labrisseau, A., Jean, P., Messier, B., & Richer, C. (1982). Fragile X chromosome and X-linked mental retardation. *Canadian Medical Association Journal, 127,* 123–126.

Lambo, T. (1962). *African traditional beliefs, concepts of health and medical practice.* Ibadan, Nigeria. University College, Medical Library.

Lambo, T. A. (1955). The role of cultural factors in paranoid psychosis among Yoruba tribe. *Journal of Mental Science, 101*(230–266.),

Lande, S. D. (1980). A combination of orgasmic reconditioning and covert sensitization in the treatment of a fire fetish. *Journal of Behavior Therapy and Experimental Psychiatry, 11*(4), 291–296.

Langevin, R., Handy, L., Russon, A. E., & Day, D. (1985). Are incestuous fathers pedophilic, aggressive, and alcoholic? In R. Langevin (Ed.), *Erotic preference, gender identity, and aggression in men: New research studies* (pp. 137–150). Hillsdale, NJ: Erlbaum.

Laufer, R. S., Brett, E., & Gallops, M. S. (1985). Symptom patterns associated with posttraumatic stress disorder among Vietnem veterans exposed to war trauma. *American Journal of Psychiatry, 142*(11), 1304–1311.

Leavitt, F. (1982). *Drugs and behavior.* New York: John Wiley.

Lechtenberg, R. (1982). *The psychiatrist's guide to diseases of the nervous system.* New York: John Wiley & Sons.

Lecompte D., & Clara A. (1987). Associated psychopathology in conversion patients without organic disease. *Acta Psychiatrica Belgica, 87,* 654–661.

Leetz, K. L., Martino-Salzman, D., & Gormley, T. N. (1991). Clinical characteristics of hospitalized military patients with narcissistic personality disorder. *Military Medicine, 156*(9), 448–452.

Lefkowitz, M. M., & Tesiny, E. P. (1985). Depression in children: Prevalence and correlates. *Journal of Counsulting and Clinical Psychology, 53*(5), 647–656.

Lefley, H. P. (1989). Family burden and family stigma in major mental illness. *American Psychologist, 44*(3), 556–560.

Lehman, A. F., Possidente, S., & Hawker, F. (1986). The quality of life of chronic patients in a state hospital and in community residences. *Hospital and Community Psychiatry, 37*(9), 901–907.

Lesch, M., & Nyhan, W. L. (1964). A familial disorder of uric acid metabolism and central nervous system function. *American Journal of Medicine, 36*, 561–570.

Lesieur, H. R. (1988a). The female pathological gambler. In W. R. Eadington (Ed.), *Gambling research: Proceedings of the Seventh International Conference on Gambling and Risk Taking* (pp. 230–258.). Reno, NV: University of Nevada, Bureau of Business and Economic Research.

Lesieur, H. R. (1988b). *Report on pathological gambling in New Jersey. Report and recommendations of the governor's advisory commission on gambling.* Trenton, NJ: Governor's Advisory Commission on Gambling.

Lesieur, H. R., & Blume, S. B. (1991). When lady luck loses: Women and compulsive gambling. In N. van den Bergh (Ed.), *Feminist perspectives on treating addicitions.* New York: Springer Publishing Co.

Lesieur, H. R., & Heineman, M. (1988). Pathological gambling among youthful multiple substance abusers in a therapeutic community. *British Journal of Addictions, 83*(7), 765–771.

Lesieur, H. R., & Rosenthal, R. J. (1991). Pathologic gambling: A review of the literature. *Journal of Gambling Studies, 7*(1), 5–39.

Lester, D. (1983). *Why people kill themselves* (2nd ed.). Springfield, IL: Charles C. Thomas.

Lester, D. (1992). *Why people kill themselves* (3rd ed.). Springfield, IL: Charles C. Thomas.

Levin, H. S., Benton, A. L., & Grossman, R. G. (1982.). Neurobehavioral consequences of closed head injury. New York: Oxford University Press.

Levinson, E. J. (1962). *Retarded children in Maine.* Orono, ME: University of Maine Press.

Lewis, N. D. C., & Yarnell, H. (1951). Pathological firesetting. *Nervous and Mental Disease Monographs, 82*, 8–26.

Lewis, W. C., & Berman, M. (1965). Studies in conversion hysteria. *Archives of General Psychiatry, 13*(3), 275–282.

Libby, J. D., Polloway, E. A., & Smith, D. J. (1983). Lesch-Nyhan syndrome: A review. *Education and Training of The Mentally Retarded,* 226–231.

Liddle, P. F., & Crow, T. J. (1984). Age orientation in chronic schizophrenia is associated with global intellectual impairment. *British Journal of Psychiatry, 144*, 193–199.

Lieberman, J. A., Kane, J. M., Sarantakops, S., Gadaletta, D., Woerner, M., Alvir, J., & Ramos-Lorenzi, J. (1986). Predictions of relapse in schizophrenia. *Psychopharmacology Bulletin, 22*(3), 845–853.

Linden, R. D., Pope, H. G. Jr, & Jonas, J. M. (1986). Pathological gambling and major affective disorder: Preliminary findings. *Journal of Canadian Psychiatry, 134*, 4.

Lishman, W. A. (1981). Cerebral disorder in alcoholism: syndromes of impairment. *Brain, 104*(Pt 1), 1–20.

Litt, C. J. (1980). Trichotillomania in childhood: A case of successful short-term treatment. *Journal of Pediatric Psychology, 5*(1), 37–42.

Livingston, J. (1974). Compulsive gamblers: A culture of losers. *Psychology Today, 7*(10), 51–55.

Lloyd, L. L. (1970). Differential Diagnosis of Speech and Hearing *Problems of Mental Retardates, 44*(4), 103–121.

Lofts, R. H., Schroeder, S. R., & Maier, R. H. (1990). Effects of serum zinc supplementation on pica behavior of persons with mental retardation. *American Journal on Mental Retardation, 95*(1), 103–109.

Lombrose, C. T. (1978). Convulsive disorders in newborns. In R. A. Thompson & J. R. Green (Eds.), *Pediatric neurology and neurosurgery.* New York: Spectrum.

Loranger, A. W. (1884). Sex differences in age at onset of schizophrenia. *Archives of General Psychiatry, 41*(2), 157–161.

Lorenz, V. C., & Yaffee, R. A. (1988). Pathological gambling: Psychosomatic, emotional and marital difficulties as reported by the spouse. *Journal of Gambling Behavior, 4,* 13–26.

Lothstein, L. M., & Roback, H. (1984). Black female transsexuals and schizophrenia: A serendipitous finding? *Archives of Sexual Behavior, 13*(4), 371–390.

Lubs, H. A. (1969). A marker X chromosome. *American Journal of Human Genetics, 21,* 231–244.

Luchins, D. J., Weinberger, D. R., & Wyatt, R. J. (1982). Schizophrenia and cerebral asymmetry detected by computed tomography. *American Journal of Psychiatry, 139*(6), 753–757.

Lucker, G. W., Kruzich, D. J., Holt, M. T., & Gold, J. D. (1991). The prevalence of antisocial behavior among U.S. Army DWI offenders. *Journal of Studies on Alcohol, 52*(4), 318–320.

Lugaresi, E., Cirignotta, F., Mondini, S., Montagna, P., & Zucconi, M. (1988). Sleep in clinical neurology. In R. L. Williams, I. Karacan, & C. A. Moore (Eds.), *Sleep disorders: Diagnosis and treatment.* (2nd. ed.; pp. 245–264.). New York: John Wiley & Sons.

Lundholm, J. K. (1989). Alcohol use among university females: Relationship to eating disordered behavior. *Addictive Behaviors, 14*(2), 181–185.

Lynn, R., & Eysenck, H. J. (1961). Tolerance for pain, extraversion and neuroticism. *Perceptual and Motor Skills, 12,* 161–162.

Mackenzie, T. B., & Popkin, M. K. (1983). Organic anxiety syndrome. *American Journal of Psychiatry, 140*(3), 342–344.

Malcolm, R., Ballenger, J. C., Sturgis, E. T., & Anton, R. (1989). Double-blind controlled trial for comparing carbamazepine to oxazepam treatment of alcohol withdrawal. *American Journal of Psychiatry, 146*(5), 617–621.

Malenbaum, R., & Russell, A. T. (1987). Multiple personality disorder in an 11-year-old boy and his mother. *Journal of American Academy of Child and Adolescent Psychiatry, 26*(3), 436–439.

Maletta, G. J., Pirozzolo, F. J., Thompson, G., & Mortimer, J. A. (1982). Organic mental disorders in a geriatric outpatient population. American Journal of Psychiatry, 139(4), 521–523.

Mannino, F. V., & Delgado, R. A. (1969). Trichotillomania in children: A review. *American Journal of Psychiatry, 126*(4), 505–511.

Manoach, D. S., Maher, B. A., & Manschreck, T. C. (1988). Left-handedness and thought disorder in the schizophrenias. *Journal of Abnormal Psychology, 97*(1), 97–99.

Marks, I. M., Basoglu, M., Lelliott, M., Noshirvani, H., Montiero, W., & Kasvikis, Y. (1988). Clomipramine and exposure in OCD: A replication. *British Journal of Psychiatry, 152,* 522–534.

Marshall, W. L., & Barbaree, H. E. (1984). A behavioral view of rape. *International Journal of Law and Psychiatry, 7*(1), 51–77.

Martin, J. P., & Bell, J. (1943). A pedigree of mental defect showing sex-linkage. *Journal of Neurological Psychiatry, 6,* 154–157.

Martin, P. A. (1971). Dynamic considerations of the hysterical psychosis. *American Journal of Psychiatry, 128*(6), 745–748.

Masters, W. H., & Johnson, V. E. (1970). *Human sexual inadequacy.* Boston: Little Brown.

Masterson, J. F., Lulow, W. V., & Costello, J. L. (1982). The test of time: Borderline adolescent to functioning adult. *Adolescent Psychiatry, 10,* 494–522.

Mathews, J. (1971). Communications disorders in the mentally retarded. In L. E. Travis (Ed.), *Handbook of speech pathology and audiology.* Englewood Cliffs, NJ: Prentice-Hall.

Matson, J. L., & DiLorenzo, T. M. (1984). *Punishment and its alternatives: A new perspective for behavior modification.* New York: Springer Publishing Co.

Matthews, W. S., & Barabas, G. (1981). Suicide and epilepsy: A review of the literature. *Psychosomatics, 22*(6), 515–524.

Mattick, R. P., & Newman, C. R. (1991). Social phobia and avoidant personality disorder. *International Review of Psychiatry, 3*(2), 163–173.

Matussek, P., & Feil, W. B. (1983). Personality attributes of depressive patients. *Archives of General Psychiatry, 40,* 783–790.

Mavissakalian, M., Turner, S. M., Michelson, L., & Jacob, R. (1985). Tricyclic antidepressants in obsessive-compulsive disorder: Antiobsessional or antidepressant agents? *American Journal of Psychiatry, 142*(5), 572–576.

Mavromatis, M., & Lion, J. R. (1977). A primer on pyromania. *Diseases of the Nervous System, 38*(11), 954–955.

May, P. R. A. (1968). *Treatment of schizophrenia..* New York: Science House.

McAlpine, C., & Singh, N. N. (1986). Pica in institutionalized mentally retarded persons. *Journal of Mental Deficiency Research, 30*(pt. 2), 171–178.

McCann, J. T. (1988). Passive-aggressive personality disorder: A review. *Journal of Personality Disorders, 2*(2), 170–179.

McCarty, L. M. (1986). Mother-child incest: Characteristics of the offender. *Child Welfare, 65*(5), 447–458.

McClelland, R. J. (1988). Psychosocial sequelae of head injury—anatomy of a relationship. *British Journal of Psychiatry, 153*, 141–146.

McCormick, R. A., Russo, A. M., Ramirez, L. F., & Taber, J. I. (1984). Affective disorders among pathological gamblers seeking treatment. *American Journal of Psychiatry, 141*(2), 215–218.

McElroy, S. L., Keck, P. E., Jr, Pope, H. G., Jr, & Hudson, J. I. (1989). Pharmacological treatment of kleptomania and bulimia nervosa. *Journal of Clinical Psychopharmacology, 9*(5), 358–360.

McFarlane, A. C. (1988). The phenomenology of posttraumatic stress disorder following a natural disaster. *Journal of Nervous and Mental Diseases, 176*(1), 22–29.

McGlashan, T. H. (1986). The Chestnut Lodge follow-up study. 3. Long-term outcome of borderline personalities. *Archives of General Psychiatry, 43*(1), 20–30.

McKeon, J., Roa, B., & Mann, A. (1984). Life events and personality traits in obsessive-compulsive neurosis. *British Journal of Psychiatry, 144*, 185–189.

McKirnan, D. J., & Peterson, P. L. (1989). Alcohol and drug use among homosexual men and women: epidemiology and population characteristics. *Addicitive Behaviors, 14*(5), 545–553.

McNeil, T. F., & Kaij, L. (1973). Obstetric complications and physical size of offspring of schizophrenic, schizophrenic-like, and control mothers. *British Journal of Psychiatry, 123*(574), 341–348.

McNeil, T. F., Raff, C. S., & Cromwell, R. L. (1971). Technique for comparing the relative importance of conception and season of birth. *British Journal of Psychiatry, 118*, 329–335.

Meador-Woodruff, J. H. (1990). Psychiatric side effects of tricyclic antidepressants. *Hospital and Community Psychiatry, 41*(1), 84–86.

Meadow, R. (1977). Munchausen syndrome by proxy. The hinterland of child abuse. *Lancet, 2*(8033), 343–345.

Mello, N. K., & Mendelson, J. H. (1970). Experimentally-induced intoxication in alcoholics: A comparison between programmed and spontaneous drinking. *Journal of Pharmacology and Experimental Therapeutics, 173*, 101–106.

Mello, N. K., & Mendelson, J. H. (1972). Drinking patterns during work-contingent and noncontingent alcohol acquisition. *Psychosomatic Medicine, 34*(2), 139–164.

Mellor, C. S. (1970). First rank symptoms of schizophrenia. *British Journal of Psychiatry, 117*, 15–23.

Mellor, C. S. (1982). The present status of first-rank symptoms. *Bristish Journal of Psychiatry, 140*, 423–424.

Melzack, R., & Wall, P. D. (1965). Pain mechanisms: A new theory. *Science, 150*(699), 971–979.

Mendels, J., & Cochrane, C. (1968). The nosology of depression: The endogenous-reactive concept. *American Journal of Psychiatry, 124*(11), Suppl. 1–11.

Mendelson, J. H., & Mello, N. K. (1979). *The diagnosis and treatment of alcoholism.* New York: McGraw-Hill.

Mendelson, J. H., & Mello, N. K. (1974). Alcohol, aggression, and androgens. *Proceeding of the Association for Research in Nervous and Mental Diseases, 52*, 225–247.

Mendlewicz, J. (1988). Population and family studies in depression and mania. *British Journal of Psychiatry, 153*(Suppl 3), 16–25.

Mendlewicz, J., Fleiss, J., & Fieve, R. (1972). Evidence for X-linkage in the transmission of manic-depressive illness. *Journal of the American Medical Association, 222*, 1624–1627.

Menolascino, F. (1977). *Challenges in mental retardation: Progressive ideology and services.* New York: Human Sciences Press.

Mercer, J. (1973). *Labeling the mentally retarded.* Berkeley: University of California Press.

Mesulam, M. M. (1981). Dissociative states with abnormal temporal lobe EEG, multiple personality and the illusion of possession. *Archives of Neurology, 38*, 176–181.

Michael, R. P., & Zumpe, D. (1983). Sexual violence in the United States and the role of season. *American Journal of Psychiatry, 140*(7), 883–886.

Miller, L. (1991). Predicitng relapse and recovery in alcoholism and addiction: Neuropsychology, personality and cognitive style. *Journal of Substance Abuse and Treatment, 8*(4), 277–291.

Miller, W. R., & Hester, R. K. (1986). Inpatient alcoholism treatment: Who benefits? *American Psychologist, 41*, 794–805.

Millon, T., & Klerman, G. (1986). *Contemporary directions in psychopathology: Toward the DSM-IV.* New York: Guilford Press.

Miniszek, N. A. (1983). Development of Alzheimer disease in Down syndrome individuals. *American Journal of Mental Deficiency, 87*(4), 377–385.

Mitchell, J. E., Hatsukami, D., Eckert, E. D., & Pyle, R. L. (1985). Characteristics of 275 patients with bulimia. *American Journal of Psychiatry, 142*(4), 482–485.

Mitchell, J. E., Pyle, R. L., Eckert, E. D., Hatsukami, D., Pomeroy, C., & Zimmerman, R. (1990). A comparison study of antidepressants and structured intensive group psychotherapy in the treatment of bulimia nervosa. *Archives of General Psychiatry, 47*(2), 149–157.

Mohr, J. W., Turner, R. E., & Jerry, M. B. (1964). *Pedophilia and exhibitionism: A handbook..* Toronto: University of Toronto Press.

Money, J., & Normal, B. F. (1987). Gender identity and gender transposition: Longitudinal outcome study of 24 male hermaphrodites assigned as boys. *Journal of Sex and Marital Therapy, 13*(2), 75–92.

Money, J., Wiedeking, C., Walker, P., Migeon, C., Meyer, W., & Borgaonkar, D. (1975). 47,XYY and 46,XY males with antisocial and/or sex-offending behavior: antiandrogen therapy plus counseling. *Psychoneuroendocrinology, 1,* 165–178.

Monteiro, M. G., Klein, J. L., & Schuckit, M. A. (1991). High levels of sensitivity to alcohol in young adult Jewish men: A pilot study. *Journal of Studies on Alcohol, 52*(5), 464–469.

Montgomery, M. A., Clayton, P. J., & Friedhoff, A. J. (1982). Psychiatric illness in Tourette syndrome patients and first degree relatives. In A. J. Friedhoff & T. N. Chase (Eds.), *Gilles de la Tourette syndrome* (pp. 335–339.). New York: Raven Press.

Moore, C. A., & Gurakar, A. (1988). Nocturnal myoclonus and restless legs syndrome. In R. L. Williams, I. Karacan, & C. A. Moore (Eds.), *Sleep disorders: Diagnosis and treatment* (2nd ed.; pp. 73–86). New York: John Wiley & Sons.

Moravec, J. D., & Munley, P. H. (1983). Psychological test findings on pathological gamblers in treatment. *International Journal of the Addictions, 18*(7), 1003–1009.

Morgan, H. B. (1985). Functional vomiting. *Journal of Psychosomatic Research, 29*(4), 341–352.

Mortimer, J. A., & Schuman, L. M. (1981). *The epidemiology of dementia.* New York: Oxford University Press.

Moskowitz, J. A. (1980). Lithium and Lady Luck: Use of lithium carbonate in compulsive gambling. *New York State Journal of Medicine, 80*(5), 785–788.

Moss, P. D., & McEvedy, C. P. (1955). An epidemic of overbreathing among schoolgirls. *British Medical Journal, 4,* 1295–1300.

Munjack, D. J., Oziel, J. L., Kanno, P. H., Whipple, K., & Leonard, M. D. (1981). Psychological characteristics of males with secondary erectile failure. *Archives of Sexual Behavior, 10*(2), 123–131.

Munro, J. D. (1986). Epidemiology and extent of mental retardation. *Psychiatric Clinics of North America, 9*(4), 591–624.

Murphree, O. D., & Dykman, R. A. (1965). Litter patterns in the offspring of nervous and stable dogs. 1. Behavioral tests. *Journal of Mental Disease, 141*(3), 321–332.

Murphy, G. E., Simons, A. D., Wetzel, R. D., & Lustman, P. J. (1984). Cognitive therapy and pharmacotherapy: Singly and together in the treatment of depression. *Archives of General Psychiatry, 41,* 33–41.

Narayan, C. (1990). Birth order and narcissism. *Psychological Reports, 67*(3, pt 2), 1184–1186.

Ndetei, D. M. (1986). Paranoid disorder—environmental, cultural or constitutional phenomenon? *Acta Psychiatrica Scandinavica, 74,* 50–54.

Ndetei, D. M., & Singh, A. (1982). A study of delusions in Kenyan schizophrenic patients diagnosed using a set of research diagnostic criteria. *Acta Psychiatrica Scandinavica, 66,* 208–215.

Ndetei, D. M., & Vadher, A. (1985). Content of grandiose phenomenology across cultures. *Acta Psychiatrica Scandinavica, 72*(1), 38–39.

Neal, A. M., & Turner, S. M. (1991). Anxiety disorder research with African Americans: Current status. *Psychological Bulletin, 109*(3), 400–410.

Nestadt, G., Romanoski, A. J., Brown, C. H., & Chahal, R. (1991). DMS-III compulsive personality disorder: An epidemiological survey. *Psychological Medicine, 21*(2), 461–471.

Norton, G. R., Dorward, J., & Cox, B. J. (1986). Factors associated with panic attacks in nonclinical subjects. *Behavior Therapy, 17*(3), 239–252.

Noshirvani, H. F., Kasviskis, Y., Marks, I. M., Tsakiris, F., & Montiero, W. O. (1991). Gender-divergent aetiological factors in obsessive-compulsive disorder. *British Journal of Psychiatry, 158,* 260–263.

Noyes, R. J., Anderson, D. J., Clancy, J., Crowe, R. R., Slymen, D. J., Ghroneim, M. M., & Hinrichs, J. V. (1984). Diazepam and propranolol in panic disorder and agoraphobia. *Archives of General Psychiatry, 41*(3), 287–292.

Nyhan, W. L., Johnson, H. G., Kaufman, I. A., & Jones, K. L. (1980). Serotonergic approaches to the modification of behavior in the Lesch-Nyhan syndrome. *Applied Research in Mental Retardation, 1*(1–2), 25–40.

Nystron, S., & Lindegard, B. (1975). Predisposition for mental syndromes: A study comparing predisposition for depression, neurasthenia and anxiety state. *Acta Psychiatrica Scandinavica, 51*(2), 69–76.

O'Brien, L. S., & Hughes, S. J. (1991). Symptoms of post-traumatic stress disorder in Falklands veterans five years after the conflict. *British Journal of Psychiatry, 159,* 135–141.

O'Carroll, R., & Bancroft, J. (1984). Testosterone therapy for low sexual interest and erectile dysfunction in men: A controlled study. *British Journal of Psychiatry, 145,* 146–151.

O'Donnell, J., Voss, H., Clayton, R., Slatin, G., & Room, R. (1976). Young men and drugs: A nationwide survey. (NIDA Monograph Series 5). Washington, DC: Government Printing Office.

O'Hara, M. W., Neuaber, D. J., & Zeboski, E. M. (1984). Prospective study of postpartum depression: Prevalence, course, and predictive factors. *Journal of Abnormal Psychology, 93*(2), 158–171.

O'Hara, M. W., Schlechte, J. A., Lewis, D. A., & Wright, E. J. (1991).

Prospective study of postpartum blues. Biologic and psychosocial factors. *Archives of General Psychiatry, 48,* 801–806.

Olczak, P. V., Donnerstein, D., Hershberger, T. J., & Kahn, I. (1971). Group hysteria and the MMPI. *Psychological Reports, 28*(2), 413–414.

Opjordsmoen, S. (1988). Long-term course and outcome in delusional disorder. *Acta Psychiatrica Scandinavica, 78,* 576–586.

Ormel, J., Koeter, M. W. J., van den Brink, W., & van de Willige, G. (1991). Recognition, management, and course of anxiety and depression in general practice. *Archives of General Psychuiatry, 48,* 700–706.

Osmond, H. (1973). Come home, psychiatry: The megavitamin treatment and the medical model. *Psychiatric Opinion, 10*(5), 14–23.

O'Sullivan, K. (1979). Observations on vaginismus in Irish women. *Archives of General Psychiatry, 36,* 824–826.

Osuntokun, B. O., Adeuja, A. O., Nottidge, V. A., Bademosi, O., Olumide, A., Inge, O., Yaria, F., Bolis, C. L., & Schoenberg, B. S. (1987). Prevalence of the epilepsies in Nigerian Africans: A community-based study. *Epilepsia, 28*(3), 272–279.

Overholser, J. C. (1989). Differentiation between schizoid and avoidant personalities: An empirical test. *Canadian Journal of Psychiatry, 34*(8), 785–790.

Overholser, J. C. (1990). Differential diagnosis of malingering and factitious disorder with physical symptoms. *Behavioral Sciences and the Law, 8,* 55–65.

Overholser, J. C. (1992). Interpersonal dependency and social loss. *Personality and Individual Differences, 13*(1), 17–23.

Paff, B. A. (1985). Sexual dysfunction in gay men requesting treatment. *Journal of Sex and Marital Therapy, 11*(1), 3–18.

Pankratz, L., &. Lezak, M. D. (1987). Cerebral dysfunction in the Munchausen syndrome. *Hillside Journal of Clinical Psychiatry, 9*(2), 195–206.

Park, S., Templer, D. I., Canfield, M., & Cappelletty, G. G. (1992). Multivariate analysis of schizophrenic dimensions. *Journal of Orthomolecular Medicine, 7*(2), 95–101.

Parnas, J., Schulsinger, F., Schulsinger, H., Mednick, S. A., & Teasdale, T. W. (1982). Behavioral precursors of schizophrenia spectrum: A prospective study. *Archives of General Psychiatry, 39,* 658–664.

Parnas, J., Schulsinger, F., Teasdale, T. W., Schulsinger, H., Feldman, P. M., & Mednick, S. A. (1982). Perinatal complications and clinical outcome within the schizophrenia spectrum. *British Journal of Psychiatry, 140,* 416–420.

Passafiume, D., Boller, F., Keefe, N. C. (1985). Neuropsychological impairment in patients with Parkinson disease. In I. Grant & K. M. Adams (Eds). *Neuropsychological assessment of neuropsychiatric disorders* (pp. 374–383). New York: Oxford University Press.

Pattison, E. M., Headley, E. B., Gleser, G. C., & Gottschalk, L. A. (1968).

Abstinence and normal drinking: An assessment of changes in drinking patterns in alcoholics after treatment. *Quarterly Journal of Studies on Alcohol, 29*(3), 610–633.

Patton, G. C., Wood, K., & Johnson-Sabine, E. (1986). Physical illness: A risk factor in anorexia nervosa. *British Journal of Psychiatry, 149,* 756–759.

Pauley, L. L. (1989). Customer weight as a variable in salespersons' response time. *Journal of Social Psychology, 129*(5), 713–714.

Pauly, I. B. (1974). Female transsexualism: Part 1. *Archives of Sexual Behavior, 3,* 487–507.

Paykel, E. S., Myer, J. K., Dienelt, M. N., Klerman, G. L., Lindenthal, J. J., & Pepper, M. P. (1969). Life events and depression: A controlled study. *Archives of General Psychiatry, 21,* 753–760.

Penrose, L. S. (1963). Measurement of likeness in relatives of trisomics. *Annals of Human Genetics, 27*(2), 183–187.

Perris, C., & Gallant, D. M. (1976), Frequency and hereditary aspects of depression. In D. M. Gallant & G. M. Simpson (Eds.), *Depression: Behavioral, diagnostic and treatment concepts.* New York: SP Books Division of Spectrum Publications.

Peterson, H. D., Abildgaard, U., Daugaard, G., Jess, P., Marcussen, H., & Wallach, M. (1985). Psychological and physical long-term effects of torture: A follow-up examination of 22 Greek persons exposed to torture 1967–1974. *Scandinavian Journal of Social Medicine, 13,* 89–93.

Petrovich, M., & Templer, D. I. (1984). Heterosexual molestation of children who later become rapists. *Psychological Reports, 54,* 810.

Peveler, R., & Fairburn, C. (1990). Eating disorders in women who abuse alcohol. *British Journal of Addiction, 85*(12), 1633–1638.

Philips, H. C. (1987). Avoidance behaviour and its role in sustaining chronic pain. *Behavior Research and Therapy, 25*(4), 273–279.

Politzer, R. M., Morrow, J. S., & Leavey, S. B. (1985). Report on the cost-benefit/ effectiveness of treatment at the Johns Hopkins Center for Pathological Gambling. *Journal of Gambling Behavior, 1,* 119–130.

Pollak, J. (1987). Relationship of obsessive-compulsive personality to obsessive-compulsive disorder: A review of the literature. *Journal of Psychology, 121*(2), 137–148.

Pollock, V. E., Volavka, J., Goodwin, D. W., Mednick, S. A., Gabrielli, W. F., Knop, J., & Schulsinger, F. (1983). The EEG after alcohol administration in men at risk for alcoholism. *Archives of General Psychiatry, 40*(8), 657–661.

Poskanzer, D. C. (1980). Neurologic disease. In J. M. Last (Ed.), *Maxcy-Rosenau public health and preventive medicine* (11th ed., pp. 1256–1265). New York: Appleton-Century-Crofts.

President's Commission on Mental Retardation. (1972). *MR 71: Entering the era of human ecology* (Report No. 5). Washington, DC: Department of Health, Education and Welfare.

Prien, R. F., Kupfer, D. J., Mansky, P. A., Small, J. G., Tuason, V. B., Voss, C. B., & Johnson, W. E. (1984). Drug therapy in the prevention of recurrences in unipolar and bipolar affective disorders. *Archives of General Psychiatry, 41,* 1096–1104.

Prince, I. (1989). Pica and geophagia in cross-cultural perspective. *Transcultural Psychiatric Research Review, 26,* 167–197.

Putnam, F. W., Guroff, J. J., Silberman, E. K., Barban, L., & Post, R. M. (1986). The clinical phenomenology of multiple personality disorder: A review of 100 recent cases. *Journal of Clinical Psychiatry, 47*(6), 285–293.

Pyle, R. L., Mitchell, J. E., & Eckert, E. D. (1981). Bulimia: A report of 34 cases. *Journal of Clinical Psychiatry, 42*(2), 60–64.

Quay, H. C. (1965). Psychopathic personality as pathological stimulation seeking. *American Journal of Psychiatry, 122,* 180–183.

Rachman, S. (1966). Sexual fetishism: An experimental analogue. *Psychological Record, 16*(3), 293–296.

Radloff, L. (1975). Sex differences in depression. *Sex Roles, 1,* 249–265.

Ramani, S. V., Quesney, L. F., Olson, D., & Gumnit, R. J. (1980). Diagnosis of hysterical seizures in epileptic patients. *American Journal of Psychiatry, 137*(6), 705–709.

Ramirez, L. F., McCormack, R. A., Russo, A. M., & Taber, J. I. (1983). Patterns of substance abuse in pathological gamblers undergoing treatment. *Addictive Behaviors, 8*(4), 425–428.

Rankin, H. (1982). Control rather than abstinence as a goal in the treatment of excessive gambling. *Behavior Research and Therapy, 20*(2), 185–187.

Ransford, O. (1972). *The slave trade.* London: Newton Abbot Readers Union.

Rapaport, K., & Burkhart, B. R. (1984). Personality and attitudinal characteristics of sexually coercive college males. *Journal of Abnormal Psychology, 93*(2), 216–221.

Rapee, R. (1986). Differential response to hyperventilation in panic disorder and generalized anxiety disorder. *Journal of Abnormal Psychology, 95*(1), 24–28.

Reich, J. (1987). Sex distribution of DSM-III personality disorders in psychiatric outpatients. *American Journal of Psychiatry, 144*(4), 485–488.

Reich, J., Noyes, R., & Troughton, E. (1987). Dependent personality disorder associated with phobic avoidance in patients with panic disorder. *American Journal of Psychiatry, 144*(3), 323–326.

Reich, T., Clayton, P. J., & Winokur, G. (1969). Family history studies: 5. The genetics of mania. *American Journal of Psychiatry, 125*(10), 1358–1369.

Reid, A. H. (1980). Psychiatric disorders in mentally handicapped children: A clinical and follow-up study. *Journal of Mental Deficiency Research, 24,* 287–298.

Reider, R. O., Donnelly, E. F., & Herdt, J. R. (1979). Sulcal prominence in young chronic schizophrenic patients: CT scan findings associated with impairment on neuropsychological tests. *Psychiatry Research, 1*, 1–8.

Reiman, E. M., Raichle, M. E., Robins, E., Butler, F. K., Herscovitch, P., Fox, P., & Perlmutter, J. (1986). The application of positron emission tomography to the study of panic disorder. *American Journal of Psychiatry, 143*(4), 469–477.

Renneberg, B., Goldstein, A. J., Phillips, D., & Chambliss, D. L. (1990). Intensive behavioral group treatment of avoidant personality disorder. *Behavior Therapy, 21*(3), 363–377.

Reveley, M., Reveley, A. M., Clifford, C. A., & Murray, R. M. (1983). Genetics of platelet MAO activity in discordant schizophrenic and normal twins. *British Journal of Psychiatry, 142*, 560–565.

Reynolds, C. F., Christiansen, C. L., Taska, L. S., Colde, P. A., & Kupfer, D. J. (1983). Sleep in narcolepsy and depression: Does it look alike? *Sleep Research, 12*, 211.

Reynolds, W. M., & Reynolds, S. (1979). Prevalence of speech and hearing impairment [in] noninstitutionalized mentally retarded adults. *American Journal of Mental Deficiency, 84*(1), 62–66.

Richardson, S. A., Hastorf, A. H., Goodman, N., & Dornbush, S. M. (1961). Cultural uniformity in reaction to physical disabilities. *American Sociological Review, 26*, 241–244.

Richardson, S. A., Katz, M., Kooler, H., McLaren, J., & Rubinstein, B. (1979). Some characteristics of a population of mentally retarded young adults in a British city. A basis for estimating some service needs. *Journal of Mental Deficiency Research, 23*(4), 275–285.

Rimel, R. W., Giordani, B., Barth, J. T., Boll, T. J., & Jane, J. A. (1981). Disability caused by minor head injury. *Neurosurgery, 9*(3), 221–228.

Ritvo, E., Shanok, S. S., & Lewis, D. D. (1983). Firesetting and nonfiresetting delinqurents. A comparison of neuropsychiatric, psychoeducational, experiential, and behavioral characteristics. *Child Psychiatry and Human Development, 13*(4), 259–267.

Roberts, A. H. (1964). Housebound housewives: A follow-up study of phobic anxiety state. *British Journal of Psychiatry, 110*(465), 191–197.

Robertson, J., & Meyer, V. (1976). Treatment of kleptomania: A case report. *Scandinavian Journal of Behaviour Therapy, 5*(2), 87–92.

Robins, L. N. (1975). Discussion of genetic studies of criminality and psychopathy. *Proceedings of the Annual Meeting of the American Psychopathology Association, 63*, 117–122.

Rodin, E. A. (1973). Psychomotor epilepsy and aggressive behavior. *Archives of General Psychiatry, 28*, 210–213.

Romme, M. A. J., & Escher, A. (1989). Hearing voices. *Schizophrenia Bulletin, 15*(2), 209–216.

Rorsman, B., Grasbeck, A., Hagnell, O., Lanke, J., Ohman, R., Ojesjo, L., & Otterbeck, L. (1990). A prospective study of first-incidence depression: The Lundby Study, 1957–72. *British Journal of Psychiatry, 156,* 336–342.

Rosenberg, C. M. (1968). Complications of obsessional neurosis. *British Journal of Psychiatry, 114*(509), 477–478.

Rosenberg, D. A. (1987). Web of deceit: A literature review of Munchausen syndrome by proxy. *Child Abuse and Neglect, 11*(4), 547–563.

Rosenthal, R., & Bigelow, L. B. (1972). Quantitative brain measurements in chronic schizophrenia. *British Journal of Psychiatry, 121*(562), 259–264.

Rosenthal, N. E., Sack, D. A., Carpenter, C. J., Parry, B. L., Mendelson, W. B., & Wehr, T. A. (1985). Antidepressant effects of light in seasonal affective disorder. *American Journal of Psychiatry, 142*(2), 163–170.

Ross, C. A., Anderson, G., Heber, S., & Norton, G. R. (1990). Dissociation and abuse among multiple-personality patients, prostitutes, and exotic dancers. *Hospital and Community Psychiatry, 41*(3), 328–330.

Ross, C. A., Heber, S., Norton, G. R., & Anderson, G. (1989). Somatic symptoms in multiple personality disorder. *Psychosomatics, 30*(2), 154–160.

Ross, C. A., Norton, G. R., & Wozney, K. (1989). Multiple personality disorder: An analysis of 236 cases. *Canadian Journal of Psychiatry, 34*(5), 413–418.

Ross, R. J., Cole, M., Thompson, J. S., & Kim, K. H. (1983). Boxers—computed tomography, EEG, and neurological evaluation. *Journal of the American Medical Association, 249*(2), 211–213.

Roth, M. (1978). Epidemiological studies. In R. D. Terry, K. L. Bick, & R. Katzman, (Eds.), *Alzheimer's disease: Senile dementia and related disorders.* New York: Raven Press.

Roth, T., Roehers, T., & Zorick, F. (1988). Pharmacological treatment of sleep disorders. In R. L. Williams, I. Karacan, & C. A. Moore (Eds,). *Sleep Disorders: Diagnosis and treatment* (2nd ed.), pp. 373–396). New York: John Wiley & Sons.

Rounsaville, B. J., Weissman, M. M., Crits-Cristoph, K., Wilber, C., & Kleber, H. (1982). Diagnosis and symptoms of depression in opiate addicts: Course and relationship to treatment outcome. *Archives of General Psychiatry, 39*(2), 151–156.

Roy, A. (1981a). Sexual dysfunction and hysteria. *British Journal of Psychology, 54*(pt. 2), 131–132.

Roy, A. (1981b). Specificity of risk factors for depression. *American Journal of Psychiatry, 138*(7), 959–961.

Roy, A. (1987). Five risk factors for depression. *British Journal of Psychiatry, 150,* 536–541.

Roy-Byrne, P. P., Geraci, M., & Uhde, T. W. (1986). Life events and the onset of panic disorder. *American Journal of Psychiatry, 143*(11), 1424–1427.

Ruch, L. O., Chandler, S. M., & Harter, R. A. (1980). Life change and rape impact. *Journal of Health and Social Behavior, 21*(3), 248–260.

Russell, D. E. H. (1984). *Sexual exploitation*. Beverly Hills, CA: Sage Press.

Rzewnicki, R., & Forgays, D. G. (1987). Recidivism amd self-cure of smoking and obesity: An attempt to replicate [Letter to the editor]. *American Psychologist*, 42(1), 97–100.

Sabhesan, S., & Natarajan, M. (1988). Delusion disorders after head injury. *Indian Journal of Psychiatry*, 30(1), 39–45.

Saeger, C. P. (1970). Treatment of compulsive gamblers by electrical aversion. *British Journal of Psychiatry*, 117(540), 545–553.

Saenger, G. (1966.). *The adjustment of severely retarded adults in the adjustment of a group of mentally deficient adults in 1948 and 1960*. Hartford, CT: The Connecticut State Mental Retardation Planning Project.

Saghir, M. T., & Robins, E. (1971). Male and female homosexuality: Natural history. *Comprehensive Psychiatry*, 12(6), 503–510.

Saghir, M. T., Robins, E., Walbran, B., & Gentry, K. A. (1970). Homosexuality: 3. Psychiatric disorders and disability in the male homosexual. *American Journal of Psychiatry*, 126(8), 1079–1086.

Salkovskis, P. M., Jones, D. R., & Clark, D. M. (1986). Respiratory control in the treatment of panic attacks: Replication and extension with concurrent measurement of behaviour and pCO_2. *British Journal of Psychiatry*, 148, 526–532.

Saltzman, V., & Solomon, R. S. (1982). Incest and the multiple personality. *Psychological Reports*, 50(3, pt. 2), 1127–1141.

San, L., Pomarol, G., Peri, J. M., Olle, J. M., & Cami, J. (1991). Follow-up after a six-month maintenance period on naltrexone versus placebo in heroin addicts. *British Journal of Addiction*, 86, 983–990.

Sanchez-Craig, M., Annis, H. M., Bornet, A. R., & MacDonald, K. R. (1984). Random assignment to abstinence and controlled drinking: Evaluation of a cognitive-behavioral program for problem drinkers. *Journal of Consulting and Clinical Psychology*, 52(3), 390–403.

Sanchez-Craig, M., Leigh, G., Spivak, K., & Lei, H. (1989). Superior outcome of females over males after brief treatment for the reduction of heavy drinking. *British Journal of Addicitons*, 84(4), 395–404.

Sanchez-Craig, M., Spivak, K., & Davila, R. (1991). Superior outcome of females over males after brief treatment for the reduction of heavy drinking: Replication and report of therapist effects. *British Journal of Addiction*, 86, 867–876.

Sanders, B., & Giolas, M. H. (1991). Dissociation and childhood trauma in psychologically disturbed adolescents. *American Journal of Psychiatry*, 148(1), 50–54.

Sanders, B., McRoberts, G., & Tollefson, C. (1989). Childhood stress and dissociation in a college population. *Dissociation Progress in the Dissociation Disorders*, 2(1), 17–23.

Sarrel, P. M., & Masters, W. H. (1982). Sexual molestation of men by women. *Archives of Sexual Behavior*, 11(2), 117–131.

Scarbrough, P. R., Cosper, P., Finley, S. C., & Smith, N. B. (1984). Fragile-X syndrome: An overview. *Alabama Journal of Medical Sciences, 21*(1), 68–72.

Schachter, S. (1971). Some extraordinary facts about obese humans and rats. *American Psychologist, 26*, 129–144.

Schachter, S. (1982). Recidivism and self-cure of smoking and obesity. *American Psychologist, 37*(4), 436–444.

Schalock, R. L., & Harper, R. S. (1978). Placement from community-based mental retardation programs: How well do clients do? *American Journal of Mental Deficiency, 83*(3), 240–247.

Scheper-Hughes, N. (1979). *Saints, scholars and schizophrenics.* Berkeley: University of California Press.

Schlueter, G. R., O'Neal, F. C., Hickey, J., et. al. (1989). Rational vs nonrational shoplifting types: The implications for loss prevention strategies. *International Journal of Offender Therapy and Comparative Criminology, 33*, 227–239.

Schmidt, C., Klee, L., & Ames, G. (1990). Review and analysis of literature on indicators of women's drinking problems. *British Journal of Addiction, 85*, 179–192.

Schneck, M. K., Reisberg, B., & Ferris, S. H. (1982). An overview of current concepts of Alzheimer's disease. *American Journal of Psychiatry, 139*(2), 165–173.

Schneider, J. A., & Agras, W. S. (1987). Bulimia in males: A matched comparison with females. *International Journal of Eating Disorders, 6*, 235–242.

Schneider, K. (1959). *Clinical psychopathology.* London: Grune & Stratton.

Schoenfeld, H., Margolin, J., & Baum, S. (1987). Munchausen syndrome as a suicide equivalent: Abolition of syndrome by psychotherapy. *American Journal of Psychotherapy, 41*(4), 604–612.

Schotte, C., Maes, M., Cluydts, R., deDoncker, D., Machteld, C., & Cosyns, P. (1991). MMPI characteristics of the DSM-III-R avoidant personality disorder. *Psychological Reports, 69*(1), 75–81.

Schuckit, M. A., Goodwin, D. A., & Winokur, G. (1972). A study of alcoholism in half siblings. *American Journal of Psychiatry, 128*(9), 1132–1136.

Schulsinger, F., Parnas, J., Peterson, E. T., Schulsinger, H., Teasdale, T. W., Mednick, S. A., Moller, L., & Silverton, L. (1984). Cerebral ventricular size in the offspring of schizophrenic mothers. *Archives of General Psychiatry, 41*, 602–606.

Schultz, B. (1932). Zur erbpathologie der scizophrenie. *Zeitschrift der Neurologische Psychiative, 143*, 175–293.

Schwartz, M. F., Kolodny, R. C., & Masters, W. H. (1980). Plasma testosterone levels of sexually functional and disfunctional men. *Archives of Sexual Behavior, 9*(5), 355–366.

Sclafani, A. (1980). Dietary obesity. In A. J. Stunkard (Ed.), *Obesity.* Philadelphia: W. B. Saunders.

Scott, A. I. (1989). Which depressed patients will respond to electroconvulsive therapy? The search for biological predictors of recovery. *British Journal of Psychiatry, 154,* 8–17.

Seagraves, K. B., & Seagraves, R. T. (1991). Hypoactive sexual desire disorder: Prevalence and comorbidity in 906 subjects. *Journal of Sex and Marital Therapy, 17*(1), 55–58.

Segraves, K. A., Segraves, R. T., & Schoenberg, H. W. (1987). Use of sexual history to differentiate organic from psychogenic impotence. *Archives of Sexual Behavior, 16*(2), 125–137.

Seligman, M. E. P. (1974). Depression and learned helplessness. In R. J. Friedman & M. M. Katz, *The Psychology of depression: Contemporary theory and research.* Washington, DC: Winston-Wiley.

Serban, G., & Siegel, S. (1984). Response of borderlines and schizotypal patients to small doses of thiothixene and haloperidol. *American Journal of Psychiatry, 14*(11), 1455–1458.

Sethi, B. B., Chaturvedi, P. K., Gupta, A. K., & Trivedi, J. K. (1982). Trichotillomania in association with psychosis—a case report. *Indian Journal of Psychiatry, 24*(4), 396–398.

Shader, R. I., Jackson, A. H., Harmatz, J. S., & Applebaum, P. S. (1977). Patterns of violent behavior among schizophrenic patients. *Diseases of the Nervous System, 38*(1), 13–16.

Shaffer, D., Schonfeld, I., O'Connor, P. A., Stokman, C., Trautman, P., Shafer, S., & Ng, S. (1985). Neurological soft signs: Their relationship to psychiatric disorder and intelligence in childhood and adolescence. *Archives of General Psychiatry, 42,* 342–348.

Shagass, C., & James, N. (1956). The sedation threshold as an objective index of manifest anxiety in psychoneurosis. *Journal of Psychsomatic Research, 1,* 29–57.

Shear, M. K., Klingfield, P., Harshfield, G., Devereux, R. B., Polam, J. J., Mann, J. J., Pickering, T. & Frances, A. J. (1987). Cardiac rate and rhythm in panic patients. *American Journal of Psychiatry, 144*(5), 633–637.

Sheikh, J., King, R. J., & Taylor, C. B. (1991). Comparative phenomenology of early-onset versus late-onset panic attacks: A pilot survey. *American Journal of Psychiatry, 148*(9), 1231–1233.

Sherwin, D., & Mead, B. (1975). Delirium tremens in a nine year old child. *American Journal of Psychiatry, 132*(11), 1210–1212.

Sherwin, I. (1982). The effect of the location of an epileptogenic lesion on the occurrence of psychosis in epilepsy. *Advanced Biological Psychiatry, 8,* 81–97.

Shields, J. (1961). Fusional reserves and psychological variables in monzygotic twins. *Acta Geneticae Medicae et Gemellologiae, 10,* 366–368.

Shields, J. (1975). Genetics in schizophrenia. In D. Kemali, G. Bartholini, & D. Richter (Eds.). *Schizophrenia today.* (pp. 57–70). Oxford: Pergamon Press.

Siegel, C., Waldo, M., Mizner, G., Adler, L. E., & Freedman, R. (1984). Deficits in sensory gating in schizophrenic patients and their relatives: Evidence obtained with auditory evoked responses. *Archives of General Psychiatry, 41,* 607–612.

Siegel, R. K. (1978a). Cocaine hallucinations. *American Journal of Psychiatry, 135*(3), 309–314.

Siegel, R. K. (1978b). Phencyclidine and katamine intoxication: A study of four populations of recreational users. In R. C. Petersen & R. C. Stillman, (Eds.), *Phencyclidine (PCP) abuse: An appraisal* (pp. 119–147). Washington, DC: National Institute on Drug Abuse. (NIDA Research monograph 21).

Siever, L. J. (January, 1990). Evaluation framework set for biologic correlates of personality disorder. *Psychiatric Times,* 17–19.

Sinclair, J. D., & Senter, R. J. (1968). Development of an alcohol-deprivation effect in rats. *Quarterly Journal of Studies on Alcohol, 29*(4), 863–867.

Slater, E. (1961). Hysteria 311. *Journal of Mental Science, 107,* 359–381.

Slater, E. (1968). A review of earlier evidence on genetic factors in schizophrenia. In D. Rosenthal & S. S. Kety (Eds.). *The transmission of schizophrenia* (pp. 15–26). Oxford: Pergamon Press.

Slater, E. T., & Glithero, E. (1965). A follow-up of patients diagnosed as suffering from "hysteria." *Journal of Psychosomatic Research, 9*(1), 9–13.

Sloman, L., Berridge, M., Homatidis, S., Hunter, D., & Duck, T. (1982). Gait pattern of depressed patients and normal subjects. *American Journal of Psychiatry, 139*(1), 94–97.

Smith, B. M. (1990). The measurement of narcissism in Asian, Caucasian, and Hispanic American women. *Psychological Reports, 67*(3, pt. 1), 779–785.

Smith, R. S. (1976). Voyeurism: A review of literature. *Archives of Sexual Behavior, 5*(6), 585–607.

Soloff, P. H., George, A., Nathan, S., Schulz, P. M., Ulrich, R. F., & Perel, J. M. (1986). Progress in pharmacotherapy of borderline disorders. *Archives of General Psychiatry, 43*(7), 691–697.

Solomon, R. L., Kamin, L. J., & Wynne, L. C. (1953). Traumatic avoidance learning: The outcomes of several extinction procedures with dogs. *Journal of Abnormal Psychology, 48,* 291–302.

Solomon, R. S., & Solomon, V. (1982). Differential diagnosis of the multiple personality. *Psychological Reports, 51*(3, pt. 2), 1187–1194.

Solyom, L., Garza-Perez, J., Ledwidge, B. L., & Solyom, C. (1972). Paradoxical intention in the treatment of obsessive thoughts: A pilot study. *Comprehensive Psychiatry, 13*(3), 291–297.

Sommers, I. (1988). Pathological gambling: Estimating prevalence and group characteristics. *International Journal of Addictions, 23*(5), 477–490.

Sours, J. A. (1983). Case reports of anorexia nervosa and caffeinism. *American Journal of Psychiatry, 140*(2), 235–236.

Spector, H. P., & Carey, M. P. (1990). Incidence and prevalence of the sexual dysfunctions: A critical review of the empirical literature. *Archives of Sexual Behavior, 19*(4), 389–408.

Speilberger, C. D., Gorsuch, R. L., & Lushene, R. E. (1970). *STAI manual [for the State-Trait Anxiety Inventory: "Self-evaluation Questionaire"]*. Palo Alto, CA: Consulting Psychologists Press.

Spengler, A. (1977). Manifest sadomasochism of males: Results of an empirical study. *Archives of Sexual Behavior, 6*(6), 441–456.

Spiegel, D., & Cardena, F. (1991). Disintegrated experience: The dissociative disorders revisited. *Journal of Abnormal Psychology, 100*(3), 366–370.

Spiess, W. F. J., Geer, J. H., & O'Donohue, W. T. (1984). Premature ejaculation: Investigation of factors in ejaculatory latency. *Journal of Abnormal Psychology, 93*(2), 242–245.

Spradlin, J. E. (1963). Assessment of speech and language of retarded children: The Parsons language sample. *Journal of Speech and Hearing Disorders*, (Monograph suppl. No. 10), 8–31, 275.

Spreen, O., Tupper, D., Risser, A., Tuokko, H., & Edgell, D. (1984). *Human development neuropsychology*. New York: Oxford University Press.

Standage, K. F. (1983). Observations on the handedness preferences of patients with personality disorders. *British Journal of Psychiatry, 142*, 575–578.

Stanton, A. H., Gunderson, J. G., Knapp, P. H., Frank, A. F., Vannicelli, M. L., Schnitzer, R., & Rosenthal, R. (1984). Effects of psychotherapy in schizophrenia: 1. Design and implementation of a controlled study. *Schizophrenia Bulletin, 10*(4), 520–563.

Starin, S., & Fuqua, R. W. (1987). Rumination and vomiting in the developmentally disabled: A critical review of the behavioral, medical, and psychiatric treatment research. *Research in Developmental Disabilities, 8*(4), 575–605.

Starkstein, S. E., Pearlson, G. D., Boston, J., & Robinson, R. G. (1987). Mania after brain injury: A controlled study of causative factors. *Archives of Neurology, 44*(10), 1069–1073.

Steffansson, J. G., Messina, J. A., & Meyerowitz. (1976). Hysterical neurosis, conversion type, clinical and epidemiological considerations. *Acta Psychiatrica Scandinavica, 53*(2), 119–138.

Stein, Z. A., & Susser, M. (1980). Mental retardation. In J. M. Last (Ed.), *Maxcy-Rosenau public health and preventive medicine.* (11th ed., pp. 1266–1282). New York: Appleton-Century-Crofts.

Steinberg, J. L., & Cherek, D. R. (1989). Menstrual cycle and cigarette smoking behavior. *Addictive Behaviors, 14*, 173–179.

Steketee, G., Foa, E. B., & Grayson, J. B. (1982). Recent advances in the behavioral treatment of obsessive-compulsives. *Archives of General Psychiatry, 39*(12), 1365–1371.

Steketee, G. S., Grayson, J. B., & Foa, E. B. (1985). Obsessive-compulsive disorder: Differences between washers and checkers. *Behavioral Research and Therapy, 23*(2), 197–201.

Stephens, J. H., & Kamp, M. (1962). On some aspects of hysteria: A clinical study. *Journal of Nervous and Mental Diseases, 134*, 305–315.

Stevens, J. R., Milstein, V., & Goldstein, S. (1972). Psychometric test performance in relation to the psychopathology of epilepsy. *Archives of General Psychiatry, 26*, 532–538.

Stevens, M., Crow, T. J., Bowman, M. J., & Coles, E. C. (1978). Age disorientation in schizophrenia: A constant prevalence of 25 per cent in a chronic mental hospital population. *British Journal of Psychiatry, 133*, 130–136.

Stewart, M. A., & Culver, K. W. (1982). Children who start fires: The clinical picture and follow-up. *British Journal of Psychiatry, 140*(4), 357–363.

Stoller, R. J. (1982). Transvestism in women. *Archives of Sexual Behavior, 11*(2), 99–115.

Stoller, A., & Collman, R. D. (1965). Incidence of infective hepatitis followed by Down's Syndrome nine months later. *Lancet 2(424)*, 1221–1223.

Stone, M. H. (1977). The borderline personality syndrome: Evolution of the term, genetic aspects and prognosis. *American Journal of Psychotherapy, 31*, 345–365.

Stone, M. H. (1986). Exploratory psychotherapy in schizophrenia-spectrum patients: A reevaluation in the light of long-term follow-up of schizophrenia and borderline patients. *Bulletin of the Menninger Clinic, 50*(3), 287–306.

Strub, R. L., & Black, W. L. (1981). *Organic brain syndromes: An introduction to neurobehavioral disorders.* Philadelphia: F. A. Davis.

Studt, H. H. (1986). [Schizoid versus hysterical personality structure: 2. Social behavioral and triggering situation]. *Zeitschrift für Psychosomatische Medizin und Psychoanalyse, 32*(4), 361–370.

Stunkard, A. J. (1983). The current status of treatment for obesity in adults. *Psychiatric Annals, 13*(11), 862–867.

Stunkard, A. J., & Burt, V. (1967). Obesity and the body image: 2. Age at onset of disturbances in the body image. *American Journal of Psychiatry, 123*(11), 1443–1447.

Suddath, R. L., Christison, G. W., Torrey, E. F., Casanova, M. F., & Weinberger, D. R. (1990). Anatomical abnormalities in the brains of monozygotic twins discordant for schizophrenia. *New England Journal of Medicine, 322*(12), 789–792.

Sutherland, A. J., & Rodin, G. M. (1990). Factitious disorders in a general hospital setting: Clinical features and a review of the literature. *Psychosomatics, 31*(4), 392–399.

Swanson, D. W. (1968). Adult sexual abuse of children (The man and circumstances). *Diseases of the Nervous System, 29*, 677–683.

Swihart, A. A., Baskin, D. S., & Pirozzolo, F. J. (1989). Somatostatin and cognitive dysfunction in Alzheimer's disease. *Developmental Neuropsychology, 5*(2–3), 159–168.

Szmukler, G. I., & Tantam, D. (1984). Anorexia nervosa: Starvation dependence. *British Journal of Medical Psychology, 57,* 303–310.

Szymanski, S., Kane, J. M., & Lieberman, J. A. (1991). A selective review of biological markers in schizophrenia. *Schizophrenia Bulletin, 17*(1), 99–111.

Targum, S. D. (1983). Neuroendocrine dysfunction in schizophreniform disorder: Correlation with six month clinical outcome. *American Journal of Psychiatry, 140*(3), 309–313.

Tarter, R. E., McBride, H., Buonpane, Z., & Schneider, D. U. (1977). Differentiation of alcoholics: Childhood history of minimal brain dysfunction, family history and drinking patterns. *Archives of General Psychaitry, 34*(7), 761–768.

Taylor, J. R., & Combs-Orme, T. (1985). Alcohol and strokes in young adults. *American Journal of Psychiatry, 142*(1), 116–118.

Templer, D. I. (1972). The obsessive-compulsive neurosis: Review of research findings. *Comprehensive Psychiatry, 13,* 375–383.

Templer, D. I. (1974). Suicide by shooting in refractory alcoholics. *Journal Supplement Abstract Service: Catalog of Selected Documents in Psychology, 4,* 49 (MS No. 628).

Templer, D. I. (1977). The subnormal intelligence of rapists. *Medical Aspects of Human Sexuality, 11,* 59.

Templer, D. I., & Austin, R. K. (1980). Decreasing seasonality of birth of schizophrenics. *Archives of General Psychiatry, 37*(8), 959–960.

Templer, D. I., Campodonico, J. R., Trent, A., & Spencer, D. A. (1991). *The neuropsychological spectrum: A theoretical formation.* San Francisco: Western Psychological Association.

Templer, D. I., Campodonico, J. R., Trent, A., Spencer, D. A., & Hartlage, L. C. (in press). The neurological spectrum of ecological validity. *International Journal of Clinical Neuropsychology.*

Templer, D. I., & Cappelletty, G. (1986). Primary versus secondary schizophrenia: A theoretical review. *Journal of Orthomolecular Medicine, 1,* 255–259.

Templer, D. I., Corgiat, M., & Brooner, R. K. (1984). A dimensional conceptualization of anxiety. *British Journal of Psychiatry, 144,* 554.

Templer, D. I., & Eberhardt E. (1980). Necrophilia: A review. *Essence, 4*(2), 63–67.

Templer, D. I., Griffin, P. R., & Hintze, J. (in press). Gender life expectancy and alcohol: An international perspective. *International Journal of the Addicitions.*

Templer, D. I., Hartlage, L. C., & Cannon, W. G. (1992). *Preventable brain damage.* New York: Springer Publishing Co.

Templer, D. I., Hintze, J., Trent, N. A., & Trent, A. (1991). Schizophrenia, latitude and temperature. *Journal of Orthomolecular Medicine, 6,* 5–7.

Templer, D. I., & Lester, D. (1974). Conversion disorders: A review of research findings. *Comprehensive Psychiatry, 15*(4), 285–294.

Templer, D. I., Ruff, C. F., Barthlow, V. L., Halcomb, P. H., & Ayers, J. L. (1978). Psychometric assessment of alcoholism in convicted felons. *Journal of Studies on Alcohol, 39*(11), 1948–1951.

Templer, D. I., Ruff, C. F., Halcomb, P. H., Barthlow, B. A., & Ayers, J. L. (1978). Month of conception and birth of schizophrenics as related to the temperature. *Journal of Orthomolecular Psychiatry, 7*(4), 231–235.

Templer, D. I., Ruff, C. F., & Simpson, K. (1975). Trail Making Test performance of alcoholics abstinent at least a year. *International Journal of the Addictions, 10*(4), 609–612.

Templer, D. I., Trent, A., Trent, N. H., Spencer, D. A., Corgiat, M. D., Munk-Jorgensen, P., & Gorton, M. (1992). Season of birth in multiple sclerosis and schizophrenia. *Acta Neurologica Scandinavica, 85,* 107–109.

Templer, D. I., & Veleber, D. M. (1981). The decline of catatonic schizophrenia. *Journal of Orthomolecular Psychiatry, 10*(3), 156–158.

Templer, D. I., & Veleber, D. M. (1982). The decline of hebephrenic schizophrenia. *Journal of Orthomolecular Psychiatry, 11*(2), 100–102.

Terman, M., Terman, J. S., Quitkin, F. M., & McGrath, P. J., et al. (1989). Light therapy for seasonal affective disorder: A review of efficacy. *Neuropsychopharmacology, 2*(1), 1–22.

Tewfik, G. I., & Okasha, A. (1965). Psychosis amd immigration. *Postgraduate Medical Journal, 41,* 603–612.

Tharp, V. K., Maltzman, I., Syndulko, K., & Ziskind, E. (1980). Autonomic activity during anticipation of an aversive tone in noninstitutionalized sociopaths. *Psychophysiology, 17*(2), 123–128.

Thase, M. E., Reynolds, C. F. III, Glanz, L. M., Jennings, J. R., & Sewitch, D. E. (1987). Nocturnal penile tumescence in depressed men. *American Journal of Psychiatry, 144*(1), 89–92.

Thiessen, D. D., & Rodgers, D. A. (1965). Alcohol injection, grouping and voluntary alcohol consumption of inbred strains of mice. *Quarterly Journal of Studies on Alcohol, 26*(3), 378–383.

Thigpen, C. H., & Cleckley, H. A. (1954). A case of multiple personality. *Journal of Abnormal and Social Psychology, 48,* 135–151.

Thigpen, C. H., & Cleckley, H. M. (1957). *The three faces of Eve.* New York: McGraw-Hill.

Thoren, P., Asberg, M., Bertilsson, L., Mellstrom, B., Sjoqvist, F., & Traskman, L. (1980). Clomipramine treatment of obsessive-compulsive disorder. 2. Biochemical aspects. *Archives of general Psychiatry, 37*(11), 1289–1294.

Tiefer, L., Moss, S., & Melman, A. (1991). Follow-up of patients and parents experiencing penile prosthesis malfunction and corrective surgery. *Journal of Sex and Marital Therapy, 17*(2), 113–128.

Torgersen, S. (1983). Genetics of neurosis: The effects of sampling variation upon the twin concordance ratio. *British Journal of Psychiatry, 142*, 126–132.

Torrey, E. F. (1980). *Schizophrenia and civilization.* New York: Jason Aronson.

Torrey, E. F. (1988). *Surviving schizophrenia: A family manual* (rev. ed.). New York: Harper & Row.

Torrey, E. F. (1991). A viral-anatomical explanation of schizophrenia. *Schizophrenia Bulletin, 17*(1), 15–18.

Torrey, E. F., & Kaufmann, C. A. (1986). Schizophrenia and neuroviruses. In H. A. Nasrallah & D. R. Weinberg (Ed.), *Handbook of schizophrenia: The neurology of schizophrenia* (pp. 361–376). New York: Elsevier Science Publishers.

Trent, N. H. III. (1990). *Dimensional structure of anxiety.* Unpublished doctoral dissertation, California School of Professional Psychology, Fresno, CA.

Tsushima, W. T., & Towne, S. W. (1977). Effects of paint sniffing on neuropsychological test performance. *Journal of Abnormal Psychology, 86*(4), 402–407.

Turk, D. C., & Rudy, T. E. (1990). Neglected factors in chronic pain treatment outcome studies—referral patterns, failure to enter treatment and attrition. *Pain, 43*(1), 7–25.

Turner, C. (1990). How much alcohol is in a "standart drink"? An analysis of 125 studies. *British Journal of Addiction, 85*(9), 1171–1175.

Turner, J. A., & Chapman, C. R. (1982). Psychological interventions for chronic pain: A critical review. 1. Relaxation training and biofeedback. *Pain, 12*(1), 1–21.

Turner, L. A., Althof, S. E., Levine, S. B., Bodner, D. R., Kursh, E. D., & Resnick, M. I. (1991). External vacuum devices in the treatment of erectile dysfunction: A one-year study of sexual and psychosocial impact. *Journal of Sex and Marital Therapy, 17*(2), 81–93.

Turner, S. M., Beidel, D. C., & Nathan, R. S. (1985). Biological factors in obsessive-compulsive disorders. *Psychological Bulletin, 97*(3), 430–450.

Tyrer, P., Lee, I., & Alexander, J. (1980). Awareness of cardiac function in anxious, phobic and hypchondriacal patients. *Psychological Medicine, 10*(1), 171–174.

Vaillant, G. E. (1973). A 20-year follow-up of New York narcotic addicts. *Archives of General Psychiatry, 29*, 237–241.

Vaillant, G. E., & Milofsky, E. S. (1982). Natural history of male alcoholism: 4. Paths to recovery. *Archives of General Psychiatry, 39*(2), 127–133.

Van Putten, T. (1974). Why do schizophrenic patients refuse to take their drugs? *Archives of General Psychiatry, 31*(1), 67–72.

Veleber, D. M., & Templer, D. I. (1984). Effects of caffeine on anxiety and depression. *Journal of Abnormal Psychology, 93*(1), 120–122.

Vermeer, D. (1971). Geophagy among the Ewe of Ghana. *Ethnology, 10*, 56–72.

Verschoor, A. M., & Poortinga, J. (1988). Psychosocial differences between Dutch male and female transsexuals. *Archives of Sexual Behavior, 17*(2), 173–178.

Victor, M., & Laureno R. (1978). Neurologic complications of alcohol abuse: Epidemiologc aspects. *Advances in Neurology, 19*, 603–617.

Victor, R. G., & Krug, C. M. (1967). "Paradoxical intentions" in the treatment of compulsive gambling. *American Journal of Psychotherapy, 21*(4), 808–814.

Villeneuve, R., Corcos, J., & Carmel, M. (1991). Assisted erection follow-up with couples. *Journal of Sex and Marital Therapy, 17*(2), 94–100.

Vincent, M., & Pickering, R. M. (1988). Multiple personality disorder in childhood. *Canadian Journal of Psychiatry, 33*, 524–529.

Vitello, M. V., & Prinz, P. N. (1988). Aging and sleep disorders. In R. L. Williams, I. Karacan & C. A. Moore (Eds.). *Sleep disorders: Diagnosis and treatment* (2nd ed.; pp. 293–314). New York: John Wiley & Sons.

Volberg, R. A., & Steadman, H. J. (1989). Prevalence estimates of pathological gambling in New Jersey and Maryland. *American Journal of Psychiatry, 146*(12), 1618–1619.

Wagner, N. N. (1974). *Perspectives on human sexuality: Psychological, social and cultural research findings.* New York: Behavioral Publications.

Wakefield, J. C. (1987). Sex bias in the diagnosis of primary orgasmic dysfunction. *American Psychologist, 42*(5), 464–471.

Waldringer, R. J. (1987). Intensive psychodynamic therapy with borderline patients: An overview. *American Journal of Psychiatry, 144*(3), 267–274.

Walfish, S., Massey, R., & Krone, A. (1990). MMPI profiles of cocaine-addicted individuals in residential treatment: Implications for practical treatment planning. *Journal of Substance Abuse Treatment, 7*(3), 151–1154.

Wallace, D. H., & Barbach, L. G. (1974). Preorgasmic group treatment. *Journal of Sex and Marital Therapy, 1*, 146–154.

Walsh, B. T., Stewart, J. W., Roose, S. P., Gladis, M., & Glassman, A. H. (1984). Treatment of bulimia with phenelzine: A double-blind, placebo-controlled study. *Archives of General Psychiatry, 41*, 1105–1109.

Walsh, J. K., McMahan, B. T., Sexton, K., & Smitson, S. A. (1982). A comparison of need satisfaction in narcoleptic and disabled individuals. *Sleep Research, 11*, 180.

Ware, J. C., & Rugh, J. D. (1988). Destructive burxism: Sleep stage relationships. *Sleep. 11*(2), 172–181.

Warmann, W. A. (1980). The use of aversion therapy for kleptomania. *Psychopathologie Africaine, 16*(1), 77–82.

Warren, L. W., & McEachren, L. (1983). Psychosocial correlates of depression symptomatology in adult women. *Journal of Abnormal Psychology, 92*(2), 151–160.

Watson, C. G., & Buranen, C. (1979). The frequencies of conversion reaction symptoms. *Journal of Abnormal Psychology, 88*(2), 209–211.

Watson, C. G., & Tilleskjor, C. (1983). Interrelationships of conversion, psychogenic pain, and dissociative disorder symptoms. *Journal of Counsulting and Clinical Psychology, 51*(5), 788–789.

Watt, J. A. G., Hall, D. J., Olley, P. C., Hunter, D., & Gardiner, A. Q. (1980). Paranoid states of middle life: Familial occurrences and relationship to schizophrenia. *Acta Psychiatrica Scandinavica, 61*, 413–426.

Watt, N. F. (1978). Patterns of childhood social development in adult schizophrenics. *Archives of General Psychiatry, 35*(2), 160–165.

Wechsler, H., Thum, D., Demone, H. W., & Dwinell, J. (1972). Social characteristics and blood alcohol level: Measurement of subgroup differences. *Quarterly Journal of Studies on Alcohol, 33*(1-a), 132–147.

Weinberger, D. R., Cannon-Spoor, E., Potkin, S. G., & Wyatt, R. J. (1980). Poor premorbid adjustment and CT scan abnormalities in chronic schizophrenia. *American Journal of Psychiatry, 137*(11), 1410–1413.

Weinberg, M. S., & Williams, C. J. (1974). *Male homosexuals: Their problems and adaptations.* New York: Oxford University Press.

Weissman, M. M., & Klerman, G. L. (1977). Sex differences and the epidemiology of depression. *Archives of General Psychiatry, 34*, 98–109.

Welti, C. V. (1987). Fatal cocaine intoxication. A review. *American Journal of Forensic Pathology, 8*(1), 1–2.

Wender, P. H., Reimherr, F. W., & Wood, D. R. (1981). Attention deficit disorder ("minimal brain dysfunction") in adults: A replication study of diagnosis and drug treatment. *Archives of General psychiatry, 38*(4), 449–456.

Whalley, L. J. (1978). Sexual adjustment of male alcoholics. *Acta Psychiatrica Scandinavica, 58*(4), 281–298.

Whitlock, F. A. (1967). The aetiology of hysteria. *Acta Psychiatrica Scandinavica, 43*(2), 144–162.

Whitney, W., Cadoret, R. J., & McClure, J. N. (1971). Depressive symptoms and academic performance in college students. *American Journal of Psychiatry, 128*(6), 766–770.

Wiggins, J. S. (1968). Personality structure. *Annual Review of Psychology, 19*, 293–350.

Wilcox, J. A., & Nasrallah, H. A. (1987). Childhood head trauma and psychosis. *Psychiatry Research, 21*(4), 303–306.

Wilkinson, D. A., & Poulos, C. X. (1987). The chronic effects of alcohol on memory: A contrast between a unitary and dual system approach. *Recent Developments in Alcoholism, 5*, 5–26.

Wilkinson, D. C., & Carlen, P. L. (1981). Chronic organic brain syndromes associated with alcoholism: Neuropsychological and other aspects. In Y. Israel,

F. Glasser, H. Kalant, R. D. Popham, W. Schmidt, & R. G. Smart (Eds.), *Research advances in alcohol and drug problems 6*(vol. 6, pp. 107–145). New York: Plenum Press.

Wilkinson, D. G. (1981). Psychiatric aspect of diabetes mellitus. *British Journal of Psychiatry, 138*, 1–9.

Willi, J., & Grossmann, S. (1983). Epidemiology of anorexia nervosa in a defined region of Switzerland. *American Journal of Psychiatry, 140*(5), 564–567.

Williams, R. L. (1988). Sleep disturbances in various medical surgical conditions. In R. L. Williams, I. Karacan, & C. A. Moore (Eds.), *Sleep disorders: Diagnosis and treatment* (2nd ed., pp. 265–292). New York: John Wiley and Sons.

Winokur, G. (1977). Delusional disorder (paranoia). *Comprehensive Psychiatry, 18*(6), 511–521.

Winokur, G. (1986). Classification of chronic psychoses including delusional disorders and schizophrenias. *Psychopathology, 19*, 30–34.

Winokur, G., Clayton, R., & Reich, T. (1969). Manic depressive illness. St. Louis: C. V. Mosby.

Witherington, R. (1991). Vacuum devices for the impotent. *Journal of Sex and Marital Therapy, 17*(2), 69–80.

Woerner, P. I., & Guze, S. B. (1968). A family and marital study of hysteria. *British Journal of Psychiatry, 114*(507), 161–168.

Wolf, E. M., & Crowther, J. H. (1992). An evaluation of behavioral and cognitive-behavioral group interventions for the treatment of bulimia nervosa in women. *International Journal of Eating Disorders, 11*(1), 3–15.

Wolf, J. M. (1967). Schooling for the retarded in overseas American schools. *Mental Retardation, 5*(4), 36–39.

Wolff, P. H. (1978). Ethnic differences in alcohol sensitivity. *Science, 175*(20), 449–450.

Wolff, S., & Barlow, A. (1980). Schizoid personality in childhood: A comparative study of schizoid, autistic and normal children. *Annual Progress in Child Psychiatry and Child Development*, 396–417.

Wolkowitz, O. M., Roy, A., & Doran, A. R. (1985). Pathologic gambling and other risk-taking pursuits. *Psychiatric Clinics of North America, 8*(2), 311–322.

Wolpe, J. (1958). *Psychotherapy by reciprocal inhibition*. Stanford, CA. Stanford University Press.

Wonderlich, S. A., & Swift, W. J. (1990). Perceptions of parental relationships in the eating disorders: The relevance of depressed mood. *Journal of Abnormal Psychology, 99*(4), 353–360.

Wood, D., Wender, P. H., & Reimherr, F. W. (1983). The prevalence of attention deficit disorder, residual type, or minimal brain dysfunction in a population of male alcoholic patients. *American Journal of Psychiatry, 140*(1), 95–98.

Wood, J. M., Bootzin, R. R., Rosenhan, D., Nolen-Hoeksema, S., & Jourden, F.

(1992). Effects of the 1989 San Francisco earthquake on frequency and content of nightmares. *Journal of Abnormal Psychology, 101*(2), 219–224.

Woodrow, K. M., Friedman, G. D., Siegelaub, A. B., & Collen, M. F. (1972). Pain tolerance: Differences according to age, sex and race. *Psychsomatic Medicine, 34*(6), 548–556.

Woodside, D. B., Garner, D. M., Rockert, W. et. al. (1990). Eating disorders in males: Insights from a clinical and psychometric comparison with female patients. In A. E. Anderson (Ed.), *Males with eating disorders.* New York: Brunner/Mazel.

Wooley, S. C., & Wooley, O. W. (1984). Should obesity be treated at all? *Research Publications—Association for Research in Nervous and Mental Disease, 62,* 185–192.

Wragg, R. E., & Jeste, D. V. (1989). Overview of depression and psychosis in Alzheimer's disease. *American Journal of Psychiatry, 146*(5), 577–587.

Yates, E. (1986). The influence of psycho-social factors on non-sensical shoplifting. *International Journal of Offender Therapy and Comparative Criminology, 30,* 203–211.

Yerevanian, B. I., Anderson, J. L., Grota, L. J., & Bray, M. (1986). Effects of bright incandescent light on seasonal and nonseasonal major depressive disorder. *Psychiatry Research, 18*(4), 355–364.

Yesavage, J. A., & Leirer, V. O. (1986). Hangover effects on aircraft pilots 14 hours after alcohol ingestion: A preliminary report. *American Journal of Psychiatry, 143*(12), 1546–1549.

Yoss, R. E., & Daly, D. D. (1957). Criteria for the diagnosis of the narcoleptic syndrome. *Proceedings: Staff Meetings of the Mayo Clinic, 32,* 320–328.

Young, L., & Powell, B. (1985). The effects of obesity on the clinical judgements of mental health professionals. *Journal of Health and Social Behavior, 26,* 233–246.

Zigler, E. (1967). Familial mental retardation: A continuing dilemma. *Science, 155*(760), 292–298.

Zuckerman, M., & Neeb, M. (1979). Sensation seeking and psychopathology. *Psychiatry Research, 1*(3), 255–264.

INDEX

S | Springer Publishing Company

PROGRESS IN EXPERIMENTAL PERSONALITY AND PSYCHOPATHOLOGY RESEARCH, Vol. 15

Elaine F. Walker, PhD,

Robert H. Dworkin, PhD, and

Barbara A. Cornblatt, PhD, Editors

Contents:

Communicatioi Deviance in Families of Schizophrenic and other Psychiatric Patients: Current State of the Construct, *D.J. Miklowitz and D. Stackman* • Understanding the Effects of Depressed Mothers on Their Children, *S.H. Goodman* • Childhood Stressors, Parental Expectation, and the Development of Schizophrenia, *A.F. Mirsky et al.* • An Information-Processing Approach to the Study of Cognitive Functioning in Depression, *I.H. Gotlib and S.B. McCabe* • On the Wisconsin, *A.M.I. Wagman and W. Wagman* • Structure-Function Relations in Schizophrenia: Brain Morphology and Neuropsychology, *R.M. Bilder* • Specifying Cognitive Deficiencies in Premorbid Schizophrenics, *R.A. Knight* • Sustained and Selective Attention in Schizophrenia, *M.F. Green et al.*

1992   336pp   0-8261-6090-5   hardcover

536 Broadway, New York, NY 10012-3955 • (212) 431-4370 • Fax (212) 941-7842

$\boxed{\text{SP}}$ *Springer Publishing Company*

MEDICAL ASPECTS OF DISABILITY
A Handbook for the
Rehabilitation Professional

Myron G. Eisenberg, PhD,
Robert L. Glueckauf, PhD, and
Herbert H. Zaretsky, PhD, Editors

A comprehensive text for students preparing for a
career in rehabilitation. Covers the medical aspects of
disabling conditions including functional presentation
and prognosis. Also serves as an authoritative
reference guide for the practitioner.

Partial Contents:

Section I. An Introduction to Key Topics and Issues

BODY SYSTEMS: AN OVERVIEW, *J. H. Ahn*

**Section II. Disabling Conditions: Their Functional
Presentation, Treatment, Prognosis, and
Psychological and Vocational Implications**

ACQUIRED IMMUNE DEFICIENCY SYNDROME
(AIDS) AND HUMAN IMMUNODEFICIENCY VIRUS
(HIV), *R. H. Remien and J. Satriano* ·

ALZHEIMER'S DISEASE, *B. Reisberg and J. A. Mackell* ·

CHRONIC PAIN, *D. E. DeGood* ·

SUBSTANCE ABUSE, *C. C. Saltz and M. Lawton*

1993   432pp 0-8261-7970-3   hardcover

536 Broadway, New York, NY 10012-3955 • (212) 431-4370 • Fax (212) 941-7842

Springer Publishing Company

THE CLINICAL ASSESSMENT OF MEMORY
A Practical Guide

Dennis Reeves, PhD, and **Danny Wedding,** PhD

This quick and useful reference for the non-specialist clinician provides helpful guidelines for the administration and interpretation of carefully selected memory tests. The volume also provides a summary of current theories of memory, as well as a summary of the neuroanatomy of memory.

Partial Contents:

Theories of Memory. The Concept of Memory • Vocabulary of Memory • A Schematic Model of Declarative and Procedural Memory • General Theories of Memory From a Neuropsychological Perspective • Three Possible Explanations for Amnesia

The Neuroanatomy of Memory. Amnesia and the Neuroanatomy of Memory • The Neuropathology of Memory • Neurological Disorders Affecting Memory • Dementia • Differential Diagnosis of Transient Global Amnesia and Psychogenic Amnesias • Depression and Memory

Psychological Tests for the Assessment of Memory. The California Verbal Learning Test (CVLT) • CVLT Clinical Applications and Group Patterns • Qualitative Scoring and Interpretation • The Cognitive Difficulties Scale

1993   240pp (est)   0-8261-7920-1   hardcover

536 Broadway, New York, NY 10012-3955 • (212) 431-4370 • Fax (212) 941-7842

Springer Publishing Company

JOURNAL OF COGNITIVE PSYCHOTHERAPY

An International Quarterly

**The Official Publication of the
International Association of Cognitive Psychotherapy**

E. Thomas Dowd, PhD, Editor

This authoritative journal is devoted to the advancement of the clinical practice of cognitive psychotherapy in its broadest sense and provides an international forum investigating clinical implications of theoretical developments and research findings. Published 4 times a year, the *Journal of Cognitive Psychotherapy* offers actual case studies, reviews of relevant theoretical developments, literature reviews on clinical topics, and articles highlighting clinical implications of current research. The editor invites manuscript submissions. All articles are refereed.

Abstracted in: Excerpta Medica, Psychological Abstracts, Mental Health Abstracts, and PsychINFO.

ISSN 0889-8391

536 Broadway, New York, NY 10012-3955 • (212) 431-4370 • Fax (212) 941-7842

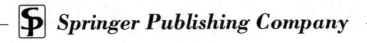

Springer Publishing Company

STRESS IN PSYCHIATRIC DISORDERS

Robert Paul Liberman, MD, and **Joel Yager,** MD, Editors,
with a Foreword by **Sherman Mellinkoff,** MD

This unique and expertly written volume describes how specific factors increase vulnerability or protect against the impact of stressors in a variety of clinical and social settings, such as depression, schizophrenia, Post Traumatic Stress Disorder, political torture, natural disasters, and the rapidly changing medical profession.

Partial Contents:

The Revolution in Stress Theory & Research, *H. Weiner* • Neuroendocrine Aspects of Stress in Depression, *R. Rubin* • Can Coping and Competence Override Stress and Vulnerability in Schizophrenia?, *S. Mackain, R.P. Liberman, & P. Corrigan* • Combat Stress Reactions: From Research to Practice, *R. Rahe* • Psychosocial Consequences of Stress Among Native American Adolescents, *D. Bechtold, S. Manon & J. Shore* • Psychiatric Implications of Stressful Methods Employed by Totalist Cults, *L.J. West* • The Psychology of Terrorism and Torture in War and Peace: Diagnosis and Treatment of Victims, *C.J. Frederick* • Stresses and the Psychiatric Professional: Coping with the Practice of a Changing Profession and Strains from the Administrative Life, *J. Yager & M. Greenblatt*

1993 224pp (est.) 0-8261-8310-7 hardcover

536 Broadway, New York, NY 10012-3955 • (212) 431-4370 • Fax (212) 941-7842